AF352692

ENTANGLED LIVES

ENTANGLED LIVES

Labor, Livelihood, and Landscapes of Change in Rural Massachusetts

MARLA R. MILLER

Johns Hopkins University Press, Baltimore

Johns Hopkins University Press
2715 North Charles Street
Baltimore, Maryland 21218-4363
www.press.jhu.edu

Library of Congress Cataloging-in-Publication Data

Names: Miller, Marla R., author.
Title: Entangled lives : labor, livelihood, and landscapes of change in rural
    Massachusetts / Marla R. Miller.
Description: Baltimore : Johns Hopkins University Press, 2019. | Series: Studies in
    early American economy and society from the Library Company of Philadelphia |
    Includes bibliographical references and index.
Identifiers: LCCN 2018060116 | ISBN 9781421432748 (hardcover : alk. paper) |
    ISBN 1421432749 (hardcover : alk. paper) | ISBN 9781421432755 (electronic) |
    ISBN 1421432757 (electronic)
Subjects: LCSH: Women—Massachusetts—Hadley—History—18th century. |
    Women—Massachusetts—Hadley—Social conditions—18th century. |
    Women—Employment—Massachusetts—Hadley—History—18th century. |
    Sex role—Massachusetts—Hadley—History—18th century. | Massachusetts—
    Social life and customs—18th century.
Classification: LCC F72.H3 M55 2019 | DDC 974.4/23—dc23
    LC record available at https://lccn.loc.gov/2018060116

A catalog record for this book is available from the British Library.

*Special discounts are available for bulk purchases of this book. For more information,
please contact Special Sales at 410-516-6936 or specialsales@press.jhu.edu.*

Johns Hopkins University Press uses environmentally friendly book materials,
including recycled text paper that is composed of at least 30 percent post-consumer
waste, whenever possible.

CONTENTS

In this addition to the series Studies in Early American Economy and Society, a collaborative effort between Johns Hopkins University Press and the Library Company of Philadelphia's Program in Early American Economy and Society (PEAES), Marla Miller examines the women in one rural community in New England during its slow transformation following the American Revolution. More particularly, Miller shows in minute detail the working lives of women in Hadley, Massachusetts, in their many manifestations and before a transition to capitalism. She peers into their shops and homes and gardens, and she gives readers the tools to understand how people in this community interacted with each other or reacted to the region beyond their village.

Miller's particular objective is to explain "how social relations of women's work and gender divisions of labor" came about in this community and how they played an essential role in shaping the responses of people in Hadley to the market opportunities presented to them after the Revolution and the ever-present constraints on those opportunities. But for Miller, the Revolution did not bring a watershed of change to Hadley; rather, the daily rhythms of working lives were only slowly changed by the advent of technological innovations or external shifts in market relations. And what lingered long into the nineteenth century were generations-old community customs and producing practices that had started in a murky past. This is a study of Hadley women who were rooted to one small place across generations. Miller elucidates the interior landscapes of their homes as rural workplaces, as well as the evolution of rural neighborhoods and the shifting landscape of shops and other small buildings where women worked.

And, as Miller argues, the physical place these laboring women occupied was deeply connected to the social and economic places they inhabited in the wider community. So Miller uses the homes, neighborhoods, and landscapes in which women labored as her point of departure for documenting concretely how Hadley women made a living, and how it mattered whether a woman was enslaved or free, a head of household or domestic servant, an employer or wage earner. The specificity of place becomes intricately woven with the specificity of women's labor. Nowhere does this become clearer in Miller's analysis than in part 2, where she guides readers through Hadley's landscapes of domestic service, cloth making, health and healing, and the hospitality trades.

It is equally true, argues Miller, that because Hadley was a rural town, the places where women labored had fewer distinctions of class, status, and wealth than, say, port cities. But if there was less diversity in broad categories of class, status, or wealth, the people of Hadley nevertheless became acutely aware of who prospered in a particular season, who had become sick and could not pay debts, who had valuable skills, who turned out shoddy goods. Moreover, the working lives of Hadley's individual women were ever changing, adapting to challenges or grasping new opportunities. There was no clear trajectory of turning outward to new market relationships far from this New England town, no easily identified evolution of laboring practices or gender (and racial) roles. Further, this was a time when women did not work merely to earn money—whether as wages or in providing occasional services; just as importantly, Hadley's women labored in myriad roles that were defined by existing available resources and an accumulation of widely varied skills needed to run a home, or a shop, or a farm. Most of them were concerned less with "fashion" than with family "comfort"—not with how they appeared to others individually but rather with how they constructed a complex household in their immediate physical landscapes.

In order to achieve this portrait of Hadley, Miller has spent years combing through not only the family papers of a few residents but also the myriad fragments that survive across a wide range of records, which when reassembled—or, re-entangled—create this portrait of one town's female economy. Nineteenth-century town histories, probate records, township maps, account books and diaries, public appeals for improvements, construction plans, and surviving household and workshop objects all become part of the deep dive we take into Hadley's history.

Cathy Matson
Richards Professor of American History, University of Delaware
Director, Program in Early American Economy and Society
Library Company of Philadelphia

The Hill

Where are Elmer, Herman, Bert, Tom and Charley,
The weak of will, the strong of arm, the clown, the boozer, the fighter?
All, all are sleeping on the hill.
One passed in a fever,
One was burned in a mine,
One was killed in a brawl,
One died in a jail,
One fell from a bridge toiling for children and wife—
All, all are sleeping, sleeping, sleeping on the hill.
Where are Ella, Kate, Mag, Lizzie and Edith,
The tender heart, the simple soul, the loud, the proud, the happy one?—
All, all are sleeping on the hill.

Edgar Lee Masters, *Spoon River Anthology*

Just as Edgar Lee Masters brought to life 244 residents of the Spoon River of his poetic imagination through short epitaphs, the men and women whose lives trace through these pages could be conjured in verse, in short sketches that would achieve more economically what I've tried to do here: to envision for readers the small and large ways that women's lives intersected with one another in the early American countryside, especially through their work. Stanzas might capture the hired woman Persis Morse as she assures her employer, Elizabeth Phelps, that the unsanctioned child she is carrying will not interfere with her duties around the farm's hearths and washtubs; or Phelps's enslaved woman, Peg, when she tells her daughters Phillis and Rose that, to seek her own freedom, she must leave them behind; or the hardscrabble Mary Trainer, taking in the sick and frightened German camp follower Mary Andries when Phelps can no longer manage her care, billing the town's Overseers of the Poor for her efforts.

Many historians feel a similar obligation to their subjects. We want readers to know them as we have come to know them, and if we cannot achieve poetry, then prose must suffice. But my aim remains the same, to introduce readers to women at work in Hadley, Massachusetts, to contemplate their lives in constellation, and to explore what they have to tell us about the broader world they inhabited, as a means ultimately to understand (gendered) social relations of labor in the early republic, and class as both process and lived experience in rural western New England in the decades following the American Revolution. I have chosen to study residents of Hadley in part because it is the town I know best. I have studied it for more than twenty-five years, and it is now the place where I live. But I have chosen it also because an unusual amount of evidence survives to shed light on its history, allowing me to investigate the entangled lives of women whose worlds elsewhere have gone unrecorded. Located in Hampshire County—which in the eighteenth century stretched across the large territory that today encompasses Hampshire, Hampden, and Franklin Counties in the Connecticut River Valley—Hadley sits in a region that has attracted a significant amount of scholarship. Its appeal to researchers stems in part from the presence of the state's flagship university but also because several historical institutions (including the Pocumtuck Valley Memorial Association, Historic Deerfield, Historic Northampton, and the Forbes Library, as well as a number of town organizations with rich collections of their own—the Hadley Farm Museum, the Hadley Historical Society, and the Porter-Phelps-Huntington Foundation) have, since the last quarter of the nineteenth century, preserved an extraordinary amount of archival and artifactual material.

What's more, the historic landscape has remained remarkably stable, creating a rare opportunity to situate families within geographies they knew. Named to the National Register of Historic Places in 1999, the Hadley Common and adjacent Great Meadow are unusual survivals of colonial New England's distinct approaches to agriculture and town planning. More than half of the houses along the common today were built before 1840, including the 1713 Porter house, believed to be the oldest extant house in Hampshire County. Footpaths crisscrossing the common, laid out by the 1791 select board, were still visible as late as the 1950s.[1] So rare and intact is this cultural landscape that the area in 2010 was named to the World Monuments Fund watch list. "This arrangement of slender, unfenced, elongated land parcels bounded by the river," the citation reads, "has endured since the time of the allotments to original settlers. Open-field farming was widespread in medieval and early modern Europe, but only the earliest New England settlements set up this type of agricultural system, and most had disappeared by the eighteenth century. This survival on such a large scale, over the centuries and through American industrialization in the northeastern United States, is incredibly improbable."[2] The town is home to three districts on the National Register of Historic Places.[3] Stones in its five historic cemeteries, if they lack the narrative force of Masters's Spoon River burying ground, mark lives that ended here.

The survival of several key structures allows us to enter interior spaces and consider spatial dimensions of women's work in more intimate settings. Importantly, the 1752 home of Elizabeth and Charles Phelps, "Forty Acres," has been preserved as a historic house museum, and the activities therein well documented by over one hundred linear feet of archival material.[4] Places like the Phelpses' house—that is, the largest house in a small town—are familiar to us as mansions of the rural New England gentry, but here I place them in another frame of reference. Between 1770 and 1816, Forty Acres was "home" to six family members—Elizabeth Pitkin Porter; Elizabeth Porter Phelps and her husband, Charles; their son, Charles; and their two daughters, Elizabeth (Betsy) and Thankful (a ward taken in as an infant)—but for more than sixty domestic servants, midwives, nurses, spinners, weavers, laundresses, gown makers, and other working women over some fifty years, it was a job site.[5] For a small family of enslaved women, it was the site of their labor as well as their captivity. For some of the community's poorest women, it was both (or, alternately) workplace and refuge.

The Phelps home was not unusual in this regard: houses all across the community functioned in these multivalent ways. Clothes and cloth-making women, nurses, and midwives moved back and forth between their clients' households and their own. Domestic servants often lived in one household to sustain another. Tavern-keeping women opened their homes as businesses. Those straightforward facts help us reconsider the hundreds of extant houses from early America as sources of insight on the history of women and work. The buildings and cultural landscapes of Hadley, Massachusetts, then, together with its archival and artifactual record, offer an uncommon opportunity to root a history of how the social relations of work changed over time in the lanes, neighborhoods, farmyards, and dwellings that both shaped and responded to those developments. Looking at how work unfolded in a range of settings in ways that proved fluid and flexible over time illuminates some of the ways that domestic, laboring, and social space were mutually constitutive, defining, distinguishing, and collapsing on each other in the half-century following the American Revolution.

In some ways—though only in hindsight—this study can be seen as completing a trilogy begun with my first book, *The Needle's Eye: Women and Work in the Age of Revolution.* In that project, I consider how artisanal skill in the clothing trades shaped the ways in which women contributed to this vast arena within the early American economy. The book argues that women entered the clothing trades in different ways and at different times that reflected their varying access to skill and opportunity, drawing them into complex webs of production that knit communities together; over time, the expansion of outwork and increased access to ready-made apparel set makers and users at increasing distance, a development with mixed outcomes for both. Arguments articulated there resonate through these pages as well. In addition, although that research surveyed much of the Connecticut River Valley, Hadley, located at the geographical heart of the valley, is also at the heart of that book, in a series of chapters that examine how women's participation in clothes making both drew women together and set them apart.[6] Some of the women whose lives informed that study reappear here. And here, as in *The Needle's Eye*, I trace the shifts in gender divisions of labor that occurred as occupations opened and closed to female practitioners in response to changing ideas about women's place in the economy.

A few years after the publication of *The Needle's Eye*, I was pleased to accept Carol Berkin's kind invitation to return to the life of one of the key subjects in that book and contribute to the series Lives of American Women a small volume that explores the life of gown maker Rebecca Dickinson, a never-married artisan from Hatfield, Massachusetts, who, like other craftswomen during the political separation from Britain, confronted the challenge posed by consumer boycotts while also enduring increasingly mean-spirited cultural prescription that left little room for women beyond marriage and family.[7] Returning to Dickinson's story allowed me to grapple with her world more fully, contemplating her faith, her family, and other elements of the artisan's day-to-day world in ways that continued to inform and deepen my understanding of gender and craft in early New England. For Dickinson, "independence" in the last quarter of the eighteenth century would come to mean not only the struggle to secure political sovereignty for newly united states, but also sovereignty of a more personal nature, as she harnessed the assets of artisanal skill to secure a livelihood and mitigate the most burdensome aspects of life alone, helping to allay bouts of loneliness and a pernicious sense of superfluity as she created a role for herself in her community grounded in craft skill and knowledge.

The volume before you revisits several of these themes, exploring how women in the half-century following Independence both navigated and drove social and economic change. The project considers how gender, class, and the production, consumption, and exchange of goods and services shaped and reflected changing social relations of labor in the early town, and the early republic. In the pages herein, across these contemplations of lives entwined across evolving landscapes, invocations of "place" are meant trifold, to signal the ways in which class-bound experiences are simultaneously rooted in work, community, and physical (interior and exterior) terrains. Place is also important to the work in ways that are analytical, methodological, and personal, since this work is inseparable from in my own thirty-year encounter with the town of Hadley. In many ways, a book of this kind takes that long to write. I have sat with these buildings and landscapes for three decades now, as a student, a researcher, and eventually a resident. I've walked these paths, and I've observed these vistas in all seasons: I have thought about Hadley's past as I've helped shape (as a voter, volunteer, and historical commissioner) its present and its future. While the project aims to offer new insight into the social relations of labor in the early republic, it also presents an intervention into larger conversations about local history, microhistory, and historical scholarship.[8] The work is necessarily entwined with my identity and long-standing practice as a public historian; it is deeply grounded in the methods and sources of (and my deep respect and affection for) local history, and it considers the role of public history practice (both in specific local institutions, and more abstractly, across the United States) in shaping popular historical understanding of (or misperceptions about) early American women's work.

Central to this book's overall aims is understanding how the lives of very different women were firmly knotted together, so thickly entangled that it is almost impossible to consider one apart from others; together these stories illuminate the braided nature of women's experience in the early republic. As any one of these women went about the business of providing for themselves, their households, and loved ones, they drew on opportunities presented as others did likewise; they also bumped up against the constraints created as neighbors pursued their own needs, competing and complementary as those activities necessarily were. Marking those entanglements of the past helps us mark them in the present. To paraphrase a watershed essay by Elsa Barkley Brown, each of us lives the lives we do because other women live the lives they do, a fact that resonates through more than four hundred years of American history.[9]

A word on quotations and spelling: The reader of this volume will note that quoted material from the period sometimes contains archaic grammatical constructions, punctuation, capitalization, or spelling. Such quotes appear as they were written. In addition, the spelling of proper names, often inconsistent across period sources, has largely been made consistent here.

This is a book about work, and how the labor of some advances the aims of others. And so I am keenly aware, as I complete this project, of the significant effort that mentors, colleagues, students, archivists, librarians, curators, editors, and friends have made through the years to help me bring this manuscript to fruition. First thanks must go to those who nurtured the project at inception. I will never tire of thanking Charles Lloyd Cohen, who first taught me how to think like a historian. Jacquelyn Dowd Hall and John K. Nelson encouraged me in this project when parts of it appeared in its earliest stages, as part of my 1997 doctoral dissertation. I learned so much from them both, but I am especially indebted to Jacquelyn for showing me what it meant to encounter the working women of the past; if I write about them with a fraction of the insight, grace, and humanity that Jacquelyn brings to her work, I will be content. Kevin Sweeney and Laurel Thatcher Ulrich read that dissertation and envisioned the books that would someday emerge from it, first *The Needle's Eye*, and now the project herein. Kevin has long been nothing short of a historian-hero of mine, as is Christopher Clark, who showed particular kindness and interest in my work way back when I began thinking about these figures in graduate school, and he has remained a much-valued ally in the years since. As this study contemplates the ways women's lives intersect through their work, though, I particularly want to recognize here Jacquelyn and Laurel, who as women faculty members in the 1990s, with tremendous pressure on their time—something I came to appreciate more each day once I became a faculty member as well—in reading my rough pages and talking through possibilities, contributed so much to my growth as a young scholar, and my development since then. The imagery that opens the introduction, of the walk along the Hadley Common, emerged from a particularly memorable conversation with Laurel, many years ago—in which she also taught me (at least in my recollection) how to create a stem chart, sketching one out on a conference hotel napkin.

At the Forbes Library, the incomparable Elise Bernier Feeley has been with me every step of the way; she has been a supporter through most of my adult life, and it has been my privilege to benefit from her generosity and expertise. More recently, her colleagues Julie Bartlett Nelson and Dylan Gaffney have helped field my many queries there; their ready assistance is also greatly appreciated. Susan Lisk, director of the Porter-Phelps-Huntington Foundation, has also seen this project evolve over more than twenty years, and has put my scholarship to interpretive work in the spaces of the Porter-Phelps-Huntington House; she has made the work feel appreciated and necessary. I am likewise grateful to the dedicated Amherst College librarians who care for the Porter-Phelps-Huntington papers, especially Mimi Dakin, Rachel Jirka, and Peter Nelson. At Historic

Deerfield, I have benefited from the expertise and good cheer of librarians David Bosse, Heather Harrington, and Martha Noblick, and also the curatorial and interpretive wisdom of Anne Lanning, Phil Zea, and Ned Lazaro. At the Hatfield Historical Society, I am happily indebted to the excellent Kathie Gow, and at Historic Northampton I thank the always-generous Betty Sharpe and Marie Panik. At Old Sturbridge Village, I have been delighted to work in the good company of Amy Hietala, Caitlin Emery Avenia, and the OSV library and museum staff.

In the Hadley Town Hall, town clerk Jessica Spanknabel and assistant clerk Janice Kangas have many times helped me access records there, and for her help reviewing records at the First Congregational Church I am grateful to Mary Thayer. At the Hadley Historical Society, I thank Ellie Neidbala and Diane Baj; I convey my posthumous gratitude as well to Hadley's longtime town historian Dorothy Russell. And at the Hadley Farm Museum, I have benefited from the enthusiasm and interest of Tom Waskiewicz. It was my privilege to serve on the Hadley Historical Commission alongside the incomparable Margaret Freeman and Peg Tudryn; their insights into the history and culture of Hadley from its founding to the present have been invaluable to me, not only as a researcher of Hadley's eighteenth-century past, but as a resident of the twenty-first-century community. Mary and Rick Thayer allowed me to spend a good bit of time in their comfortable dining room poring over the account book of the Pomeroy tavern, and kindly reviewed my prose on that space, while Jordi Herold graciously included me on a tour of the Cook house while it was under renovation, and shared photos with me of the interior spaces during construction.

Over the many years that this project has been in some form of development, friends and colleagues have been kind enough to review a passage, read a chapter or two, or in some especially heroic cases, tackle the whole thing. For their perceptive comments and perplexed questions, for lines of inquiry proposed and turns of phrase suggested, for cheering me on when I was ready to throw in the towel—for all this and more, I am deeply grateful to Christopher Clark, Barbara Clark Smith, Bruce Laurie, Alice Nash, Pamela Sharpe, Cathy Kelly, Jessica Lepler, Laura Jane Moore, Rebecca Shrum, Linda Ziegenbein, Margo Shea, Sarah Leavitt, Mary Kelley, Betty Sharpe, Betsy Carlisle, Anne Lanning, Kate Viens, Susan Brandt, Laura Miller, Emily Hamilton, Paula Michaels, and Ritchie Garrison. Ruth Herndon read the manuscript in full at a key moment and offered encouragement and feedback essential to the project's completion; Cathy Kelly and Jessica Lepler merit still more thanks for their ongoing intellectual companionship and the many ways they have buoyed my spirits. Others, thanked in the notes too for their more specific and timely contributions, include Marge Bruchac, Myron Stachiw, Sharon Mehrman, Peggy Hart, and Bill Flynt. I have learned so much, too, from material culture specialists and friends Bonnie Parsons and Lynne Bassett; their expertise and insights also inform these pages. I am grateful to have met in the course of this work the wonderful graphic artist Kate Blackmer; her astute questions as she prepared a number of images herein improved the analysis as well as illustrating it. The readers for Johns Hopkins University Press—Karen Halttunen and a second unidentified reader—provided support and sage direction. And, of course, I am so grateful to Cathy Matson, who took on this project and helped me deepen and sharpen my thinking at key points along the way. While the project was in development I benefited greatly from the editorial assistance of Debby Smith and Mary Child. More recently, at Johns Hopkins University Press, I am happy to have worked with Laura Davulis, Andre Barnett, Esther Rodriguez, and others on that terrific staff, as well as copyeditor David Goehring and indexer Susan Ferentinos. I am deeply grateful to them all for their care, thoughtfulness, and patience as I brought this long-standing work to completion.

Over the years that this project has been in process, a number of students at the University of Massachusetts Amherst contributed to the research. No one except my husband will be happier to see this book in print than Melissa Burke, who helped with the research on enslaved women in Hadley while she was a sophomore Honors Fellow in Commonwealth College. Melissa graduated in 2002; if she learned anything from that experience, I suspect that it is just how long a book can take to prepare. For their capable assistance and archival camaraderie at various points along the way, I thank Nolan Cool, Katherine Fecteau, Katherine Garland, Peggy Hart, Mona Minor, and Sandy Perot.

I have been fortunate to secure financial support for this work from a number of sources, including a National Endowment for the Humanities fellowship, and the Samuel F. Conti Faculty Fellowship at the University of Massachusetts Amherst. My deep thanks to those funders, and also to colleagues who helped support me in those endeavors, particularly Dan Horowitz, Mary Kelley, Ritchie Garrison, Barbara Clark Smith, and again, as always, Jacquelyn Hall. I am also grateful for permission to incorporate previously published work in these pages. Chapter 4 is drawn from "Eggs on the Sand: Domestic Servants and Their Children in Federal New England," in Peter Benes and Jane Montague Benes, eds., *Women's Work in New England, 1620–1920,* Proceedings of the 2001 Dublin Seminar for New England Folklife (Boston: Boston University, 2003), 184–95. Chapter 8 is drawn from "Labor and Liberty in the Age of Refinement: Gender, Class, and the Built Environment," in Kenneth Breisch and Alison K. Hoagland, eds., *Building Environments: Perspectives in Vernacular Architecture,* vol. 10 (Knoxville: University of Tennessee Press, 2005), 15–31.

As I was finishing this book, a dear friend sent me a card that read, "Behind every great woman is another great woman replying to her frantic texts in the middle of the night." Indeed. And so, for their many years of warm friendship, unfailing support, and stewardship of my general sanity, I thank (and admire and adore) those friends whose presence in other areas of my life has brought so much joy, comfort, and serenity: Christine Cooper, Anne Whisnant, Laura Jane Moore, Dena Grinder, Laura Gant, Nancy Barker, Barbara Schlaefer and Rebecca Wright. Lastly, though no words can capture my gratitude to my husband, Stephen Peck, for the many ways in which he makes everything possible, I thank him for his love and support over these many years.

ENTANGLED LIVES

Placings

Walk with me down the Hadley Common. It is nightfall. Look north, and you will see a half-mile of tree-lined lawn stretching toward the steep dike straining to stave off the Connecticut River; look south, and you'll see another long lawn just like it, leading to the old Bay Road heading east to Boston. Glance up, and you can spot the white fleck that is the historic Summit House atop the sculptural expanse of the Holyoke Range. Double rows of silver and sugar maples—successors of long-gone elms, willows, butternuts, and buttonwoods—mark our path. People are just beginning to switch on their lamps. If you're willing to take a bold look, it is possible to see into some of the houses. You can just make out a picture on the wall, a shelf of books, the style of furniture, whether the rooms are painted or papered, or the blue glow of the television. Sometimes you can see the people inside, in motion: here someone is in the kitchen, starting dinner, there someone is in the living room, reading the newspaper. People move in and out of our view as they go about their business, unaware that we are outside looking in. Some houses are lit up brightly; almost every window affords a glimpse into some corner of their lives. But some houses are dark; we can't see in at all.

Like the Hadley Common of our imagined walk, the eighteenth-century village we might stroll through in our historical mind's eye is brightly lit in some areas, shadowy in others. We can glimpse people at work and at leisure. A woman enters a shop; we see her for just an instant as she selects her goods and accepts the debts that accompany them. But we cannot see the husband, parents, or children whose shared needs those purchases may fill or whose preferences helped determine them. When our subjects are ensconced in their homes, as they are on our walk, we see them only apart from the world from which they've retreated, separated from the neighbors whose actions and conversation gave tone to the day just past. We might spot some of the items the purchaser's work has secured—the prints on the wall, the books on the shelves, the candles or lamps that light our view—but we do not now observe the labor it took to secure them. Nor can we tell from the presence of these objects anything about their selection, whether they were bought with a sense of purpose and pleasure or begrudgingly acquired only because they were functional.

And, just as there are some rooms that we cannot spy from our vantage point, some corners of early American lives are tougher to observe than others. Looking hard demands a sharp focus and a steady gaze.

Observing closely as a single, rural community—Hadley, Massachusetts—made one part of its slow journey toward modernity reveals how social relations of women's work and gender divisions of labor evolved and overlapped in the decades following the American Revolution. Examining the work women did in this rural setting in the years between political independence and the emergence of the economic order and class relations we associate with the market revolution suggests ways in which women's labors both curbed and accelerated the development of what would become the rural middle class. As we visit and revisit the common we just walked along, we can see women's work drawing together the households that surrounded that landscape, both directly and at a distance. The opportunities and the constraints that shaped women's lives on this ground were products of larger contexts, long-standing relationships, cumulative choices over the span of lives and generations, and sometimes, simple chance.

Thinking about place in this way creates an opportunity to think anew about social relations of labor in the early rural republic. Metaphors of space and location, as scholars from a range of fields have observed, have long denoted where or how someone is situated socially, culturally, and economically. "Place," as others before me have noted, has been synonymous with employment (obtaining a "place" in a shop or a bank, or as a servant, caregiver, or other household worker, and so forth), a situation or set of circumstances (as in, "if I were in your place"), or a responsibility (that is, whether or not it is one's "place" to do something); "place" can serve as a synonym for identifying someone (when our memory cannot "place" her) while the phrases to "know your place," or to be "put in one's place" have signaled an awareness of one's social "position" or station.[1] This analysis takes notions of "place," in these many senses both social and spatial, as a point of departure from which to explore the wide range of ways women in postrevolutionary Massachusetts could gain livelihoods. It tracks those occupations through the flowering of the market economy, and it situates them on the evolving landscape—dwellings, neighborhoods, and townscape—of Hadley, Massachusetts, a town in the heart of New England's Connecticut River Valley, a region with its own distinct history and culture (figure I.1). It investigates the labors of African American women in slavery and in freedom, and it follows the efforts of young white women to manage (that is, to enter, negotiate, and abandon) domestic service. It considers the roles of women of the rural gentry as producers and employers, and it explores the work of Native American women as domestic servants, basket makers, and healers. And it shows how "place" is a product of this web of ever-shifting

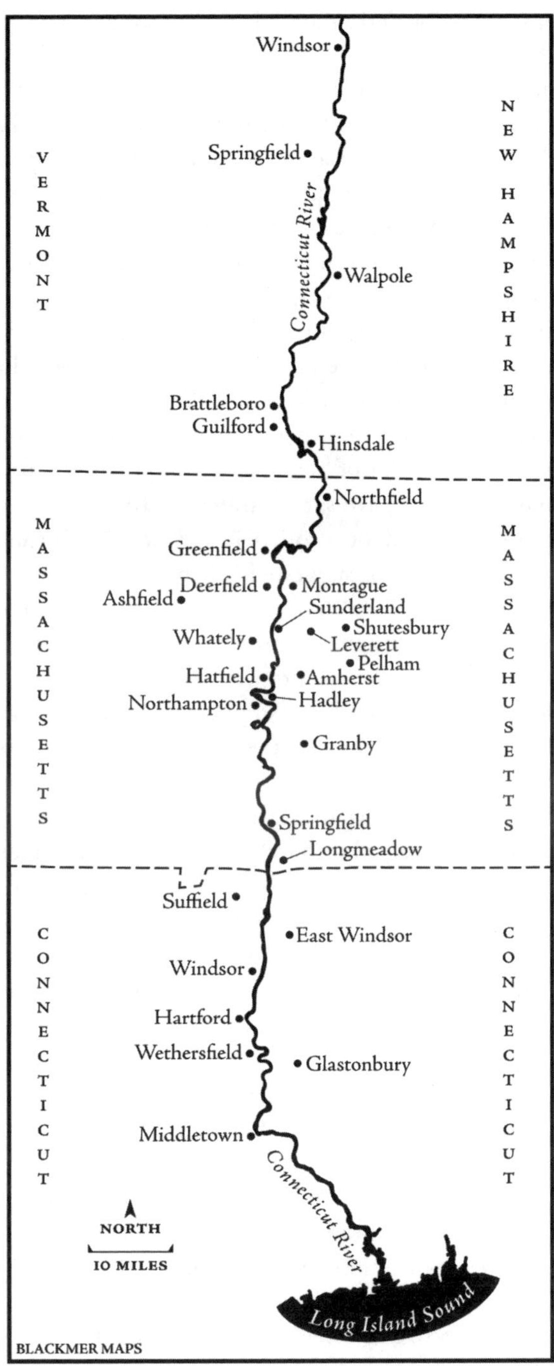

Figure I.1 Hadley in the Connecticut River Valley. Map by Kate Blackmer

social relations, its tangible and intangible manifestations constantly and mutually constitutive.

In New England society manifestations of place were everywhere. One need look no further than the seating within the New England meetinghouse to understand how social and spatial status were entwined, both here and hereafter, the "dignity" of the pew being matched as closely as possible, in assignments made by church authorities, to that of its occupants. When men and women gathered for worship on Sunday mornings, the seat they took in the pews reflected the position their neighbors understood them to hold in the community. Committeemen appointed to map out the meetinghouse placed leading families at front and center, the less prominent in the back and sides, enslaved women and men in the back or in galleries. No record survives of the means by which Hadley made these determinations, but generally such assignments were based on a calculus of "age, estate and places of trust."[2] In Hadley, women and men appear to have sat separately until the early 1760s, when a shift in seating opened the door to other innovations with subtle but important effect. As Laurel Ulrich has suggested, when "the first families of the town began to sit together in pews" (a change that appears to have come to Hadley later than elsewhere) "the distance between wealthy women and women of ordinary status became even more pronounced."[3] Meanwhile, already wide distances between white and black worshippers remained so; race was a determinative factor in the topography of the meetinghouse into the nineteenth century (gender prevailing here longer, too, as black men and women remained separated after white families began sitting together).

The relative rank as assessed by church committeemen was a matter of constant contestation, commanding the regular attention of town meeting, though tensions became acute the same years that witnessed the deepening imperial crisis.[4] In the 1760s, objections rose when some felt their pew assignments to be unacceptable, and residents unhappy with their placement "crowded into higher seats"; apparently the disgruntled had taken direct action: in May 1760, Hadley selectmen determined that "sundry persons of late have been disorderly on the Sabbath by refusing to take such seats as have been appointed them by the seaters . . . and have presumptuously gone into seats higher than those assigned them to the great injury of those that were seated there, and to the disturbance of all the Congregation." Four years later, once again, when seating was recalibrated, "persons were aggrieved."[5] Tempers also flared in the early 1770s, when the committee charged with seating the meetinghouse found their recommendations rejected, over and over.[6] In time, Hadley (like its counterparts across the region) would abandon the seating of the meetinghouse. Old systems of deference died away, and new sentiments about equality flourished in their stead, as resettlements of meetinghouse real estate would both reflect and prefigure larger upheavals in class, gender, and landscape unfolding in the early republic.

Thinking about what class may mean in early America—in rural areas, among women, or more particularly among rural women—no metaphor seems as useful as that of place. In the towns and villages of eighteenth-century rural New England, it is difficult to approach the subject of gender and class in their usual definitions and terms.[7] In recent years, scholars writing about class have shifted the center of gravity from cultural or political constructs to material constraints, but the conversations continue to emphasize perceptions of commonality among men and women in like circumstances over perceptions of difference. Simon Middleton has proposed that the "social power" of class relations "implies more than the force exerted by one class over another to attain its particular ends," and is "best conceived" as "a field of relationships and interactions that pulls as much as pushes men and women into social and cultural arrangements with particular economic outcomes while remaining constantly in flux: contested, negotiated, and rarely, if ever, static."[8] Seth Rockman in particular has urged students of early America to reconsider how we think about notions of class disentangled from class consciousness, to affirm the material context of class position, to plunge toward the center of multicultural communities, and to explore the interdependent relationships between all forms of labor along a continuum of slavery and freedom. He has suggested that, in order to gain new insights about class relationships, we need to look at them anew, on the ground and in constellation.[9]

To be sure, in the towns and villages of New England, gradations were often subtle, fluid, and contentious; the distance between a community's greatest members and its least was a fraction of what one might observe in some colonial and early national cities. As Mary Fuhrer finds in Boylston, Massachusetts (a town about sixty miles to the east), with the exception of apparel, "distinctions of wealth could be found mostly outside—in the form of land and livestock."[10] In Revolutionary-era Hadley, property was distributed fairly evenly. More than 67 percent of Hadley heads of household in 1771 were taxed for a dwelling; the top tenth of these taxpayers held just under 39 percent of the wealth.[11] The six hundred acres amassed by Charles Phelps was rare among Connecticut Valley towns (in Northampton, only one in five farmers held more than one hundred acres, and in Hatfield, one in four), catapulting this family to the top of the social order, but on the whole the profile was flatter than many other places across the Atlantic World.[12]

In that setting, the men and women of western Massachusetts did not always construct or construe identity in terms of the people most like themselves; rather, they watched for evidence of difference. These early American women understood themselves and their families principally in terms of their position in the community relative to others; in this "culture of appraisal," their points of reference were less those who seemed most like themselves than those who were decidedly not. In Hadley and towns like it, women knew whose financial situation was either clearly better or clearly worse, and whose social status was plainly superior or plainly subordinate.[13] Class was less a position than a process.

In his masterful 1990 book, *The Roots of Rural Capitalism*, Christopher Clark posits that rural farmers, over the final decades of the eighteenth century and the early decades of the nineteenth, turned gradually toward distant markets, exchanging an economic culture grounded in long-standing personal relationships for another shaped by cash transactions. Women's decision making around their work was integral to these developments, as they both accepted and pursued the new forms of labor (particularly outwork, as well as factory and shop settings) that advanced their households' interests in this evolving economic terrain. Clark later observed that there was work yet to be done before we fully understand "how inequities shaped farm families' adaptation to the processes of change on the countryside."[14] This project seeks to contribute to that larger effort by contemplating the vastly different lives and opportunities contained in this single town, and by exploring rural poverty alongside success, plumbing in earnest lives that, while deeply entangled, led in very different directions.

Such arguments resonate with a proposition offered by historian Jeanne Boydston, who suggested in a landmark article that students of early American women's history should revisit the ways in which gender has been construed as a "category of analysis." Contemplating how other sources of identity have contributed to our understanding of the past, Boydston observes that gender was inextricably entwined with other categories in which people place themselves and one another, constituting one set of threads in the "complex fabric of processes and meanings that constitute a social or cultural history."[15] Looking closely at labor and landscape in Hadley reveals ways in which markers like male and female moved together with markers of race, social and economic position, family, ability, and even time in place (longevity on the land, that is) to shape present circumstances and future prospects.[16]

At the same time, the way historians understand work in this period has become increasingly complex and expansive. Observations of the multiple ways women's "place" was constructed are imbricated alongside discussions of the evolution of social and gender relations of work. Since women's history emerged as an enterprise with scholarly force in the wake of the modern women's movement, historians have given working women in the early modern Atlantic World significant attention. Important questions have revolved around the work that has been understood as appropriate for women to perform—or in more academic terms, gendered divisions of labor—and the past thirty years have witnessed a tremendous outpouring of research that tracks shifting currents in how an array of tasks and occupations were assigned gender across time in a wide range of localities. How societies think about what work is appropriately performed by men and by women has never been stable: that thinking varies by race and by class, and certainly by time and space. It is shaped by cultural expectations as well as structural social and economic conditions, and it is always in flux as it responds to and drives other developments in the economy and culture. For residents of Britain's North American colonies, the decades surrounding the creation of the United States were decades of especially volatile change.

As Maria Ågren writes in a landmark book on women's work in early modern society, "the point of departure for research cannot be whether women worked"—because of course they did—"but rather what they did for a living."[17] Rethinking what we mean by "work"—how we understand what motivated (and motivates) people to work, how we approach the role of work (or lack thereof) in constituting identity and how we define the boundaries of enterprise—has yielded an array of important insights. Our twenty-first-century lives are focused on occupations as sources of income (to the exclusion of almost any other motivation, it often seems), but in the eighteenth century the management and stewardship of existing resources—that is, the skills and knowledge constituting "housewifery"—were every bit as important as the generation of new revenue.[18] Many have placed consumer desire at the center of their conception of what motivates people to work, giving short shrift to other forces, including the genuine desire to provide a comfortable home for one's family—motives at least as compelling as the desire for ever-newer and still-shinier things. As Nancy Folbre and Julie A. Nelson caution, we should beware the false dichotomy that "one works either for love or for money—that is, out of spiritual values, affection, and altruism, or out of crass materialism, self-interest, and greed."[19] This project joins others that emphasize multiple, simultaneous, and overlapping contexts and seek to understand how "calculation and interest enter into the very heart of emotional relations," the "cost of reciprocity and its conventions," and the "role of long-term relations in the build-up of trust between partners in trade."[20] Many women were then, as now, driven by a range of desires. The appeal of luxuries small and large competed with the aim to satisfy the more quotidian needs that create our own comfort and that of our loved ones. Women's work responded to needs both immediate and aspirational, driven by necessity and expectation (their own, and those of others), and satisfied both tangible and intangible demands.

One way to transcend abstract constructs, to accept Boydston's challenge to "focus instead on the complex fabric of processes and meanings that constitute a social or cultural history," and to embrace the most encompassing perspectives about the motives that underlay labor, is to track the tangible world in which women were embedded, and explore how experience is mirrored by and constructed through material landscapes, in the homes, neighborhoods, and communities that otherwise gave shape to their lives.[21] As Doreen Massey has written, "It is not just that the spatial is socially constructed; the social is spatially constructed too."[22] To quote yet another observer of these phenomena, the geographer Tim Cresswell, "Class, gender and race are often treated as if they happened on the head of a pin," but a discussion of the geographic and material environments in which women's work relationships were enmeshed can provide another means by which to understand the forces that shaped their economic lives.[23]

This book, then, explores place as a metaphor for class position while also examining the ways that real, physical landscapes shaped and reflected those meanings for individual women and for the families to whom they belonged. The chapters herein consider the interior landscapes of the homes of the gentry as rural workplaces, the evolution of rural neighborhoods, and other ways that place and space both shaped and reflected social relations. Conversations about poverty and charity take in the shifting geography of poor relief, as public support attached to individual households scattered across the community gave way to a more centralized approach in the form of a town poor farm. What did it mean when some of the town's least advantaged members ceased to circulate through the households willing to take them in and became instead concentrated together in a single place on the local landscape? Contemplation of the "social centrifuge" that was the market revolution tracks the ways changes in architecture reflect new demands for liberty and opportunity among employers and employees alike. Taken together, these stories reveal how, in the decades following the American Revolution, relationships between place, in the sense of geography, landscape, and material environments, and "place," in the sense of society, class, and status, changed, even in a rural New England town.[24]

The heart of this investigation lies in the early years of the American republic. Though from time to time we'll glance backward, to the mid-eighteenth century, and forward, to the early nineteenth, the center of gravity here lies in the five decades immediately following Independence. I am most interested in how social relations of work among women transformed between the 1780s and 1820s, a period Clark has termed one of "involution," when western Massachusetts families intensified their market activity.[25] As Clark has shown, in these years the rise of urban markets coupled with population growth and land shortages altered Massachusetts' household economy, increasing emphasis on cash transactions and drawing ever-larger numbers of women into outwork.

These changes strengthened ties between western Massachusetts towns and the cities that supplied markets for goods and labor. A number of historians have together built a compelling picture of the ways in which the second quarter of the nineteenth century saw the emergence of more defined and observable social classes, as new consumer goods, systems of production, built environments, and other cultural priorities helped middling families articulate distinct sensibilities.[26] This study joins those in an effort to help us better understand more generally how social relations of labor, particularly among rural women in the early republic, are created, reconfigured, unsettled, and sustained, and how opportunities that shape class, wealth, and access to education are formed by constellations of circumstances.

Periodization, however, is complicated by the range of subjects considered here. How change comes to rural places like Hadley is difficult to narrate; tidy timelines can overstate or artificially privilege some areas of human activity and perception over others.[27] Now and then turning points are clear, driven by leaps in technology or some political, environmental, economic, or cultural rupture; more often, though, change comes more slowly, unfolding gradually over lifespans and generations.[28] Continuity necessarily emerges from the daily exchanges of men and women, from generations of inhabitants, as they go about their everyday lives, earning a living, raising families. Christopher Clark found that, in early Hadley, at least among the town's white women, persistence was more prevalent than migration: of 227 women listed in Lucius Boltwood's "Genealogies of Hadley Families" who are noted as having been born in the years 1780–1789, at least 54.2 percent, and perhaps as many as 71.4 percent, remained in Hadley or in a nearby town.[29] For the women considered here, the drama of the American Revolution sat alongside the quotidian rhythms of daily life over decades, the advent of technological innovations, new patterns of work, and other disruptions absorbed incrementally.

Even the end of legal human bondage came slowly, as freedom came to some Connecticut Valley residents long before others (Connecticut opting for gradual emancipation), while others continued to live in conditions much unchanged from their involuntary status. The decades in focus here, then, must be seen as part of incremental and uneven trajectories in women's labor history over the long seventeenth and eighteenth centuries and through the Federal Period in the United States. Following (for instance) three generations in the family of Peg, enslaved by the Phelps family until she secured her own freedom in the 1780s, alongside three generations in the lives of the family of domestic servant Susanna Whipple, Susanna's unsanctioned daughter Submit, and Submit's own unsanctioned daughter Philina, demonstrates powerfully persistence amid change.[30] The developments described herein are multilayered and untidy, events that occurred decades apart sometimes making sense in juxtaposition.

Decisions reflect short- and long-term calculations, their results accumulating gradually, probably at times imperceptibly to the families who witnessed them.

The patterns observed here can be located among larger understandings of women's work over time, and before the transformative effects of industrialization as described by historians of gender and labor in American cities as well as the United Kingdom, Europe, and beyond. No place, of course, is "typical"—to see what matters here, we must look constantly to ways that this site is both like and unlike other places nearby and farther afield. Several scholars have traced the lives of working women elsewhere in eighteenth- and early nineteenth-century New England, particularly in the port cities of Boston and Newport.[31] A lively community of historians devoted to the study of early modern women's work have recovered an astonishingly detailed view of laboring women's lives in the context of the Atlantic World.[32] Particularly important here is the insight articulated by Maria Ågren and her colleagues (engaged in the pathbreaking collaborative initiative, "Gender and Work in Sweden in the Period 1550 to 1800") that "when European women's labor force participation declined sharply in the nineteenth century, only to rise again in the twentieth," it was "after an unprecedentedly high level" of participation in the late eighteenth century.[33] Researchers abroad and at home have shown that gendered divisions of labor are fluid, shape-shifting, and sometimes unpredictable, and that the transition from "two-supporter" model to "single-breadwinner" model across the Atlantic World unfolded differently, at different paces in different places. As Ågren and her collaborators assert, "We need both the big map to find our way in the terrain," they continue, "and the magnifying glass to spot subtleties on the ground."[34] This study applies that magnifying glass to Hadley, Massachusetts, to illuminate how that transition looked "on the ground" in western New England.

Focusing the lens on this singular landscape, the study plumbs the world of female labor in one small town and considers the ways in which women's labor bound communities together, while also sustaining (if transforming) the hierarchical structures on which they rested as well as the spaces those structures occupied. As I explore several means of livelihood available to women in eighteenth- and early nineteenth-century Hadley, I map some members of the community's female workforce, with the hope that we will better understand the economy of rural New England (both for women and for men) by looking closely at work as it unfolded and evolved across households in a single Massachusetts town.

Such sustained contemplations of one small place sit in no way at odds with other impulses to locate our subjects in broad global contexts. The men and women of Hadley, Massachusetts, were every bit citizens of the world. The clothes they wore, the food they ate, the ideas they debated all flowed to and through the small town from points around the globe; their livelihoods and comforts depended on the faraway families who would eat their grains, vegetables, and fattened cattle, who would smoke Hadley tobacco or sweep their floors with Hadley brooms. Hadley men died in the same worldwide colonial and imperial struggles that drew the globe together in conflict, and Hadley dinner tables absorbed conversations as loud as anywhere about rights, slavery, nation, and empire. But the way Hadley families experienced that world was necessarily shaped too by their own lived experience. For some, that meant travel (often as soldiers) to points around the world; for others it meant encounters with other families with common interests in commerce or politics. Knowledge of the wider world was filtered through encounters with travelers who brought news to local taverns, churches, and parlors. In time, as families sifted through the information that came their way, embracing some ideas, rejecting others, the local responded to (and so continued to direct) the global. In this way, the village participated in broad developments sweeping across Britain's North American colonies and the republic to emerge from them in ways reflective of distinct local and regional circumstances and culture.

Source Subjectivities

Our imagined walk down the Hadley Common, and our ability to see clearly into some houses and not at all into others, reminds us of those vagaries of historical inquiry, how we can know a great deal about some things and almost nothing about others. A very bright light, for instance, glows from the household at Forty Acres, because the wealthy Porter family (which later became the Phelps family, and then Huntington) who lived there in the eighteenth and nineteenth centuries generated pages and pages of diaries, letters, accounts, and other documents preserved by descendants.[35] At the age of sixteen, likely at the encouragement of her elders, young Elizabeth began keeping a journal, which she called a "memorandum book," perhaps to supply some companionship, perhaps to comply with imperatives surrounding the monitoring of one's spiritual life embraced by her Congregational church.[36] For the first several years of the journal, she recorded only the biblical text of the Sunday sermon. But then, in the autumn of 1766, something unusual happened. A townswoman named Submit Gaylord delivered a stillborn child and then died. The diarist, just weeks shy of her nineteenth birthday, found the events shocking, even portentous. Submit and her husband, Samuel, had only been married in April; her death just six months later and the death of their child seemed sure punishment for Submit's having been intimate with Samuel before a wedding occurred. The following week, the minister seized on the events to remind parishioners of the fury of God's wrath. From that week forward, and over the next nearly five decades, through her 1770 marriage to Charles Phelps, the births of her children Charles, Elizabeth, and Thankful, and the upheaval and aftermath of Revolution itself, Elizabeth's memorandum book became a versatile record, part spiritual journal, part account book, part confidante.[37] In its pages she documented the men and women who visited her home, the people who came to work there, and the labor accomplished. She drew on these entries for reference; when a question arose about the tenure of one visitor to the house, Phelps could write to her husband, "Should you be at a loss how long Mrs Payson was here I can tell you I have searched my records and find she came the 9 of March."[38]

I too have searched Phelps's records, and find Payson and hundreds of other women in the pages of her text, most of them from her own small town, and many others from neighboring towns like Amherst, Hatfield, and Belchertown, but also from places more distant too, such as Spencer, Brookfield, and Boston in Massachusetts, and Hartford, Wethersfield, and other towns in Connecticut, and even women from worlds away—from England, the Netherlands, and Germany, to West Africa and the West Indies. In any given year during the decades between 1780 and 1800, some two hundred visitors crossed Phelps's worn threshold.[39] Moreover, Phelps's house still stands near the banks of the Connecticut River and is today a historic house museum (figure I.2). We can see well into the kitchens, chambers, and parlor of this well-appointed home, supported by working women across the community. We can examine Phelps's possessions, read her letters, or scour her memorandum book, with no risk that she will discover us snooping. We can read along with her daughter as Phelps complains about the domestic servants in her employ or heads out for a full morning of "errands." We smile to picture her falling asleep while trying to knit a mitten, recognizing in her dozing an experience we have all had at the end of a long day. And we cringe at her earthy descriptions of "puking" while nevertheless trying to get through her morning's chores, and nod in recognition as she complains about the pressure of keeping the housework up as she gets older and frailer.

But the bright archival glow that emanates from the Phelps farm also exaggerates its importance, skewing our perspective by making some individuals and households loom inappropriately large, as if they were more central, more widely known, more influential in their worlds than they in fact were. Where do shadows lengthen beyond their sources, distorting size and shape? To be sure, Forty Acres was probably among the most important employers in early Hadley. But for the women who crossed that threshold only a handful of times as employees of the household, those visits may have been barely memorable, negligible events on the periphery rather than the center of any woman's orbit. We must use such forceful texts with caution, attending to absences as well as strong presences. And we must strain to contemplate how the men and women

Figure I.2 Forty Acres in the 1920s. This photo of Forty Acres shortly before its transition to a historic house museum shows the size and form of this influential family's home as Elizabeth Porter Phelps and her household knew it. Visible here (*right to left*) is the three-story, gambrel-roofed house, the large south kitchen ell and dairy spaces, corn barn, and carriage sheds; a large barn stood just out of view at left. The Porter-Phelps-Huntington Foundation, Inc., Porter-Phelps-Huntington Museum, Hadley, MA. Photograph P050: November 19, 1922, Edward Hubbard, Hadley, MA, photographer

whose lives are described herein might have described those moments differently in the telling of their own lives. If through Phelps's records we can observe indirectly the activity of the domestic servants, spinners, weavers, midwives, and other women whose work brought them in and out of this house, others leave us in the dark. In the summer of 1788, for instance, Phelps rode out one morning "do to business with Mrs Sweetser." But what sort of business she does not say, and we can no longer discover: Mrs. Sweetser's house is almost entirely dark.[40]

The pull of compelling documents like Phelps's papers is offset partly by the work of local historian Sylvester Judd (1789–1860), whose conversations in the second quarter of the nineteenth century with Hadley residents of the Revolutionary generation would help shape his view of Hadley's past. Many historians of western Massachusetts have drawn on the research of Hampshire County antiquarian Judd, whose monumental *History of Hadley: Including the Early History of Hatfield, South Hadley, Amherst and Granby, Massachusetts* was published in 1863. His dozens of fat notebooks, at rest in Northampton's Forbes Library—covering topics from Connecticut and Massachusetts history to various Hampshire County towns to, wonderfully, nearly twenty volumes dedicated to miscellany, and capturing content gleaned from a vast range of sources published and unpublished—teem with observations on everything from the price of flax in the 1670s to the topography and biodiversity of Mount Holyoke as he walked it in the 1820s. But of particular value here are the conversations he recorded, as he sought to understand Hadley's past, with about twenty residents, at least nine of them local women, inviting them to reflect on their own lives, and on others in their community. Judd's notes are full of these testimonies, noting what this or that person "says" or "mentions," adding when possible their year of birth to help situate them in time. Though the women Judd spoke with are a small and select group, his notes capture some glimpse into the perceptions of Hadley women—Sophia Cook Clark, Thankful Richmond Hitchcock and her daughter Martha Richmond Smith, Abigail Dickinson Newton, and others—as they looked back over the course of their own lives and shared their recollections of the community.[41]

But he and his informants inherited traditions that were still older. Rebecca Crow Noble (1712–1802) was one of the community storytellers whose memories were long and imaginations vivid. Her own story was dramatic enough that versions survived in local memory through the nineteenth century. Another local historian, Clifton Johnson (1865–1940), recorded that "in her youth" Rebecca Crow "had been a girl of superior beauty and much admired." A man from Hartford had supposedly wooed her, but in a jealous fit she spurned his suit, and when regrets came, they came too late. The disappointment changed her. She grew older and wiser, people said, but "with none of her former beauty and sprightliness."[42] When she was just shy of fifty she married Daniel Noble of Westfield, but after his death she returned to Hadley, where she died in poverty at the age of ninety.

Rebecca Crow Noble was supported in her final years by the town. In the eighteenth century, Massachusetts communities assisted the poor among them by placing them in the care of a household, and then compensating that household for the expenses they incurred in the effort. In 1783, Noble agreed to sell everything she owned but her bed and to give herself over to public support. From then on, the town reimbursed whoever provided room and board for her at a rate of four shillings six pence per week in summer, and an additional shilling per week in winter, presumably her share of increased expenses for heat and light.[43] In exchange for the necessities of life, Rebecca recounted stories learned in her youth, pirate tales and stories about settlers battling Indians. She told about her grandfather, killed in the celebrated—or notorious—Falls Fight of May 1676, and her grandmother, who lived through the tumultuous days when Mary Reeve ("Moll") Webster was accused of witchcraft. Though tried in Boston and acquitted, Moll Webster was strung up by the young men of Hadley until she was nearly dead and then buried in the snow, only to spring back to life. In time, those stories came to new generations of Hadley citizens, some of whom, like Sylvester Judd and later Clifton Johnson, wrote them down for posterity.[44]

Other kinds of records appear less ephemeral, though they too can be deceptive in their illusion of veracity. Account books and ledgers of various sorts tell us of the many ways that women contributed to the upkeep of their families by making shirts, weaving cloth, churning butter, making cheese, knitting, or weaving. Probate records in which the estate is debited for the final care of the deceased tell us who served as nurses in their communities. The houses and outbuildings that survive on the landscape, the paths that are now roads, the extant patterns of fields and farms also contain hints about the ways women sustained themselves and their families. The study of objects to answer questions not easily addressed in the archival record offers another means by which to explore the past. Though we are rarely able to discover what affective meanings working women made of their environments, the evolution of domestic architecture can be harnessed to contemplate changes in their lives. As employing families reconfigured workspaces inhabited by employees, we get glimpses into how the early national economy altered the experience of families of means and the people they employed, as well as the shifting relations between those groups. If we move our vantage point and take in houses in constellation, contemplating what historians term the "cultural landscapes" of the village, we gain insight into larger patterns. We see how neighborhoods form and relate to one another, and how the village's position with respect to the larger world changed as bridges supplanted ferries, and circulation patterns changed in response to the building of roads, turnpikes, railroads, and new centers of commercial activity, while the village itself stayed still.

Looking carefully at the narratives preserved in notebooks like Johnson's, and the still-older volumes created by Sylvester Judd, both as evidence of the eighteenth-century past and subsequent interpretation of it, suggests how the cultural work of memory in popular and scholarly imagination—what we remember, why and how we remember it, what we forget—can also inflect these pages. Judd and his informants had their own preoccupations and prejudices, engaged here not as biases to be read past but as evidence themselves of the anxieties of an age. Judd, as Altina Waller has explained, immersed himself in the past as his present became increasingly frustrating: schisms across communities of faith, rising political tension and the expansion of opposition parties, and the collapse of the once "homogeneous, unified agricultural community" as Northampton became an "economically diverse, politically and religiously pluralistic town." These tensions, all coupled with his own business failures, drove him to the study of history in part as a means of escape.[45] Likewise the notes Clifton Johnson kept for a never-published book about the mid-century town, "An Old Town in New England," offer insight into how Victorian and Progressive-era Hadley remembered its Federal past, as do writings of descendants of Elizabeth Porter Phelps (grandson Theodore Gregson Huntington, great-granddaughter Arria Huntington, and great-great-grandson James Lincoln Huntington), as well as choices those descendants made, as they dealt with their family's tangible legacy, about what to preserve, and what to discard. This study engages such sources sometimes as repositories of information unrecorded elsewhere, and often as avenues of insight into changing beliefs about, and understandings of, local (and regional and national) history.[46]

However rich these sources may be, the slices of life captured in the archival and artifactual detritus of history nonetheless also remind us how flat the world of the past can get when compressed onto two-hundred-year-old paper. In her day, for instance, the plain, shrewd, and cross-eyed Sarah Pomeroy was a legendary Northampton mimic who could "imitate the voice of any person or animal." Now we can know little more about Sarah's life than the value of her husband's estate and what the household paid in taxes from year to year—we can't hear her impressions of her neighbors, and even if we could, we probably wouldn't get the joke.[47] Likewise, despite the wealth of documents left behind by Elizabeth Porter Phelps, we can only know what she committed to paper. Forty Acres is so quiet now that it is hard to picture the hustle and bustle of the working farm: the bleating sheep, whinnying horses, cackling hens in the barnyard, barking dogs, and cows lowing in the barn. Butter is not churning in the dairy, flax is not bundled on the stoop to be scutched, fattened cattle are not restlessly awaiting the long drive to Boston. No longer do wagons piled high with barrels rattle in and out of the farmyard; carts bearing trunks stuffed with grandchildren's coats, bonnets, and mittens are not unburdened on the porch. Seasons of planting and harvests have given way to the rhythms of New England tourism and the quieter work of museum interpretation and preservation. Hired help still congregates in the large kitchen, but the dairy and field hands bent over tubs and hatchels have been replaced by students bent over keyboards in what is now the office of the Porter-Phelps-Huntington Foundation staff.

That quiet is misleading. When we lose the sounds of everyday life, the aural environment of the past, our ability to imagine that world is diminished. And so we depend on these written records, amplified by our historical imagination, to remind us that Phelps's world, like ours, could be loud and cluttered and that she and her neighbors, like us, sometimes found their nerves jangled, their minds distracted. When Sylvester Judd was recording people's recollections of the town's eighteenth-century past, for instance, one thing many people remembered was the geese. The street and common were once full of geese, their cackling heard at all times. One woman remarked that when one honked, they all did, a phenomenon that led to some "loud night noise." Elihu Warner recalled that the geese used to gather around people leaving the meetinghouse and made a terrible ruckus. Oliver Smith, too, mentioned how all that "squaking" made a "world of noise." Mrs. Ephraim Smith commented that "almost every family had a flock"—although she did add that Charles Phelps had refused to keep geese because of the racket. Giles Crouch Kellogg likewise remembered the "street full of geese, and full of feathers. Their noise was incessant. They made so much noise in time of public worship that you could not hear the minister." Long-gone songbirds and even the bell of the meetinghouse— some sounds that were so familiar then are hard to conjure now.

But if the sounds, sights, and smells of working farms have long since vanished, the physical fabric of the Phelps house remains, and continues to speak, if only in signs, of eighteenth-century Hampshire County. The noisy geese that once stalked the town common become metaphors of more substantive tensions that were part of the nature of and variety across early American laborers' lives. Understanding the multitiered human and material communities in which those variations played out enables us more fully to understand those larger developments, and to assess their consequences as well.

The Lay of This Land

A few paragraphs are in order to map the lay of the analytical terrain ahead. To entangle the working women of early Hadley and explore the ways labor both brought women together while also setting them apart, part 1 follows a handful of women, observing how their lives and work were enmeshed with the lives and work of their neighbors. An initial chapter surveys the society, culture, landscape, and economy of the village of Hadley from its founding through the era of the American Revolution, sketching the town's histories of settlement and enslavement and describing its eighteenth-century economy and culture while also introducing the families whose cultural, political, and economic influence shaped life in Hadley. This and the next two chapters together limn portraits of women whose lives remind us how wide the gaps were that separated the mothers, wives, and daughters of Hadley, even in a rural Massachusetts community that might at first glance seem comparatively homogeneous. In order to approach gentility as both a social category and a distinct occupation in and of itself, we enter the dairying spaces of Elizabeth Porter Phelps and observe her work there as well as the labors of other women—the African American dairywomen Sarah Jackson, onetime (Anglo or African American) hired woman Zerviah Ford, and the Native American woman

Assinah, whose labor was essential to Phelps's own. We meet the African American families—the Prutts, Bostons, and Ways—as well as the enslaved men and women of the Phelps farm who lived in and around an array of Hadley households, struggling to create and sustain family ties, during enslavement and after. And we consider the ways poverty, public welfare, and economic (legal, illegal, and marginally legal) activities positioned less fortunate women within the larger community—women like the resourceful laborer Mary Trainer and the resourceless immigrant Mary Andries.

An important intervention in recent scholarship on the history of working women has been the reconsideration of slavery and freedom as distinct categories.[48] To better understand the lives of these enslaved women and other women, black and white, who labored under contracts that bound them to a household or enterprise for some given period, Ruth Herndon and Ella Sekatau remind us, we need to replace conceptions of a polarity between confinement and liberty with another model that accommodates degrees of freedom and unfreedom.[49] Women in Hadley found their actions circumscribed by a number of legal, cultural, and social institutions, including pauper apprenticeships, compulsory indentures and apprenticeships, and various sorts of interventions by selectmen and other town officials. Looking closely at the work women did helps us understand not only gender, class, race, and place, but also how those institutions functioned in rural New England towns.

Part 2 turns to some of the most significant categories of work for Hadley women: domestic service, cloth making, health and healing, and hospitality trades. Many researchers—myself included—have opted to organize their studies by focusing on specific occupations: millinery, midwifery, tavernkeeping, brewing, weaving, and so forth.[50] But I do so here with caution, as I have come to believe that grounding our questions principally in occupation, whether of men or of women, risks misrepresenting to greater and lesser degrees lived experience, as it does not account well for variation over time or through seasons, and masks the extent of multiple employments. Moreover, it can exaggerate our perception of occupations, overdrawing distinctions and creating misperceptions about the ways occupations were practiced and understood, implying stability where there was fluidity.[51] Studies focused on particular occupations can overlook small, interconnected processes that facilitate larger systems (an effect that often neglects, for example, important roles played by children), as well as ways that women's work itself facilitates and lubricates the larger community and social systems described herein. As an organizational strategy, it can obscure occasions when an activity that is work for one person is leisure for another and flattens levels of relative expertise. And it overstates, if only by implication, the degree to which identity was entangled with occupation in the early American past.[52]

Yet this approach remains methodologically valuable, and in many ways appropriate as a means to marshal evidence and understand how certain tasks were accomplished, production organized, and labor needs met in early American communities. Women's work in clothes-making trades was every bit as entangling as the occupations addressed in this volume, but that subject is amply covered in *The Needle's Eye*; here the analysis turns to changes in cloth production as a lens into larger shifts in social relations of labor. Other chapters consider domestic service, hospitality trades, and women's work in health care and healing, the latter two in particular allowing us to consider work grounded in service rather than production. Yet several arenas of women's labor are not examined here. Because this study explores ways that work generated and shaped relations between women from different households, it does not dwell on the labor women undertook to care for their own families—tasks like the endless knitting, mending, or laundering required to keep families clothed, or the daily labor involved in tending animals, cooking and cleaning, gardening, and preserving food. That effort, to be sure, was mighty, and work for one's household and labor for the market entwined, sometimes indistinguishable, both within and across households.[53] Likewise, throughout the eighteenth century and in Britain's North American colonies, for instance, women were deeply involved in agriculture.[54] Native American women had farmed long before European settlement, while African American women farmed whether enslaved or free. European women farmed as well. They also worked in family gardens producing vegetables and fruits to supplement the household's diets and herbs for medicinal purposes. They raised poultry for the meat, eggs, and feathers; they cared for the cows that provided meat, milk, and butter, and the sheep that supplied meat and wool. They labored in fields, planting and tending crops, hoeing, and harvesting, and they processed the fruits of those labors once they were out of the ground and in the barn.[55]

Other ways by which women earned incomes in early America are also absent from these pages. Some women in early America generated revenue, for instance, by providing financial services, but little evidence survives of that activity in early Hadley or Hampshire County, though Elizabeth Porter Phelps's intriguing reference to her neighbor "Landlady Smith" raises questions about women acting principally as rent seekers.[56] Shopkeeping, while important elsewhere, does not jump from the pages of local sources. Though family-owned shops engaged a handful of women in eighteenth-century Hadley, they were small in number and do not appear to involve women as employees.[57]

This project also joins others that emphasize multiple, simultaneous, and overlapping contexts and seek to understand how "calculation and interest enter into the very heart of emotional relations," the "cost of reciprocity and its conventions," and the "role of long-term relations in the build-up of trust between partners in trade."[58] Many women were then, as now, driven by a range of desires; the appeal of luxuries small and large competed, as it does now, with the aim to satisfy the more quotidian needs that constitute our own comfort and that of our loved ones. Their labor, prompted by both everyday needs and emotional ties, drew them into other relationships that were no less emotionally charged. This study, then, harnesses what's helpful about occupational study (the chapters that make up part 2) while also revealing the deeply entangled ways that work, identity, and both conflicting and cooperative needs bound together people across a community, and with others very far away.

Finally, in the concluding chapters that form part 3, the lens widens to take in the larger community, and we turn again to the work of entanglement, with particular attention to place. Chapter 8 focuses on a single building in this community—the mansion house of the Porter and Phelps families—and suggests how these developments can be observed in a domestic landscape. The concluding chapter contemplates how the real and metaphorical places women inhabited were transformed in the first decades of the nineteenth century, years of dramatic alteration in the social, commercial, and domestic landscapes of Hadley and beyond. Finally, a coda returns to the questions of women, work, and the gestures of remembrance with which these pages opened, contemplating how early Hadley's working women have fared in the town's collective memory in an effort to understand the contours of historical understanding today.

Each of the chapters here explore ways that changing configurations of women's work shaped and reshaped relationships in response to broader changes in the New England economy in the generations around and following the American Revolution, reconstellating lives that shared a common ground in rural western Massachusetts. In these pages, we meet women both as the protagonists of their own story and as supporting players in those of others; at times we visit and revisit the same sources, even the same passages, to see how the glimpses they afford might alter by subtly shifting our angle of vision. Looking closely in this way at women, work, and landscape in this single locale, entangling lives in and around the material environment in which they unfolded, affords a broader aspect on larger questions of social change in early New England.

WOMEN, WORK, AND COMMUNITY

From Nolwotogg to Hadley

Hadley, Massachusetts, was more than a century old when Elizabeth Porter Phelps started filling in the pages of her memorandum book, and as the recollections of Sylvester Judd's informants hint, memories in Hampshire County ran deep and long.[1] English families embraced Puritan understandings about their destiny in the region as well as long-standing beliefs about family, position, and pedigree to orient themselves among their neighbors. Women and men of wealth engaged an assumed cultural consensus to maintain positions of authority, while white families who had migrated just as early but whose fortune and influence were less great depended on their longevity on the landscape to assert their own claims. Newcomers navigated accordingly. Native American women certainly knew the history of their people's contact with the English settlers as they navigated the valley and the local economy. For many of the African and African American women brought unwillingly to western Massachusetts, that long sense of a grounded past was among the many assets stolen from them in their captivity. But these many pasts, and women's sense of where they and their families entered those timelines, shaped not only the ways they encountered systems of labor, but how they understood themselves in relation to neighbors and employers. As always, understanding the past that was in place for Hadley families in the era of Revolution helps us understand the (revolutionary and postrevolutionary) present.

English Settlement

I begin with Elizabeth Porter Phelps's family, the Porters, since the history and concerns of this influential family are inseparable from the history and concerns of Hadley itself. Elizabeth's forebears, the pious men and women who emigrated first from East Anglia and then north from Connecticut, belonged to a larger social movement of families anxious to purify a corrupt Church of England by reestablishing itself in its true form in what they perceived to be the American wilderness. After a few decades of settlement, though, considerable differences of opinion had emerged as to how best to achieve their aims. Founded in the 1650s and 1660s, Hadley was the refuge of men and women whose disagreements with their church over matters of faith became so profound that they felt they had to leave one community and establish another. In May 1653, men from Windsor, Hartford, and elsewhere in Connecticut petitioned the Massachusetts General Court for permission to settle lands several miles north of the settlement at Springfield. John Pynchon obtained a deed from the native occupants of the land in September 1653, and settlement of the community of Northampton commenced in 1654. Not long thereafter, controversy within the churches at Hartford and Wethersfield caused a number of families from Connecticut to settle a second tract of land set out by the General Court. The causes for division, as is usually the case, were multiple. Personal rifts played a role, and the death of founding minister Reverend Thomas Hooker led to disagreement over the choice of his successor. That disagreement was exacerbated by dissent over several theological issues, including qualifications for baptism, church membership, and the "rights of the brotherhood"— that is, the relationship among congregations of believers. In the late 1650s and early 1660s, migrants made plans to try once more in the town they christened Hadley. But even as they left the Connecticut outposts that had nurtured them, Hadley's eventual leaders remained closely connected to the political and religious revolutionaries who had toppled King Charles. After the monarchy was eventually restored in 1660, several local households harbored two of the fugitive regicides, Edward Whalley and William Goffe, events that even today remain a source of local pride and identity.[2]

In April 1659, a group of men gathered at Nathaniel Ward's house in Hartford and entered into an agreement to settle land upriver. Negotiations ensued with people of Nolwotogg in the middle Connecticut River Valley, which became present-day Hadley, Amherst, Hatfield, and Northampton.[3] The word *Nolwotogg* (also sometimes *Nonotuck* or *Norwottuck*) roughly translates to "the midpoint of the river." Culturally and linguistically, the Nolwotogg are part of the eastern Algonkian family of indigenous peoples that includes much of eastern Canada and all of New England. At first, the Nolwotogg were open to dealing with the newcomers. In a series of deeds, they conveyed to the English arrivals portions of the middle Connecticut Valley lands. In 1658, "the Indians of Nolwotogg" sold to John Pynchon, acting on behalf of the Hadley settlers, land on the east side of the Connecticut River. Three Nolwotoggs—Umpanchla, Quonquont, and Chickwalopp—signed the document that solemnized the arrangement. The natives reserved the right to occupy these lands from time to time and to extract firewood from them. In 1662, the English gained additional lands when a native family whose lands lay south of those already deeded also sold some land; Wequagon and his wife, Awonusk, and their son, Squomp, yielded land in the neighborhood that the English called Hockanum, as well as the future towns of South Hadley and Granby.[4]

When Nolwotogg Indians conveyed land at Northampton to English colonists in 1653 (both men and women signed these agreements, reflecting their society's understanding of men's and women's roles in political decision making), and in Hadley in 1658, they did so with intention, as they could see some advantages to having the English settle among them.[5] But they also saw a need to articulate several protections. For instance, in a written agreement signed in July 1660, the Nolwotogg reserved to themselves the right to hunt, fowl, and fish, and in some cases, the right to set wigwams and firewood on the commons. Before King Philip's War broke out in 1675, native families moved freely through English settlements. Men and women of the two communities exchanged goods, services, and knowledge, the Nolwotogg trading furs, venison, baskets, and mats for English goods, especially cloth and metalwork.

Taking the broad central street at Wethersfield as a model, proprietors laid out an unusually wide common—a generous mile in length and twenty rods (330 feet) wide—lined with forty-seven home lots, one reserved for the minister, one for the town, and another for the ferry.[6] The "Great Meadow" just to the west was divided into strips, marked by merestones, assigned to individual "engagers." By their April 1659 agreement, each English family would occupy a home lot of eight acres. Such an emphasis on equal distribution would not extend to the allotment of lands beyond the home lot, however, which were made according to the wealth each proprietor brought to the new settlement. Among the earliest proprietors, the largest share of land was approximately five times larger than the smallest.

Fifteen years later, in 1675, Wampanoags, Nipmucks, Pocumtucks, and Narragansetts all joined in a bloody war to drive the English out of their territories. Amid this conflict, now remembered as King Philip's War, Hadley's leaders decided to "set up [a palisade] for the defense and security of the town on the east and west side . . . that on the west side [of] the street to defend the meadows from spoils and damage, and to be subject to the inspection of the fence viewers, and no man in any part of the fortifications above said shall have or make any particular outlet for himself or cattle into meadows or lots."[7] Their protective palisade was constructed of "two rows of pales, stakes or posts about ten feet in length, having two feet in the ground and eight feet above the ground . . . set close together in the earth, and were probably fastened to a piece of wood near the top."[8] The fortifications persisted into the 1690s, but as the threat of attack waned, so did interest in these defenses. In time, they were dismantled or allowed to crumble.

Another sign of the colonists' sense of increasing security was the laying out of new streets. In the 1680s, optimistic inhabitants voted to create new home lots to the east of the settlement around the common.[9] This second street, or "back street," though envisioned, would not be settled until after the threat of violence had subsided. By 1720, fifteen families had settled along this new street. As late as 1770, that number had risen only to twenty-two, households that included both those of free black men Ralph Way, Ralph Way Jr., Hammon Way, and white physician Giles Kellogg.[10] A half-century later, the families along this pathway would come to possess growing economic power, but in the last quarter of the eighteenth century, the Back Street probably had more huckleberry bushes than residents.

Over time, gentry families like the Porters consolidated their position at the top of economic, political, ecclesiastical, and cultural orders. Their influence was significant and radiated well beyond Hadley, but in the town itself they were big fish in a small pond. By 1765, Hadley counted nearly ninety houses sheltering close to one hundred families. There were 150 men and 151 women, while boys (males under sixteen) numbered 125 and girls 127. The enslaved population had risen slightly, to thirteen men and seven women.[11] In 1770, about 110 families made up the town's six hundred or so residents.[12] When authorities made the 1771 Massachusetts tax valuation, Hadley's report listed 132 taxpayers, but the number of houses had held steady at eighty-nine.[13]

From Hadley's beginning, the households that made up the town relied on networks of exchange for the necessities and the small luxuries of everyday life. To develop these networks residents cultivated relationships voluntary and involuntary. In rural places like Hadley, one's choices about who to trade with to obtain certain goods were limited. There were only so many fullers able to prepare textiles, for example; there were only so many shops that carried the wanted goods, and they stood where they stood. In such places, tacit assumptions about reciprocity guided local exchange. Sometimes the rules—embedded in increasingly formal institutions necessary to guide transactions between strangers—were explicit and unambiguous (for example, if you fail to settle your account at my shop I will take you to court), but more often they were intangible and implied (if I come to your quilting, I will expect to see you at mine). Forces both centripetal and centrifugal were constantly at work, pulling the community together at the same time that they drove people apart.

Those relationships unfolded across the town and within the neighborhoods that constituted the eighteenth-century community, from the mills north and south of the town center to the village of Hockanum to the south. Mutual exchange was key. Account books and ledgers, usually kept by men, tracked some kinds of obligations; diaries kept by women tracked others.[14] But both systems devised to record financial exchanges and systems also monitored less tangible debts sustained and reflected larger cultural ideas about long-term relations between individuals and families. In an economy grounded in long chains of credit only periodically settled, memories were long, and careful—a cultural demeanor that carried over to other aspects of community life. Sometimes things went awry (someone overcharging for goods or services, or failing to deliver as promised) and conflicts among neighbors upset immediate and distant equilibriums. Other hitches occurred when the same watchfulness that allowed neighbors to know when someone was in need of help led to unwelcome prying or unflattering gossip. The power of familial and individual identity on which these relationships depended, however, usually supplied the social ballast that sustained the system over decades, even generations.[15]

Indeed, a number of vehicles beyond the formal devices of daybooks and account books served as economic aide mémoire among the households of western Massachusetts. For Hampshire County healer and midwife Rhoda Childs even chalk markings on a door might provide a record of exchange.[16] In this rural economy, cash changed hands infrequently; instead, debts were noted in records maintained with varying degrees of formality, and only "reckoned" or "settled" at long intervals. This system ensured that families were knit together in complex relationships that endured over years; beneath the give-and-take of day-to-day life lay tacit knowledge of the long-term debts and obligations. As Christopher Clark warns, such "obligations should not be sentimentalized. Frequently enough they gave rise to conflicts. But they were real, and they embodied the distinctive moral demands made by rural people on each other when they exchanged goods, labor, and other services."[17]

Hadley's commercial life on the eve of the American Revolution thrived. In 1771, three shops offered a wide range of goods.[18] A handful of dedicated workshops sheltered the community's craft enterprises, including two shoemakers, a hatter, a potter, a cooper, a blacksmith, two joiners, and a maltster. Other artisans—such as the town's tailors, gown makers, and seamstresses—worked from their homes, and in the homes of their customers. After a hard day's work, people could find refreshment at several local taverns.[19] Two gristmills and two sawmills harnessed water power to improve the town's ability to process grain and wood products. The agricultural economy was diverse, not specialized: eighty-two barns and thirty-nine cornhouses sheltered livestock and stored an array of agricultural products. The town's farmers raised some 11,000 bushels of grain, produced close to 370 barrels of cider, and mowed well over 800 tons of hay. But no household could supply all of their own needs, nor did they aim to; rather, the agricultural products raised and sold allowed them to secure needs and comforts from farther afield—candles from Boston, tools from England, sugar from the West Indies, tea from Asia, cloths woven from Indian cotton. Hampshire County men and women made use of imported goods, some that traveled in ship's holds to merchants in Boston and Hartford, and others that traveled by wagons and boats to shelves closer to home.

Slavery and Antislavery

In July 1771, Elizabeth Phelps recorded that a "negro man" in Hadley had "melted himself dead with the violent heat."[20] Little more than this single, heart-stopping image is necessary to grasp the nature of northern slavery, and so slavery in eighteenth-century Hadley. Africans and their African American descendants were present in the community from nearly the beginning, first as captives, and later as free men and women. Although the number of enslaved men, women, and children in eighteenth-century Hampshire County was never large, they were a visible presence in the river communities of the Connecticut Valley from the outset of European settlement, and integral to the rural culture and economy.

The earliest years of enslavement in the valley are glimpsed in the accounts of the Puritan entrepreneur William Pynchon, who in the 1650s, Sylvester Judd's records note, paid a man for "bringing up my negroes."[21] The first record of slavery in Hadley is found among the probate records of Richard Fellows, whose 1664 estate was overcharged for an enslaved man appraised for a higher value than he could be sold for. In March 1670, Margaret, enslaved in the household of the town's minister, John Russell, was whipped fifteen stripes for bearing a child out of wedlock.[22] The unsanctioned child's father, John Garrett, was whipped twenty-four stripes and ordered to pay Russell seven pounds ten shillings for the added expense of the unwanted infant.[23]

Patterns of slave ownership in Hampshire County reflected less a household's real labor needs than their desire for affirmations of affluence.[24] Less than one-tenth of the New England labor force was enslaved, yet most of the leading Connecticut Valley families had at least two enslaved laborers, generally an adult man and woman. Many ministerial families in New England—including each of Hadley's first four ministers—enslaved workers, giving the practice religious and moral sanction.[25] John Russell, in addition to the enslaved woman Margaret, asserted ownership of a man named Cyrus as well as a child, while Reverend Isaac Chauncey claimed possession of Arthur and Joan Prutt and their several children. When Reverend Chester Williams died in 1753, his wife, Sarah (the daughter of the Honorable Eleazer Porter), received his enslaved woman Phillis as part of her legacy. When Sarah married her husband's successor, Reverend Samuel Hopkins, in 1756, he moved into the house that Sarah and Phillis kept. Sarah was accustomed to supervising enslaved workers, as her father held at one time at least six: Thankful, "Tab," Agnes, Boston, Simon, and "Josh."[26] Clearly, then, enslaved African Americans were closely associated with the prominent families of Connecticut Valley society. Indeed, one study of enslavement in New England found a correlation between the construction of imposing gambrel-roofed houses and the ownership of slaves: both were highly visible symbols of status that demonstrated to the community wealth, power, authority, and at least some degree of leisure.[27]

Other Hadley families profited from the slave trade. Judd records, "Ezekiel Kellogg was a trafficker in many things and used to buy and sell Negroes for gain." According to an oral tradition in circulation when Judd was making his notes in the second quarter of the nineteenth century, Kellogg used to shave off the hair of those he offered for sale "to make them look young."[28] Most of the slaves who arrived on Boston's Long Wharf had passed through the West Indies, where the city's merchants and traders had thick commercial ties. Other enslaved people in the Connecticut Valley had come through the vigorous slave market in Rhode Island, while centers of trade along the Connecticut River included Hartford and Middletown. The local press regularly carried advertisements of shipments of "new Africans," or parcels of "men, women and boys, directly from the Gold Coast."[29] Enslaved women, men, and children made their way north as Massachusetts families traded with other river communities, and genealogical threads bound together black families strung along the waterway much as they did white; enslaved workers moved across the region as they circulated among family members, often deployed as wedding gifts to newlyweds striking out on their own.

Patterns of transferring human property raise important questions about the nature and extent of African American community in early New England. Though it is true that, throughout Hadley, Hatfield, Deerfield, Northampton, and Amherst, a small number of African Americans lived and worked in the households of a few wealthy English families, it is also the case that those who claimed possession of any enslaved people were as likely to claim several, and so many captive laborers worked alongside others. Historians' evaluation of the prospect for developing community under these conditions has varied, some suggesting that the dispersed nature of enslavement forced captives to assimilate into English culture, while others argue that men and women of color in areas of comparatively high concentration could cultivate a distinct African American culture.[30] But even across households, the communication of a small number of enslaved workers might be considered an occasion, if sometimes fleeting, for creating community. A poignant moment is preserved in the memorandum book of Elizabeth Porter Phelps, who on an evening in October 1768, recorded that their "Negro woman went to Live at Col'l Partridges, his Negro's wife being lain in they wanted help a little while."[31] It was the Partridge family's need for labor that prompted the move, but the two enslaved women may have been glad to be able to spend some time together, and the new mother happy to have the companionship of twenty-six-year-old Peg, now the mother of two little girls, Rose (sometimes Rosanna) and Phillis. Some years later, when Rose herself had her first child, a woman named Phillis in the household of the Warner family would come to Forty Acres, again presumably to aid the new mother and also to cover her duties.[32] Such encounters were brief but likely welcome chances for these women of color to share news about the well-being of people they knew in common around Connecticut Valley households.

Bernard Herman and Dell Upton have considered the implications of the domestic landscapes where masters and servants in this era, slave and free, lived in close quarters. Herman posits that the very omnipresence of slaves in cities facilitated a certain sort of privacy. "The habit of their masters' gazes," he writes, "was the servants ally," in that their movements up and down stairs, through yards and along streets and passages were so routine that they "failed to register . . . except when service went unexpectedly right or very, very wrong."[33] Dell Upton's scholarship has also considered ways in which ubiquity was associated with a certain invisibility, as well as the ways in which white and black families negotiated those shared spaces responded to subtle changes over the course of the day.[34] In a rural place like Hadley we might also consider seasons of the year. In warmer weather, for instance, men were often able to escape their employer's eye in the fields and barns.

In moments of privacy enslaved women and men could sometimes draw on deeper cultural resources for sustenance. Because captive men and women were often compelled to practice traditions in secret, the evidence of those activities is necessarily scant.[35] Archaeological evidence suggests that some men and women created cosmograms, patterns of objects intended to harness spiritual forces.[36] Other traditions survived as well. The Victorian-era Deerfield antiquarian George Sheldon reported a local tradition about Jenny Cole, who had been brought to Boston's waterfront in the 1730s from Guinea when she was about twelve; if the story of her capture and sale is accurate, Jenny would have been an exception: of the two hundred captives traded through the Boston newspapers in the 1730s, only eighteen are described as having come from Africa.[37] "All her long life," Sheldon writes, "she was gathering, as treasures to take back to her motherland [at the time of her death], all kinds of odds and ends, colored rags, bit of finery, peculiar shaped stones, shells, buttons, beads"— "*anything* she could string." Her son Cato would likewise gather "trinkets," especially brass or copper buttons.[38] Jenny and Cato may have been gathering *minkisi*, charms in which protective spirits could reside, sources of comfort and strength that she could share with her son, born into New England slavery.[39] Such practices helped these captive workers sustain cultural ties with homelands, with family members, and with other African Americans in their community.

The day-to-day work of enslaved New Englanders was hard and dangerous. Fully a third of advertisements for runaway slaves in New England mention limps, scars, and other evidence that they may have been injured in the course of their labors or at the hand of their masters.[40] Records of the Hadley physician Richard Crouch document those hazards. Crouch, for instance, treated Moses Marsh's "negro man" when he ran a fork through his wrist, and again later the same year when he cut his leg with an axe; he also cut and treated the blisters of Marsh's "negro girl."[41] At Forty Acres, the elder Charles Phelps offered to remake tools to accommodate the enslaved Cesar's hand, which had become lame in the course of his work.[42] Enslaved women experienced the same dangers known by all women who worked in and around kitchens—burns and scalds and the promise of arthritis born of long days spent on knees, scrubbing floors—while also facing acute threats of violence and sexual coercion.[43]

Enslaved women and men sought ways to escape bondage, though, as Catherine Adams and Elizabeth Pleck explain, "Black women's quest for freedom during their lifetimes was different than that of black men because men had more opportunities to gain skills, even during slavery, more personal mobility," and possessed more confidence about their ability to succeed; they also were less encumbered by children.[44] The columns of Hartford's *Connecticut Courant*—the valley's main newspaper before the *Hampshire Gazette* appeared in 1786—are filled with advertisements seeking the return of runaways, though women were far less likely than men to pursue this form of self-emancipation. Before the outbreak of hostilities between the colonies and England, only one notice in the Connecticut paper mentions a female runaway, a thirty-four-year-old woman who in summer 1770 ran away in the company of a man.[45] Once Revolution was afoot, the number of enslaved women willing to risk it on their own grew. Nineteen-year-old Hannah, "country born," took off with only the clothes she had on: a striped tow (that is, a comparatively coarse fiber recovered during flax or hemp processing) and linen gown, an old red shag shortcoat, a linen and woolen petticoat, and a striped tow apron. And fifteen-year-old Zil, "small for her age," absconded from her master's home, headed (he presumed) for contacts in Lenox.[46]

Some black women took another tack: between 1716 and 1783, eight sued for their freedom in Massachusetts courts—seven successfully (and the eighth result unknown).[47] Most famous among these is Elizabeth Freeman, or "Bett" as she was known before freedom. Freeman had migrated from one family to another; she had been a member of the Claverack, New York, household of Pieter Hogeboom, but after his death, she and her sister Lizzy moved to the household of his daughter Annetje (or Hannah) and her husband, Colonel John Ashley, in Sheffield, Massachusetts. In 1771, tax assessors found five enslaved laborers in their household, one of fourteen Sheffield households that held enslaved people. As relations between the Crown and the colonies unraveled, Ashley chaired a 1773 committee that drew up the Sheffield Declaration, a statement asserting: "Mankind in a State of Nature are equal, free, and independent of each other, and have a right to the undisturbed Enjoyment of their lives, their Liberty and Property." In 1781, Bett joined the dozens of others enslaved in Massachusetts embracing that language to press the Commonwealth to realize those principles. But if these ideological conversations provided a tool, another incident provided more immediate motivation. Freeman, among the first to use the courts to dismantle the institution of slavery in the Commonwealth, would later recount that the event that finally pushed her to sue her master was the day she lunged to protect her sister from a "heated kitchen shovel" in the hands of her angry mistress. Freeman sustained lasting damage to her arm, a permanent reminder of the circumstances she had escaped.[48]

Some white families liberated, or "manumitted," their slaves through their wills, though the General Assembly at the turn of the eighteenth century had required masters to post bonds when they freed their slaves, to guarantee that any newly freed African would not become a town charge.[49] Such manumissions reflected the region's growing discomfort with slavery. Antislavery agitation followed soon after the arrival of slavery in colonial Massachusetts. Samuel Sewell's pamphlet, "The Selling of Joseph" (the first antislavery tract to be published in New England), appeared in 1700, and opposition to slavery surfaced periodically in Massachusetts throughout the century. Those sentiments intensified in strength and volume as British North Americans voiced their own sense of injustice surrounding their changing place in imperial policy in the language of slavery and liberty. In the 1770s, several bills and petitions opposing slavery and the slave trade were introduced in the Massachusetts General Court and debated in towns across the Commonwealth.[50] While such efforts helped begin to reshape the opinions of the Commonwealth's political leadership, some enslaved men—pursuing a path unavailable to enslaved women—chose military service as the fastest route to personal liberty and freedom.[51] Upon his appointment as Commander in Chief, General George Washington prohibited the enlisting of blacks, except those already present. But when so much manpower was needed and was less forthcoming after the initial flush of patriotism, policy changed to accommodate exigency. As Sylvia Frey notes, "Convinced that the outcome of the war hinged 'on which side can arm the Negroes faster,' Washington publicly advocated the recruitment of blacks in the Continental Army" to prevent them from being recruited to the British forces.[52]

In Hadley, Charles Phelps Jr. took a wagonload of provisions to Cambridge and left his enslaved man Cesar there to join the army, enlisting for a three-year stint.[53] In a letter home to Forty Acres (whether written by Cesar himself or dictated to another we cannot now know), he asks the Phelps family to send a few things he needs at camp and complains that he is not receiving his wages as promised, suggesting that Charles may need to intervene. He also sends his good wishes to all, adding: "Sir, I take this opportunity to enform you that I don't entend to live with Capt. Cranston [where he is working for wages, some portion of which he appears to have kept] if I can help it." Apparently reconciled to the possibility that Phelps might detach him from the family circle at Forty Acres, he says, "if you determine to sell me I Want you Should Send me my Stock [a man's neck cloth] and Buckle." He adds, "I want to know how all the Folks Do at home" and asks that everyone keep him in their prayers while he is "in the [service]."[54] Cesar was at Fort Ticonderoga when it fell, although his history after that is unknown. But Peg, enslaved alongside Cesar at Forty Acres, spent the war years in Hadley, very much like she had spent every other of her twenty-some years of enslavement there. The Revolution would not come to her until the Commonwealth of Massachusetts concluded that slavery was inconsistent with the new state constitution.

For African American women in Hadley, postrevolution emancipation technically conferred legal freedom, but within a context constrained by racial prejudice. In early America, both captivity and freedom could be confining, ambiguous, fragile, relative, and transitory. It is tempting to think of manumission as an event, a discrete moment at which an enslaved person gained freedom. But in truth, freedom was more often a process shaped by local relationships than an event codified in a legal document.[55] Whether a man or woman of color was free or not was as much determined by his or her relationships with others in the community as it was legal status. Freedom required the consent and acknowledgment not only of the former owners and their families but of neighbors, relatives, and other third parties; captives were free when their communities perceived them to be.[56] And even in the years following the dismantling of slavery as an institution in Massachusetts, racism and poverty constrained free black women's choices. As we shall see, some women seized the opportunity to relocate, charting new courses in communities far from Hadley. Others continued to perform labors not unlike those assigned during enslavement, though now under new conditions that afforded some to live in families of their choosing.

The Porter and Phelps Families at Forty Acres

By the era of the American Revolution, Hadley was more than a century old, and it encompassed residents of European, African, and Native American descent. On the eve of the imperial crisis, in 1771, when a tax valuation measured Hadley's prosperity, the town contained some 110 families, and roughly 600 residents. In addition to the scenic town center (in the same year, a young John Adams, traveling in Connecticut, exclaiming on the "beauty and fertility" of Wethersfield, was told that no broad street in all of America could compare, except in Hadley), a collection of families had gathered around the mills north

of the town center, and another in Hockanum to the south—the latter neighborhood sufficiently unfamiliar to residents of the former that Elizabeth Porter
Phelps sounded it out phonetically: "Hauk a numb."[57]

When that 1771 tax valuation was made, Elizabeth Phelps was a newlywed.
Both families—her own and her husband's—as they traced their paths from
England to America, and ultimately to this Hadley farm, embodied the aspirations that defined much of British colonial America. Like most migrants to
New England, the progenitors of the Porter and Phelps families had aimed to
be something in the New World that they had not been in the Old, to enlarge
their economic prospects and their social opportunities. By the last quarter of
the eighteenth century, members of those families counted among the most
successful and influential residents of the region whose stories open up the
ways in which aspiration, arrival, and appearance shaped and reflected one
another in early New England. In this brief genealogical sketch, separating the
threads of family ties is not my goal; instead, it is the web itself that I hope to
highlight, the closed knot of kinship that bound together the most influential
men and women of Hampshire County.[58]

By the mid-eighteenth century, the Porter name was among the oldest and
most respected in the Connecticut Valley. Family interests transplanted to the
New England colonies in 1634 by John Porter were nurtured by his son Samuel
and blossomed under the careful cultivation of Samuel Porter Jr. A prosperous
merchant and farmer like his father before him, the younger Samuel served as
a Hadley selectman and county magistrate; he was later elected to the governor's council. At the time of his death, he had almost fifty times the wealth of
the average Connecticut Valley yeoman; moreover, "if the distance between
Porter and his neighbors was already evident in 1722, it gained visibility for his
son [Eleazer Porter] in the 1740s and was glaring when his grandson [Eleazer
Porter Jr.] inherited the farm in the 1760s."[59]

The next generation of the Porter family in New England continued to order Hadley's political and economic life. Eleazer's sons, Eleazer Jr. and Elisha
(Esquire Porter and Lawyer Porter, respectively, as they were known to Elizabeth Porter Phelps), inherited the lion's share of the Porters' political power:
Eleazer was appointed justice of the peace, justice of the Inferior Court, and
probate judge, while Elisha served as an officer in the military, and as county
sheriff. Samuel Porter III's son Samuel graduated from Harvard in 1730 and
settled in Sherborn, where he was ordained in 1734. His brother Moses Porter
(Elizabeth Porter Phelps's father) pursued a career in agriculture, but his life
was cut short in 1755, when he was killed in military action at Lake George.

Advantageous marriages strengthened the Porter family position and confirmed existing alliances among powerful families. Porters intermarried with
members of Northampton's influential Edwards family, as well as the family of

the so-called Monarch of Hampshire County, Israel Williams, and Connecticut's influential Pitkin family. In a few generations the Porters in Hadley had "established a strong tradition of success based upon financial wealth, political power, and social prestige. At the same time, it had become one of the leading families of the Hampshire County magistracy and certainly the most powerful and influential within Hadley." By the mid-eighteenth century, the Porter family had moved "from aspiration to tradition."[60] They were well-established members of a group then and now recognized as "River Gods"—interrelated families (the Ashleys, Dwights, Partridges, Porters, Pynchons, Stoddards, and Williamses) who dominated the economic, military, political, religious, and social life of the eighteenth-century Connecticut River Valley.

Members of these families demonstrated and perpetuated their positions of leadership through their material environment. As scholars of eighteenth-century architecture, furniture, and gravestones have found time and again, the rural gentry used objects to assert their knowledge of and ability to manipulate fashion, to demonstrate wealth and authority, and to extend patronage to local labor. Most patriarchs of these families, for instance, erected large "mansion houses," containing four rooms on each floor divided by a spacious central hall, often with another half-story contained under the gambrel roof. The scale of these houses alone was enough to report the confidence of influence, while their gambrel roofs added an association with political authority in the valley: the Hartford state house and the Springfield town hall carried gambrel roofs, as did the houses of several justices of the peace, who occasionally held court in their homes. Fashionable effects—fielded paneling, scalloped corner cupboards, and elaborately carved doors and window surrounds—further established the standard of polite architecture in rural western Massachusetts.[61]

In Revolutionary-era Hadley, the Porters defined gentility, members of this extended family enjoying large and stately homes.[62] Around 1761 or 1762 Elisha Porter added a scrolled pediment to the doorway of the impressive two-story house the first Eleazer Porter had built on the Hadley Common in 1713, demonstrating in his selection of classical pilasters and pediments his "intimacy with the classical knowledge that formed the basis of a true gentleman's liberal education."[63] At the same time, the double-door entrance surrounded by elaborate carving and joinery work, like the gambrels, cued associations with other buildings of authority.

Elizabeth Porter Phelps's life began brightly as the cherished daughter of Moses Porter and Elizabeth Pitkin Porter, a young couple at the pinnacle of local and regional society. Moses was the son of Samuel Porter and Anna Colton Porter, while Elizabeth Pitkin's family was among the leading families in the colony of Connecticut; her relatives included the onetime governor William Pitkin. In 1743, Elizabeth Pitkin wed Moses Porter and moved to Hadley.

When their daughter Elizabeth was born, the new family was living with Moses's parents on the Hadley Common, but the new mother had no desire to live under the watchful eye of her mother-in-law: according to family tradition, living with "old people" (Samuel Porter was almost sixty that year, and Anna Colton Porter sixty-three) dragged down her spirits.[64] In 1752, Moses built a mansion house in the countryside two miles north of town. The large and imposing house was the cutting edge of fashion in its day, boasting a wide center hall when nearly all houses in the valley were still close affairs arranged around center chimneys.[65] It was clad in wooden siding carved and painted to look like stone blocks, an architectural wink, since the framing of the house also made clear that it was constructed with wood. The young family's future sparkled before them. But when fighting broke out once more between France and England, the two empires continuing their decades-long struggle to control this section of North America, Moses was called to war. The separation was a difficult one. Neither Moses's letters to Elizabeth nor her replies reliably found their way to their intended recipients. In Fall 1755, Elizabeth got the news she had long dreaded. Moses had been killed in a surprise attack at Lake George; she was a widow. Whether by choice or circumstance, Elizabeth Pitkin Porter never remarried. Certainly her wealth, inherited from her father as well as her husband, enabled her to remain single. But she was also without much in the way of familial support, with only three sisters living, in Connecticut, and both parents gone. Her daughter Elizabeth was now fatherless, and in time she became virtually motherless, too, as Elizabeth Pitkin Porter gradually succumbed to an opium addiction.[66]

Fifteen years later, Elizabeth Porter was an eligible young woman poised to inherit that large estate. In 1770, as Charles Phelps Jr. surveyed the large home and prosperous farm of his prospective bride, he felt that he himself had "done pretty well" in making such an advantageous match. His family in Hampshire County had long been associated with craftwork, representative of middling to successful artisanal families steadily rising through the social and economic ranks of seventeenth- and eighteenth-century New England.[67] In 1655, Nathaniel Phelps had been among the original settlers of Northampton, migrating north from Windsor, Connecticut; his sons and grandsons were for generations successful bricklayers, stonecutters, and silversmiths. Phelps family masons built chimneys for some of the most powerful households in the county. At the same time, several women in the family were known for their mastery of needle trades: Charles Phelps's mother, Dorothy Root Phelps, was a gown maker, his aunt, Catherine Phelps, was for many years Northampton's most prominent tailor, and another aunt, Abigail Phelps Lankton, was a Northampton shoemaker.

Charles Phelps Sr. in time read law and became one of the most controversial figures in the public life of Hampshire County, remembered for his strong personality and outlandish clothes. Perhaps purposefully, then, his son Charles would become as well known for his sobriety as his father had once been for his eccentricity. "Altogether a self-made man," the younger Charles had "none of the advantages of education except those of a very common school. . . . He was endowed with good, plain, practical common sense, and possessed a pretty accurate knowledge of human nature."[68] These qualities may explain why he was engaged to assist widow Elizabeth Pitkin Porter in managing the large farm. Daniel Worthington, another distant relative who had been living at Forty Acres and running the farm since 1762, left town for a few weeks in the spring of 1768, and Phelps was engaged for a time to help out. Charles and Elizabeth seem to have met, and perhaps began to court, in the summer of that year.

Two years later, over the opposition of her family, Elizabeth Porter and Charles Phelps Jr. published their banns; they were married in June 1770.[69] Admitting Charles to the family fold certainly proved no error. Before long, Charles and Elizabeth Phelps were among the very wealthiest people in town.[70] To be sure, Elizabeth brought most of their wealth to the marriage: as newlyweds, the couple's net worth was second only to that of Eleazer Porter Jr. and his wife, Susanna Edwards Porter.[71] But Charles Phelps did not simply savor the fruits of the Porter vineyard: he developed Forty Acres into a large enterprise consisting of hundreds of acres of the valley's richest farmlands.[72]

By 1790, no one in Hadley rivaled the Phelpses in sheer material wealth. The farm has long been known as Forty Acres, but it was never that size: the name was a reference to the Forty Acres Meadow north of the village, allotted by the town's proprietors in the 1660s. When established by Moses Porter in the mid-eighteenth century the farm already occupied hundreds of acres and would encompass some six hundred acres at its peak productivity.[73] The house itself had been dramatically remodeled over the course of several years to meet and set current fashion. The grounds boasted flower and fruit gardens maintained by a Scottish gardener. The first carpet in Hadley lay on the floor of the Phelps parlor. The well-traveled president of Yale University, Timothy Dwight, remarked that the Phelps estate at Forty Acres was "the most desirable possession of the same kind and extent, within my knowledge."[74] And with economic success came political influence: Charles Phelps served on Hadley's Committee of Correspondence and was elected to twenty terms as selectman, as well as nine terms in the House of Representatives.[75] Authority with regard to church matters also accrued to Charles and Elizabeth, who occupied and enjoyed the most prominent seats in the meetinghouse, front and center on the broad aisle.[76] Charles became a deacon of the church and sat on several church committees. Meanwhile, Elizabeth asserted the family's importance to the congregation by donating communion silver.[77] Charles and Elizabeth's large and influential household came to include two children of their own, a young ward, and Elizabeth's invalid mother, as well as many hired men and women and a handful of enslaved workers. Charles Phelps ran this farm until his death in 1814; Elizabeth Porter Phelps remained mistress of the house until her death in 1817.

When Moses Porter in 1752 purchased those lands, two miles north of the Hadley meetinghouse on the banks of the Connecticut River, little stood between his property and the village proper. Though the land lay near the intersection of two major highways, one leading east to Boston and another south to Hartford, the closest houses were across the Connecticut River at Hatfield; in fact, the steeple of Hatfield's Congregational church was clearly visible from the walk around the Porter home. By the time Elizabeth Porter Phelps became mistress of this house, several families had erected homes on the highway stretching up to what was then known as the "Upper Mills and School Meadows"; still, no dwellings were situated between the Phelpses' and Hadley's Back Street. So placed, the estate became a destination in and of itself, and a convenient stopping place for travelers. For their part, the family at Forty Acres saw in the crossroads and the Connecticut River their links to the trade and society of the region's larger port towns.

But it was the narrow path that led south to Hadley, the ferry that bridged the river to Hatfield to the west, and the road leading east to Amherst and the hill towns above it that bound them to the local community, to the sources of their social and economic status, and to the networks of labor and skill necessary to maintain them.[78]

CHAPTER TWO

Women, Work, and the Business of Gentility

The View from Forty Acres

Mrs Allen Clark says the women of Hadley nearly all worked, and were in the kitchen and elsewhere. She thinks Windsor Smith's family despised labor as much as any and were above work. He and some daughters have ended poor. Mrs Huntington and Mrs Hitchcock were sent to school. John Hopkins wife was not brought up to work. Rev Mr Hopkins' girls were brought up to work, as were Rev. C. Williams. Colonel Moses Porter's wife was a worker, and the wife of Dr William Porter and General Samuel Porter worked, though less than some. Some who worked had hired help, having a large family. In general all whites sat at the table, except when there was company and there was need of servants to wait on the table. The wife of Charles Phelps was industrious.

Sylvester Judd interview with Sophia Cook [Mrs. Allen] Clark (b. 1793)

These were the recollections of sixty-six-year-old Sophia Cook Clark as she conveyed them in September 1859 to a seventy-year-old Sylvester Judd. Judd was once a newspaperman in Northampton, Massachusetts, but on the day of this interview journalism was not on his mind. Instead, he was embarked on a project to preserve what was left of a world that was fading away before his very eyes. Every now and again he would travel over the Connecticut River from Northampton to Hadley to interview men and women there about the not-so-distant past. Clark was a regular informant, regaling him with stories about the Hadley of her girlhood: the people she remembered, how they spent their time, the way life used to be. It was a world that Judd remembered, too. Born in Westhampton in 1789, he recalled fondly the Massachusetts of his childhood, when the Commonwealth was a young state in a young nation. By 1859, the future of that nation no longer seemed at all certain. The world Clark described was a world Judd cherished, and one he feared would soon be lost to obscurity.[1]

The question that elicited Sophia Clark's response above is not recorded, but Judd was preoccupied, in his researches, with how the women he knew as an adult compared with the women he remembered from his own childhood "on the stony slopes of the Berkshire foothills."[2] Judd remembered the hard work of the past—the great kettles of soap every spring, vats of lye and potash for bleaching linens in summer, the smell of blood, meat, and salt during slaughtering and sausage making in the fall. Women in the mid-nineteenth century, Judd worried, were china dolls compared to the hearty goodwives of generations past, women like his mother, Hannah Burt Judd, who had raised four children on the family's hardscrabble farm. Whether Sophia Clark shared Judd's assessment, she knew a lot about the women of her town, what they did, and what they didn't do. Among the various sights and sounds of her youth, Clark mentioned that every house had a well—"the crotch, swipes and poles were seen in every quarter"; the creak of the buckets as they were drawn up and down announced the filling of the neighbor's morning kettle. In this squeaky way, households knew when their neighbors' day had begun.[3]

Clark remembered several sorts of women, some hardworking, some lazy, some privileged, some less so. For the women related to the prominent Hadley merchant Windsor Smith, who "ended poor," their pride (Clark mused) went before their fall. "Mrs Huntington and Mrs Hitchcock"—that is, Elizabeth Phelps's daughter Elizabeth (known as Betsy in her youth, and in this study) and her ward, Thankful Richmond (later Hitchcock)—attended school; they were not expected to contribute their labor at home. Because Phelps could afford a constant supply of hired women, her daughters were able to turn their attention to the cultivation of other sorts of skills: reading and writing, ornamental needlework, and even dancing. "John Hopkins wife"—that is, the Newburyport gentlewoman Lydia Thompson—"was not brought up to work." The daughter of the merchant Thomas Thompson, Lydia grew up in a genteel urban environment where women, especially women of privilege, did not master the skills that even wealthy women in rural communities needed to develop.

Clark also recalled women who pitched in around the house and farm. Those girls "brought up to work" included the several daughters of the town's revered ministers, Samuel Hopkins and his predecessor, Chester Williams: Mabel Hopkins Hubbard, Hannah Hopkins Spring, Jerusha Hopkins Austin, Polly Hopkins Colt, Lucy Hopkins Riddel, Elizabeth Hopkins Worcester, Penelope Williams Gaylord, Martha Williams Emmons, and Sarah Williams. Perhaps it was the strain of raising a large family on a ministerial salary that prompted Sarah Porter Williams Hopkins to bring up her daughters to be accomplished housewives. And indeed, Martha, Hannah, Jerusha, Lucy, and Elizabeth each went on to head ministerial families of their own. Other "workers" recalled were Amy Colt Porter (the wife of Colonel Moses Porter), and Charlotte Williams Porter (the wife of the merchant and physician William Porter). Lucy Hubbard Porter (wife of General Samuel Porter) worked, too, "though less than some" (apparently unlike her sister-in-law Sarah Porter Hillhouse; figure 2.1). And finally, "the wife of Charles Phelps," Elizabeth Porter

Figure 2.1 Sarah Porter Hillhouse (1763–1831) portrait, ca. 1810. Elizabeth Porter Phelps's cousin Sarah Porter Hillhouse—related to several of the women recalled here—married and moved to Georgia, where she became an early newspaper publisher; she returned occasionally to Hadley and remained in touch with family there. Courtesy of Alexander and Hillhouse Family Papers, 1758–1998 (The Louis Round Wilson Special Collections Library, University of North Carolina at Chapel Hill)

Phelps, "was industrious," an assessment confirmed in her own family's extensive records.

This chapter and the one that follows explore the working women of Hadley, from the town's most affluent families to its least. First we look at the "industrious" Elizabeth Porter Phelps and the ways in which her labor in her farm's dairy reflected her household's wealth while also augmenting it and at the same time bringing Phelps into steady contact with a wide range of laborers in her community. Next we turn to the town's least privileged residents, and consider the networks that shaped their own position across the town's landscapes of labor. If we can imagine the shared enterprises that linked these women as threads that cross back and forth across households, from one home to the next—up and down, back and forth, again and again—in time we can picture the dense fabric those threads eventually create.

The Business of Gentility

It is easy to dismiss the countless references to teas and quiltings in the writings of early American women of privilege as evidence of leisure, but the business of gentility was complex and serious. Gentility, especially women's gentility, is sometimes understood as having the freedom not to work. But constructing and maintaining gentility itself involved real but often hidden (to their peers, and to us) labor. For instance, though quiltings have for us today the appearance of leisure, quilting was a serious enterprise among women of the rural gentry. Expectations concerning visiting and the collaborative work of quiltings could be challenging elements of genteel women's everyday lives and constituted only part of the demands on their time, energy, and abilities; Elizabeth Porter Phelps found the need to make and receive visits a real chore—"don't tell of it . . . I owe visits to all," she once confided to her daughter—but understood that it was an obligation she could not forgo.[4] As elite women traveled to one another's homes, devoting hours and even days to the production of richly ornamented quilted petticoats, often made in silk and other beautiful fabrics, they cemented the bonds that linked and perpetuated the region's most influential families while at the same time producing tangible symbols of that influence.[5] This skilled labor—associated most closely with the relatively young members of these powerful families, women who had not yet married and taken on the demands of housewifery—was made possible by the laboring and enslaved women whose efforts in kitchens and other work spaces kept these women's own homes running smoothly in their absence.

Women of the rural gentry worked in other ways, too, that shored up their families' prosperity and influence while thickening ties with other women in the area. Despite her position as mistress of one of Hadley's wealthiest families, for instance, Elizabeth Porter Phelps by no means escaped household and farm work. While Phelps's hired woman Susanna Whipple "washed all the chambers," for instance, Phelps herself tackled the windows.[6] As she advised her daughter Betsy, while the latter was setting up her own household in Litchfield, Connecticut, "you must see to and really do a great deal about the housework yourself."[7] Sophia Clark remembered Elizabeth Phelps as particularly "industrious" among the women of the town, and indeed, Phelps well knew the end of a hard day. In particular, she channeled much energy into the production of milk, butter, and cheese, for her household and also for the market.[8] Dairying meant keeping cows and calves, milking, churning butter, and undertaking a range of activities surrounding the cheese press as well as identifying, securing, and supervising hired help. Phelps was regularly up at three and four o'clock in the morning to churn in the cool of the day. As much as her gentility depended on the production of stylish articles of clothing created in collaboration with her peers, it was grounded, too, in the labor she performed in her own household's dairy, as she and Charles pursued an increasingly aggressive agenda to generate income from cheese produced for the Boston market. Phelps's own effort and expertise was essential to the enterprise, though the venture also depended on the farm's access to hired help. Like Phelps's quilts and caps, her churn and cheese basket were instruments of affluence. All of these things together reflected the real and the symbolic labor required to sustain rural gentility.

The need for dairy products linked families across communities, whether wealthy or struggling. In the third quarter of the eighteenth century, each pound of butter required two to three gallons of milk. If a person consumed one or two pounds of dairy goods each week, then women whose households included six members would have to produce some three hundred to six hundred pounds of butter and cheese, requiring two or three times as many gallons of milk each year. To meet even the minimum standard would have required three cows.[9] Yet while most families in this era had access to one cow, only a quarter of estate inventories note as many as three. In 1771 Hadley, 222 cows were distributed across 114 households, with some households holding none, and others as many as nine.[10] To get access to the milk products they needed, most Massachusetts families had to turn to the marketplace—a fact that created opportunities for women of comparative privilege like Elizabeth Porter Phelps. Some families pooled the milk they produced in order to have enough to work into butter or cheese, but Charles and Elizabeth's comparatively large herd (which would reach thirteen cows) enabled them to meet their family's needs and to supply local and distant markets as well.[11]

Milk was a critically important part of early American diets. In addition to cheese and butter, children and adults consumed milk with bread or hasty pudding for breakfast and supper. Fruits and berries were coupled with milk and bread, too. For most of the seventeenth and eighteenth centuries, dairy and meat products were closely linked, since, as a source of animal protein, dairy products filled the gap when supplies of salted meat had been exhausted. Sarah McMahon points out that "most farmers avoided 'overwintering' their cows, preferring to keep them in a 'mean' state until they could graze on fresh grass in the late spring." That practice meant that dairy production was suspended during the winter and resumed in the spring, after the calves had weaned, and continued into the summer and fall, filling in during the months when the "salt-meat barrels stood empty." Over the course of the eighteenth century, those patterns would shift, in part because new approaches to feeding livestock in the winter extended the season for butter production, and in part because some families simply began producing more, creating surpluses that lasted longer. As supplies of salt meat also grew, reducing the pressure on dairy products to fill the gap during the warmer months, supplies of dairy products also lasted longer.[12]

Cheese was consumed at home, traded locally, and sent to distant markets. Cheeses made of unskimmed milk, or new milk cheeses, contained the most fat and were therefore the most valuable. Sometimes milk from more than one milking was combined for a "two-meal" cheese. Butter could be purchased in the last quarter of the eighteenth century for about five or six pence before the American Revolution, but its price rose to six or seven through the rest of the century, and topped eight and nine in the years after 1800.[13] Sold in rounds typically weighing from three to five pounds, valued at a shilling or a shilling and six pence, cheese could be exchanged for goods and services in the neighborhood or town or transported through shopkeepers to more distant markets. The Phelps family sometimes used a "factor," or middleman, to take their product to market: as Phelps wrote one November, "the man to take the Cheese etc is to be here very early this day."[14] The December 1793 invoice of Eleazer and William Porter provides a glimpse into the process as it describes the movement of thirty-four cheeses received by a "Capt Chapman," who sold them on the Porters' account. They had sent thirty-seven; three had broken into pieces en route and could not be sold, but the remaining cheeses, at a remarkable 17 pounds each, together weighed 586 pounds, which sold for seven shillings and two pence a pound. Less Chapman's 5 percent commission, the cheeses brought in eighteen shillings and four pence in revenue.[15] Other years were less promising: in 1802, the market was so poor that the Phelps household did not send any cheese at all to market.[16]

Cheesemaking was undertaken largely by women in families of privilege, not least because it required the presence of several cows, which only a minority of households could afford. In the mid-1770s, most Massachusetts families lacked the animals or equipment to generate cheese and milk for a household of six.[17] Yet Elizabeth Porter Phelps's mother, Elizabeth Pitkin Porter, was apparently producing cheese some twenty years earlier, for the farm's tools in the 1750s included a cheese ladder, cheese tubs, and a skimming dish. At that time, Porter and her servants were milking six cows. After Moses Porter died in 1755, the men appointed by the court to inventory the household's possessions listed pounds of stored cheese among the couple's considerable assets.[18]

Cheese production began in the late spring, when the cows had "freshened" by returning to green pasture. Fresh cows' milk was heated to eighty degrees and then poured into a vat. Rennet was added to cause the milk to curdle. The cheesemaker then brought the whey out with a ladle and moved it to a basket where it could drain further. Next, the cheese was put in a hoop lined with cheesecloth and placed in a cheese press, where it might stay as long as twelve hours. Once removed it would cure for several months before it was ready for eating. As Phelps's note concerning the factor suggests, most surplus was sold in the fall: in nearby Deerfield, Massachusetts, for instance, 60 percent of the cheese transactions occurred in October and November.[19]

Elizabeth Phelps and the women of Forty Acres also produced butter. In summer 1807 Phelps wrote, "it seems like holding breath, churning every other day sometimes."[20] The amount of butter a particular cow's milk could produce varied widely. One Northampton man remembered that six quarts of milk from his best cow would make a pound of butter, but that it took far more than six quarts from his second-best cow, and that he'd known cows with milk so poor that up to sixteen quarts of milk were needed to make a single pound of butter; ten or twelve quarts was not unusual.[21] The quality of the milk and the amount of marketable product that could be gleaned from it depended in part of the quality of the animal, and in part on luck, as natural variation from animal to animal, as well as the grass and fodder on which cattle were feeding, could mean a good bit more, or a good bit less, effort and profit for the owners.

Work in the dairy had long been cast, at least among the western European cultures to which Hadley looked for precedent, as women's work. As Elizabeth Porter Phelps wrote her daughter, "the cheese and butter falls pretty much to my part."[22] The work was too arduous, however, to tackle alone, and a competing desire to spend time with her married daughter necessarily removed her from the house during some dairying seasons. Hired women, then, were essential to the process. Dairying families employed women who specialized in the operations of butter and cheese production, although women hired as general domestic help also contributed to dairy production. In the summer of 1801, for instance, Elizabeth was terribly ill but trying to work, skimming the milk and (in her own language) puking. Finally she gave up and went to bed. Ten-year-old Mitte West, the daughter of a hired woman, "came a number of times to ask what was to be done—but I told her to let me alone shut up the doors & [their hired woman, Judith] must make the cheese and work the butter & do all she could." Later, in November, Phelps wrote,

Here I am once more alone. Polly [Randall, a live-in domestic servant] went to Pelham on last Satt, & is to be gone all this week visiting about among her folks. How clever it seems to be alone, now we have so very few men, only John and Samuel Smith (Elisha's brother) & they out husking. . . . Tomorrow I shall have churning, & cheese, and no time to write, no body to help—perhaps Polly may come by night—old Phillis [a former enslaved woman still living in Hadley] has wash'd for me this day and done very well, offer'd to scour afterwards,

& wash the floor, & all done very well. Since we came home have put down two firkins of butter, one is sent to Boston and the other to you, which you may consider as paying for your braclets if you please.[23]

From time to time Charles and Elizabeth were able to get some help by engaging the services of Sarah Jackson, a black woman from Shutesbury, a small town in the hills above the Connecticut Valley about fourteen miles northeast of Hadley. Sarah, born in 1761 in Colchester, Connecticut, was at least a second-generation African American. Her husband, Peter, was African, born in 1746 during the crossing of a slave ship bound to the Americas. He and his parents were purchased by planters in the southern colonies, and sometime, perhaps in the chaos surrounding the American Revolution, Peter escaped slavery; local legend recorded that "he had been a fugitive."[24] By 1800 Peter and Sarah headed a free black family that included their three children: four-year-old Richard, two-year-old Catherine, and an infant, Dolly. Sarah was not always available when Charles and Elizabeth needed her; in May 1803, looking for a "dairy woman," Charles set out to see Sarah, but, unable to get an immediate commitment from her, he rode on to New Salem, a hill town about twenty miles northeast of Hadley, and "agreed with Zerviah [Zerviah Ford] to come for 4 weeks," while asking Jackson to come within three weeks. Charles and Zerviah "took the calves immediately and made three cheeses."[25]

In May 1803, at least two women contributed to cheese production in Elizabeth's absence: Zerviah Ford, and a Native American hired woman named Assinah. Zerviah had the year before been a domestic servant in the Phelps house. She had come in May 1802 from her New Salem home to help out at Forty Acres while Elizabeth traveled to Connecticut to attend the birth of a grandchild. She remained until the fall; in October, Phelps recorded that Polly Seymour had come "to make Zerviah's silk gown" (suggesting the settling of accounts at the completion of an indenture) just a week before Zerviah left Phelps's employ.[26]

Assinah (also called Assanah in Phelps family records) was a Native American woman who had been hired in the wake of Zerviah's departure.[27] Little is known about this woman, but she apparently came to the Phelps household after a term in the employ of Mercy Eastman Kellogg and husband Daniel, and was apparently from a local family: her mother lived close enough by that she could travel home for a visit now and then.[28] Phelps perceived her as both of her community, and apart from it: in December 1802 she wrote to tell her daughter "what a terrible cold week" they had had, and added that "such a wind as last Thursday I scarce ever knew." She told Betsy that "our Sena came here on foot that day from the lower end of Amherst 7 or 8 miles She had something due to her there"—that is, unpaid wages from Mrs. Kellogg—"&

went on Tuesday—chose not to ride—the wind turn'd & grew very col here, before midnight. We all spoke of her a number of times, hop'd she would not set out, for I really fear'd she would perish—but just at dusk in she came, puffing along—& glad was I to find she was not froze—pure hardy race."[29] Assinah apparently became quickly integrated into the Phelps family as well: by the end of January 1803, Phelps would write her daughter that when "Sena" cleaned the fireplace, she took care not to disturb a "small bit of sealing wax, stuck tight" on the hearth by little Charles (Huntington)—apparently a memento of toddler hijinks that each of these women remembered with affection.[30] But those ties notwithstanding, Assinah would leave as soon as she was able; by spring, Charles wrote that the hired woman "talks much of going as soon as she has paid what she owes us," suggesting that she had not yet come out ahead in her relationship with the Phelps family.[31]

For her part, Assinah might have brought more to the project than a strong back and willingness to rise early. Native basketry skills may also have contributed to the work of the dairy, as cheese baskets were among the essential tools. Broad, round, woven-splint baskets made and sold by native women served as strainers; lined with cheese cloth, the baskets' broad hexagonal openings allowed women to separate the curds from the whey.[32] Perhaps Assinah brought the skills to make such baskets as well as to use them, since basket making and related competencies were cultivated by native people of the Connecticut Valley.[33] As Hadley housewife Abigail Dickinson Newton recalled, when she was a girl in the 1780s native men and women would come to Hadley and "peddle brooms and baskets"; Judd himself remembered these figures from his own boyhood, recalling the native men and women who moved "about these towns when I was young, and sometimes built a hut on the edge of the woods or an old field, and lived there . . . [They] made brooms, baskets, mats, and bottomed chairs—all done with wood made into splints."[34] For his part, Phelps's grandson would note that, during his boyhood in the 1810s, basket makers "came mostly from Shutesbury," which he described as "a sort of unclaimed territory beyond Leveritt," in the hills northeast of Hadley—land associated with Nipmuc peoples.[35]

Cheese baskets, laundry baskets, baskets for gathering and storage, round and square, open and covered, small and large, utilitarian and decorative— western Massachusetts homes were once filled with baskets serving a wide range of purposes, and they represent another way that native women's work was entwined with that of Anglo women. Of 273 probate inventories from five Hampshire County towns (Hadley, Hatfield, Northampton, Deerfield, and Springfield) taken between 1760 and 1810, nearly a third (89) contain some sort of basket, and several as many as a dozen or more.[36] Baskets came in a range of forms, for a number of purposes. Bread baskets and strawberry baskets served in the kitchen; forks and knives might await mealtime in cutlery baskets; flax baskets in workrooms and storage spaces stored raw materials for cloth makers.[37] Baskets—not unlike today—served as catchalls in the homes of early Hadley: one might spot a basket of nails here, or a basket of rags there, while hanging baskets kept stored materials away from floors and rodents.[38] Corn baskets (that is, closely woven baskets used to sift corn meal) were especially common in sheds and outbuildings, while clothes baskets and cheese baskets appear in county probate inventories with regularity as well.[39] The native men and women who fabricated these articles were present in at least this indirect way in rooms across the community.

The cheese basket in the Phelps dairy, then, suggests another way in which native and European women's labor intersected, though today we know nothing about its maker.[40] But all of the objects in the Phelps house take on new valences as we consider the native women who handled them in the course of their work as domestic servants in late eighteenth- and early nineteenth-century Hadley. As archaeologist Stephen W. Silliman has observed, scholars unfortunately tend to consider objects in early American houses "to be always fundamentally and categorically European / Euro-American artifacts in European / Euro-American households, regardless of who handled them during the day."[41] One result is the "invisibility of Native Americans in colonial settings, typically where they worked as laborers, because the labeling of objects by their origins in production has obscured the everyday activities, such as handling dishes and glassware, that brought these into others' hands and, likely, others' meanings."[42]

Directly and indirectly native women contributed to the work of Phelps's farm. With the help of Assinah and other women, Phelps became so successful at her lucrative "making-cheese business"[43] (as she called it) that her husband, Charles, wanted to add cows to their small herd, a decision to which she acquiesced only with apprehension: "Your father," she wrote to her daughter, "seems to have set his heart very much upon a dairy (16 cows this summer) which puts everything in a family into confusion, but so it must be." "It surely is foolish perhaps sinful," she added, "to feel anxious about the matter."[44] Between 1777 and 1806, the number of cows grazing Forty Acres rose from eight to thirteen. As early as 1797, when Charles and Elizabeth built a large ell stretching south from their house, they added a dairy room lined with shelves to store the products of Elizabeth's labor. The room (which survives intact with the contemporary historic house museum, now converted to office space; see figure 8.1), approximately fifteen feet four inches by seven feet nine inches, is lit by a single, west-facing window that could be closed with a sliding shutter.[45] The wide planed and beaded tongue-and-groove boards that line the room's walls have never been painted. Two large wooden bins nestled against the west wall provided storage, beneath enough shelves to store as many as seventy cheeses. The room's door retains a keyhole, evidence of the value of the contents stored therein.[46]

Good dairy production depended on other choices, too. The wooden containers in which salted butter was transported, for instance, were preferably of oak and without iron hoops, which could undesirably alter the butter's color. Seasoning and maintaining the vessels took added care: they were filled with scalding water that was allowed to cool inside, and the interior rubbed with common salt. An excerpt from "Anderson's writings" published in the summer 1802 *Hampshire Gazette* advised that a "sweeter and more marrowy" butter could be had if the maker exchanged the usual preservative—common salt— for a mixture of sugar, salt, and nitre (saltpeter), one ounce for every fifteen ounces of butter.[47] That same edition of the *Gazette* included a short article that promised to cut the time "farmer's wives" spent over the churn by more than half—news that surely made Elizabeth Porter Phelps sit up straight, if no one else. The author suggested that, the day before churning, makers scald the cream in an iron kettle; then, taking care not to allow it to boil over, as soon as it reached boiling they were to strain out the milk particles (which could "sour and change the butter," that is, become rancid) and then place the vessel now containing the cream into a tub of water to cool. The result, the author claimed, was that the cream would take far less time to convert to butter.

Perhaps Elizabeth embraced this technique, and perhaps it actually did reduce her time spent in butter production, since by June 1805, the household seems to have been considering an alteration to another product that would increase Elizabeth's workload. That summer she wrote her daughter, "Your father has propos'd several times to have a few cheeses made with all the cream in them, so now we make night milk into a cheese every night which takes up the time pretty busily till 10 or 11 & it is rather slow tonight tis not broke up yet."[48] It was common practice to skim the cream off of milk to make butter and then make cheese with the remaining milk (often referred to as skimmed milk cheese, which was generally cheaper and considered to be of a lower quality). Charles seems to be suggesting that Elizabeth leave the cream in in order to produce a richer and perhaps more valuable product. But the technique came with some additional hurdles: with the increase in fat, it could take longer for the cheese to "turn," for the rennet to take effect. A cool night could also extend the time needed for producing curds; hence Elizabeth's reference to the "rather slow" process. Charles and Elizabeth also seem to have been making use of the variable water and fat content between day and night milking. Making cheese at night may also signal that they were combining the morning and evening milking to produce a larger quantity of cheese (another possibility is that they may have used the morning milk to make butter and the skimmed milk for cooking or eating).[49]

Family Enterprise

During those times that Elizabeth was away visiting her children, Charles was left to oversee production. His letters suggest that Elizabeth indeed controlled the dairy operation but that he participated as well. One spring, Charles wrote that neither he nor their hired woman Assinah could find the tools they needed to continue in her absence: "We have searched the house to find the new cheese cloths . . . but can find none. I wish you would write what we are to do—as yet we have made use of the old ones but they are poor—Asanah says the new ones were made before you went away—but where they were put is the puzel."[50] Elizabeth replied that, though she could give but "poor account" of the cheese cloths, she suggests that they are either in the cupboard in the sitting room or "upon the top shelve in the closet, by the Clock." Less sure than Assinah, she reported that she "cant remember whether there is any new one made."[51]

Elizabeth's success drew visits from other women who hoped to learn how they too might profit from their dairy skills.[52] In spring 1807, for instance, Elizabeth wrote, "Mrs John Hibbard is here, she came last night and lodged here to see the whole process of cheese making, as they are setting out in the dairy line."[53] The two families' operations were closely intertwined; in 1808 Charles and Elizabeth rented the use of John Hibbard's bull to serve their twelve cows.[54] John Hibbard and Whately's Irene Belding had married in January 1792. Their first child died in infancy in April 1793. A son, Elias, was born the following February, and another son, John, was born in 1795, but he, too, died before he was much more than a toddler. Their first daughter, Lucy, arrived in February 1797, and another son, named John after his brother, was born in the summer of 1798. Three more boys—Albert, Chester, and Eliphaz— were added to the family in 1800, 1802, and 1803. Perhaps the care of their farm, with just seven-year-old Lucy to help, contributed to the bout of depression that Irene apparently endured in the winter of 1804; Elizabeth's letters to her daughters that season refer to Mrs. Hibbard's being of unsound mind, and deep in despair.[55] By the time John sent Irene to Forty Acres to learn the tricks of the dairying trade, Irene had given birth to a second daughter and namesake, Irene, and was apparently ready for new challenges. In time, the two families may have sent their products to market together; Elizabeth recorded that "tues morn Mr P set out for Boston, Bidy Till, who lives here (he & his brother Bill came here to live one year in last December, week after Thanksgiving) set off for Boston to carry our Cheese, in company with Thaddeus Hibbard (John's brother)."[56]

John Hibbard and Charles Phelps were clearly behind their wives' work in the dairy line, urging them to undertake and expand their efforts. But they were also integrally involved in the work. Repeated queries from Charles to Elizabeth when she was traveling document both his proximity to the dairy operation and his distance from it. At the turn of the nineteenth century, however, as cheese and butter production became increasingly lucrative, men began to take a greater interest in the operations of the dairy. The tide had already begun to turn in England, when Joseph Twamley published his 1784 tract *Dairying Exemplified, or the Business of Cheese Making*. Agricultural associations investigated ways to increase productivity, and, as the income-generating potential of dairying rose, so did the interest of male entrepreneurs. Charles Phelps quickly joined the Massachusetts Society for Promoting Agriculture, incorporated in 1792. The following year saw the appearance of the *Laws and Regulations of the Massachusetts Society for Promoting Agriculture*, which included Twamley's "Account of the Manner of Making Cheese in England."[57]

As Charles and Elizabeth aged, cheese making became physically more difficult, but they continued on. In May 1813, an elderly Charles had to stay home from Sunday meeting, having been "hurt by the cheese press."[58] Later that year, she and Charles were still "stubbing about"—Charles "hoes or ploughs the corn, mother makes the cheese," and both "appear to do very well indeed."[59] Later that summer, Elizabeth observed that "the cheeses do pretty well, I should be well pleased could you have when and what you wanted of 'em. Your father helps a great deal. We have not made one upon a Sabbath this summer. Get what cream we can and give the hogs the milk."[60] Around this time, it seems that they began to rely on yet another generation, as their granddaughters began to help with work. Keeping up with the dairy was increasingly difficult for Elizabeth, now in her sixty-sixth year:

> You say perhaps my low spirits proceed from over fatigue—you forget my difficulty of breathing is now increasing as the weather is growing cold particularly in the morning when I rise, it does not hardly appear proper to carry round the Country such a wheezing hacking old woman as your mother. Indeed I don't feel as if my help could be of any great service to you, and here I think I can, for daughter eno[ugh] to do with all the exertion I can give we make about 3 cheeses in a week and consequently have a great deal of butter to attend to, and you know the cheese and butter falls pretty much to my part.[61]

Phelps wrote regularly, in her later years, of her fatigue at the "burden of caring for the great house and farm."[62] Chores too often kept her from her letter writing: "I wanted to write, but how could that be? Zerviah must go home that day, & baking bread, two sorts & pies, & churning, & cheese, & a deal to do in the cheese room—about 10 men to get dinner for . . . the next day worse than that—never took off my morning cloathes till they were taken off to go to bed—last night about 8 she got back & now for one day I am a little more at liberty—tho next Monday we purpose to begin whitening & that you can easily guess what rest it will afford."[63] The following summer was a bit easier, as Elizabeth reported to her daughter, "we have another woman to do the cheese, so that I feel myself much at ease—I work in the morning, and Sally [her daughter-in-law] superintends the dinner when we have company, and is a great relief to me in afternoon company."[64]

Phelps's "ease"—and her lack of it—rested, then, on a fragile constellation of activities among women and men from near and far. In order for her to meet her obligations as a member of the rural gentry and attend to the demands of "afternoon company" without compromising the productivity of the dairy, she depended on access to the labors of women like Zerviah Ford—as well as Sarah Jackson, Assinah, and others through the years—and those of her daughter-in-law Sally, who assumed her own distinct responsibilities in the Phelps household. Dairying would be transformed in the decades to come, as men asserted greater control over this sphere of agricultural production, eventually boxing out women like Phelps.[65] But first, it would assume an integral place in the economic activities of larger numbers of western Massachusetts families as more and more families like the Hibbards embraced dairying as part of their overall strategy. The reduced flax cultivation that accompanied the reconfiguration of cloth production (considered in chapter 5), as Christopher Clark has explained, "helped farmers shift toward . . . increased livestock production." In the 1820s, dairy produce "was the principal item brought in by all the women who traded in their own names."[66]

At Forty Acres, however, dairying was no longer among the labors of the woman of the house, as Elizabeth Phelps's daughter Betsy, the wife of the Reverend Dan Huntington, shared neither her mother's interest in nor her aptitude for the dairy.[67] In 1816, Dan and Betsy moved back to Forty Acres. They would raise eleven children there, on proceeds from the farm (farm production as well as the sale of land), income Dan occasionally received as a clergyman, teacher, and principal of Hopkins Academy, and the profits from a North Hadley shop that he and his son Edward, and in time other partners, managed together.[68] If Elizabeth Porter Phelps's time was spent managing the work of a large farm, her daughter's life would revolve around the raising of her family. Elizabeth Whiting Phelps and her adoptive sister Thankful Richmond, as Sophia Cook Clark notes in the recollections that open this chapter, were "sent to school," and today Elizabeth Huntington is remembered best for her theological deliberations.

Clark's recollections capture the range of ways women of privilege in early Hadley related to the labor required to keep their families afloat. Some women were "brought up to work"; others were not. Differences of degree and kind, alongside inclination and temperament, separated the labor performed by middling and affluent women in Hadley, as circumstance and opportunity shaped their working lives. But Clark's comments also offer sightings, if brief, of other women whose options were more circumscribed: women of color, women in service, women who found themselves in poverty. Revisiting Hadley's landscapes of labor from the vantage point of women at the edges of Clark's memory—shifting our perspective from the spaces of Forty Acres to the households along Hadley's Back Street—offers alternative views of these comparatively comfortable households as well as the community around them.

Women, Work, and "Economies of Makeshifts"

The View from the Back Street

Most of the women Sophia Clark recalled at the behest of Sylvester Judd were connected in one way or another with the town's leading families, including the Porters, Williamses, and Hopkinses, but a glimpse into other women's lives, if an oblique one, is captured in her observation that "some who worked had hired help, having a large family." The phrase "having a large family" reminds us that the bearing and raising of children was a tremendous part of almost all women's working lives; this reproductive labor, though not our focus here, necessarily threads through all of these discussions, and includes not only the ways that affluent women drew on the labor of servants and enslaved women to care for the household's children, but also the efforts hired women made to keep their children alongside them in their workplaces, and the contributions children often made to the employments of their parents. Some women, as Clark notes, had the means to secure help to manage their substantial households, though she had little to say about the dozens of domestic servants and enslaved workers—not to mention laundresses, tavern keepers, gown makers, midwives, craftswomen, and others—whose labors kept her community supplied with everything from clothing to crockery.[1]

Sylvester Judd did not interview any of Hadley's women of color, nor did he sit down with any of the many less privileged women whose point of view would have differed markedly from that of Sophia Clark and her peers. Piecing together their stories is more challenging, but doing so reminds us that the lives of a handful of middling and affluent white women cannot stand in for the vast range of experiences present in the eighteenth-century village. Looking outward from the farm at Forty Acres from the point of view of Elizabeth Porter Phelps and women like her yields one view of women's work in early Hadley; looking toward that same farm from the point of view of enslaved and later free black women like Peg, hired women like Zerviah Ford and Assinah, and other working women who crossed those thresholds, yields another. Likewise, looking outward from the Back Street homes of Mary Trainer, the Way family, and other struggling families whose lives intersected in places like this, yields still others. Here, as we consider in turn the community's women of color, women who relied on their neighbor's charitable impulses, and others

who scraped together livings by whatever means presented themselves—
"economies of makeshifts," to borrow Olwyn Hufton's memorable phrase—
we are reminded how varied the community of women workers was across a
town's neighborhoods, even in small rural settings like Hadley.[2]

Labor and Family among Hadley's Women of Color

One summer day in the mid-eighteenth century, Hadley minister Chester
Williams called on the local physician concerning his "Negro girl," asking the
doctor to apply a "strength plaster" to her back.[3] Dr. Richard Crouch's patient
was likely the woman named Phillis whom Williams would bequeath the following year to his wife. Williams's daughters were among the women Sophia
Clark would in time remember as having been "brought up to work," but their
labors were supported by those of Phillis and other enslaved women.[4] The
symptoms or events that led to Crouch's treatment are no longer known, but
there is no doubt that a strong back was important for women like Phillis, in
rural New England as much as elsewhere. Newspaper advertisements seeking to buy and sell black women emphasized the desire for "strong, healthy"
workers, "likely" and "lively" women and girls who "understand all kinds of
housework," or know the "business in a family."[5] On more rare occasions, a
notice might mention a woman's value as a "good breeder."[6] There were about
eighteen enslaved men and women over the age of sixteen in Hadley at the
time Phillis was treated. She, together with Joan Prutt and her daughters Elenor and Chloe, as well as Thankful, Tabitha, and Agnes Boston, and Peg, Rose,
Smardin, Maria, and a number of other women named Phillis, help constitute
the community of African American women, both enslaved and free, who
did the hard work that kept many white Hadley families fed and clothed, in
clean houses.

Understanding these women's lives is not easy. A paucity of sources makes
it difficult to press beyond generalities. We know that women of color were
assigned the most tedious and backbreaking chores necessary to support
eighteenth-century households, and reviewing those tasks helps fill in a picture
of what these laborers did from day to day, season to season, and year to year.
But it is important, too—and first—to consider these women's lives beyond
hearths, wells, and farmyards, in order to understand where household labor
fit into larger trajectories, and how these women worked to control, insofar as
they were able, the ways their roles as wives and mothers intersected with their
status as enslaved laborers—and later as free women of color—in early Hadley.

Across Hadley, black families were knit together by their own multigenerational networks of kin and culture, and they also knit together the white families who claimed ownership of their labor.[7] Joan and Arthur Prutt were in the
possession of Isaac Chauncey, Hadley's second minister, and his wife, Sarah

Blackleach Chauncey. The large household on the Hadley Common included the Chauncey's nine children as well as Joan and her substantial family: her first surviving child, George, was born in August 1722, and a daughter, Elenor, followed in 1724. Son Ishmael followed in January 1726, and Caesar in June 1727; two years later, in August 1729, a fourth son, Abner, was born, joined by Zebulon in August 1731. Joan and Abner's final child, a daughter named Chloe, was born in July 1738. The Chaunceys were not committed to preserving the Prutts' familial integrity: just months after Isaac Chauncey died in May 1745 his daughter Jerusha sold Zebulon, then a boy of about fourteen, to Moses Porter (Elizabeth's father) for £150 (Joan was surely relieved that he didn't go any farther than the Porter farm two miles to the north).[8] Twenty years later, as a man in his thirties, Zebulon would take matters into his own hands when he ran away from Forty Acres; the family must have thought he might try to head downriver, because they placed an ad in the *Connecticut Courant* posting a ten dollar reward for his return.[9] Somehow he was recovered—whether he made it as far as Connecticut is unknown—but Porter nevertheless decided to sell him to another local family, the Warners.[10] The Prutt family would remain a significant presence in the area into the early nineteenth century, though the few records that survive indicate that most if not all eventually left Hadley; George survived (in Whately) until 1794, Zebulon in Amherst until 1802, and Caesar (also in Amherst) until 1807—the latter both in the care of the Overseers of the Poor. The lives of Elenor and Chloe are, unsurprisingly, less well documented, but neither appear to have remained within the community of black women laborers at work in the town.[11]

The Boston family shared a similar history. Eleazer Porter's 1757 will does not make claims to human property, but his estate inventory lists four enslaved people who are not assigned a dollar value—Boston, Thankful, Tabitha, and Simon—as well as Joshua, valued at twenty pounds (and about seventeen years old at this time), and Agnes, valued at eight pounds.[12] The fates of the three women are largely unknown. Thankful and Agnes Boston largely vanish from the known archival record. Tabitha Boston appears as an unmarried free black in Hadley in October 1761, when she filed an intention to marry Thomas, a free black of Amherst. The newlyweds moved to Amherst, but that town promptly warned them that, should they be unable to maintain their household, they would not be eligible for public support.[13] Tabitha in time returned; at least Phelps noted her December 1796 death. Other members of the Boston family also persisted in Hadley. Joshua Boston remained well known in the community for decades, highly regarded by townspeople. Sylvester Judd wrote that Boston was "represented by those who knew him well, as tall, erect, and portly; he was well dressed, gentlemanly in his manners, and there was much native dignity in his appearance. His dignified aspect attracted attention in the street, and when he entered the meeting-house."[14] Elizabeth Phelps Huntington told her children that she believed Boston "had a prince's blood in his veins."[15] This romanticizing tells us more about Hadley's white community than it does about Boston himself, but it does suggest that he possessed a certain status in the village. As we shall see, he became a conduit for public support, and his home a refuge for some of the town's women of color as they advanced in age.

Hadley families like the Prutts and the Bostons strained to preserve familial ties. The community respected at least some unions among people of color; between 1766 and 1808, the town's Reverend Samuel Hopkins solemnized the marriages of at least five African American couples.[16] Yet African and African American women struggled to protect the unity of their families. Occasionally Connecticut Valley owners took steps to preserve enslaved families: downriver in Windsor, Connecticut, for instance, Joseph Phelps's will ordered "that my Negro man Servant Zickery and my Negro woman Servant Citty that are Husband and wife Shall not after my decease be parted asunder, but have Liberty to chuse their master and mistress among my children to live with."[17] But such relationships were generally unprotected: in his study of enslaved people enumerated in seventeenth- and eighteenth-century Boston probate inventories, Peter Benes found that slaves' family relationships were rarely noted; in more than fifteen hundred inventories, words like "wife" or "daughter" appeared only a handful of times.[18] Enslaved mothers like Joan Prutt had little ability to control the futures of their children, and even when they remained united, faced the many and obvious challenges of parenting in the context of enslavement.[19]

Other black families likewise saw multigenerational histories unfold in Hadley. In 1754, Elizabeth Porter Phelps's father Moses purchased Peg, about twelve years old at the time (her life dates, then, were ca. 1742–1792), who lived and worked in the Phelps family for almost twenty years. In the 1760s, Peg gave birth to two daughters, Rose or Rosanna (1761–1781) and Phillis (1765–1775). The identity of the girls' father or fathers is unknown, though the Porters also claimed possession of Zebulon Prutt in the 1760s, when Peg was in her late teens and twenties. She would raise two girls while she labored at Forty Acres. Surviving evidence suggests that Peg later became involved with Cesar Phelps, a man about eighteen years old when purchased by Charles Phelps Jr. in March 1770, on the eve of Phelps's marriage to Elizabeth Porter.[20] But over the years to come, Peg made a change. In 1776, Charles Phelps Sr. wrote his son from Vermont offering to purchase Cesar and move him to his own farm. His letter suggests that tension between Cesar and Peg had contributed to some bad behavior on Cesar's part and inspired this offer to move him to Vermont: "I am persuaded that he is more Peevish and fretful in Pegs resistance of his former indulgences and freedom with her than otherwise he would [be,] that she is a pernicious temptation and incitement to him to a number of vices by her Peremptory [*sic*] Denial and resistance of his those [*sic*] former gratifications." If, Phelps added, "high living" was injurious to even the "best younger people," then "judge ye how much more so in him so depraved as he and all others of that Nation are when in the full vigor of life."[21] Phelps's proposal suggests that Peg had altered her feelings about Cesar, or may not have had full control of her body in the past, but was exerting it now.

Peg had, it seemed, formed a union with another enslaved man, one that she hoped to secure in marriage. In 1772 she and Jon Warner's slave Pomp persuaded their respective owners to sell them both to Stephen Fay of Bennington, Vermont, in order to facilitate their marriage. Pomp and Peg had been pressing for this arrangement for over a year, since at least May 1771, when the town clerk, Josiah Pierce, recorded, "Jon Warner's Pomp desires to be published with Charles Phelps's Peg." Pomp told Pierce that "the masters are consenting," but when Pierce's son tried to confirm the matter, according to Pierce, Warner "denies consent . . . and says he shall forbid, if published."[22] Given the circumstances, Pierce refused to publish the banns. But after a year of what must have been persistent lobbying, the deal was eventually struck, and Peg went to Vermont, leaving her children behind. Elizabeth Phelps apparently was lukewarm if not overtly resistant to the plan: when Peg was finally gone, she wrote: "this Day our Peg who has Lived with us near 18 years of her own Choice Left us and two children was sold to One Capt. Fay of Benington with a Negro man from this town all for the sake of being his wife."[23] Phelps seems to have found Peg's effort to marry Pomp foolish; perhaps she opposed the plan too as the marriage would deprive her of her ability to control Peg's labor.[24] Peg, on the other hand, was so determined that she was willing to leave her daughters behind in order to secure the partner of her own choosing.[25]

The joint sale may have been an effort to secure residency in a common household, and also to mitigate tensions at Forty Acres. It is also possible that Pomp was the father of Rose and Phillis. As Gloria McCahon Whiting writes, "Enslaved wives and mothers in the region rarely, if ever, had the opportunity to enact both their own freedom and that of their kin," but perhaps Peg's action was part of a larger, longer-term effort to provide for her family, and to "fulfill the cardinal requirements" of traditional definitions of "family: coresidence and submission to the household head."[26] Whatever the situation, for several years Peg was separated, at least much of the time, from her daughters. In time, Rose became pregnant at fourteen, and Phillis grew desperately ill. Charles and Elizabeth carried Phillis from healer to healer and doctor to doctor, but nothing, it seemed, could be done. In a twist of fate, in April 1775 Rose gave birth just as Phillis lay dying; Rose would name her daughter after her dead sister (Phillis, 1775–1783), and raise the child at Forty Acres until her own death in 1781.

In March 1778, the new mother regained the help of her parent when Charles Phelps repurchased Peg, who returned to the Hadley household.[27] The discussion of Cesar's bad behavior after Peg began to refuse to satisfy his former "indulgences"—likely because of her union with Pomp—suggests that Peg had been coming to Forty Acres during the years of her marriage. Now, two years later, Peg (perhaps now widowed?) desired to return to her daughter and granddaughter. The departure of Cesar, who left to serve in the Revolutionary War and never returned, helped clear the way, but Fay's decision to sell may also have been prompted by the July 1777 ratification of the Vermont constitution, which declared slavery to be illegal in the fledgling state. But as Massachusetts followed Vermont's lead, entertaining a series of lawsuits that by 1783 would abolish slavery, Peg—with both daughters now dead—"went off free" in May 1782.[28] Whether the Phelps family believed her to be emancipated or manumitted her themselves is unclear; the previous August, Phelps records that Peg "went out for herself," so perhaps somehow she was able to purchase her own freedom.[29] Peg did arrive at least once more at Forty Acres, coming back after a year away to nurse her ailing granddaughter, Phillis, in her own final illness.[30] In the end, Peg outlived both her daughters and her granddaughter, surviving until 1792. When she died, she was living with Ralph Way Jr.'s family, having joined this locally prominent household of color.[31]

Peg's ability to make choices involving her family was circumscribed by her legal status and her race; she had to appeal to the good offices of her owners when seeking marriage, and she had little say over the care and disposition of her children. When Phillis and Rose were sick, Peg had only limited ability to make decisions about their treatment; instead, Elizabeth and Charles Phelps chose how to treat them and paid the bills that followed. Indeed, few Hadley families of color were able to protect their familial sovereignty, but those that did became notable and long-remembered figures in the fabric of the community. Two of these—the Prutts and the Bostons—had once been enslaved by leading local families and continued to sustain some sort of connection to them long after slavery was dismantled in Massachusetts. The Way family has a hazier history, but it appears to have been a family of free blacks present in the community from the mid-eighteenth century—whose declining fortunes by the early nineteenth century found them (as we shall see) in the town's poorhouse.

In the decades after the abolition of slavery, black women in Hadley, like their counterparts across New England, struggled to carve a place for themselves in the new American republic. Some, unable to claim any community as home, moved from place to place, struggling to find a home. Others remained near their former owners, taking whatever advantage they could find in long-standing neighborhood relationships. But most continued to labor in poverty. Women who moved from slavery to freedom experienced an uneven transition; their legal status may have changed, but they remained residents of a society whose racial prejudice had made slavery possible for well over a century.

Long after the demise of slavery, Hadley's women of color continued to perform the hardest chores associated with early American households. While Peg, Phillis, and Rose were members of the household at Forty Acres, their labors touched on every aspect of life in the farm, from the preparation of food to the cleaning of pots, pans, and plates after meals. They surely supported Elizabeth Porter Phelps's dairy operation by keeping the spaces and tools associated with that work clean and orderly. They likely helped keep the family's clothing laundered and in good repair, contributed to the work of cloth production, and helped with the significant amount of entertaining required to maintain the status of this influential family. In the decades following the end of slavery in Massachusetts, Hadley's black women continued to perform these chores—apparently into their old age. Phelps would write that "old Phillis" has "wash'd for me this day and done very well, offer'd to scour afterwards, & wash the floor, & all done very well." Although it is unclear which of the several Hadley women named Phillis Phelps refers to here, apparently this woman's distinguishing characteristic in Phelps's eyes was that she was "old" at the time.[32]

Poverty, Charity, and "Economies of Makeshifts"

It is possible that the "Phillis" referred to by Phelps was Phillis Aberdeen—one of a handful of workers of color who participated (as beneficiaries or recipients) in systems of charitable support and the labor of caregiving. In the early years of the nineteenth century, Poll Sampson, along with Joshua Boston, found "house, room and firewood" for Aberdeen.[33] Around the turn of the twentieth century, local historian and "self-styled folklorist" Clifton Johnson would record this little joke in the pages of his notebooks, apparently because the picture it painted of his neighbors' lack of generosity amused him: "There was once a man who was condemned to either be hung or to beg his living in the streets of Hadley. He came to the town and tried it, but in a very short time he went back and asked the court to please hang him."[34] But poverty was a serious problem in Hadley, in Johnson's lifetime and in the two centuries that had passed before. Women on the margins of the economy struggled to make ends meet and to spare themselves the scorn of neighbors who might resent having to contribute to their support. For her part, Phillis Aberdeen, after a lifetime of labor, spent her final years benefiting from the efforts of other caregivers of color in Hadley.

To understand poverty in early British North America, one must also understand public welfare and poor relief as well as other strategies that allowed some families to keep their heads (just) above water. Social welfare in early America had a spatial dimension that would shift as approaches to the support of the poor changed. For much of the eighteenth century, town leaders tried to limit the cost of public support by instructing the poor to migrate away from their coffers. Barry Levy has also suggested the importance of the warning-out system to the protection of local labor systems.[35] Town authorities sought to ensure the health of the households with a legitimate claim to their aid by discouraging unwanted competition from newcomers. The practice makes landscape definitive: the boundaries that articulated the town itself determined the work relationships that might legitimately unfold within them.

Stories of poverty and relief in Hadley cross two local institutions important to the decades examined here: the Overseers of the Poor and the Hampshire County House of Correction. It is not coincidental that Charles Phelps was associated with each, though in very different ways. While women like Mary Trainer (as we shall see) faced the indignity of confinement, Charles Phelps had the power both to put people there, and to keep them out. The seat of Hampshire County, Northampton, had had a jail for most of the first half of the eighteenth century. In 1773, however, increased need prompted the town to buy land and build a more suitable structure—although just how suitable it was may have been in the eye of the beholder, since, according to one description, the "cells were scarce four feet high, and filled with the noxious gases of the privy vaults through which they were supposed to be ventilated. Light came in from two chinks in the walls."[36] In 1800, that pitiful structure was supplanted by a stone building, forty feet by twenty-eight feet, and sixteen feet high. Charles Phelps served on the committee charged with erecting the new two-story facility, which opened in 1801 with space for debtors on the second floor, to keep them separate from the criminal element below.[37] Some fifteen women were imprisoned there for debt between 1793 and 1819, and another twenty-three for a variety of criminal offenses, including nine for theft and burglary.[38]

English systems of public support had been transplanted to British North America with its founding, and, though some Massachusetts men and women drew aid from the colony's treasury, most were assisted at the local level. Town boundaries marked the range of public support, as communities committed to taking care of their own—men and women who had been born in the town or had formed a recognized relationship grounded in property ownership, marriage, or an apprenticeship contract—and equally committed to denying responsibility for the support of those eligible elsewhere. Exceptions were made, however. If a person from outside were too ill to send home, for instance, a town might take on the financial burden and bill the recipient's town of origin for his or her expense. Selectmen and Overseers of the Poor monitored the needs of the community's most marginal residents, locating sources of support and compensating providers appropriately; they also watched the fortunes of inhabitants for whom the town felt no responsibility and warned them accordingly not to expect public assistance. Public charity was supplemented by private charity, by individuals, and (increasingly) by societies, organizations, and institutions that also provided aid to families in need.[39] But despite these well-meaning efforts, pride prevented some women and men from accepting aid. In Deerfield, for instance, Esther Birge, despite her family's impoverished state, refused to accept the good will of the local Overseers of the Poor when they attempted to supply her with a cloak; the overseers found such attitudes exasperating, but for women like Birge, no cloak at all was preferable to one that would be marked, in her mind at least, with the stain of condescension.[40]

Across eighteenth-century Massachusetts, as the population grew, so too had the numbers of landless men and women, transients who moved from place to place in search of a foothold in the economy. Local gown maker Rebecca Dickinson was dismayed by "how the inhabitence of the Earth are a walking and a stalking up and down the Earth"—sentiments shared by town leaders.[41] To manage the number of claims on public resources, a community's political leadership, or selectmen, occasionally advised men and women who had moved into the town from another community that they would not be eligible for town support should they fall on hard times. This practice, called "warning out," did not necessarily evict people from their homes; it was generally used to caution them about what they could and could not expect to receive in the way of help. In Deerfield, anxious town selectmen warned out "Abel Rice, Sarah his wife, Ethel, Polly, and baby unborn"; still in her mother's womb, Sarah Rice's child was already unwelcome there.[42]

After 1780, the number of transients and paupers demanding Hadley's attention rose markedly, putting increased pressure on the warning-out process and systems of public support. In the winter of 1784, for instance, Elizabeth Phelps witnessed the enforcement of such an order when the constable arrived to remove a woman and her four children who had been abandoned by her husband and were lodging temporarily at the farm.[43] Many of these rural men and women eventually made their way to Boston; indeed, hundreds of migrants from the Massachusetts countryside tried to establish residency in Boston in the early 1790s.[44] That movement reminds us that the labor markets of Hadley and Boston were thoroughly entwined, women flowing from city to country and from country to city as exigency and opportunity directed. Many of these women would work as domestic servants.[45]

In the years following the abolition of slavery in Massachusetts, newly freed blacks were often the targets of warning out, since in many cases they had come to a place via the internal slave trade, and, as residents born elsewhere, had no recognized claim to assistance. In Hampshire County in 1788, three newly freed black women—Chloe, Hannah, and Lydia—ferried over the Connecticut River from Hatfield to Hadley, a new community that perhaps already contained their parents, siblings, or children, purchased by the neighbors of their owners. But the town of Hadley wasn't as welcoming as the women had hoped; in mid-February the town warned them out: they would not be eligible for town support should they be unable to take care of themselves.[46] In 1796, the town warned out Caesar Prutt, despite the fact that he was born in Hadley in 1727 to parents claimed by the Reverend Isaac Chauncey. Prutt had served the newly established community of Amherst during the Seven Years' War and made his way back there after the warning—a natural decision since that was where his sister Chloe and brother Zebulon, at one time enslaved by the Porter family, were living. By 1801 town meeting voted that he be "set up at vendue, to the Lowest bidder for Victualling and Beding."[47] Did he feel relief when a local farmer won the contract for a dollar a week, or was this a painful reminder of his earlier enslavement? We cannot know, but in 1807 the now eighty-year-old Prutt was still on public relief and his support still being auctioned off to the lowest bidder.[48]

But while people of color often appear in records as the recipients of charitable relief, they also appear as purveyors of that aid. In 1808, for instance, Hadley's Overseers of the Poor compensated Polly Sampson for the care of Phillis Aberdeen and Ishmael Pratt as well as white residents Jabez Seldon (the onetime neighbor of Ralph Way on the Back Street), Rebecca Smith, and Olive Lathridge.[49] Like Mary Trainer, who also was both a recipient of assistance (in Spring 1813, when Charles Phelps provided almost three cords of firewood) and the vehicle for aid (as we shall see, when she cared for Mary Andries and other neighbors), Sampson benefited from the efforts of the Overseers of the Poor at different times as both a recipient and a supplier of support.[50]

In Hufton's look at the poor in eighteenth-century France, economies of makeshifts encompassed everything from seasonal labor and odd jobs, to theft and prostitution, to mendicancy. In my own usage, the phrase "economies of makeshifts" encompasses these activities and more; that is, the term also signals the many ways women found sources of support outside traditionally recognized occupations.[51] While most Massachusetts women worked within and beyond their homes in jobs that were very much familiar to all, some found unusual ways to sustain themselves. The small number of women who managed to enroll in military service during the Revolutionary War and escape detection while they collected small bounties, payroll, or maintenance would fall into this category, as would the activities of women who were able to secure livings as actresses or performers, an uncommon occupation in rural New England.[52] Sometimes, women seeking their livelihoods simply had to be creative and enterprising.

Some women confronted more than just systemic poverty; women disabled from birth or as a result of injury or illness were especially vulnerable in this regard. So little evidence of these early American lives survives that it is particularly hard to document their experiences, but we must pause to remember that some women entered the marketplace with added difficulty. Among women for whom physical conditions presented unusual challenges, some—like the multitalented performer Martha Ann Honeywell—were able to join a "community of disabled artists and entrepreneurs."[53] Honeywell, whose "singular body" lacked most limbs (she had only one foot), "capitalized," as historian Laurel Daen shows, "on new cultural and commercial opportunities in the early republic as well as long-held conceptions of disability in productive ways."[54] Honeywell tapped deep-seated expectations about gender and genteel bodies and demeanors while carefully crafting performances that engaged public interest in silhouette-making, paper-cutting, and other forms of aesthetic expression.

Honeywell toured for a time with another woman, who likewise carved out a career at the intersection of art, disability, and performance. In 1807, a notice in the *Hampshire Gazette* invited the "benevolent and curious" to come to the Pomeroy family's inn, and, for twenty-five cents (children half-price) view a "singular and surprising instance of the wonderful productions of nature" in the body of a "young lady" whom "nature has deprived . . . of the use of hands and feet." Twenty-year-old Sally Rogers, "born of poor but respectable parents" in Lempster, New Hampshire, had "taught herself to perform several kinds of employment with the assistance of her mouth only, which she has consented to perform in public," including painting flowers and landscapes, writing, threading a needle, and cutting both paper and cloth (figure 3.1). Like Honeywell, Rogers framed her exceptional performance in the context of familiar expectations for women of New England's middle class. "Her features are regular, handsome and expressive of a great degree of sensibility," the paper's perhaps hesitant readers were reassured, "and her countenance exhibits the smile of affability, resignation, and good nature." Hours of exhibition ran daily from nine to noon, two to five, and again from six to nine in the evening—nine hours over a twelve-hour day of taxing physical and emotional work.[55]

Sally Rogers successfully harnessed toward her own aims human curiosity about bodies far outside one's own experience. She traveled to Boston, New York, and as far as Charleston, South Carolina, exhibiting her physical challenges as well as her ability to surmount them. In many ways, her work reflects

Figure 3.1 Sally Rogers (c. 1789–1871) watercolor, 1806–1815. An artist without use of her arms or legs, Rogers traveled across New England and beyond, supporting herself through exhibitions and sales of her work. Hall and Kate Peterson Fund for Paintings, Prints, Drawings and Photographs. Reproduced by permission of Historic Deerfield (HD 2006.14.2). Photo by Penny Leveritt

many of the same themes identified in Honeywell's, in the effort to tap new cultural currents to carve out a career in the arts. But Rogers's promotional material also seems to have deployed themes that Honeywell did not, as she suggested that, in supporting her work, audiences could also engage their philanthropic impulses and sensibilities. A pamphlet published the year before Rogers's Hampshire County appearance, titled "A Real Object of Charity," positions Rogers as a deserving recipient of public benevolence, suggesting that the money spent to see her exhibitions or to purchase the pamphlet itself should be seen as way to satisfy natural curiosity while generously contributing to the support of a worthy yet disadvantaged woman. As Rogers drank tea, threaded needles, sewed and knit, and demonstrated how she moved across a room without use of her limbs, she was acutely aware, as the pamphlet's author noted, that she had "no other resource for a living," but was nevertheless "verily industrious."[56] Unable to perform some of the usual tasks necessary to earn a more conventional living, Rogers pursued a transient life as a traveling performer, hoping that curiosity would bring her New England neighbors into whatever venue she could secure, and that their empathetic, emotional responses would move them to further contribute to her support. Hampshire County women likely watched Rogers with fascination, and probably no small amount of admiration. Rogers's public appearances represent one way that women bereft of other choices secured a living under exceptional circumstances; like other itinerant artists, musicians, and performers, Rogers supported herself by selling access both to her unusual experience, and to the works of art that, for buyers, captured the act of witnessing it.

Hardscrabble Hadley

Another economy flourished under the radar of public regulation in which men and women engaged in economic behavior in conflict with the law— illegally producing and selling alcohol, running an unlicensed tavern, theft, or prostitution—in order to create or supplement their livelihoods.[57] Sometimes, these activities were embedded in the legitimate work of domestic service; they might include skimming a little for yourself when preparing your employer's flax or spinning her yarn. Sometimes, theft was more outright. As historian Serena Zabin has written, "larceny and consumerism come together as a matched set."[58] The theft of goods from homes, taverns, and shops, and their resale, Zabin's scholarship shows, was part of a larger informal economy in which consumer goods circulated illegally, outside the channels tracked by account books and ledgers. Impoverished wives, mothers, and daughters were often involved in larceny, distributing and hiding stolen goods or resorting to theft to amplify meager household incomes. It might mean snitching the unattended belongings of others and selling them on the used-clothing market, or trading them at the shop for other things you need more. Whatever the opportunities taken, these activities on the margins of the visible economy were an important part of life in early American communities, in small towns as much as urban centers, in the countryside as much as the city. One need not have been completely destitute, or devoted to a life of crime, to avail oneself of small opportunities to acquire goods off the books; rather, the degree to which men and women participated in economies of makeshifts varied over time, providing the better part of some livelihoods during periods of real desperation, or simply avenues toward an occasional necessity, or the rare luxury, among laboring households.

For some women, theft became essential to survival. Hampshire County women confined for larceny in the county jail in the last decades of the eighteenth century and the first of the nineteenth routinely included women of color, whose options, severely circumscribed by racial prejudice, pushed them to the margins of the local economy. In February 1792, for instance, twenty-five-year-old Meribah, an "Indian woman" from Hatfield, was incarcerated in the county jail for her participation in a theft, together with a native man. He escaped in April, but, for whatever reason, Meribah didn't go with him; she was released by order of the local sheriff in June of that year. Northfield's Catherine Loomis was a thirty-two-year-old African American woman who spent nearly a year jailed for theft.[59] Other women too, described as "light" and presumably white, both transients and county residents, also appear in the ledger of the local jail, incarcerated for both theft and burglary. Laying claim to goods or raw materials that could be converted to cash or otherwise offer sources of support was for some women the only way to close the gap between immediate needs and available resources.

One Hadley family who struggled on the periphery of the local economy, and apparently at the edge of the law, was the Trainers. In 1768, Elizabeth Porter Phelps noted in the pages of her memorandum book that Mary Clark Trainer gave birth to a "large child" on September 25, when the Trainers had only just married in February, seven months earlier.[60] Her mention of the child's size meant that the baby did not appear to be premature: she intended her subtle note to record that the child must have been conceived before Mary had married the teenaged Hadley tailor Francis Trainer (also Trayner).[61] This infant was stillborn, but Francis and Mary brought another child, a daughter, Nelly, into the world in November 1769. Their next child, another daughter, was born and died in August 1771; three more girls followed: Jane (born July 1772); Elizabeth (November 1774); and Isabel (December 1776). Other children came in due course: James, born in August 1778; Mary, born in February 1781; and William, born in June 1784. Another son was born and died in April 1786. The last of their several children, Sarah, was born in the summer of 1787. Mary Trainer, then, had eleven children between 1769 and 1787; several appear to have died as infants, but most survived childhood.

The family lived on the Back Street, on the north end near the bend in the Connecticut River.[62] Just south stood the households of John Clark Jr. and his wife Mary—presumably Mary Clark Trainer's parents.[63] Francis and Mary Trainer's family often struggled to make ends meet. Francis's trade, tailoring, was not a lucrative occupation in eighteenth-century New England, occupying a lower rung of the artisanal ladder in terms of both prestige and income. As a result, the Trainers looked to a number of strategies to keep body and soul together. During the Revolutionary War, Francis enlisted again and again for a variety of service. He had already marched with Eliakim Smith's company when the alarm came from Lexington, and he went on to join the men encamped at Cambridge.[64] He later served thirty-nine days in the summer of 1777, marching to Moses Creek, New York, to reinforce the Continental Army troops led by Major General Philip Schuyler; he then enlisted in the company of Samuel Cook of Colonel Woodbridge's regiment, serving with the Northern Army for three and a half months. The following year, Francis took a position in the company of Abner Pomeroy, securing the bounty offered the so-called nine-month men.[65] He would serve in Colonel Ezra Wood's regiment, manning artillery.[66] After a short return to Hadley, he reenlisted, serving from July to the year's end. In January 1782, Francis was "hired by Class No. 6 to serve in the Continental Army for the term of 3 years, agreeable to resolve of Dec. 2, 1780."[67] Trainer may well have kept enlisting in the army in large part for the steady support it offered, but he clearly believed in the cause as well: years later, when he sold property on the auspicious date of April 19, 1786, his deed noted with pride that the transaction occurred in this, the "tenth year of American Independence."[68]

Through these periods of separation, Mary cared for their growing family alone. Francis made it home often in breaks from camp, and the couple's family grew over the course of the war. Running a household without the help of a husband was not easy for soldiers' wives, and Mary Trainer was surely no exception. After the war's end, they continued to struggle. In the 1780s, the household took in some income by providing shelter and sustenance for one of the town's poor, a woman named Mary Battis.[69] Entering the town's public relief system as providers perhaps enabled the Trainers to get some financial help in meeting their own household needs. In the mid-1780s the Trainers, like many families in postwar Massachusetts, were struggling to make ends meet. In April 1786, Trainer sold two acres of Back Street land and the house thereon for thirty pounds.[70] But in May, he lost a suit for debt: he owned John and Lucretia Walker five pounds, five shillings, and ten pence, plus another three pounds, nine shillings, and seven pence in court costs.[71] The court instructed the sheriff to collect those sums—plus another two shillings for the writ instructing him to do it, and any costs he incurred in the work to boot. Trainer was falling in deeper by the minute. The officer was instructed to take him to jail, in Northampton or Springfield, until these debts were cleared. In June 1787, three court-appointed Hadley residents arrived to assess Trainer's home, an acre of land on the west side of the street. The men found the whole to be worth just over nine pounds, sixteen shillings, which they "set apart" for the Walkers, "in full discharge" of the debt.[72]

Where the Trainer family went at this point is not known, but it wasn't the last time they would lose a home: just five years later, Trainer was in court yet again for debt. The household—which in 1790 included Francis, Mary, and five children—had continued to expand, in ways that increased the family's expenses. In April 1792, Mary and Francis's oldest and still-unmarried daughter, twenty-two-year-old Nelly, delivered a son she claimed was the child of Hatfield farmer Moses Wells. She went to court to have him held responsible for the costs of the child's support. Like most men in similar situations, Wells pleaded not guilty. What is surprising is that the justices *found* him to be innocent—a rare exception in a system that often preferred to find a plausible father rather than to have the child and its mother turn to the town for aid. Nelly found herself not only denied ongoing support but instructed to pay Wells's court costs as well.[73]

This entire episode must have been trying for Nelly's parents, and Mary in particular, who now added a grandchild to her family of seven, while her own youngest—Sarah—was still just five years old. But the year of trouble wasn't yet over. In June, Francis had acknowledged in court a debt to a Northampton merchant—thirteen pounds, eighteen shillings, and ten pence—that he couldn't pay.[74] When it was still unpaid in July, once again the sheriff was dispatched. Francis was to be taken to jail, again in either Northampton or Springfield, until the debt was settled. And once again, three neighbors were appointed to appraise his belongings. These three-man teams were meant to represent the competing interests in play—those of the creditor, the debtor, and the courts—with one individual being appointed to stand for each party; but Francis, perhaps despairing of any fair treatment, refused to participate in the selection of his representative. Neighbor Samuel Gaylord was asked to step in on his behalf. The men "viewed a certain dwelling house in the back street as it is called in Hadley . . . in which the said Trainer and his family now dwells, which stands upon land claimed by the town of Hadley."[75] They found the "dwelling house and its privileges" to be worth fifteen pounds, and so they "set apart the same dwelling house" to satisfy the debt. Trainer's creditor seems not to have been particularly eager to separate the family from their home, but "not being able to find any personal estate" to take instead, accepted the house, and in early August, the sheriff seized possession.

Again, where the family went is unclear, though the federal census of 1800 suggests that they had remained in roughly the same neighborhood, on the Back Street or the road north, near the families of Joshua Boston, George Andries, and other figures on the edges of both Hadley's town center and its economy.[76] Before long, Francis, in some state of desperation, turned to theft: in the spring of 1794, the county justices heard the case of *Commonwealth v. William Davis*, a former resident of Hadley who had stolen thirty pounds of tallow (worth twenty-five shillings), and thirty pounds of flax (worth another eighteen shillings)—perhaps as much as he could carry—from Hadley's Noahdiah Warner. Davis pleaded guilty. Francis Trainer, identified to the court as a "laborer," was involved in the affair, as was Levi Prutt, another laborer who also seems to have been involved (and a figure who contributes to the picture of racial diversity around the Trainers: Levi, who was probably related to the Zebulon Prutt mentioned above, is described as "mulatto," and was married to a Nonotuck woman; his wife Anne was the daughter of Joseph Sampson, one of the so-called last Indians to live in Hadley).[77]

Francis was still head of household in 1800, but his contribution to the household's upkeep appears to have been uneven. Mary Trainer's debts to the neighboring family of Solomon and Tryphena Newton Cook shed light on her activities at the turn of the nineteenth century.[78] In spring 1800 she became indebted to Solomon for his work in building a well box for her, for his harrowing flax, and for renting his horse to go to the mills. In August, she purchased forty feet of oak timber as well as slitwork (thin boards that have been split or roughly sawn lengthwise into long strips, usually to be used in building construction, particularly as laths for plasterwork, suggesting that she was undertaking some sort of construction). Charges for "finding vitling for three men one day" and "finding vitles for two hands two days" also suggests that some project was afoot at the Trainer home during those weeks. In September, she again used Solomon's horse to go to Northampton and to the mill. In October, he carted loads of wood for her, while she rented use of his oxen and purchased a bushel of potatoes. In January 1801, she owed Solomon again for taking his horse to the mill, and for using his team (and his time driving it), for part of a day. Other debts were for cider, loads of wood, and sundry agricultural products.[79]

In order to repay the Cooks for these goods and services, Mary produced what she could for that family, including some weaving and quarts of ale, but primarily hat making. She sold the Cooks a castor hat priced at one pound, four shillings, three more hats (at seven pounds, six shillings) in 1802, another three (at five shillings) in 1804, plus one more in 1808 to offset most of her debt to this family.[80] Mary Trainer also performed domestic work for neighboring families, helping with hard chores associated with the agricultural year. For several winters, for example, she helped the household at Forty Acres butcher hogs.[81]

In the early nineteenth century, Mary also participated in the broom-corn boom that revolutionized farm production in Hadley, as the village committed acres of land and other resources to the raising of this useful plant—not corn at all, but more like a tall grass whose tassels made for excellent sweeping—and the assembly of brooms. The enterprise came from Hadley's communities of color. Sylvester Judd's informant Elihu Warner remembered that it was an African American man named Cato who first planted broom corn in the community, though "Levi Dickinson from Wethersfield was the first that cultivated it to any extent."[82] John Cook (born in 1776, Judd noted) also remembered his uncle Aaron raising broom corn when he was a boy, and that the "old Indian brooms were used by all—Indians and squaws used to peddle them." Brooms were in fact closely associated with other Native American skill in the making and repair of baskets and chair seats; the broom-making industry, which is central to Hadley's history and civic identity today, almost certainly has its roots in this native craft.

Cook, too, remembered Levi Dickinson's early interest in this crop, observing that "people thought he was crazy, but he made the brush into brooms and sold them and enlarged his business. Shipman next began and there was some strife between them to get the market." "No great quantity was raised by either for some time"—at least before 1800—Judd added.[83] The early role of African Americans is also suggested in the recollections of Levi's son Harvey, who remembered his father hiring a "colored" person named Heber to tie the brooms.[84] The following year Dickinson, who lived very near the Trainers at this time, put in a half-acre, from which he produced between one and two hundred brooms. He sold them locally at first, but quickly expanded into Berkshire County and then Connecticut. William Shipman, Levi Gale, Solomon Cook, and others (again, all near neighbors) joined Dickinson in the endeavor by about 1801, although early on "the business was looked upon as low and Indian"; Harvey Dickinson later recalled, "We were sometimes mortified with taunts."[85]

Mary's work with broom corn may have been entwined with her racial and cultural communities, as the Trainers appear to be one of several multiracial Hadley households with white, black, and Native American members. Mixed-race households were not uncommon among families at the edges of the economy, as people of color, generally on the margins of English society, worked alongside one another in fields and kitchens, or lived alongside one another in garrets, outbuildings, and neighborhoods, and formed unions of love and necessity. For instance, when Zebulon Prutt ran away from the Porters, the notice in the *Connecticut Courant* posting a reward for his return noted that Prutt had a "whitish complexion" (perhaps hinting that he was of mixed race himself), and that he was "suppos'd to have a Squaw in Company."[86] The Trainer family likewise appears to have included Native American and African American members. Hadley historian and folklorist Clifton Johnson collected notes on an indigent woman named Jenette Trainer (b. 1795), whom he understood to be of mixed race, "part Indian, part African, and some white." People remembered her as having a copper-colored complexion, Johnson recorded, and recalled that she and her brother lived in a "long black shanty" on a lane associated with the homes of people of color.[87]

Johnson also noted that these Trainers earned a living from basket weaving and other crafts. This reference to basketry links the Trainer household with an area of craft work closely associated with Native Americans, as we have already seen. In December 1805 Mary Trainer earned eighteen shillings cutting an acre of broom corn for Solomon and Tryphena Cook, and in that same month she paid Solomon to make fifty broom handles for her.[88] Over the next ten years she would continue to participate in broom-corn production. It was not easy work. In the fall, after the corn, planted in rows of small hills, had broomed out and yellowed, it had to be tabled—that is, the stalks were bent over and attached to the row opposite, creating long lines of two-and-a-half-foot-high green tables, yellow broom tassels hanging over the edge to be cut away. To harvest the brooms, around the time of the first frost, a worker moved along one side of the table with a knife, slitting the stalks while pulling on the brooms. In 1805, Mary Trainer's accounts with the Cook household reflected her labor in the field, cutting an acre of broom corn—work that seems to have taken her nine full days.[89] As late as October 1812, Trainer—now likely in her sixties—would be credited for two days' work cutting broom corn for the Cooks.[90]

By 1808, life had become very difficult, and Mary surely searched for other ways to earn a living. All her children had grown up and were probably out of the house by this time (her youngest daughter, Sarah, was twenty-one in this year). Despite an infusion of cash ($150) when she sold a small amount of property (just a half-acre) that had likely come to her from her father, Mary seems to have fallen on hard times.[91] Like others pushed to their limits, she appears to have tested the law in her effort to secure a livelihood: in April 1808, she spent ten days in the Northampton jail for keeping a "house of ill fame." In March 1809, the town reimbursed William Hodge (a local tailor whom she may have known especially well through Francis's work) $9.39 "for defraying the expense in committing to gaol Mary Traynor for keeping a house of ill fame."[92] It seems that some activity in the household had occasioned concern for some time: two years before, in March 1806, Charles Phelps together with Deacon Seth Smith "went to talk with Mrs Trainer" about unnamed, but apparently untoward, activities in her household.[93]

Just what a "house of ill fame" meant in this case is not entirely clear. As early as 1703, Massachusetts women of "ill fame" had been prohibited from "receiving or entertaining lodgers in their houses," legislation affirmed once more in 1720 and after.[94] In the 1730s and 40s, in order to protect women who ran legitimate public houses, the Commonwealth affirmed that "women of ill repute are not allowed to entertain lodgers in their houses but women of good repute are not to be hindered from engaging in lawful employment as a means of livelihood with approval of selectmen and overseers of the poor."[95] John Adams would later remark that houses run by marginal proprietors "became the eternal haunt of loose, disorderly people."[96] Trainer's "house of ill fame" may have been an illegal tavern; alternatively, Trainer may have simply been allowing excessively rowdy behavior, gambling, or providing intoxicating beverages to mixed-race gatherings in her neighborhood.

The sale of intoxicating beverages (as we shall see) had long been carefully monitored in Massachusetts. Since the colony's founding, great pains had been taken to regulate both taverns (which sold alcohol by the glass) and retailers (which sold alcohol in bulk quantities). After 1681, the colony's General Court stipulated that selectmen screen applications from those hoping to sell wine or distilled beverages, after which a license—which must be renewed annually— might be granted by the county court. But the state's desire to supervise and manage these activities was in endless tension with public demand for them: retailers were constantly accused of allowing drinking on their premises, and illicit gathering places were a constant source of concern. As early as the late seventeenth century, one group especially invested in relaxing alcohol policies were the poor, who saw the production and sale of alcohol as a way out of poverty. Licensing authorities had long preferred to sanction only those deemed capable of running a well-ordered establishment, but by the turn of the eighteenth century they began to see the issuing of a license as a potential form of relief.[97]

In an economy grounded in credit and barter, possession of a license meant at least the prospect of future income, giving these women greater access to channels of exchange than they otherwise might have enjoyed. Town officials may have been simply looking the other way if Mary Trainer was supplementing her income with off-the-books sales of drinks.[98] After 1786, the law concerning the "due regulation of licensed houses" in Hampshire County held that "no person whosoever, may presume to be a common Victualler, innholder, taverner, or seller of wine, beer, ale, cider, brandy, rum, or any strong liquors, by retail, or in a less quantity than twenty-eight gallons," without a license from the county justices of the peace; any person who was found selling "spirituous liquors, or any mixed liquor, part of which is spirituous, without license" duly obtained, would face a stiff fine.[99] There is no record of Trainer having received formal permission to sell alcohol in any quantity, so perhaps her transgression here was along these lines. But perhaps local officials were content to allow Trainer to support her household with some informal commerce (perhaps preferable to adding anyone to the list of those in need of public support), until they became uneasy with the interracial nature of the gatherings; the spring 1806 warning may have been an effort to urge her to keep better control of her patrons if she hoped to enjoy their continued indulgence, especially since from the middle of the eighteenth century colonial law barred white tavernkeepers from serving patrons of African descent.[100]

Today the term "house of ill fame" tends to connote prostitution, and if Mary Trainer engaged in or sheltered some form of sex work, she would not have been alone among Hampshire County women. Other women jailed for sexual offenses in those years include Sally Williams, a thirty-year-old African American woman who spent over five months in the Northampton jail, and Sarah Smith, a thirty-eight-year-old Hadley tailoress who spent two and a half months in the county jail before she was transferred to the state prison.[101] The Massachusetts courts had only recently turned their attention to prostitution when Trainer came to official notice. Commerce in sex had not yet been addressed specifically in colonial law; only in the decades after the American Revolution did the courts begin prosecutions in this area (then, as now, concentrating on female prostitutes, and not male customers), the first clear case appearing in Boston in 1800.[102] In the first two centuries of Massachusetts government, such activity was attacked within a rubric of "lewd and disorderly" behavior or houses. But, by the decade that Trainer found herself in trouble with the law, prosecutions were rising: about three in any given year during the first decade of the nineteenth century (and never more than six). By the 1810s there would be more than twelve, and by 1820, fifteen.[103]

Whether Trainer was permitting drinking, sexual commerce, or both (or neither, as it is certainly possible that she was unfairly accused or that the transgressive behavior was something else), the law clearly considered these activities to come as a set; when Boston clamped down on the city's houses of "ill fame," indictments charged proprietors with facilitating their customers' "drinking, tipling, whoring and misbehaving themselves."[104] Whatever the allegations, Trainer's home clearly made community leaders anxious. Committed to the still relatively new stone jail in Northampton, Mary spent more than a week in the room set aside to incarcerate women.

In the years to follow, in addition to participating seasonally in the broomcorn economy, Mrs. Trainer turned again to the care of the needy, taking in Mary Andries, the ailing widow of George Andries.[105] Andries was perhaps a Hessian soldier who had remained in Massachusetts after the conclusion of the American Revolution. He and his wife Mary had come to Forty Acres in 1782; the following year Charles Phelps had a house built on the property for the two tenants. They would live there for some twenty-five years, and among other things, they introduced the Phelps household to the German traditions associated with Christmas, which the two couples celebrated together in 1785, 1788, and 1793.[106] When Andries fell ill late in 1809, the community in and around Forty Acres had been braced for his death—"As to Andries," Elizabeth Phelps would write to her daughter, "he grew gradually worse, the last week he declines faster, some of our folks were there the greatest part of the time night & day—Mr. Hair and John set up there satturday night between 4 & 5. John came to our window & said he had stop'd breathing without a struggle or a groan." Charles Phelps "rose immediately & with those two men laid him out decently (we had every thing ready)—but his wife could not reconcile herself to being alone in a strange place." Mary Andries "seem'd to be much agitated," Elizabeth Phelps wrote, wailing "what shall I now doon? What shall I now doon? O mine Andries, &c." Elizabeth told Mary that she "must come and live" with her, but that she "must leave all her dirt and rags there."[107]

Mary Andries was paralyzed with grief. "'I can ne I can ne' was the most she would say," Elizabeth wrote, "However, after the corps was taken away, after 2, she was put into the wagon & brought here sett directly before our kitchen fire—having been previously wash'd and cleanse'd & dress'd in decent, clean cloaths. Thus you see what door opened." Having Mary in the household was a real burden for Elizabeth: "It is troublesome you may depend, she can understand so little what we say to her, & we so poorly understand her, that it is rather difficult to get along. . . . She appears to be in prayer great part of her time," Phelps added, "up lifted eyes, with folded hands in the attitude. She seems to have a great dread of returning to the old house again, frequently breaks out 'O mine Andries, mine Andries.'" But in her better hours Elizabeth felt real compassion for Mary. "How should I feel," she mused, "was I such a poor helpless creature in a strange land without any person to depend on? No where else by on clear, pure providence, indeed I can't but hope her eyes are fix'd, trusting on God." Elizabeth pulled out a large chest that they had made into a bed by the fire when their enslaved girl Phillis died, and put it "against the outward east door in the kitchen, put straw at the bottom then a bed—that is her night accommodation." Mary's health was poor—she could no longer dress or undress without assistance, and apparently could no longer walk— and so demanded the constant attention of Elizabeth and the other caregivers in the household.

One can certainly sympathize with the widow's distress: having followed her husband into a new country, she was utterly lost when he died and left her alone there, without friends, family, or financial resources. And if Elizabeth Phelps found her to be a burden, Mary Andries seemed sometimes little grateful for her new circumstances. But the displaced widow had few choices. As was customary, the Phelps family was compensated by the town for their expenses taking on responsibility for her care: Charles received $31.50 from town coffers toward his costs for twenty-one weeks of her upkeep, just a fraction of the total time she spent under his roof.[108] In time, perhaps exhausted by the effort, the Phelps family made a change; widow Andries went to Mary Trainer's household in May, where she remained until her death in October, a move that, as Trainer also received compensation for her effort, perhaps solved a problem for both women.[109] In fact, after 1810, the aging widow Mary Trainer would become a significant figure in the town's system of public welfare, suggesting that whatever had troubled the town's leaders just a few years earlier had put no permanent blemish on her local reputation; in some years as much as a fifth of the town's poor relief funds passed through her hands.[110]

Women like Mary Trainer well knew the uncomfortable edge of a marginal existence. With little in the way of special skills or financial resources, these women lived catch-as-catch-can, always on the lookout for opportunity. They surely felt the fragility of their situation. But of course, the most vulnerable women in Hadley were those brought there in captivity, or the children and descendants of these coerced residents. Whatever Mary Trainer's financial situation at any given time, or the interracial unions by some members of her household, Mary was understood to be a member of Hadley's white community; poverty limited her choices in ways that race did not. When she transgressed the law she found herself confined to the local jail—though not for long. Mary Trainer crossed boundaries of law and custom and crossed back again; from field to farmwork to household chores and carework, she provided for herself and her family together with others in and around her household as chance and circumstance allowed.

For many women in Federal Hadley, these were years of what they in their own time would have called "straightened" circumstances. Perhaps then it is no wonder to find that in the decades between 1770 and 1810, fertility rates in Hadley declined while the age at the time of a woman's marriage rose, trends historian Christopher Clark ascribes to the increasing scarcity of land and the comparatively "poorer future prospects" of local families.[111] How women responded to and experienced those circumstances depended on their position relative to them, and to one another. Elizabeth Porter Phelps, Sarah Jackson, Irene Hibbard, Zerviah Ford Packard, Assinah, Peg and her daughters, Joan Prutt, Sally Rogers, Mary Andries, and Mary Trainer each led lives different from the others, and yet so thickly entwined that it is almost impossible to consider one without the others.

Like their counterparts across New England, the women of early Hadley looked across the community at the different sorts of women with whom their own lives entangled. If we, at our contemporary remove, tend to see the circumstances that united the women of rural places like Federal Hadley, those women readily perceived the differences of race, ethnicity, ability, education, and opportunity that both created and constrained their own options. From the dairy at Forty Acres to its parlor, from North Hadley to Hadley Center to

Hockanum, from the substantial homes that lined the town common to the dwellings huddled along the river, from the households of families enslaved, free, and something in between, women looked out their own doorways and toward the households of others, viewpoints filled with prospects topographical and economic, commanding and close.

PART TWO

LIVELIHOODS

CHAPTER FOUR

Domestic Service

Each day opened with the scrape of a bucket coming up out of the well. Fires were built, stoked, banked, and doused. Water was carried, food prepared, dishes scoured and put away. Kitchen floors needed to be swept; beds made up or put away; chamber pots emptied, rinsed, and replaced; lamps and candles lit and doused. Children were bathed, dressed, fed, nurtured, generally kept from harm, and tucked back into bed again. Most weeks, clothing and household textiles were washed and mended, and the baking was done. And then there were the more seasonal tasks, such as the dairy work (which picked up after calves were born in the spring and continued through the summer), and the making of everything from soap to sausages.[1] The labor of the domestic servants who helped keep households running smoothly fell into these general categories: the production, preparation, and preservation of food; the production and maintenance of clothing and household textiles, including knitting, spinning, mending, and making, as well as the production of soap, and washing and ironing; the care of children; and the care and cleaning of the house itself. Elizabeth Phelps and other women of the rural gentry participated in these activities as well, but they also had the option of avoiding the most backbreaking chores. For example, although Phelps certainly toiled in her dairy and could frequently be found churning in the wee hours of the morning to take advantage of the cool of the day, it was often a hired woman who scoured out the chamber afterward.[2]

Throughout the eighteenth-century Atlantic World, domestic service "provided the standpoint from which other female employments were judged."[3] More women earned livings as domestic help than in any other occupation. In Hadley, as elsewhere, parents with too many mouths to feed—or with a few boys but not enough girls, or plenty of girls but too few boys—placed their children out as servants in the households of others. As one historian has written, "family security frequently depended on getting a girl a place. As a result, the majority of servants were girls in their early teens who presented themselves as maids of all work."[4] Most affluent households had some sort of "hired maid" all the time: the household of Hadley's Reverend Samuel Hopkins, for instance, saw more than a dozen hired women pass through, in succession, between 1767 and 1797.[5] The getting of servants was not a phenomenon of elite households only: Hadley tailoress Tryphena Newton Cook employed Jemima Boynton to help do the work of the house, and even Joshua Boston had a Native American woman, Polly Sampson, keeping house for him in the last years of his life.[6]

The story of domestic service in Federal New England is a story of relationships and how they responded to the evolving preferences of both employers and employees. In the intimate landscapes of family homes, work cannot be disentangled from the everyday associations in which they were entwined. Employers and employees shared spaces, but not necessarily values or objectives, prompting negotiations small and large, tacit and overt, that would help trigger the gradual reshaping of landscapes of labor as hired women both claimed and were relegated to dedicated workspaces within (kitchens and ells) and beyond (factories and workshops) the household. The situation could be as unique as each pairing of servant and mistress, turning as those pairings did on personality and circumstance as well as larger structural systems in which those relationships were embedded. Our focus here is on relationships between employers and employees, and between mothers and their children (as some servants coped with the challenges of parenting while at the same time assuring an income for themselves and their child), though others run through the narrative as well, including hired men and hired women, debtors and creditors, and families and local government. What emerges is a picture of employed and employing women striving to shape their circumstances, day-to-day and in the long term.

Mobilities and Migrations, Security and Stability

Domestic help in early America was not necessarily limited to young women who circulated among households within their neighborhood; instead, hired girls tended to come from middling and less fortunate families well beyond the local community.[7] In urban centers like Boston, rural women seeking work as domestics constituted a significant proportion of the people migrating through the city in search of work.[8] Holly Izard's findings on Shrewsbury's Ward household in central Massachusetts also suggest that "neighbors' daughters did *not* casually move in and out of the Ward household in work relationships centered in mutuality during the early years; nor were they replaced by strangers in calculated non-reciprocal wage-based service relationships later on." Izard's study of domestic work, workers, and work relationships from the late eighteenth to the mid-nineteenth century confirms patterns present in Hampshire County, too, where "the preponderance of hired girls throughout the entire time span" were drawn from "artisanal and laboring families outside of the local face-to-face community." Hired women in both Hadley and Shrewsbury "often worked for fairly long terms for set wages in relationships that, while congenial, reflected an inequality of status." Ross Beales, in a study of a similar household in Westborough, Massachusetts, concluded that there, too, female servants socialized and attended church together with their employers, but that they also had "agreed upon wage rates and settled work accounts; they were hired help and they had their 'place.'"[9]

Patterns of employment in Hadley confirm these findings, suggesting that economic relationships between early American women were more complex than are often imagined. Of the more than twenty hired women whose names appear in Elizabeth Phelps's diary and correspondence, only one seems to have been living in Hadley when she moved to Forty Acres. Most were drawn from nearby settlements like Pelham and Leverett (both about eleven miles east), but a nearly equal number came from towns farther afield—Brookfield (thirty-one miles), Hardwick (twenty-nine miles), Spencer (thirty-eight miles), and Ashfield (twenty-two miles).[10] After Phelps's children married and moved away, to Litchfield, Connecticut, and Boston, she constantly quizzed them as to likely girls in their areas who would be willing to come to Hadley to work.[11] Phelps's Hadley neighbors likewise employed hired girls from Boston, Vermont, and other distant places. Sarah Hopkins's maid Naomi Phelps came from Cold Spring (today Belchertown, twelve miles to the east, on the other side of Amherst). Lucretia Johnson, who worked for Samuel and Lucy Porter's household in the mid-1780s, is described as "a girl Mrs Porter got from Boston," suggesting perhaps that the Porters had consulted the city's Overseers of the Poor.[12] In Hadley, as throughout the eighteenth-century Atlantic World, a job in domestic service was among the most common reasons for women's travel.[13]

Some of those servants were drawn from indigenous communities. By the mid-eighteenth century the English colonists had seriously reduced the populations of native nations, but by no means had they eliminated them from the New England landscape; in fact, European and native families had been exchanging goods and services for well over a century. From the outset of European colonization in New England, English and native communities had negotiated and sustained a fragile balance of power, but after cataclysmic war broke out across New England in the 1670s, relations between English colonizers and native nations were forever changed. Native communities became increasingly scattered, sometimes reconfigured in new villages that embraced members of a number of nations. A 1765 Massachusetts census reported no Native Americans living in Hampshire County, but it is more likely that the census failed to identify the native men and women who lived there only part-time, or who had married or changed their names, thereby obscuring their native heritage. State and even national boundaries were not especially relevant for many indigenous families. Some women and men moved between European and native settlements, living in northern villages in the winter (in Vermont, New York, or Canada), and coming south during the summer to sell splint baskets and other woven goods.

Some native women in the eighteenth-century Connecticut Valley chose less migratory lifestyles and found work in domestic service. At mid-century, Elisha Williams's Wethersfield household included an "Indian maid servant and her two children," as well as an unrelated Native American girl; these servants shared space with an English domestic and a "Negro boy."[14] In Northampton, Sally Maminash (a niece of the Mohegan preacher Samson Occum) appears at least for a time to have been a servant in the family of Warham and Sophia Clapp. The daughter of Joseph Maminash (most likely a Nonotuck, Pocumtuck, or Podunk Indian) and Elizabeth Occum (of Connecticut's Mohegan community, Samson Occum's older sister), Sally in the later years of her life would tell Sylvester Judd that after the death of her mother she supported herself by "spinning and weaving in different families."[15] Sally may also have woven baskets and chair seats, a craft practiced, as we have seen, by many Native Americans in the Connecticut Valley (figure 4.1).

Indian women were a steady presence in Hadley and at Forty Acres. We have already met the hired woman Assinah, who remained with the Phelps family only a few months.[16] Years later, when hired girl Persis Morse left the farm's employ it was an Indian woman who filled her place. Rachel, another Native American whose family lived in Ashfield, stayed with the family for nearly two years before she married Ralf, a hired man, and moved out of town.[17] Years later, in the spring of 1815, Phelps recorded in the pages of her memorandum book, "This day an Indian woman came here to live & work for us."[18] In a letter, she elaborated on the household's labor situation, reporting that the two hired men they have now are both excellent, and that "one more kind providence I must mention, an Indian woman is come to us, from Connecticut, who appears to be everything we can wish."[19] Unfortunately for us today, Phelps added that "her story is almost too long and particular to relate on paper"—a tantalizing allusion to what must have been a fascinating conversation between the prospective employee and employer. But Phelps was already smitten: "She has been with us two days & you don't know how pleased daughter and I are." Her next words present the kind of mystery that is the bane of all historians: "The girl we had before, we was released from in a very peculiar manner only one day before this one came."[20]

Phelps's pleasure at the new servant's arrival would not last long; just over a week later, the woman was gone again, collected by her husband and taken home.[21] Phelps was deeply disappointed: "She did a deal of hard dirty work, and did it indeed very well. We anticipated a great benefit from her strength and good management. Where we can find one we know not. Daughter gets

Figure 4.1 Ladder-back chair with an ash-splint seat, belonging to Sally Maminash (ca. 1765–1853). It is possible that Maminash herself, whose mother was from Connecticut's Mohegan community, and whose father was identified with Podunk, Nonotuck, and Pocumtuck communities, wove the cane seat. Photo courtesy of Historic Northampton, Northampton, MA

along for a week past, with what little I do, but thinks when the cheese comes on, we shall fail."[22] Why the servant left and where she went are unknown. Perhaps she had abandoned her husband, only to be returned to him when he found her at work on the Phelps farm. Or maybe she had gone to seek employment to contribute to their shared household income and found service at the Phelps's farm too demanding—she perhaps being less enthusiastic about the completion of this "hard, dirty work" than was Elizabeth. Like the "peculiar release" of her predecessor, we'll likely never know.

Thinking about domestic help along another axis—age—also helps move beyond long-standing conceptions of servants as white adolescent girls or young adults working for families around town and reminds us that children sometimes traveled far from home to obtain work and housing. Boys as young as five were routinely bound out by Overseers of the Poor, assigned to families that could convey the principles and practices of husbandry, and officials relieved the reputed father of an unsanctioned child from the burden of further financial support when the child (if healthy) turned seven.[23] John Davis was just five when Boston's Overseers bound him to the household of Hadley's Oliver Smith, where he was to remain until he reached the age of majority (twenty-one for men) in the summer of 1775, while Mark Noble was seven when bound to Moses Marsh, also until he reached the age of twenty-one, in 1774.[24] Mary Craigie was twelve when the Boston Overseers assigned her to the Northampton household of Nathaniel and Elizabeth Phelps (uncle and aunt to Charles Phelps, husband of Elizabeth), where Mrs. Phelps would instruct her in "knitting and sewing and all other parts of good housewifery."[25] Help-wanted ads sought girls as young as eight.[26] When Northampton's Overseers of the Poor bound out "Mary Dwight a poor female child of Mary Lyman of said Northampton" to the Allis family in Hatfield, she, too, was "to be taught or instructed in spinning, sewing, and knitting, and the other common occupations of labouring women."[27] Girls could be put to work around the house almost as soon as they could walk. Children could help clean wool until they were old enough to spin, and they could undertake little errands around the house and farm.

The work given domestic servants was, unsurprisingly, hard—and sometimes led to injury. Hadley correspondence and the accounts of physicians and healers are full of references to workplace injuries, from cuts and bruises to accidents involving animals and vehicles. Burns, in particular, were familiar occurrences among the women of eighteenth-century Hadley, and are mentioned routinely in Phelps's memorandum book, at Forty Acres and elsewhere. Hired woman Lucy Marshall gave herself a bad scald when she accidentally stepped in a pail of boiling water, while on another occasion, the servant Rachel burned her foot "bad eno,'" in Phelps's words.[28]

What drew women and girls into domestic service? In Shrewsbury, Massachusetts, Holly Izard has observed, the usual motivation for entering service was "sheer need": young women like Lydia Stone worked to offset her father's indebtedness; another servant, Nancy Newton, was the oldest child of twelve in an "economically marginal family."[29] Similar circumstances brought young women into the Phelps household. The death of a male provider was associated with many women's entry into some form of service. Seventeen-year-old Sarah Ayres of Granby, Massachusetts (a town just over the Holyoke Range), for example, came to Elizabeth Phelps as an orphan. Ayres's mother had died when she was eleven, and her father drowned in the Connecticut River only three years later, during the winter of 1768, when Sarah was fourteen. The seventh of ten children, Sarah came to live at Forty Acres in May 1771. She had just been gruesomely reminded of her parent's death—her father's body had the month before surfaced below the falls at South Hadley, the spring thaw raising his corpse more than two years after it had disappeared into the Connecticut's current.[30]

Most female servants were recruited by way of the business and social relationships that brought neighbors into contact with each other throughout the area. In 1796, Charles Phelps encountered Lydia Atwood in Spencer, probably while traveling to or from Boston, and engaged her services from December 1796 to September 1798; in April 1802, he "went to meeting at Pelham, brought a little girl to live with my son, Martha Hatchman."[31] Many servants at Forty Acres were the daughters of families Charles encountered on his business travels, or neighbors of the Phelpses' friends and families scattered throughout New England, invoking a geographic element, even rationale, in the selection of hired women. Indeed, distance itself may have been part of a girl's appeal; perhaps the employing of hired help from towns beyond their near neighborhood reflected an effort to keep servants' family members at bay, and thus to exert greater control over these workers.[32] It also helped discourage employees from absenteeism, since it was harder to run home.

Though Phelps did not record her criteria for hiring or retaining help, correspondence with her daughter Betsy contained much discussion of servants, and the correspondence suggests that both had three general requirements: an even temper, good moral character, and an aptitude for heavy labor. "I never expect to have another girl so kind, and willing to wait on me," Phelps wrote on one occasion; another woman was praised for being "so good f[or] business, and so good natured too." She appreciated the extra effort of another woman who "washed for me this day and done very well, offered to scour afterwards, & wash the floor, all done very well."[33] Finally, good servants were honest and trustworthy. Incidents involving theft and embezzlement of products of the farm were common. On one occasion, she worried about a hired hand whom the family apparently did not know as well as they might have liked: "There was three men here yesterday who appeared well acquainted with our Clark when he lived in Boston (I find he has lived in many places)." The men said not "one word good of him. . . . I really feel concern'd for he has all the chance any one can desire, threshing and dressing flax, tis easy for him to pay himself."[34] A good servant could be trusted with the goods of the household, whether the products of the farm ready for market, or the little comforts of life scattered around any home.[35]

The position that servants held within the household seems to have varied widely. Those who remained with a family for several years—like Lucy Marshall, who lived in the Phelps household off and on for nearly a decade—were almost members of the family, garnering a fair amount of security and stability.[36] Persis Morse, who spent four years at Forty Acres, was particularly popular with the grandchildren, while others maintained less intimate relationships with the family. Though passages in both the diary and correspondence suggest that Elizabeth became genuinely fond of some of the women who worked in her household, another woman, she observed, had a disagreeable "temper." Still others could become a little too familiar as a result of a long tenure in the house. She wrote of one young woman who had apparently become presumptuous in her encounters with her mistress: "Her long tarry has made her assume too much importance." The woman, she wrote, "has been here perhaps nearly long enough."[37] It is worth noting that Phelps felt it was critical when dealing with servants to "take hold right sharp."[38] Her neighbor Dorothy Williams phrased it more gently when she wrote her mother that "business cannot go on without a leader."[39] Hired women had to be instructed, nurtured, corrected, and praised; they required "a great deal of flattering and scolding"— which, Phelps joked with her daughter, "you know I could administer very handily."[40] Something of the grooming of servants, and the skills it involved for both women, is captured in Betsy Huntington's letter home describing her efforts with a newly hired girl: "You may wish to know how I succeed with my new girl—she is quite young and awkward, but I hope by patience and constant attention, to be able to make her good for something."[41]

Sometimes, of course, a genuine fondness developed between a servant and the family who employed her. Certainly Lucy Marshall demonstrates an example of the sort of affection that sometimes grew between families and servants. But in other instances—and it seems increasingly so as the rhetoric of the Revolution changed the nature of social relations—a servant and her employers simply could not get along. As Elizabeth Phelps would say, "some help is hardly worth the having."[42] Some miles downriver, in Suffield, Connecticut, Thaddeus Leavitt registered his frustration with one servant when he wrote in the pages of his diary, "this morning sent to Boston in stage to her parents Mary Davis a girl fifteen years old and which has lived with us five years and by agreement was to have lived with us until eighteen years, but after long experiment and hard endeavors to instruct and reform her, she still continued to be deceitful, unfaithful lazy girl for which reason I gave her a final discharge."[43] Leavitt had made preparations for the fateful event some two weeks earlier when he purchased from Matthew Thompson "a Negro female servant named Mille," a fifteen-year-old girl for whom he paid thirty-five dollars. Mille arrived the day after Mary departed, prompting Leavitt to "hope and expect she may prove a good girl and be a great help to Mrs Leavitt if so she will be used with tenderness" (Leavitt left no word on how she would be "used" if not).[44] Sometimes severance seemed mutual: when Easter Green left the Porters, Susanna Edwards reported that "if they had been a little slower she should have saved them the troubles." But despite "the mortification of being turned away," Easter seemed unconcerned. For her part, Elizabeth Phelps recorded her suspicion that, wherever she wound up, Miss Green "will be no great benefit to others."[45]

Other partings were less fraught. Sometimes young girls, unaccustomed to living away from home, simply got homesick. In May 1783, Elizabeth Phelps recorded "Satt my husband went and got Lucy Baker to come and Live here." But, less than three months later, Lucy's term as a servant ended prematurely. In July, Elizabeth recorded that Mrs. Baker had visited her daughter in her new situation on the 8th and 9th; by Saturday the 12th, she wrote that she "went and carried Lucy Baker home—she been poorly ever since here mother was here."[46] Young Lucy had lived in Hadley just ten weeks, but apparently after the visit with her mother was overcome with homesickness and returned home. Some hired girls found spouses among the hired men in their orbit, and left off work in domestic service as they worked instead for and within their own family. And of course, countless young women reached the conclusion of their terms of service with little fanfare, collected their things, and moved on.

Labor Strategies

The circumstances of any given position varied widely and were a constant source of negotiation—and negotiation (as the affective nature of relations between employers and employees and other members of the household) continually shaped the conditions under which women worked. Relationships between the mistress of the house and any given servant were one important element in establishing the nature of the position, but so too were relationships with other members of the household—particularly young children and other employees. Women in a position to hire help engaged in a constant calculus that was not merely financial, but weighed personalities, convenience, family privacy, and a host of other intangible factors.

Elizabeth Phelps and her daughter Betsy Huntington were often exhausted by the problems that hired girls and women brought into their homes, and preferred, when possible, to hire people to help out with specific tasks, which freed them to perform the other work of the house themselves. Textile-related chores lent themselves particularly well to this strategy. Hiring different sorts of women workers was necessary to balance competing household needs. Huntington wrote home that her hired girl Polly helped "a great deal . . . I must keep her sewing," adding, though, that she had "brought enough of her own to last till spring." Huntington continued, "next week I intend to get somebody to come and make Mr H's shirts and my shifts."[47] Alternately, having a hired girl in the house to help with the general work of the household gave Huntington the time she needed if she wanted to do the sewing herself. In late June 1801, when pregnant, Huntington wrote that she was "ready to set down to sewing," since her hired girl Candace would be with her "constantly" through the end of her service: "Today," the young mother-to-be could then write, "I shall cut out my new gown for it is time I think."[48]

Balancing sewing with other housework and deciding how best to use hired women to facilitate those chores occupied Huntington's mind much of the time. She would have preferred to avoid the trouble and expense of hired help, and to do what she called the "common work" of the household herself (figure 4.2). When Huntington first set up housekeeping, she wrote home that her husband had almost immediately "engaged a black girl of 13 years, who can do all the common work, and there is a black woman will assist me in washing."[49] But it was this so-called "common work" that most often competed with sewing chores: "If I do the work of the family," she wrote on one occasion, "I shall be obliged to hire all my sewing."[50] In Hatfield, Mary Graves Miller chose not to hire a domestic servant; she did the common household chores herself, employed women like "black Cynthy" to perform the particularly laborious work of washing, and "put out" her sewing. For Huntington, conversely, hiring help to do the household chores enabled her to do her own needlework: "Since Clara [an African American woman] has been with me, I have had time to do much of my sewing and indeed have nearly work'd myself out, or rather, have done those things that were more immediately necessary."[51] Another year, while worrying about her next delivery, and complaining about the heavy burden her body was carrying, Betsy was grateful for the hired help that lightened her load: "How thankful i should be that my situation is so comfortable—I have help to relieve me of most of the labor, except sewing and knitting and seeing to the children."[52]

Determining when to hire help and when to do without, whether to do one's own sewing or put it out, was also of course a financial calculation. In the 1770s, for example, sewing could be hired at roughly a shilling a day, while domestic servants generally were paid between two shillings, eight pence and three shillings, six pence per week, depending on their duties. Betsy Huntington weighed a similar disparity when, some thirty years later, she wrote her mother that her hired helper "Miss Hotchkiss is here yet; I have a great deal of sewing to do, and think it cheaper to keep her two or three weeks longer, than to hire a girl by the day."[53] With the hired woman in the house to take care of the food preparation, cleaning, and so on, Huntington

Figure 4.2 Elizabeth Whiting Phelps Huntington (1779–1847) portrait by Simon Fitch, ca. 1801. Elizabeth ("Betsy") Phelps grew up at Forty Acres, and watched her mother manage the large workforce employed there. In 1801 she married the Rev. Dan Huntington and moved to Litchfield, Connecticut; in 1809 the couple and their children moved to Middletown, Connecticut. To support her husband's ministerial work and raise their eleven children, Huntington relied on a steady stream of domestic servants. In 1816, the Huntingtons moved to Hadley, where they took over the family farm. Portrait P036 in the collection of the Porter-Phelps-Huntington Museum, Hadley, MA

would be free to take care of her own sewing, thus avoiding the higher daily rate. Around the same time, Huntington's sister-in-law Sarah Parsons Phelps had written Elizabeth Porter Phelps that "upon trial I found it more expensive to hire my washing than to keep steady help. I have therefore got a girl to live with me this winter."[54] Apparently each of these women preferred not to keep a hired girl in the house but both found sending work out to be so much more costly than keeping servants that they continued, if reluctantly, to employ live-in help.[55]

Sexuality, Motherhood, and Domestic Service

Balancing competing concerns was a struggle known not only to women employers; women who became mothers while employees knew well that same challenge. While the Christian ideal may have encouraged women to wait until they were married to experience sexual union, children born early in marriages or out of wedlock altogether were not uncommon in eighteenth-century New England, and their numbers increased during the colonial and early national eras.[56] Some women, in what they perceived as an impossible position, terminated the pregnancy, and if they were able to do so before their condition was known, they could escape censure.[57] Other women felt compelled to take desperate measures and took the life of the child after it was born. Elizabeth Porter Phelps noted the death of "a poor squaw hanged at Northampton for murdering her infant babe" in 1785, although the most talked-about case in late eighteenth-century Hampshire County was surely Abiel Converse, a twenty-three-year-old woman hanged in 1788 for the murder of her newborn, apparently the second time she had turned to such extreme measures.[58]

Servant romances and premarital pregnancies seem to have been almost more the rule than the exception among Phelps's household help, a fact that caused both Elizabeth Porter Phelps and her daughter no small share of concern.[59] Popular imagery about early America suggests a uniform conservatism when it came to sexual behavior, but in fact different women embraced different values in this area, depending on their religious orientation, class status, and other factors. On one visit to Northampton, Phelps "saw she that was Fanny Dickinson, & she told me, that there was said to be 9 girls pregnant in Northampton, that they principally were of the lowest class, Mary Wire, &c." With some horror she added that "two of the new converts were tho't to be of that number." One woman, she hints, found a way to terminate her pregnancy: "They had not behaved with that solemnity as others had done . . . one of them had been very unwell for some time, but had got cleverly."[60]

Raising one's children in one's workplace was, of course, not new in Federal New England. African American women had been doing it for generations, in the north as well as the south, and under much more trying conditions. As we have seen, Peg raised her little girls Phillis and Rose at Forty Acres until 1772, when she and Jon Warner's slave Pomp persuaded their respective owners to sell them both to Stephen Fay of Bennington, Vermont, in order to facilitate their marriage. The circumstances of her life after emancipation are more difficult to track, but it seems possible that Peg, like other freedwomen in Hadley, continued to perform household labor for local families. The Anglo-American women who worked for the Phelps household had more alternatives. Though their marginal economic status surely constrained poor white women's employment options, this was especially the case among unmarried white women with children in rural New England. These women often sought positions as domestic servants, which required them to find ways to care for their children while working. Some women opted to keep their children with them in their places of employment, acting simultaneously as mothers and wage workers. Others left their children with relatives. Whatever choices they made, the balancing act was a difficult one.

Susanna Whipple came to the Phelps household in December 1791 at the age of seventeen with a six-week old baby in tow, named Submit, or "Mitte," West. The child was apparently her daughter with nineteen-year-old Daniel West Jr., whose family lived on the south end of town.[61] For whatever reason, Susanna could not compel a marriage, and so she found herself in need of shelter and employment, both of which were secured at Forty Acres. In the following months, she nursed the infant in between chores for the Phelps household.

Susanna would not remain a single mother for long; on March 16, 1794, Susanna married Samuel Blodgett, a nineteen-year-old hired man who was also living on the property. Born in Lexington, Massachusetts, Samuel and his father Timothy had moved to Hampshire County sometime during the tumultuous years of the Revolution. Blodgett came to work at the Phelps farm in the years before Susanna's arrival, and apparently the two young workers cultivated a mutual attraction over the first year that Susanna was living at Forty Acres, for at the time of her marriage, she was three months pregnant. Two weeks later, the newly married Blodgetts moved out, first to a house in North Hadley, and in time farther north. In Susanna's place, Phelps engaged a "Mrs Hancock," the sister of neighbor John Montague's wife (suggesting something about the networks through which servants and employers found one another), who herself brought two children along with her. The Hancock family would remain in the Phelps household for just over a year, until the fall of 1794, when they moved to Whately.[62] By July, however, Susanna was having a difficult time managing both her pregnancy and little Mitte, prompting her to ask whether she might return the child to the Phelpses. On the 21st of September, Susanna gave birth to twins, a boy and a girl. On the 28th, Elizabeth Phelps recorded in the pages of her memorandum book "we had our little girl Submit West christened," suggesting that already the little girl had made her way into the Phelps family circle.[63]

Susanna Blodgett may have initially assumed that she and her new husband would eventually retrieve little Mitte, but for whatever reason, that was not to be. In the spring of the following year, the Blodgetts and their twins moved north, to Deerfield, but Mitte, now three-and-a-half years old, did not join them. Instead, she remained with the Phelpses, where she was raised as a member of their household—not quite the adopted daughter that Thankful Richmond was, but a loved child, whose status seemed part servant, part ward. She learned to knit, spin, help with the milking, and perform other chores typically undertaken by children; at the same time, she became a treasured companion for Elizabeth Porter Phelps, whose own daughters were just leaving the nest. In August 1794 Phelps reported to her daughter that she made Mitte "a little bed by ours every night and sometimes She will be in it at night others she will be up and down a number of times jest as she happens to feel—but on the whole she makes not much trouble in the night . . . indeed she is a great deal of company for me." The toddler was a steady source of amusement: "I love dearly to hear her talk. Yesterday it rained a little she was standing at the door looking out very serious then turning to me 'I is paid twil 'ain on Besse—un tamp un Porter'—I told her I thought there was more danger of its raining in on her—there she talks all day and is very diverting I can tell you." But even at the age of three, there were early signs that the young girl would not be easy to raise; Elizabeth assured her daughter Betsy that Mitte "is a much better girl than when you was here no body to flee to now—but expects to do as I bid her."[64]

Over the next several years, Mitte's unruly behavior became a source of constant worry for Elizabeth Phelps and her daughter. She was apparently uninterested in contributing to the work of the family, and she had a willful streak. Her conduct was a constant topic of conversation for Elizabeth, who regularly observed how "Mitte plods on, sometimes good and sometimes bad."[65] In 1801, Phelps carried Mitte up to her mother's, so that she could attend a school kept there.[66] When Betsy offered to take Mitte into her home in Connecticut, Elizabeth called it a "relief."[67] Mitte shuffled between the Hadley and Litchfield households until November 1804, when she left the Phelps household to live with her "grandmother West," fifty-five-year-old Mary Cook West. Exhausted and disappointed, Elizabeth sighed, "O how pitiful I feel for her. I commit her Lord unto thee, do thou dispose of her as seemeth good in thy sight."[68]

Mitte wasn't the only one whose conduct Elizabeth Porter Phelps found difficult to control; Phelps constantly had a hard time enforcing among her hired help the same codes of behavior embraced by members of her family. As the eighteenth century gave way to the nineteenth, Elizabeth found her household affairs regularly disrupted by the sexual behavior of the people in her employ.[69] Although labor contracts from the latter half of the eighteenth century routinely forbade fornication, Elizabeth Porter Phelps had little luck controlling her servants' sexual activities. Not only did it create havoc with the affairs of the household: it was simply awkward, evidence of Phelps's inability to control her employees, and a crack in the household's genteel facade. One unhappy consequence of unsanctioned intimacies concerned a hired woman named Judith who had arrived sometime before February 1801.[70] The family had been quite satisfied with her work, but when she became pregnant in the winter of 1802, her condition was an embarrassment, so much so that when Elizabeth was away visiting Betsy in Litchfield, she instructed her husband Charles, if company should come, "don't introduce Judith."[71]

By mid-March, it was becoming increasingly difficult for Judith to keep up with her duties: "Jude is quite feble. She has made out to dress a fowl for her Self, and a few other chores, she discharged her blood on Wednesday. Mrs Prince has been here to help her ever since. But I hope to get along if I can hire the washing."[72] Though she was "not certain how it will be," whether Judith would indeed "venture off," she took the opportunity to inquire whether her daughter-in-law in Boston, Sarah Parsons Phelps, might be able to help secure Judith's replacement: "If you could find a good black girl down there I should be willing to give a good price, or a white girl, tho a black one would be best on some accounts for us."[73] Phelps's desire to hire women of color probably stemmed from long-standing cultural preferences among Connecticut Valley elites concerning access to black labor, but it seems possible, too, that she hoped that women of color would find fewer opportunities for romantic entanglements in Hadley than their white counterparts.

Elizabeth seemed truly torn by her employee's difficult situation. She hoped that Judith appreciated "her own mercies" (perhaps a reference to kindnesses she had heretofore received at Forty Acres), but she felt too that Judith had perhaps begun to take her (longtime) position in the Phelps family for granted.[74] For her part, Betsy recognized how few options were available to single mothers: "I pity poor Judith—should she be unable too work for her living, what would become of her?" Her father, she believed, would never turn her out, "destitute and distressed," but apparently Judith had no other means of support beyond her own labor.[75] By May 1802, for whatever reason or by whatever means, Judith had left the household.

The experience left a lasting impression on both Elizabeth and Betsy, the latter a young woman of twenty-three when Judith became pregnant. In January 1804, when discussing the care of Susanna Blodgett's daughter Mitte, Betsy suggests that she might come to live with her in Litchfield: "I feel as if she was not in so great danger here, as she was with your girls—from some things I understood from her, Persis is a poor example for a girl of her years, [and] Meriam [Wire] was quite as bad."[76] Well aware of the circumstances surrounding Mitte's own birth, Betsy was especially concerned that the young woman seemed a little too "sociable" in the kitchen with the hired boy Almond, a situation particularly troubling to her since twelve-year-old Mitte had already "had the sign" that Betsy and Elizabeth did not get until they were fourteen. Betsy's concern for the girl proved well-founded: in a month's time Persis *was* pregnant, by another of the hired boys, nineteen-year-old Reuban Debell, who had lived at the farm since he arrived there in April 1791, at the age of five.[77]

Persis Morse had joined the Phelps household in October 1803.[78] Reuban Debell had lived at the farm nearly his whole life, having been brought there as a small child whose father was apparently dead, though he had other relatives in the area, and his mother visited him from time to time.[79] The first hint of trouble for the two young laborers came by early February 1805, when Elizabeth wrote to remind her daughter of "one thing I forgot to desire you to keep a profound secret, you recollect a Suspicion I mentioned of a person in our family—whether it be true, or false, keep it close."[80] A month later, with Persis now nearly three months pregnant, Elizabeth reported to her daughter Betsy that Reuban had "took leg"; he told his employers that he was going to see his brother and sister in Vermont, and proposed to return at the beginning of the next week, but when the week passed with no sign of the young man, the Phelpses concluded that Persis had been abandoned.

Persis herself seemed oddly unconcerned. She "ventured to say he would not be seen here again," and Elizabeth concurred, adding that "if lifting a finger would have kept him I'm sure mine would have try'd hard to have lain still." Still, Persis's calm puzzled her: "I should think it was of some consequence to her where he was—but as she appears to be well pleased." As to Charles and Elizabeth, they tried to keep out of it as much as possible—"we say not much"—though Elizabeth remained concerned: "Sometimes I almost tremble—& can tell you, I do now feel, as if I hardly dare go to bed."[81] Within a few weeks the family heard that Reuban was back, and was living with an uncle nearby, though he "has not been near here *that we know of,*" conceding that the young couple might have been in greater communication than she realized. Though Elizabeth was genuinely fond of Persis, this situation presented a real dilemma. Betsy encouraged her mother to dismiss Persis, but Elizabeth was less certain:

> Pierces does not seem to have any inclination to quit here, says she can do as
> much work as last summer, says work does her no hurt, indeed she is as good as
> ever for ought I see. . . . yesterday [she] did all of the washing and all the work
> in that part of the house, cleard out that buttery, which you know is a great job,
> scoured it and replaced all the things, washed the floor done all and set down to
> knitting before four. I never expect to have another girl so kind, and willing to
> wait on me, and yet I know some things are very disagreeable. Your father and I
> talk, and talk, about it, and leave it just where we begun.[82]

Persis's exemplary work in this period—washing the kitchen, scouring the buttery, getting everything back in order before four o'clock, and sitting down then to knit—may have been a calculated effort to convince Charles and Elizabeth that her pregnancy would not interfere with her responsibilities at work. And the campaign was working. In the summer, Elizabeth described to her daughter a difficult week in which they had not only entertained important guests, "Col Chester and his Lady," but had also fed more than a dozen hired men. "I don't know how it is," she sighed, "but I do think Persis is really the best help I ever had, or ever shall have." Partly inclined to release Morse from her duties, Elizabeth was equally afraid that Persis herself would announce her departure, a prospect so disconcerting that Elizabeth was "almost in tremors every time I leave home."[83]

That is exactly the conclusion Persis intended her employers to draw. While Charles and Elizabeth were stewing over what the outcome of this troubling situation might be, Persis herself was imagining her future at Forty Acres. In July, she provided Elizabeth with some new information that she hoped would put her employer more at ease, and secure her place:

> P. is jest [illeg] as ever . . . she says when she [illeg] other one, she did not mind it, any more than a [illeg] was round doing any thing in a few days—& [illeg] was no trouble, quiet as a lamb, she went back [illeg] time to the place where she liv'd before, & did all the work of a large tavern—the child liv'd about 2 years—& before it died, its work used to be to go round into all the rooms and chambers, & gather the candlesticks for P. to clean, that it was a very forward child. Thus stands the matter.[84]

It is unclear whether this was the first Elizabeth learned of Persis's other child, or whether Persis only just revealed this chapter in her life in order to persuade her employer to keep her on. It's worth pausing to note Persis's reference to the utility of the expected child in view of recent scholarship on children in the early American workforce, the mother citing the usefulness of her toddler padding from room to room retrieving candlesticks.[85] In any event, Persis hoped to reassure Elizabeth that, the last time she found herself pregnant, while employed at a "large tavern," her child proved to be no trouble at all, and in fact helped Persis complete her regular duties. "She continues jest as alert as ever," Elizabeth concluded, adding that "perhaps she intends to go way—but she takes care not to tell of it—"[86]

Finally, on Wednesday August 10th, at about 11 p.m., Persis gave birth to a daughter, named Dolly. Although she was living under the same roof as Elizabeth Phelps, she did not call her employer until after the child had arrived, and there is no mention of the midwife arriving until the next day, when Charles brought a Mrs. Montague to the house to see to the new mother and child.

Elizabeth hired an African American woman to come in and help with Monday's wash, but on the following Tuesday, true to her word, Persis came down to do some chores, and "gained a little in the business every day" thereafter.[87] By the twenty-eighth, Elizabeth reported that "she is now nearly as good as ever. The child is very quiet, & she pays every attention to it, that is necessary. I dare not let her do the washing this week, tho she said she could."[88]

For almost two years, Persis and Dolly remained members of the Phelps household. No records survive to shed light on how well the two families coexisted under the same roof, but Persis's departure late in 1807 seems to have come on awkward terms. A year earlier a letter from Elizabeth hinted that having Dolly in the house was starting to strain her nerves: early one Saturday morning she wrote, "I feel just as unable to write now as last night—for my patience is so much try'd with this young one that it really disturbs my peace—I beg for more patience if I must have this thorn in the flesh or in the spirit I don't know which—we were quite dirty eno' I tho't before, but now it is much worse than ever."[89] By spring, Phelps was again asking Betsy to be on the lookout for new help: "If you could find a good Negro woman for us, I hope we should be thankful, as our present help is nearly worn out."[90] Phelps recalled that her hired woman had been "very kind to me, & very good tempered the first part of the time," but "the trouble which is attached to her now, and the crosses which we have to bear, is rather troublesome, how long we shall have it I can't guess, unless she should be so kind as to say she will tarry no longer, which I am something suspicious will take place."[91] The nature of the "trouble attached to her" remains unstated, but eight months later, in November 1807, Elizabeth sighed to her daughter-in-law Sarah "I suppose [Persis] will leave us soon . . ."[92]

Whether or not Phelps drew a distinction, the woman they ultimately hired was not African American, but the Native American woman Rachel. As Persis left, "bag and baggage, child and all," Phelps noted, "I wish her & her child well," and added that "Thurs there came an Indian woman here to try if she could suit."[93] After a trial period, apparently both Rachel and Elizabeth concurred that Rachel's employment at Forty Acres would suit them both, and she remained through the winter. By the spring, both parties agreed that Rachel might stay on a good bit longer. In March, Phelps noted that the hired man Ralf had driven Rachel up to Ashfield, "after her household stuff."[94]

Rachel remained through the whole of the next year, though not without some tension. Eighteen months into Rachel's tenure, Phelps wrote her daughter that "your help is poor—I don't know I dare say mine is poor—Rachel is quite as good & better than I expected—don't perade herself off so much as in the winter."[95] What Phelps meant about "perad[ing] herself off" isn't entirely clear, but perhaps her heightened awareness of flirtations among the hired help had made her aware of its dangers. Still, the situation was agreeable enough that Rachel remained another year. Then, in July 1809, Phelps recorded that Rachel, "an Indian woman (who has lived here about one year and seven months) left us and all her furniture."[96] Later she narrated the following series of events to her daughter:

> On Thanksgiving, Ralf was called for (he was to take care at the barn, & John was to roast the old cock Turkey that was all we had) no Ralf was to be found. Finally, J took the horse, but no R. we had no body but John [Morrison] from that time to Monday morning (which made your father's work very hard). Then R came to reckon, as he had done here—went away again immediately—it is said Rachel and he are gone away together, I heartily wish they may come to good, but no tears have been shed because they are gone.[97]

Who knows when affection blossomed between Ralf and Rachel? Perhaps it was as early as that long wagon ride to Ashfield to retrieve her things. Whatever the answer, Rachel's departure meant yet another vacancy for a domestic servant, and this time Phelps chose to hire an English woman, Polly Randall, although this new relationship, too, had its complications.[98] Persis Morse actively promoted her ability to raise a child while keeping up with her household assignments, even suggesting that a child could contribute to the household labor; other women took a different tack, struggling to sustain families far distant from their places of employment. Polly Randall, like both Susanna Whipple and Persis Morse, had a small child in her care when she worked at Forty Acres. But Randall did not wish to bring the child with her to her new workplace. Instead, she left her young child with an aunt in the hill town of Pelham, about eleven miles to the east.

In making this choice, Polly joined other single mothers who decided not to try to balance domestic service and parenting. In the 1760s, Mary Turner, a young woman from Boston, "in consideration of £4/yr, . . . put herself a servant to Charles Phelps, Esq., wife Dorothy and heirs, for four years." Charles and Dorothy Phelps agreed to "find her sufficient meat, drink, and lodging and take care of her in sickness (excepting the Physicians Bill)" during that time, while Mary agreed to live with them and "obey al their lawful commands."[99] Mary, like Polly Randall, was the mother of a small child at the time she entered service; two years earlier, in the middle of September 1766, Turner had given birth in the Boston almshouse. That the child was of mixed races—"a daughter Negro"—may have added to Turner's reluctance to bring the toddler with her to Hadley; certainly it is easy to imagine Charles and Dorothy's objections to the child, for a number of reasons.[100] Where her mixed-race child was living (if she was indeed still living) when Mary traveled out to work in Hadley is unknown.

Some forty years later, Polly Randall was perhaps more fortunate, as she had a circle of support in Pelham. She came to work at Forty Acres in July 1809 and remained until November of the following year. She may have been the Polly Randall born in Rochester, Massachusetts, in 1787; if so, by the summer of 1809 she was twenty-two, unmarried, and the mother of an eleven-year-old son, Silas Allen Jr., probably born out of wedlock in April 1799.[101] Her child's father appears to have been a good deal older than she was; the likeliest candidate is Silas Allen, born in Bridgewater, Massachusetts (thirty miles north of Rochester), in his forties when the child was conceived. While the genealogies of working women, and especially births outside marriage, are often difficult to trace, Polly Randall considered Charity Packard Burr, whose family emigrated from Bridgewater to Pelham in the 1770s, her "aunt," and Allen's mother was Mary Packard Allen, also of Bridgewater.[102] Polly and Silas, like many other men and women from Plymouth County and southeastern Massachusetts in the years following the American Revolution, were among those who migrated west to the hill towns of Hampshire County. Perhaps Polly and Silas knew each other when both were living in the eastern part of the state, or perhaps they crossed paths only in Hampshire County. In either case, Allen's family, as the Wests ultimately did with young Mitte, assumed some responsibility for the unwed mother of Silas Allen's child whether or not Allen himself did.

In any event, the spring and summer of 1809 were months of upheaval for Polly Randall, as the town Overseers of the Poor took an interest in her circumstances and intervened. The past ten years had seen Polly struggling to make ends meet for her small family, and in the month before she went to work at Forty Acres she accepted public assistance when her son was "struck off" to George Macumber at two shillings, eight pence per week.[103] In fact, accepting the "assistance" of the town may not have been altogether voluntary; at the April town meeting, the selectmen had voted to appoint a committee to "look up the residency" of three members of the community: Zenas Canady, Olive Montgomery, and Polly's child.[104] In June, Silas was placed with Macumber, and Polly arrived at Forty Acres in July. Perhaps any apprehension Polly felt at leaving Silas in Macumber's care was partly alleviated by the presence in Pelham of her elderly aunt Charity Packard Burr to keep an eye on Silas. Born in 1733 in Bridgewater, Massachusetts, Burr had been widowed in July 1797, and left with few sources of support.[105] For her niece, Seth Burr's death meant one more mouth for Polly Randall to feed, but at least she had someone to help raise Silas.

On the other hand, unlike many of the young women who became domestic servants at Forty Acres, Polly had family nearby to draw on for emotional, if not financial, support. While Polly tried to get to Pelham when her aunt Charity was unwell, so too did Charity and Silas come to Forty Acres when Polly was sick.[106] Charity's daughter Huldah visited Polly from time to time; a grand-daughter, Suky, also worked as a domestic servant in Hadley (at the home of the town minister, Samuel Hopkins, and his wife, Sarah Porter Hopkins) while another, named Nancy, also visited Polly from time to time at Forty Acres.[107]

The period of Polly's employment at Forty Acres was a difficult one, both for Polly and for her employers. Polly was trying to juggle the care of an elderly aunt and her own young child with full-time work in the Phelps household. Elizabeth recorded Polly's regular trips home to Pelham (and so regular ab-sences from her duties) in the pages of her memorandum book; sometimes Polly waited as much as four weeks between visits, but when circumstances demanded—the December when her Aunt Charity was ill, or the March when she needed to find a new place to live—she went almost weekly to Pelham.[108] Elizabeth Porter Phelps keenly felt the inconveniences Polly's family obliga-tions caused her own household. In writing to her daughter Betsy, she ex-plained, "I was obliged to break off abruptly last Wednesday as Polly went away last Tuesday to Pelham, & has not got home yet, she has a great deal to do, to take care of her old Aunt & her own child, I think it uncertain whether we shall be able to get along with her much longer."[109] Polly was apparently trying to find new lodgings for her aunt, who had been sick for most of the winter. Nearly once every two weeks she had been borrowing a horse from the Phelpses and riding to Pelham to attend to matters there "without any charge made of it," leaving Elizabeth without reliable help: "Now I have had the work to do about three days & when she will come is altogether uncertain." As to Polly's dilemma, trying to raise a child on her own while working in the households of others, Elizabeth was unsympathetic: "Her folly, & sin, has been the occasion of a great deal of trouble to her & others."[110]

Randall struggled on through the spring, summer, and fall, but by the end of the year had decided that enough was enough. In mid-December, Randall quit her position and returned to Pelham. Her wages were a dollar a week with the Phelps family, but she found that, burdened with the care of both her el-derly aunt and young child, she could not make ends meet. Elizabeth Porter Phelps seemed a bit dismayed at Polly's decision, or at least at the circum-stances surrounding it. "I am the only female in the house and have been about two weeks," she reported to her daughter in December 1810; "We gave Polly great wages, & she could not support a family at Pelham and half cloath her-self, so she tho't best to try some other method, & braiding straw hats was the one proposed."[111]

New Opportunities, New Geographies of Labor

Like growing numbers of girls in central and western Massachusetts, Polly Randall had embraced a new source of income that would allow her to remain at home, converting locally grown rye into lengths of straw plaits that were then woven into women's bonnets.[112] In December 1810, this enterprise was still a relatively new one; the first advertisements for braid appeared in Worcester's *Massachusetts Spy* only in the previous year, but straw-hat braiding would become a significant industry in western Massachusetts.[113] In 1809 Hardwick shopkeeper Jason Mixter also began accepting straw braid from customers, and in 1810, he began paying teamsters to cart straw to Worcester.[114] Mixter's braiders were drawn from Hardwick's least prosperous households, those on the margins of the town's economy. Single women and widows were particularly active in the work. That Polly Randall seized on braiding so quickly is telling; here was an alternative to service that she pursued as soon as it became available to her in Pelham. In fact, Randall was not alone in her eagerness to leave service for other sources of income, and she was not the first servant at Forty Acres to do so. As we shall see, as early as the summer of 1796, Elizabeth Porter Phelps recorded that her domestic servant Persis Leonard "left us to go to the mills and spin"; apparently Leonard was as struck as Randall by the opportunity to leave service as soon as an alternative presented itself.[115]

With the prospect of earnings from home work, Polly, like legions of young women throughout New England, abandoned domestic service in favor of new opportunities that allowed her to remain in her own home. In August 1810, four months before she would tender her resignation, Polly retrieved a month's wages in goods from the Porter store, charged to the Phelpses' account; what she purchased is not recorded, but it seems likely that a supply of goods and groceries made their way soon thereafter to her family in Pelham.[116] She apparently continued to trade on her account with the Phelpses. At end of Polly's tenure at Forty Acres, Charles Phelps's records show that she owed the family $25.98 for the purchase of gloves, wool, a shawl, shoes, and other miscellaneous items, as well as several visits to the doctor. She was also in debt for pork, cheese, butter, and sugar, which she supplied to her aunt in Pelham. Subtracting some $19.00 in unpaid wages, Polly Randall left Forty Acres with a balance due of $6.65—the equivalent of more than a month's work as a servant.[117]

Polly returned to Pelham, and, despite whatever income she was able to generate from braiding hats, she continued to rely at least in part on support from the town in order to make ends meet. Apparently none of her relatives were in a position to take Silas in, and in 1810, Polly's son and some others were left "in the care of the selectmen."[118] Silas was "struck off" (that is, assigned by the select board) to Israel Conkey, "at thirty cents a week for one year unless otherwise disposed of by the selectmen."[119] They further stipulated that if Silas remained with Conkey for any extended period of time, then he was to attend school. When the town "voted to advertise the poor," Polly's son was once again "bid off at twenty cents by George Macumber."[120] This was Silas's third year with Macumber.[121] In 1812, town reports indicate that Polly was compensated for her efforts to support her aunt, who otherwise would have become a town charge; she received $43.43 that year for Charity Burr's maintenance (in the same year the town also voted to pay Charity's doctor's bill, in the amount of $9.47, probably in her final illness). At the same time, George Macumber was credited for supplying the funds to clothe Silas, now thirteen.[122]

Negotiating Change

What became of these women, their children, and their employers? As is too often the case, once servants' paths diverged from that of their better-educated and more affluent mistress, fewer records survive to shed light on their lives. Susanna Whipple Blodgett and her husband Samuel remained in Deerfield for a time and later moved to the nearby hill town of Conway. When Susanna had another child in January 1802, Elizabeth Phelps wrote her daughter Betsy that she may inform Mitte or not, as she pleases.[123] At the turn of the nineteenth century, Mitte left the Phelpses' care and moved in with the family of her father, the Wests. But by 1805, she had already moved on, living probably as a domestic servant, with the family of William Dickinson.[124] The following fall she changed circumstances again, joining the household of Jacob Smith.[125] She remained there only seven weeks before gathering her things once more and moving in with the family of Andrew Cook, to "stay there a while to help his wife."[126] Apparently, Mitte was unable to settle into life as someone else's servant; as historian Karen Parsons writes, "bad behavior cost the teenaged Mitte four jobs in eighteen months."[127] In May 1808 she relocated once more, this time back into the Phelpses' extended family circle; Elizabeth and Charles's son Charles had just moved back to Hadley after several years in eastern Massachusetts, and Mitte West joined the household to help Charles's wife Sarah Parsons Phelps, who by 1808 had two small children underfoot (and was grieving the loss of a third). In the months to follow, Mitte and Elizabeth became parts of one another's everyday world once more, picking whortleberries in the summer, riding together to do errands in town.[128] In June 1809, however, Mitte moved once again, this time to Conway, perhaps to be near her mother.[129] Susanna Whipple Blodgett (occasionally spelled with just one *t*) had continued to have children through the years; in addition to the twins who followed Mitte's birth, Susanna carried another six children.[130] Moving to Conway reunited Mitte with her mother's large family and a flock of younger stepsiblings.

Mitte West had a good reason for wanting a change of scenery, for she had undergone a significant change in circumstances. Susanna's daughter, despite the continuing concern and efforts of the Phelps and Huntington families, had remained unreconciled to social constraints; in January 1810, Phelps recorded that "last Thurs a man come from Conway says Mitte West had a child there at one Mr Grays alone, twas alive & well. Lord it is a sore grief to me, may my sins be set before me—my neglect forgiven."[131] Clearly Elizabeth and Mitte hadn't seen each other in some time, for Elizabeth was caught completely by surprise. She blamed herself for Mitte's shortcomings; despite her best efforts, she had failed to impress Mitte with the beliefs and values to which she herself ascribed. And for Phelps the news only got worse: Charles rode to visit their former charge, and he brought home stunning news: the child was "a negro"— it was a "shocking affair."[132]

The child's father, the household in time learned, was Prince Cooley, an African American hired man who lived in the North Hadley neighborhood near Forty Acres and was an occasional employee of the farm.[133] While Massachusetts was among the first states to eliminate slaveholding, miscegenation was still considered "shocking" in the turn-of-the-century Commonwealth, though it was by no means unknown. Interracial marriage had been outlawed in Massachusetts in 1705. That policy was reasserted in 1786 when the Commonwealth of Massachusetts revisited the issue; though the prohibition on fornication itself was relaxed, public opposition to interracial sex was in full force when Mitte became pregnant in the summer of 1809—and West and Cooley lacked the option of the quick wedding a white couple might choose.[134]

When Sarah Parsons Phelps heard the news about Mitte, she wrote her mother-in-law, "My heart sickens within me when I think of her or Prince, what will become of her I know not."[135] Eighteen-year-old Mitte must have been about three months along in June when she decided to leave her situation with Charles and Sarah Phelps and join her mother in Conway (Charles Phelps billed the town two dollars for his time and trouble taking Mitte to her mother's, Mitte being considered without resources and eligible for public support).[136] The prospect of motherhood surely encouraged Mitte to seek out the comfort and advice of her own mother, who had found herself in much the same position eighteen years earlier. Perhaps she also hoped she could conceal the event entirely from Hadley's disapproving eyes by leaving town.

Susanna had been just seventeen herself when Mitte was born; how did she now react to seeing her own daughter following so closely in her footsteps? How did she react to the news that the child's father was a man of color? For whatever reason, Mitte gave birth—to a daughter, whom she named Philina— "alone" at a Mr. Gray's house (like Persis Morse, perhaps, without a company of women to assist her), and moved again to her mother's house some three weeks later.[137] Like Morse, she may have been working through the final months of pregnancy, giving birth in the home of her employer. The following week her stepfather, Samuel Blodgett, made a trip to Hadley to gather what remained of Mitte's things. The event occasioned an outpouring of grief that is almost unparalleled in Elizabeth's journal:

Fryday eve at a meeting at Dr Porters, When home, found Mr Blotchet here. Satt we loaded off his wagon, if he can keep Mitte it appears best, but we have been taught by experience so often that when we were endeavoring to do our best it has eventually been productive of the most unhappiness. Therefore O lord we desire to look to that direction, and submit all to thy disposal, and if thou seest best that we should be more tryed, and grieved by her misconduct, may we say and feel in truth, thy will be done. Lord, there is one favour for her, which I may beg for. . . . may she be an heir of eternal mercy thro Christ—may the riches of sovreign grace be exalted, in the salvation of her, and her poor destitute child. We have dedicated her to the Lord in baptism and thou Lord canst cause her to subscribe in truth, and verity, with her own hand unto the Lord. She is thy creature do with her as seemeth thee good. Wherein soever we have done wrong, may we all be forgiven and have true repentance.[138]

Mitte's mother and stepfather did indeed assume care for the child at least, if not for Mitte. In April 1811, Hadley's Overseers of the Poor compensated Blodgett for "supporting the child of Submit West one year ending Dec 31 1811." But then, for reasons unknown, the infant was passed along to others in the community. In spring 1812, Caleb Smith billed the town $2.50 for supporting the child, now just over two years old, for five weeks, suggesting that his wife, North Hadley's forty-five-year-old Olive Hibbard Smith, cared for Philina for a time. And in summer 1813 the town settled a debt owed a Captain Jonathan Cunnabel for supporting her for just over a year, since March 1812.[139]

Several years went by with what appears to have been little or no contact between Elizabeth and Mitte. Then, in the late summer of 1816, when Elizabeth Porter Phelps was a widow in her sixties, she records in the pages of her memorandum book that Submit West "came here with her child to try to do our kitchen work."[140] Submit was perhaps eager to return to work in familiar, even fond, circumstances, and Philina, now six, was old enough to begin contributing to the work of the farm. Perhaps Elizabeth saw an opportunity to repair her earlier failings, to help Submit learn to be what Phelps would consider a responsible mother, and even, perhaps, to have a hand in raising her child. Almost twenty years earlier she had taken in Submit's mother, Susanna, when she was a single mother, and now here she was again, bringing mother and child into her employ, care, and supervision. Eight months later, the last entry Elizabeth Porter Phelps was to write before her death noted that "Tues Mrs West and her husband's sister Hannah here[;] brought out Submit's child which they have took home to keep."[141] Phelps was now almost seventy; perhaps she found the presence of a small child once more under her roof too tiring to manage, or perhaps she couldn't overcome her aversion to Philina's mixed-race parentage.

Although we don't know how long Mitte remained at Forty Acres, in time she too left. Whether the mother and child were separated for any significant amount of time is unknown; perhaps they left Hadley altogether, and like her mother and stepfather, Susanna and Samuel, migrated west to New York. Susanna's life would end in Antwerp, New York, in 1840; Samuel lived another nine years before he passed away in Saratoga County. Or perhaps she in time returned to Hadley and resumed her life there; the archival record contains some hint that she later formed a union with another man in the constellation of Forty Acres and settled in North Hadley.[142]

Polly Randall and her son Silas returned to Pelham. Their subsequent fortunes apparently did not improve; Polly was committed to the Hampshire County House of Correction in August 1816, for a bad debt of some eleven dollars. She spent a month confined in the same Northampton jail that her onetime employer Charles Phelps had helped build. But she was apparently unable to raise the funds: when she was released in late September, it was on the oath of neighbors.[143] Persis and Dolly Morse, too, vanish from local records; whatever happened for them in the years to come, Elizabeth Porter Phelps seems never to have learned.

With increasing numbers of young Anglo-American girls able to find an income by spinning, braiding, shirt manufacture, and button making, fewer and fewer were willing to subject themselves to domestic service, creating a good deal of scarcity among potential employers. As Springfield's Thomas Dwight wrote to his wife Hannah,

> I am extremely sorry to learn that you have lost your maid, not that I ever thought her very extraordinary help, but she was better than none. I do not know that it is in my power until I get home to offer you any consolation in this loss unless it be to tell you that wherever one goes, half the conversation is on the extreme difficulty of getting any servants worth the having or any decent help—they tell me here that they pay the most enormous wages to their kitchen folks, and when this is done, they are very indifferently and in many instances very unfaithfully served.[144]

This scarcity shifted some economic power to the women who remained willing to work as domestics. At the close of the eighteenth century and into the early nineteenth, increasing numbers of working women chose to abandon domestic service to focus on another enterprise. Doing so was an effort to gain greater control over their lives: new industries and new organizations of labor for some women meant the chance to work at home alongside their children, or to take in outwork in systems that allowed them to set their own pace and conditions of labor.[145] As early as 1793, notices in the *Hampshire Gazette* seeking workers to "do house-work in a family" promised the "highest wages" to "young and middle aged women" willing to apply.[146]

As domestic help became increasingly scarce, those women who did elect to hire out as domestics were in high demand, and it seems they could almost name their wages. In the summer of 1801, newlyweds Dan and Betsy Huntington sought to hire a black woman, Chloe, with a three-year-old daughter, in tow; the anxious family offered her three shillings per week plus the board of her child. "If we can get her, we shall be highly favoured," the anxious employer noted, but Chloe insisted that she was worth five, a figure too "extravagant" for the Huntingtons to manage, and negotiations collapsed."[147] Later that same year, Elizabeth Phelps Huntington was still trying to find a servant whose labors she could afford. Her sister-in-law Sally's hired girl "promised to try to get one for me—but our income," Huntington had come to realize, "will not allow us to hire good help, because they ask so great a price."[148]

Among the working mothers who lived for a time at Forty Acres, the brief tenure of each suggests some of the strategies employed by working mothers in Federal New England. Each woman chose different means by which to cope with the challenges of parenting while at the same time assuring an income for themselves and their child. Sometimes those strategies came at a cost, whether it was the price of a horse to Pelham, or a jeopardized relationship between mother and child. Their stories shed important light on the larger world of laboring women and children in early New England. At the midpoint of the eighteenth century, enslaved women like Peg had very few options when it came to improving their situation; when she became pregnant with Rose, and later Phillis, she had little choice but to raise them alongside her in the spaces of her enslavement. With the abolition of slavery in the 1780s she exercised her newly gained liberty, but she was called back to care for her granddaughters. The white women of English descent would also see changing options, as they increasingly embraced millwork and industrial home production, and rejected domestic service. Whatever the circumstances, close examination of these laboring women, their relationships with their employers, their choices in raising their own families, and the consequences of those decisions for their children, allows us to imagine the world of early America's working women as they struggled to balance their own needs, desires, and values with the needs, desires, and values of their employers.

CHAPTER FIVE

Making Cloth

In the 1850s, Sylvester Judd noted that "sixty and fifty years ago . . . flax was an important crop in old Hampshire." But by the time he was writing, Judd mused, so "complete a change" had taken place that now "few persons under thirty years of age, have ever seen a woman hatchel flax or card tow, or heard the buzzing of the foot wheel, or seen bunches of flaxen yarn hanging in the kitchen, or linen cloth whitening on the grass."[1] The older women he interviewed remembered "great bunches of yarn hung against the walls" of their childhood homes, and Judd himself could still picture flax dressers covered in dust, dirt, and plant detritus; he remembered fondly the steady percussion of flax brakes and swingling knives, the rhythmic click of the clock reel.[2] But by the time Judd was recording these glimpses into Hadley's past, most men and women had only sketchy memories of preindustrial production processes. Flax and the linen cloth it yielded had itself been marginalized by the rising popularity of cotton, which could be produced more cheaply and easily. The spinning wheels and flax brakes of Judd's youth had been relegated to sheds and attics as cloth production moved from domestic to factory settings.

The transformation of cloth making meant the transformation of communities. As Susan Ouellette has argued, from the seventeenth century onward "domestic textile production was a major form of social organization, especially in early Massachusetts. Textile-producing networks clearly served to draw households, neighborhoods and regions together in particular ways. From the processing of fibers to the finishing of cloth, intense cooperation and an extensive system of corporate labor were key elements of textile production." Women and men, children and adults, from the hands that picked debris from fleece to those who wove complex fabrics—many different kinds of laborers and labor were "necessary to the success of the industry."[3] "More than the work of any single gender or household," Ouellette continues, "one aspect or another of domestic cloth production was visible in nearly every part of New England's social landscape," from the fields where sheep grazed and flax flowered to the barns, farmyards, and lofts where fibers were cleaned and prepared, to the ells, kitchens, and shops where it was spun and woven to—finally—the mills where it was fulled.[4] The warp and weft that lay over the land in the seventeenth century covered it still in the eighteenth and nineteenth, though like the fashion that evolved over those years, new patterns constantly prevailed.

While narratives tracking cloth production's inexorable march from colonial hearthsides through Samuel Slater's Rhode Island mill en route to Lowell's manufacturing plants are common, in truth the industrialization of textile production in North America—encompassing the spinning, weaving, fulling, and dyeing of wool, linen, and cotton—advanced in fits and starts.[5] What's more, different fibers industrialized differently, as the particularities of any given fibershed influenced how any given place or people experienced changes in textile production. The ways in which households were clustered in community or dispersed along roads and rivers and the relative ease with which they could access transportation and trade routes, coupled with the presence, nature, and cost of labor, specialized and unspecialized, joined together with the sources of fiber rooted in the earth itself—from the plants that thrive to breeds of animal able to flourish—to shape how cloth making unfolded and developed, town by town.[6]

At the remove of centuries it can seem as if these developments came all in a flash, but the advent of new sources of power would transform the spinning of fibers long before the weaving of cloth. Cloth production in places like Hadley in the decades following the Revolution did not gradually recede like raindrops shrinking out of sight, but rather evolved and reconfigured, expanded and contracted, as new technologies and production practices gained purchase in different places and at different times for different reasons. The decades between 1790 and 1830 witnessed acute transformations in home cloth manufacture as the introduction of new tools and systems—specific to the demands of the relevant fibers—reshaped spinning, weaving, and finishing.[7] As entrepreneurs and innovators searched for ways to make the steps required in cloth production more efficient, spinning mills, carding mills, and other forms of mechanization began appearing on the New England landscape. But to call these changes a "revolution" is a misnomer; change was gradual, uneven, incremental, and unfolded over decades. As Christopher Clark has ably explained, "while dramatic changes in rural production and exchange undoubtedly occurred in the half century after the Revolution, they did so substantially within the household-based economic structure that had become so powerful" in Connecticut Valley towns; the flowering of spinning and carding mills would "serve rather than supplant" household production.[8]

Much of this story, even as it pertains to the Connecticut Valley, has been well told, particularly by historians Christopher Clark and Laurel Thatcher Ulrich.[9] This chapter aims to plumb the evolution of cloth production as it unfolded in Hadley, and to connect this story to other developments in the life of the community—particularly intersections with domestic service. Because so much literature already documents changes to the work of spinning and weaving, these pages also focus on the lesser-known work of fulling (that is, the process by which woven cloth was cleaned, tightened, and otherwise finished), and touch on the making and maintenance of wheels, looms, reeds, and other textile production tools and equipment.[10] After discussion of Hadley women's labor in and around cloth production in the decades around the American Revolution (the 1760s through the 1780s), attention turns to changes that began surfacing in the 1780s and 90s, following them through to the 1820s, by which time, most accounts concur, home cloth production had dwindled in Hadley. How were social relations of women's work in Hadley altered as cloth production evolved?

Textile Production in Revolutionary Hadley: A Closer Look

Linens, silks, woolens, and (increasingly) cottons traveled to Hadley on backs and in trunks, laid across tables and enclosed beds. The fibers from which a given fabric were constituted made up only part of its physical presence; consumers then were far more familiar than we are today with what can appear to be a dizzying array of weaves, weights, and treatments that produced a wide variety of materials from alamode (a thin, glossy silk) to zanella (a cotton and worsted serge).[11] Fashionable fabrics constituted a large part of the consumer goods pouring in from Europe, and Hadley shoppers well appreciated quality linen from Ireland, or a beautiful Spitalfields silk. Most Hadley families in the last half of the eighteenth century availed themselves of imported textiles for their better apparel.[12] But if the men who compiled Hampshire County estate inventories rarely described the garments they found as "homemade," the opposite was true of household textiles. Some needs were better met locally. The beds in John Dickinson's house in the 1760s, for instance, were warmed by eight blankets described as "homemade," and three "boughten."[13] Likewise, only one blanket in Samuel Marsh's house was described as "boughten" when his estate was submitted to the probate courts in that same decade. Awaiting attention were three runs of worsted yarn, eighteen run of cotton tow, and twenty-five run of linen yarn, with eight pounds of hetcheled flax in the barn ready for spinning, and more besides.[14]

Historians have observed both the extensive, even pervasive, nature of domestic cloth production as well as the importance, across rural New England, of community-exchange networks—features of early American cloth making that were inextricably tied.[15] "Boughten" and "homemade" fabrics flourished side by side as families expanded cloth-making activities in part to expand their access to imported fabrics.[16] William Porter, whose shop stood on the Hadley Common at the turn of the nineteenth century, would advertise that he "still wishes to encourage the Industrious Females," by receiving checked flannel as well as "linen, bed ticks, brown and white tow cloth, fulled cloth and meal bags." Porter offered to take "county produce of all kinds and many useful manufactures" as well as cash in exchange for "colonnade" (perhaps meaning "cottonade") as well as laced and cambric muslin for gowns.[17]

Decades earlier, on the eve of the American Revolution, some Hadley families possessed not just wheels, but the apparatus to complete nearly every stage of textile production, from the preparation of fibers to the weaving of cloth.[18] David and Hannah Smith's household was among the nearly 15 percent of Hampshire County families equipped, on the eve of Independence, for most stages of cloth production.[19] When David died in 1771, his household contained a foot wheel and a large wheel (that is, a wheel to spin flax and another for wool) as well as three pairs of the wooden cards needed to comb fibers and a dye tub in which to color yarn. They also possessed a "loom and all its utensils thereto belonging" valued at two pounds, two shillings—a little more, by way of comparison, than his red steer. In their storage space lay almost forty pounds of wool gleaned from a flock of some twenty-four sheep. "Grass in the homelot, flax and seed" was valued at two pounds, five shillings, while another eight pounds of flax lay in storage, though some of it had been converted to ten runs of tow yarn.[20] Not least, the family enjoyed the labors of six daughters, three of whom were still living at home when their father passed away, making good use of his investment in cloth-making materials. One of the wealthiest families in town (in 1770, Smith's estate was valued at just over £106, more than double the town median of £52, and well above the town average of £70), the Smiths could afford the outlay without difficulty, and had access to the labor to make it worthwhile.[21]

But few families matched the Smiths' material success, and rarely did single households possess this amount of cloth-making equipment. For instance, on the other end of town, Eliakim Smith was worth almost as much as David Smith, but the household he shared with his wife Mehitable contained no cloth-making tools at all.[22]

Cloth production required collaboration, cooperation, and interaction across households. Some relationships were grounded in kin, others long-standing neighborhood associations, and still others required contact with strangers. Evidence from Hadley affirms that some phases of cloth production were widely practiced throughout and across communities, while others required the tools and talents of specialists. As many as sixteen months could pass between the time the flax was sown to the completion of the finished cloth— months during which households nurtured ties as long and as durable as the yarn they produced.[23] At Forty Acres, Elizabeth Porter hired women like Eunice Pomeroy, Peggy Clark, and Amherst's Lodema Ingram to weave.[24] Other women, like Amherst widow Marcy Rolf, traveled to the Phelps house to comb wool, while Elizabeth Montague was hired to spin, as was Alice Hyde.[25] And while the work of cloth production bound together women across the community, the maintenance of the necessary tools associated with the work engaged men around town as well.

In the southern village of Hockanum, for instance, innkeeper Mindwell Pomeroy coupled her work in support of her family's tavern with other skills, particularly in cloth and clothing production. With six daughters and two sons, Mindwell had plenty of help around the tavern and the farm. The couple's account book shows her steady contributions to the household coffers by sewing simple garments for men (never for women) in the neighborhood, including coats, jackets, trousers, and breeches.[26] The Pomeroys availed themselves of the services of weaver Esther Alexander, and hired Stephen Fairchild regularly to help prepare flax; his accounts also refer to weaving, though the identity of the weaver is unknown. While the girls were still small, the family hired help with spinning: someone in the households of William Brace and Moses Taylor regularly earned something from the Pomeroys by spinning wool and cotton yarn.[27] But when the girls were old enough, they began contributing to the work of spinning: one November, Mindwell and her husband Ebenezer hired joiner Brace to construct two great wheels and to make a new rim for a third, presumably so that the three oldest girls (Eunice, Abigail, and Elizabeth, the latter just a month shy of her eleventh birthday) could spin wool.[28] As each of the Pomeroy girls married, they were supplied with a great wheel and a foot wheel for their own households, together with three sheep to ensure a steady supply of fiber.[29]

The first step in the long series of tasks required to produce cloth was transforming plant material or animal products to yarn. But even before that work could begin, another series of agricultural tasks, specifically the raising of flax to make linen, and the raising of sheep to produce wool, had been accomplished.[30] Sheep ownership in Hadley was concentrated in the hands of a minority of families; about one-third of the men on tax valuation lists from the 1770s and 1780s owned sheep, and of these, one-third owned more than two-thirds of the total number.[31] Households that chose to raise sheep generally kept about five to eight in their flock, though over thirty households kept more than ten.[32] But only half of the households that possessed sheep also owned wool-spinning wheels, suggesting that at least some sheep growers found others in the community to do their spinning.[33]

In early Massachusetts, the average sheep might produce four pounds of wool per year; if so, then a small flock of two or three sheep might generate eight to twelve pounds of wool, enough to spin five or six pounds of yarn, which in turn might be converted to five or six yards of cloth.[34] When it came time to shear, the fleece was cut from the animal while removing sections from rump, belly, and head that were soiled. Fleeces were rolled up and put somewhere to dry until harvest was past and people turned their attention to processing fibers.[35] The wool was sorted, finer and coarser fibers already destined for their final form, as coats or blankets, respectively. Soiled wool was not just discarded; rather, someone was charged with picking out the debris, and this wool was then soaked, rinsed, and dried for use in felting, stuffing, and other purposes. The finer wool was greased, carded, laid in bats, and spun.[36]

Linen was as necessary as wool in New England households, and many families devoted between a quarter- to a half-acre to flax cultivation.[37] The Connecticut Valley was an important center of flax production in the years before the Revolution, raised both for seeds (processed in mills for linseed oil and exported raw) and for fiber (tow, in particular, was exported to Newport, Rhode Island, where it was traded for wool, molasses, sugar, indigo, and tea).[38] Flax plants grow to about four feet in height and bear blue or white flowers that mature into bolls containing seeds (ten in each). The eventual purpose to which the plant would be put shaped the way in which it was planted. If a household planned to convert the flax to fiber, it was best to sow the plants densely, which prevented branching, and the plants were gathered before they matured. When the aim was instead to sell flax seed, the plants were sown sparsely, and allowed to develop and fruit.[39] Passers-by could readily deduce the intent of the owner of any flax they might pass on the landscape.

In Hadley, the plant was more often grown to be processed into cloth than for seed. In 1787, for instance, "well-dressed flax" could satisfy one's tax bill at the rate of eight pence per pound.[40] Typically pulled in early August, flax was spread and turned in September and taken up toward the end of October.[41] To obtain the fiber, growers first stripped the stems of their leaves and tied them in bunches. Next came a process called "retting," necessary to separate the fiber within from the extraneous plant material that surrounded it. In order to activate microorganisms that can weaken the fiber's binding to the plant material around it, the flax was wetted or dampened. It might be immersed in warm water (which could yield results in only a few days) or in cool water (over one or two weeks); sometimes flax was simply spread out on grass and exposed to the morning dew over several weeks. After retting, the flax was "dressed" in a series of steps. The dry stems were first put through a flax brake (which snapped the plant into pieces), scutched (that is beaten, with a tool called a scutching sword or swingling knife, which scraped away more plant material) to pull out the fibers. Lastly, a combing process (called hackling or hatcheling) continued to clear away any remaining nonfibrous material. In time, these multiple and successively finer treatments prepared the fiber for spinning. Any flax remaining in the teeth of the hatchel, called tow, was also recovered, spun, and used to make coarser fabric.

The next step was converting these fibers to yarn. While some tasks were sometimes performed by children—one way these young laborers served as adjunct workers. But spinning usable thread required practice, the nature and difficulty of the work depending on the raw materials to be used, as well as the intended purpose of the yarn to be made. Olive Cleveland Clark, penning a memoir in the nineteenth century (in which she, like Hadley's Sophia Clark, felt moved to compare work among the women she knew), at first said that "when she was young every girl in Northampton used to spin," but upon reflection qualified her statement, noting exceptions that she could recall among the town's "ladies."[42] The daughters of Williamsburg's Joseph Strong were taught to spin, but their mother "was brought up a lady," and never learned.[43] Fibers had to be uniform if the yarn and cloth made from it was to be smooth and consistent. Uneven yarn might adequately serve if it were intended to be used in a cloth that would eventually be further finished (that is, fulled and napped), but not when the warp or weft would be visible. Skill at spinning determined not only the quality of the yarn produced, but also its quantity. Elizabeth Porter Phelps considered spinning "one run of linnin yarn" to be "two thirds of a days work for a maid."[44] A better spinner might produce more, a weaker one less.

Correlations between spinning and youth, and spinning's place in a woman's life cycle, are well known, and the young women envisioned at the wheels of popular historical imagination are not incorrect. But the age at which Hadley girls first began to master the work nevertheless seems striking.[45] Writing about her granddaughters, Elizabeth Porter Phelps wrote that little Elizabeth, just nine-and-a-half years old, "has spun near 2 run last Satt." But apparently so much spinning could be hard on the hands: on Sunday the child's "forefinger on her left hand begun to have a sore come upon it like Martha's, and it was been increasing ever since, & I think it not likely she can spin some time." Elizabeth's injury proved "a good chance" for seven-year-old Bethia, who had "been very busy trying her possibles." Little Bethia "has worked out her own way pretty much nearly half a run I guess in all, but," Phelps observed, "she inclines to spin too coarse." Nevertheless, Bethia wanted her grandmother to be sure and tell her mother, "I have learned to spin." Sister Elizabeth, on the other hand, the proud grandmother could report, "spins pretty yarn."[46]

In the years around the American Revolution, many, but not all, houses across Hadley contained the tools necessary for spinning. Elizabeth Pitkin Porter had both a great wheel and a foot wheel, and a reel to measure their output; when the death of Moses Porter occasioned an inventory of his possessions, more than one hundred runs of yarn lay ready for weaving.[47] More middling families were comparably equipped. Aaron Goodrich's 1769 estate inventory included a Dutch Wheel, two great wheels, and a reel, as well as a pair of cards (described as "old"), while Josiah Dickinson had collected no fewer than three foot wheels as well as a great wheel, but no dye tubs, looms, or other tools for processing.[48] Carole Shammas found that, in the year 1774, the percentage of probate inventories of Hampshire County households reporting linen and woolen wheels as well as a loom, sheep, and flax was 14.8.[49] Widening the lens to include all Hadley households documented by probate inventories between 1760 and 1790 reveals that about half (56 percent) appear to have possessed at least one flax wheel, while just under half (48 percent) appear to have had at least one wool wheel. But only 39 percent possessed wheels to spin both flax and wool, and just 13 percent of inventories mentioned a loom.[50]

But those counts are still only rough approximations, as other sources suggest the presence of wheels in homes unvisited by court-appointed assessors. Woodworker Samuel Gaylord's ledgers, for instance, suggest wheels as well as other tools associated with cloth production in households unrecorded in the Registry of Probate. While he rarely produced complete spinning wheels, Gaylord could be found making and maintaining hetchels and reels, and producing hetchel boards,[51] whorls for spindles,[52] and parts for looms (trundles, or treadles),[53] as well as other fiber-processing tools.[54] Altogether, he helped craft and repair cloth-making tools for more than thirty Hadley households, from the comparatively modest home of free black Joshua Boston to the comparatively affluent Reverend Samuel Hopkins.

The different equipment required for the spinning of linen and the spinning of wool also demanded different spaces within the home. A flax wheel might measure a yard or so in height and width and was light enough to be portable. The motion associated with the device required minimal floorspace: a spinner at a flax wheel was stationed in a seated position near enough to work the treadle that caused the wheel to turn. Conversely, a wool wheel was larger—perhaps some sixty inches high and seventy inches long; moreover, a spinner of wool stood and moved (the spinning of wool on large walking wheels was a vigorous activity—"dancing is vapid by comparison," one observer would later write); a long day at the "great wheel" might mean walking more than five miles.[55] At Forty Acres, then, flax was spun in a kitchen, a room large enough to harbor a wheel (like the thirty-six by thirty-three-and-three-quarter-inch version that survives in the home today) alongside all the many other tools in active use there, but the wool wheel inscribed *EH* (likely the property of Elizabeth Huntington), which stands fifty-nine inches tall and extends sixty-one inches, was housed and used in the corn house, where a spinner could move more appropriately.

Although spinning was expected of domestic servants, it was also a ready source of income for women in Revolutionary Hadley. Spinning was paid by the run, generally about seven or eight pence per run, depending on whether the yarn produced was fine or coarse, tow, linen, or wool.[56] In some cases, an itinerant spinner might also receive board and lodging: Sally Maminash, as we have already seen, supported herself by "spinning and weaving in different families," and when one Northampton wife was abandoned by her husband, she was remembered to have carded and spun "about the town."[57] This latter reference reminds us that spinning sometimes also provided a means to dispense private ad hoc charity. In September 1768, when a pregnant Betty Goodrich found herself evicted from her father's house, she and her sister Sarah made their way to the Phelps farm at Forty Acres. The two young women arrived late—"Monday about 9 o'clock at night came here Sarah Goodrich with her sister Betty Daughters of Josiah Goodrich. Betty being with child had no settled place of abode." Twenty-year-old Elizabeth Porter noted that her mother "was a going to set her spinning for her a week or two she not expecting to lie in these three months." After what was certainly a very long and late conversation, the women all went to bed. But the decision to take in the pregnant Betty and give her work was cut short that very night when Sarah woke the Porters and told them Betty seemed to be going into labor. Elizabeth roused a hired man, who rode into Hadley to bring up Aunt Porter, "then turned straight about" to find midwife Mrs. Dickinson. Dickinson could not get there in time: the child, three months premature, arrived about a half-hour before the midwife, and "lived not an hour."[58]

Sarah had been living and probably working for Aunt Porter in town when her sister Betty showed up pregnant and scared. Sarah must have thought she would find a sympathetic ear in Elizabeth Pitkin Porter, and apparently she did. Aunt and Uncle Porter "rode up in a Chaise and carried the Corps" of the infant into town; young Elizabeth Porter attended the funeral and the following night Polly Porter and her good friend Penelope Williams sat up with the distressed mother. On Sunday, the minister preached "two rousing sermons" in which he openly referred to "two illegitimate children born the year past—one of Mary Cook the latter part of February confidently denied by the person she Fathered it upon and likewise the person Betty Goodrich charged with hers professes not to own it; these persons being all present but Betty, did hear a good honest sermon."[59] It was just a week later that Elizabeth would learn that Mary Clark Trainer had also been "delivered of a large child still born."[60]

If the Porter household taking in Betty Goodrich suggests spinning and neighborly largesse, Elizabeth also knew that spinners and their employers could find themselves in terrible tension. The year before, a spinner in the

Marsh family had set fire to some bundles of linen yarn in order to hide the fact that she had "made false ties" in the skeins—that is, cheated the Marshes by short-skeining the yarn.[61] Elizabeth had recorded the burning of the house a month earlier, in January: "Capt. Moses Marshes house burn[ed] to the ground—some few things saved blessed be God all their Lives." Apparently people suspected that the fire had been no accident. By mid-February, "Sarah Bartlet that Lived with Captain Marsh was brought to own that she willfully set his house on fire . . . to burn some yarn that she had been discovered to make false ties in. She is now at Springfield jail."[62] It seems that sometime during the day, Hannah Marsh began to suspect that there was something wrong with the skeins of yarn the young woman had been producing: they didn't seem to have quite the right heft. When Sarah short-skeined the Marshes, it was not just that she had produced less than she said she would; the lie could also undermine the weaver's subsequent efforts. The spinner may have realized that her dishonesty would be revealed at the loom, or perhaps Marsh made her suspicions known. Either way, around midnight Sarah—desperate to cover her tracks—apparently slipped into the room where the materials were stored and ignited "a Certain Bundle of Linnen Yarn and also a certain Bundle of Flax & Tow."[63] Though the young woman had initially confessed—she "was brought to own"—that she had purposefully burned the yarn, in court she initially pleaded "not guilty," and then replaced that plea with another that the "indictment may be quashed for the insufficiency thereof."

For Elizabeth Phelps, this case was a real awakening to the dangers posed by domestic servants. The young diarist had at first assumed that the fire was caused by any one of the numerous things that sparked house fires in early America: she was stunned to learn instead that it was the result of arson at the hands of hired help. For the hired spinner, the temptation to cut these small corners had been irresistible, though apparently she came to fear the consequences of her actions. For Phelps, nineteen when forced to confront the implications of these events, this was an early but enduring lesson in the sort of wariness she would bring in the future when choosing and supervising employees.

For some women, then, spinning was a part of their larger work in domestic service. But Sarah Bartlet was not the only woman who found spending two-thirds of a day at the wheel tedious: Elizabeth Phelps's hired woman Persis Marsh, too, "had much rather knit than spin."[64] Luckily the work was seasonal. One Hadley woman recalled that the spinning of flax typically began as soon as Thanksgiving had passed, and "might take through May."[65] Wool naturally and necessarily operated on a different schedule, being spun in the summer, after the sheep had been sheared in June. Spinning occupied attention, it seemed, nearly the whole year 'round.

Weaving

The next step in cloth production was weaving—that is, converting yarn of whatever material into fabrics. Weaving was a task altogether distinct from spinning, requiring different tools, knowledge, and skills entirely separate from spinning. And the act of weaving was essential in ways beyond cloth making as it is generally understood. For instance, in time Hadley women also wove horsehair for the sieves used in bolting or sifting flour. But it is cloth making that occupied most women's attention, and that occupies ours here.

Weaving also responded differently to gendered ideas about women's work and men's work. While spinning had long been gendered female, weaving was less clear and less stable. For centuries an artisanal trade reserved for men and protected by guilds in Europe, weaving in New England by the eighteenth century was work undertaken by both men and women, and increasingly the latter.[66] That change—which long predated transformations to power and technology—was readily visible to observers like Sylvester Judd, who himself noted how gendered definitions of labor had evolved by the 1850s when he wrote that "women had long been gaining ground in this employment, and it is believed that men seldom, if ever, learned the trade after the Revolution."[67]

Men who had earned livings as weavers in pre-Revolutionary Hadley included Samuel Gaylord II (1711–1785) and Jonathan Smith (d. 1768), and possibly Samuel Wright, whose 1793 estate inventory included a loom together with a set of twenty-two reeds and harness, and another of thirty reeds and harness, alongside a dye pot, two great wheels, wool cards, and other equipment associated with the production of wool cloth.[68] Gaylord and Smith also had shops—the dedicated sites in which to undertake their craft that became a key marker of artisanal identity.[69] Gaylord's shop stood on the east side of the Hadley Common, just south of Samuel Hopkins's home, close to the middle highway that ran through the town, while Smith's stood on the west side, below the middle highway, each establishment convenient to slightly different constellations of customers.[70] Gaylord's account book tracks the weaver at work, and offers a sense of the relative value of skills and weaves. He wove tow cloth and linen for just five or six pence a yard, while the weaving of fine linen sometimes ran to nine. Something heavy and coarse, like sacking, might cost only three or four pence per yard. For linsey-woolsey, Gaylord charged eight pence, and the same for a good quality plain woolen. Checked linen and checked woolen also cost eight pence, and checked cotton slightly more. For cloth appropriate for bedtick, he charged nine or ten pence per yard. More complex weaves cost still more: for diaper—a comparatively sophisticated herringbone twill—he sometimes charged close to a shilling per yard, while diamond (another complex twill) for table linen cost between eight and nine pence. Striped or streaked cloth, crape, and blanketing all cost eight pence per yard. For a full coverlid, he charged six shillings, eight pence.[71]

Gaylord's accounts help illustrate the difference between "vernacular" and artisanal weaving.[72] For home-produced textiles, two weave structures were most common: plain and twill. The former was generally used for sheets, pillowcases, shifts, and so forth, and the latter for blanketing.[73] The looms worked by most home weavers had four shafts, counterbalanced.[74] This sort of weaving one might consider "vernacular weaving" (meaning that knowledge was acquired by watching others do it, rather than through a period of formal training), mainly performed by women.[75] But "fancy weaving" was a different enterprise. These artisans made blankets, coverlets, worsteds, and diapers on a loom that was very different, with up to sixteen harnesses, each moving differently.

Contemporary historians have confirmed what Judd reported in the 1850s, that New England women over the course of the eighteenth century had moved into weaving as a source of livelihood—in fact, earlier than Judd realized. "Long before the Revolution and more than half a century before the opening of the first mechanized spinning factories," historian Laurel Thatcher Ulrich writes, "New England women began to weave."[76] The shift in gender divisions of labor can be tracked in part by observing patterns in the ownership of tools used in textile production. For instance, as Ulrich explains, "in an artisan system, where families carried their homespun wool and flax to a local weaver, one would expect to find many more households with wheels than with looms, and that is exactly what one discovers in early American inventories." But over the first half of the eighteenth century, the number of looms distributed across households rose much more quickly than the number of wheels—numbers that signal change in both how cloth making occurred, and who was seated at those looms.

In Hampshire County in 1671, Ulrich finds, "barely 35 percent of inventories listed spinning wheels, and looms were so rare as to be virtually invisible"; almost six decades later, "two-thirds of households had wheels and an astonishing 20 percent had looms."[77] The shifting ratio of wheels to looms tells us, Ulrich argues, that something was happening to the structure of textile production: weaving was becoming an occupation undertaken by women. Those aspiring to perform this work learned not through periods of dedicated instruction (as male artisanal weavers once had, and as those women aspiring to work in clothing construction would still do), but rather through observation and practice. By 1774, Hampshire County had "one weaving household for every 2.5 households with wheels, producing a loom-to-wheel ratio of 0.40"; this "high proportion of looms to wheels meant dispersed household production," Ulrich concludes, and that "work that had once belonged to male artisans had become a part-time occupation for women and girls."[78]

Too few inventories survive from 1774 Hadley to test the town against that statistic, but one study of domestic cloth production in late eighteenth-century Hadley found that between 1760 and 1800, one of every six Hadley residents owned a loom; about one-third of the inventories contained 85 percent of the total number of wheels listed, while almost half of the inventories she reviewed contained none.[79] My review of inventories taken between 1760 and 1790 finds that, among households in possession of spinning and weaving equipment at the time an inventory was taken, about a third contained a loom. The town's loom-to-wheel ratio over these three decades appears to have been about 0.20.

The meaning of the data is complicated by the fact that looms were resources that households shared. In the 1770s, for instance, Molly Snell, a tenant of the Phelps family, came to Forty Acres to weave "for herself," completing her work just before Eunice Pomeroy settled in for the month.[80] The women of Francis Newton's household had three foot wheels, two great wheels, and a loom worth thirty shillings (worth fully as much as the horse shed on the property, and more than twice the value of the horse within).[81] But the Newtons did not need to use their own tools to profit from their skill at the loom. Teenager Betty Newton had taken that expertise into the Phelps household together with her sewing ability, working the loom at Forty Acres as early as the summer of 1778.[82] In doing so, she joined a number of local women who made cloth at Forty Acres, though she may not have—at least at that time—possessed a great deal of skill herself: Betty's arrival came on the heels of a "Mrs Pierce," who came to "put in a piece of overshot" (a patterned weave that can produce a range of geometric motifs, including curves and circles)."[83] Betty may not have (yet) had the knowledge or skill to warp the loom to produce overshot, but with the loom prepared by another hand, she spent a week doing the weaving, work that itself demanded greater skill than the production of other less complex fabrics.[84]

Eight women appear in Phelps's memorandum book as living with and weaving for the household, earning income at that loom. At Forty Acres, weavers came twice a year, in the spring (typically April) and again in the fall (often October, but sometimes November).[85] It was not unusual for weavers to remain the better part of a month: when Eunice Pomeroy came in the mid-1770s, she usually stayed about three weeks.[86] Peggy Clark arrived in November 1777, remaining almost the whole month, accompanying Phelps to the fuller at the end of her stay.[87] In addition to skills, then, another difference separating spinners from weavers stems from the spatial and seasonal relations the work generated, as weavers lodged in the homes of employers for these seasonal, finite terms, creating relationships marked by regularity and intimacy, but also fixed terms and distance.

Pomeroy, like a striking number of Phelps's weavers, was from Amherst rather than Hadley, though this may be largely a function of shifting borders and nomenclature: in 1759, Hadley's eastern land, created as a "precinct" in 1735, was established as the separate district of Amherst (it would be incorporated as its own town in 1775), named for the British army's Lord Jeffery Amherst, celebrated for his victories over France in the Seven Years' War.[88] In search of land and opportunity, Eunice Pomeroy's parents Simeon and Abigail had sometime in the 1740s moved to the gathering community east of Hadley Center, into a home on the east highway in the town's southernmost neighborhood; Eunice, then, didn't so much live in a different community as she lived at a considerable distance within the Hadley of Phelps's experience.[89] As an unmarried woman in her twenties, Pomeroy traveled seasonally to Forty Acres, and perhaps other households as well, lodging while performing the labor required to produce the year's necessary textiles. After Pomeroy's tenure came to a close with her marriage, in the early 1780s, women from another Amherst family, the Ingrams, worked the loom at Forty Acres.[90] Diademia Ingram arrived in December 1780, after which Lodema—the oldest of Philip and Experience Ingram's ten children—would become a steady presence at the farm.[91] Lodema was in her early twenties when she first appeared at Forty Acres, and she wove for the Phelps family annually until 1782, after which she was in turn succeeded by Lucy Marshall.

Lucy Marshall would become a long-term member of the household at Forty Acres, remaining as live-in help until her own marriage (her departure would bring Susanna Whipple into the family).[92] Her sister Dolly then came to help with the weaving.[93] The entwined histories of the Marshall and Phelps families illuminate the fluidity between the work of weaving and domestic service. Lucy Marshall "of Leverett" first appears in the memorandum book of Elizabeth Porter Phelps in spring 1783, when she came down from the hill town to work at weaving.[94] She appears to have stayed on for some weeks before moving on to the Hubbard household. But when Lucy Baker, the servant who became homesick after her mother's visit, left Forty Acres, Phelps apparently invited Marshall to return to work as a domestic servant.[95] A year later, the Phelps family's reliance on the Marshalls deepened when Lucy had a mishap with the horse and wagon: driving the Phelps family's cart into town in late September 1784, she met another team on the road; as she turned her vehicle, the cart hit the hind leg of the horse, causing the vehicle to overturn. The cart wheel passed over Marshall's torso, and her leg was broken in two places. Lucy would be brought back to Forty Acres "on a blanket fastened on poles" carried by a "great number of men."[96] Lucy's sister Dolly was summoned—surely to comfort and care for her sister while also replacing her labor—and would stay on in Lucy's stead until mid-January.[97]

Lucy Marshall would remain with the Phelps household for the better part of a decade, but Dolly, too, became a reliable figure in the social and working life of the family, and in time would go to work for Elizabeth Phelps's sister and brother-in-law, Dorothy and Lemuel Warner, after which she moved on to the family of Samuel Hopkins.[98] Lucy and Dolly both contributed to the work of cloth production in these years, Lucy in her capacity as a domestic servant and Dolly—who arrived from time to time to spin (staying a week), and also to weave (staying a month)—as a seasonal worker.[99] But Phelps still found need to hire other temporary weavers. In spring and fall 1787, for instance, a Polly Smith from Amherst came to help with the household's weaving.[100] But again, lines between cloth producers and domestic servants were blurry at best: Smith, for instance, was hired to weave seasonally, but when Lucy Marshall inadvertently stepped in a pail of boiling water, Dolly returned to fill in around the hearths and washtubs while Lucy's injuries healed.[101]

Fulling

Cloth production in Revolutionary Hadley was not necessarily complete with the conclusion of the weaver's work; once the cloth was taken from the loom, other steps remained before the fabric was finished. While linens were often bleached and dyed, woolens were fulled, a process that shrank the cloth, tightened the fibers, and gave the cloth the desired weight and sheen, as well as some resistance to water and flame. Households without access to a fulling mill might achieve some measure of these effects by wetting the cloth, beating it with implements, rinsing it, and wringing it out to dry.[102] But men and women who brought their cloth to a fulling mill could have it scoured, fulled, dyed, napped, sheared, and pressed, representing a "considerable investment even when cloth was woven at home."[103] And in Revolutionary Hadley, the fulling mill was overseen by Mehitable Cleveland Dean.

People who brought cloth to a fulling mill usually knew what they intended to do with it once it was ready; in fact, the planned garment shaped decisions about the fabric's finishing. Account books refer to cloth intended "for your great coat," and so forth, being brought to the mill for fulling, and identified by its final purposes in the columns recording the client's debts. Indeed, knowing both the final product and the eventual wearer was integral to the fulling process, since cloth dressed for men's garments and for women's was treated differently, in response to gendered fashions and functions. Fulling mills also "refreshed" old clothing.[104]

A full-fledged fulling mill was a significant investment, expensive to build and difficult to maintain.[105] As the historian Adrienne Hood observes, "fulling was one of the earliest textile processes to be mechanized using waterpower to drive the hammers that pounded the wet cloth to condense it. During this last stage of production, therefore, the household ceased to be the primary location of the work as artisans operated out of water-powered fulling mills scattered around the countryside."[106] Constructing the mill building and acquiring the necessary equipment and materials demanded far more capital than the loom and associated tools used in cloth making. The most sophisticated operations included a mill—typically a building set alongside a source of water power with a waterwheel on the side, driven by harnessed river water reserved in a millpond—where fabric was washed and shrunk. To access power, the fuller channeled the water through the millrace; the force of the water over the wheel, which the fuller controlled, determined the speed of the fulling hammers, which fell against cloth in a basin. This process caused the fabric's fibers to lock together; the cloth contracted and became denser. A dyehouse filled with large copper or tin vats housed the fuller's cleansing agents as well as dyestuffs (like madder or redwood, fustic, and indigo), and mordants—metal salts that set the dye or prepared the fiber to accept color—such as alum, green vitriol (an iron sulfate), and blue vitriol (copper sulfate).[107] Other facilities included tenter yards, where fabric was stretched across frames to take shape and dry, and a "dress house," where cloth was brushed and clipped, with teasels mounted in frames to help raise the cloth's nap and large shears used to trim the nap to the desired length. Finally, some establishments included a press shop, where cloth was pressed and made ready for use.[108]

Executing these tasks demanded considerable skill. As Hood notes, "cloth fulling was a far more complex process than saw or flour milling because the fulling itself took knowledge and skill and the finishing required even more expertise. Fullers had to understand the operation of a mill sufficiently to control the action of the hammers so they did not over shrink and ruin the cloth. Moreover the further processing could destroy the cloth if not done properly."[109] Some glimpse into the effort behind fulling can be found in the memorandum book of Elizabeth Phelps; in the summer of 1783, for instance, she wrote, "Tues morning up to the Mill to put on a new bolt found it was too fine Thurs up at the Mill to sew on some cloaths, to fix the Bolt—but it did not—stayed a little while at Mr. Days then up to Mr Worthingtons Sat morn up again did the work to the Bolt at Mr. Worthington. Aug 30—Tues up at Mr. Days to work on the Bolt once more."[110]

Hadley residents like Phelps traveled to the village at "the mills" (today known as North Hadley) to get their fulling done. By the summer that Elizabeth Phelps struggled to get her cloth finished just right, the community had had access to their own proper mill for only about eight years. The history of fulling in western Massachusetts is still largely unknown. While a number of fulling mills were established as early as the 1640s in eastern Massachusetts, a century later only a handful were present in the Connecticut Valley.[111] When the assessors to the Massachusetts General Court gathered information on mills in 1771, Hadley reported only gristmills and sawmills; the only nearby fulling mill reported was Caleb Ely's in South Hadley, on the other side of the Holyoke Range. In Williamsburg (a small village just west of Northampton), Joseph Williams kept accounts related to fulling in his miscellany book. In addition to farming, Williams was part owner of a fulling mill in town and noted the yards of cassimere and wool sold to his neighbors, as well as customers from Hatfield and Northampton. His wife Submit's work at tailoring, too, was noted.[112]

Hadley's first fulling mill opened in 1775.[113] Beginning in that year, Hadley families could make use of the North Hadley enterprise of Faxon and Mehitable Dean. The Deans were at that time relatively new to the community: Faxon had been born in 1718 in Dedham, Massachusetts, where his family had lived for several generations. His wife, Mehitable Cleveland, was born in Canterbury, Connecticut, in February 1727/28.[114] The young couple had married in Connecticut in mid-October 1746, and together they had children Samuel (born in 1755 in Mansfield), Mehitable (born in 1760 in Brimfield), and Sarah (born in 1762, also in Brimfield). Two more—Olive, born in January 1766, and Orange, born in September 1767—would follow after their move to Hadley.[115]

Faxon Dean was the son of Dedham clothier Joseph Dean.[116] Joseph died when Faxon was just two years old, his brother Thomas inheriting the family real estate. Thomas maintained the clothier's business until his death in the 1740s, and so young Faxon would have learned the trade as a young man. But having inherited no real property, he took the funds he received and eventually hit the road. He apparently made several attempts to succeed as a clothier but had trouble making a go of it. He married in Connecticut and then moved north to Brimfield before relocating again, in the mid-1760s, to Hadley. At first, the Deans had been decidedly unwelcome there: at the May 1765 meeting of the court of General Sessions of the Peace, the list of men and women warned out of town included "Faxon Dean and his wife Mehitable and Samuel, Mehitable, and Sarah, their children."[117] The Deans, forewarned that the town had refused any responsibility for their upkeep should they not find work, nevertheless set about establishing themselves.

Faxon Dean's relationship to the work of a clothier is easy to spot in legal records that list his occupation and those of his father and brother. But clearly his wife had also mastered elements of cloth finishing at some point during her life; though she was the daughter of joiner and cooper Samuel Cleveland, Mehitable's extended family tree also included clothiers, including John Marsh, a clothier who was among Hadley's first settlers.[118] In Hadley by 1765, and at work finishing cloth by 1767, the Deans apparently did not yet have the resources to build a fulling mill, and would not for eight years.[119] Perhaps at first it did not look like they would stay; by 1769 Faxon had acquired land and a house in Hadley, but he was already looking to sell it to Eleazer Porter Esq., receiving twenty-five pounds, five shillings, and seven pence for "a certain dwelling house in Hadley viz the one in which I now live."[120] But the following year Mrs. Dean joined the Congregational church, signaling an intent to settle, and the Dean family continued to thrive among the small community gathered around Hadley's "upper mills and school meadows," though theirs was among the more modest households: while Charles Phelps's estate in 1770 was valued at £250, and Benjamin Smith's at £101, Faxon Dean's estate came in at just £18.[121]

Mehitable and Faxon's business was a joint effort. Unlike other references in the memorandum book, it is striking that Elizabeth Porter Phelps speaks, variously, of tapping the expertise of both Faxon and Mehitable Dean. Adrienne Hood has noted that among Pennsylvanians, "wherever it was practiced, cloth finishing was men's work."[122] Of the fullers in Chester County, Pennsylvania, only two women are known, and in both cases the mills had belonged to their husbands. Widows, she suggests, may have run their husbands' business with hired labor or rented the equipment out to others, but they would not have performed the manual labor the work demanded, even if their husbands had.[123] But Elizabeth Phelps's memorandum book contains mentions of both Mr. and Mrs. Dean. In one instance, Phelps's reference notes "Mrs Dean here in the fore-noon to shew me about some colouring"; a week later, Eunice Pomeroy arrived to weave. Another time, Phelps had occasion to note, "Mr. Dean here to visit about colouring otter."[124] The fulling operation of Faxon and Mehitable Cleveland Dean seems to have been a shared enterprise.

The expertise cultivated by women like Dean was significant. An array of recipes needed to be mastered if the craftswoman was to help her clients achieve the desired color, different ingredients, and techniques being employed to produce the correct shade of green, to distinguish crimson from scarlet, and other subtle but important differences.[125] Mehitable Dean likely knew how to tell when a dyestuff had gone bad, and how to take the sap out of sumac lest the dye leave spots. If she was good at her work, then she knew not to let her indigo get cool, not to overcrowd her vat, just how much camwood would give her a nice light cinnamon, and how a little decoction of logwood could convert a sturdy snuff brown to a subtle London smoke. She could apply just enough water and soap to the raw cloth to raise the grease in wool fibers, and she knew that baize would be warmer if napped on both sides. Even the growing of teasel—a plant used to raise the nap of a cloth—had ins and outs of its own, from the placement of seeds (about eight inches apart) to the thinning of rows (when the plants have acquired six or seven leaves), to the harvesting for use (cutting about eight inches of stem once the blossoms have fallen). This and much more constituted the specialized knowledge possessed by Mehitable Dean and fullers like her.

But Hadley apparently failed to provide the market the Deans craved. In 1782 they prepared to make another move, selling their entire operation in December of that year to Horace Day, a Southington, Connecticut, clothier, for £175.[126] The reasons why are obscure, but part of the Dean household's success had hinged on the work of the town's spinners and weavers (as Hood observes, "a profitable cloth-finishing business required newly woven fabric to process"), and the number of weavers in 1780s Hadley may have been insufficient to keep the mill active.[127] Elizabeth Porter Phelps notes having ridden to "Mr. Fields respecting some colouring" in March 1781, suggesting that another clothier was already at work nearby, and perhaps the competition was worrisome.[128] Elizabeth Phelps seemed sorry to see the Deans go; she and "Hitty" had become friends. The two women traveled back and forth regularly to one another's homes, and in January 1782, Phelps had seen Dean through an unusually tough time in childbed; when they left, she sighed in the pages of her journal, "One Mr Day came to live at Mr Deans—bo't it of him—they are gone."[129]

The Transformation of Cloth Production in Federal Hadley

For Elizabeth Porter Phelps, the 1790s were a period of acute change. Her mother, Elizabeth Pitkin Porter, died, and the whole house—top to bottom and side to side—was renovated in anticipation of the hoped-for (but unrealized) return of Phelps's son and his (eventual) family.[130] Landscapes both nearby and far afield began to see the arrival of new stores and new means of transportation, from canals to roads to turnpikes; meanwhile, the appearance of a new woolen mill at Byfield, as we shall see, drew Phelps and other curious families eager to glimpse this new development in cloth production.[131] In fact, cloth production at Forty Acres began to look very different beginning in the 1790s. Though Phelps's memorandum book continues to teem with references to the work of quilting, soap, and candlemaking, the baking of mince pies and making of sausages, and other labors in and around the farm, the last reference in that source to any woman coming to the farm to spin was the March 1796 visit of Dolly Marshall. Marshall's return the following month to weave is the last reference in those pages to any woman coming there to work the loom.[132] Instead, we see (in Phelps's memorandum book, as well as her correspondence) her daughters carrying yarn to Amherst to weave, Phelps riding to Muddybrook "after cloth," and Charles Phelps and Elizabeth both retrieving wool they had had carded and colored, also in Amherst.[133]

Indeed, cloth production in Hadley and across the region was transformed in the decades between the 1790s and the 1820s, when Sylvester Judd observed the waning of household cloth production in Hadley. It is worth noting that the scenes of Judd's particular nostalgia were very much focused on the production of flax, and less so wool (with the exception of his fondness for the memory of girls on horseback carrying wool to be carded). His palpable nostalgia for the sights and sounds of cloth production ("few persons under thirty years of age," he would muse, in phrases laden with disappointment, "have ever seen a woman hatchel flax or card tow, or heard the buzzing of the foot wheel, or seen bunches of flaxen yarn hanging in the kitchen, or linen cloth whitening on the grass") evidences in part a measurable eagerness among rural families to abandon that work at least in favor of other fibers.[134] The conversion of flax to linen proved comparatively difficult to mechanize, and so, the more cotton fabrics became readily available, the less linen contributed to the sartorial vocabulary of western Massachusetts. Paul Rivard posits that flax was "possibly the first crop abandoned by New England farmers"; by the time of the 1810 manufacturing census, linen would account for less than six percent of Hampshire County's textile output.[135] In the decades between 1790 and 1830, some aspects of home cloth production boomed, then, while others dwindled.

But this is not a story of industrial processes supplanting hand production; rather, as Laurel Thatcher Ulrich has explained, "the most successful early industries built on rather than competed with household manufacturing." The boom in household cloth making would have consequences for women working in related industries as well. As early as May 1791, for instance, the *Massachusetts Magazine* reported on Boston's thriving business in the making of wool and cotton cards, some eight thousand dozen pairs being made in that city every year; one house alone, the author reports, produced six thousand dozen pairs per year, employing some sixteen hundred women and children in their assembly.[136] Over the next two decades, home cloth production engaged the attention of women across the region. "Of the 19,276,043 yards of cloth made in New England in 1810 and recorded in the federal census of that year," Ulrich continues, "only 4 percent was produced in 'manufactories.' The remaining 96 percent was woven 'in families.'"[137] "Helping to sustain this household production," she adds, "was a host of water-powered carding and spinning mills."[138]

By 1810, some fifty-seven carding machines and sixty-seven fulling mills were scattered across Hampshire County (almost one-third of Massachusetts' total), while Hadley itself was producing some 60,000 yards of linen and over a million yards of other cloth.[139] Those fulling mills, which handled over 225,000 yards of cloth in that year, represented fully a quarter of the fulling mills in Massachusetts. And those carding machines handled close to 260,000 pounds of wool (more than 30 percent more machines than the next largest producer, Worcester County, and handling almost 40 percent more wool). The census reported some 5,745 "looms for clothes of cotton, wool, etc." (again, 25 percent greater than Worcester County to the east, and more than twice the number in Berkshire County to the west).[140] In 1810, the annual production of linens, wools, and other cloths in Hampshire County was valued at an average of $7.87 per capita—the highest of any county in Massachusetts.[141]

Hadley together with the whole of the Connecticut Valley had long been witnessing attempts to mechanize and reorganize the time-consuming and labor-intensive work of cloth production. Jane Nylander has explained that "from 1765 to the beginning of factory production of textiles," the Connecticut Valley saw "efforts to stimulate and to improve the quality of domestic production and reduce the reliance on imported, mainly British goods."[142] A September 1790 editorial in the *Hampshire Gazette* suggests some of the ways in which domestic cloth fell short: if a yard wide and just three or four yards long, the cloth when fulled shrunk to perhaps three-quarters of a yard in width—"too narrow to cut to advantage for clothing."[143] Moreover, sloppy sorting produced cloth with remnants of other fibers visible. The author recommended some standardization, too: wool should be woven, fulled, and bleached so it could be reliably described as "flannel of a yard wide," and "brought to market white."[144] Merchants would begin to convey their needs with more specificity, as we shall see, in the columns of the *Gazette*.

In the late 1780s, Northampton merchant Levi Shepherd also began building what would become a considerable textile-producing enterprise.[145] In March 1788, the Massachusetts legislature, in an effort to boost manufacturing, created a bounty that paid makers "eight shillings for every piece of Topsail-Duck and other stouter Sailcloth," an offer the Northampton entrepreneur found too good to pass up.[146] Duck—a strong, untwilled linen (or cotton) that was like canvas, but lighter and finer, and widely used in the making of sails—was needed to supply both fisheries and commerce. By July, Shepherd (observing how "our country is so well suited to the raising of flax, and [yet there is] so little demand for it, either in its natural state or manufactured in any other form") posted a notice in the *Hampshire Gazette* inviting proposals from "any who has a sufficient knowledge in manufacturing Duck, and will undertake to make it," asking respondents to stipulate their price by the bolt, the number they could produce, and the time it would take them to deliver; a month later, he had placed another notice offering half cash and half dry goods for one thousand pounds of "water rotted flax."[147] By October he had received enough samples to conclude that the best pieces were those twenty-four inches wide and forty-one yards long, noting that "this sort is a lighter cloth than the duck formerly made in this county"; as such, it won't draw as much per bolt, he cautioned, "yet there will be a greater proportion of the expense in making it, labor of consequence the more profitable in every kind of manufacturing that is produced with the least stock, turns out uniformly to the greatest advantage to the industrious mechanic."[148] By the end of 1789, he alerted readers of the

Gazette that he aimed to expand his commitment, having "erected large buildings for the purpose"; he "wish[ed] to engage four young women more" (to an existing work force of how many is not known), "for a year or longer in his manufactory."[149] He allocated space for weaving in one part of the building and spinning in another (a ropewalk was also contained in the building). A year later he expanded the operation further, placing constant ads for "well-dressed flax."[150]

In the space within Shepherd's manufactory that was dedicated to spinning, the "distaff with the flax for the warp was fastened to the side of the spinner," one description reads, "and the tow or filling spinners held the carded tow in their hands while walking up and down."[151] The four young women Shepherd hoped to engage "for a year or longer time" may have been these in-house spinners.[152] But much of the flax was spun by families at home and delivered to Shepherd's enterprise. In spring 1791, for instance, he advised readers of the *Gazette* that he was seeking a "quantity of good linen yarn, made from good flax," weighing sixteen ounces per run.[153] Several Hadley families embraced the opportunity to spin for Shepherd's enterprise. Chloe Moody soon found herself delivering spun flax to the manufactory, as did women in the families of John Dickinson, Joseph Cook, and Samuel Cook.[154]

The processing of wool fibers was also transformed. In the last quarter of the eighteenth century, Elisha Pitkin (part of Elizabeth Porter Phelps's mother's family in East Hartford) had developed one of Connecticut's first water-powered wool carding machines.[155] The first American effort at a woolen mill—which opened in Hartford, Connecticut, in 1788—involved "two carding-engines," which one observer described as having "two large center cylinders in each, with two doffers, and only two working cylinders, of the breadth of bare sixteen inches, said to be invented by some person there."[156] Families still had to sort and clean the raw wool, but they found that "mechanically carded wool was not only much easier to spin but enabled them to produce twice as much yarn from the same amount of wool."[157]

During the spring of 1795, Phelps and her son Porter rode to Byfield, Massachusetts—some thirty miles northeast of Boston, almost to the New Hampshire line—to see the new mill there.[158] The Newburyport Woolen Manufactory, a mill housed in a multistory wooden building (105 by 32 feet), produced broadcloths, flannels, and blankets on a water-powered loom and a spinning-jenny of forty spindles produced by brothers Arthur and John Scholfield.[159] Phelps's trip shouldn't surprise us. Charles and Elizabeth had some connection to the new enterprise, in that their son Charles Porter Phelps had since 1792 been studying law under Newburyport attorney Theophilus Parsons, an investor in the enterprise (Charles would in time wed his mentor's niece, Sarah Parsons), which brought them to visit Newburyport. But they were not the only curious observers: years later, Newburyport's Sarah Smith Emery—seven years old when the mill opened—would later recall that "the erection of this mill created a great sensation throughout the whole region. People visited it from far and near"—so many that the manufactory charged a ten-cent admission fee.[160] Eight decades later, Emery could still recall the wonder she felt as a child viewing the manufactory for the first time: "Never shall I forget the awe with which I entered what then appeared the vast and imposing edifice. The large drums that carried the bands on the lower floor, coupled with the novel noise and hum, increased this awe, but when I reached the second floor, where picking, carding, spinning and weaving were in process, my amazement became complete."[161]

Entrepreneurial families like Charles and Elizabeth Phelps weren't the only ones taking notice of new facilities like that at Newburyport. In the summer of 1796, Phelps complained that her hired woman Persis Leonard "left to go to the Mills to spin" (Anna Bigelow "came to do the work").[162] Leonard had come to Forty Acres to work as a domestic servant in September 1794, when Mrs. Hancock and her two children left the farm.[163] Apparently, the moment an opportunity came to exchange domestic service for work in a spinning mill—possibly Levi Shepherd's Northampton duck manufactory—Persis took it. A few years later, Phelps's daughter Betsy Huntington in Middletown found herself in a similar position when she reported that "Sally quit this morning, she has gone to Mr. Kirby's to spin," as apparently "her Doctor recommends that instead of housework." Sally's decision was likely a boon for Kirby, as Huntington called Sally "very profitable help," adding that she "does all the work—last week began to spin, has done five runs, intends to do another tomorrow." Sally, like Persis, opted to exchange the backbreaking (and intimate) labor of domestic service for the more predictable, and impersonal, work of spinning. For her part, Huntington assured her mother—in a phrase that rings a bit hollow—that she and Mitte West now "expect to get along alone."[164]

In Byfield, the mill operatives were mainly men, though a few "young girls" were "employed in splicing rolls."[165] The mill's presence reverberated throughout its community, and "brought quite a revolution," Emery would observe, "in the domestic manufactures of the neighborhood."[166] Hand carding had already been abandoned as families opted instead to take their wool to local clothiers to be converted into rolls; now this larger mill captured that activity. When the mill shifted to cotton, yarns were spun and dyed at the factory; men working looms in the factory produced heavier cloths like ticking, "but much of the lighter stuffs" (a lighter, blue and white striped or checked cloth suitable for aprons as well as summer fabrics for men's and boy's clothing) "were taken into families and woven on the common house loom." Meanwhile, the work created a "new occupation" in households around the manufactory as women were drawn into the necessary work of cleaning the cotton, separating the seeds from the fiber.[167]

As the eighteenth century gave way to the nineteenth, Arthur Scholfield embraced what he quickly perceived to be an opportunity in the making of carding mills; he moved to western Massachusetts, leaving cloth manufacture to produce the carding machines themselves.[168] As early as November 1801, he alerted the "inhabitants of Pittsfield and the neighboring towns" that he had set up a carding machine just west of the meetinghouse, where families "may have their wool carded into roles [*sic*] for 12.5 cents/pound," and 10 cents if they "find the grease, and pick and grease it" ahead (families still needed to do the cleaning—wool needed to be sheared, sorted, picked, and scoured before it could be carded, with no more than a pound of grease to every dozen pounds of wool—but carding mills brushed the wool into rolls ready for spinning or for use as batting). He also offered a "small assortment" of woolens for sale.[169] The following summer, the advertising columns of area newspapers were filled with notices alerting readers to the advent of new carding machines. In a single season, Hampshire County residents learned that Roger Wing & Co. had made a carding machine available in Williamsburg; Joel Norton & Co. installed machines in both Westfield and Chesterfield; and Daves & Worthen had brought one to Wilbraham.[170] Women "soon discovered they could spin twice as much wool in a day by starting with the soft rolls produced by machine carding."[171]

A carding mill appears to have opened in Hadley as early as 1802, with another following, in North Amherst, in 1803; yet another could be found at Hadley's "lower mills" by 1805.[172] The household at Forty Acres made use of these enterprises. In November 1804, Phelps records that her husband made a trip to "Amherst after wool which he yesterday carried to carding mill," and the following fall he again traveled to the "upper part of Amherst" (the neighborhood soon to be christened "Factory Hollow") "to get wool carded, coloring done, etc." Christopher Clark suggests that the Phelps household used the Amherst enterprise when it became available, but shifted their business to Hadley when a carding mill opened there.[173] In fact, Charles and Elizabeth Phelps helped advance the spread of such enterprises when they committed ten dollars to a subscription for a miller named Lamson: the couple brought wool for carding, and also paid Lamson for weaving a coverlid.[174] Sylvester Judd remembered Hadley girls on horseback carrying "bundle[s] of wool almost as high as their heads" to be processed.[175] While no ledgers are known to survive from the carding mills of Hadley or Amherst, the compass of trade was likely much like Ambrose Church's mill in Middlefield in the hills about thirty miles to the west, which carded wool for nearly every family in town; his ledger lists at least 129 of the 134 families who lived there.[176]

At the turn of the nineteenth century, while Phelps's memorandum book no longer mentions the arrival of women hired to spin, the household at Forty Acres remained very much caught up in spinning, now with the aid of these new machines to prepare the fibers. When just around ten years old, servant/ward Mitte West would brag that she could spin three run of yarn per week, sometimes ten or eleven knots in a day.[177] A decade later, it was Phelps's granddaughters who sat at Forty Acres' wheels: nine-year-old Elizabeth proudly spun ten run over the course of a two-week visit from her home in Connecticut.[178] As we have seen, Phelps's granddaughters took considerable pride in their ability to contribute to the work of the family. When just about seven years old, Bethia "has told me several times," Phelps reported to her daughter, "be sure tell ma'm 'I have learned to spin.'"[179] Meanwhile, an aging Mary Trainer continued to prepare fibers for this new generation of Phelps family spinners: in March 1814, she offset part of her debt for a peck of onions, a gallon of cider, and almost five pounds of cheese by hatchling flax.[180]

Ulrich's study of wheels, looms, and changing patterns of cloth production considered the "mix of casual and committed weavers" in early nineteenth-century New England towns, and notes that an unusual source from New Salem—just twenty miles northeast of Hadley, and the source of some of the Phelps family's labor—"inadvertently provided evidence on this point by counting the output of looms rather than of households. As the proportion of loom-owning families in New Salem (46 percent) is similar to that in other parts of the region," these "records give some hint about how weaving might have been distributed elsewhere." One New Salem family produced 1,000 yards in 1810, while eight others made 500 yards or more. "The collective production of these high producers," Ulrich notes, "accounted for only 19 percent of the cloth made in the town in 1810. The remainder was scattered among 148 households, about a third of which wove more than 200 but fewer than 500 yards. The town mean was 186 yards, the median 130. Clearly, casual weaving," she concludes, "was the norm."[181]

In Hadley, probate records for the period 1800–1815 show 76 percent of households with wheels, and 35 percent with looms.[182] Those loom-owning households included those of joiner and carpenter Elihu and Cynthia Cook, as well as a number of farming families, from the comparatively substantial operations of Warham and Martha Smith (who lived next door to the Newtons), and Benjamin and Patty Kellogg (Patty being the daughter of Warham and Martha), John and Sybil Montague, and Zera and Eleanor Green, to the modest household of Josiah and Eunice Nash.[183] Merchants and their counterparts in nearby towns continued to seek locally made cloth, sometimes in large quantities. One called for "brown or whitened yard-wide tow cloth"; another wanted "3,000 yards check'd woolen shirting," further noting that it should be "made in the following manner, 3–4th wide—half blue, and 4-4th check."[184] In summer 1810, the Conway firm of Charles Billings and Obadiah Smith advertised their desire for a thousand yards of yard-wide tow cloth; Obadiah Smith & Co. of Hadley sought another five hundred yards.[185] That same month, Hadley's William Porter reminded readers that he accepted "most kinds of country produce" as well as tow cloth and meal bags in exchange for goods in his shop."[186] In 1813, William Porter sought one thousand yards of the aforementioned white flannel, as well as one thousand pairs of socks and mittens, and one thousand meal bags, brown and white.[187] Meal bags, in fact, constituted an important category of local production: one merchant sought some five hundred meal bags, twenty-two inches wide and thirty-six inches long, plus another one hundred, "common size," telling us a bit more about the quantities of cloth needed for these important containers, and also reminding us of women's role in this aspect of agricultural production and exchange.[188]

In 1813, Nathaniel Coolidge Jr. (whose shop, still extant, stood on the Hadley Common near the meetinghouse) also alerted readers that he had "received a quantity of cotton yarn," and hoped to "get twenty thousand yards of cloth wove"; Coolidge offered "factory prices," and would pay in either goods or yarn. "Those who are disposed to engage in weaving," he assured his audience (women and men alike), "can have constant employ."[189] It was a staggering, even audacious amount of yardage to aim for; whether he was able to meet that figure is unknown, but apparently Coolidge was ambitious, and saw great opportunity in the production of cotton cloth.

In the eighteen-teens, the area would see the emergence of several mills, the most important of these initiatives being the Northampton Cotton & Woolen Company, which would produce most of the area's wool cloth for some thirty years after its launch.[190] Newspaper notices suggest that early on, proprietor James Shepherd had difficulty obtaining labor. As a result, he sought to engage whole families, who would live in company-owned houses and work in the mill.[191] His notices tell us a bit about how the work was organized by gender and age, and remind us once again that youths were considered essential workers: "Wanted—at the Manufactory of James Shepherd & Co.," one notice read:

> A steady and industrious family, consisting of man and wife and two girls of from 15 to 20 years of age, and two or three boys, from 12 to 18 years of age. Constant employment will be given to the whole family. The business of the girls will be to pick wool. And of the boys to tend carding machines and indoor work. Convenient house is ready for such a family, where they can live by themselves, rent will be cheap, price of wood is also cheap. They also have a House to rent at Manufactory suitable for a Widow and small family, to whom constant employment will be given.[192]

In November 1817, Shepherd announced a new partnership with a Samuel Jones, with whom he would carry on "woolen manufacturing." The firm offered "work for the industrious"—as "those who wish for employment can have the wool left and received at their houses." "Three or four industrious girls" may also "find employment at the factory in sorting wool."[193] By the 1820s, Shepherd's factory employed 118 workers, almost half of them (54) women and girls.[194] In the period 1825–1827, "girls" were tending the mechanical shearing machines, which required "one superintendent at \$32 and seven girls at \$8/mo, including board, and these attend twenty pairs of shears." Women were also employed in burling (that is, removing knots), linting, and marking cloth.

Unlike smaller operations, this enterprise utilized power machinery from the outset, selling its goods in outside markets. Manufacturing was carried on at the facility, though some spinning and weaving continued to be executed by workers in their homes. Like its Byfield counterpart, this mill employed women who participated in production processes from home: as late as 1818, advertisements appeared in the newspapers for home workers to pick wool: "Shepherd & Jones have 7000 lbs of Spanish Wool" (probably referring to wool from merino sheep) "which they wish to have picked. Those who wish employment can have the wool left and rec'd at their houses, by leaving their names at Captain Dickinson's store."[195]

In this, a classic example of a putting-out system, Hampshire County women brought work home from manufactories, completed it in their own homes, and returned it when they were ready for more.[196] Women who pursued outwork found a way to expand earnings while reducing some of the burdens associated with other forms of employment, from the drudgery of domestic service to the intimacy of work that required laborers to live-in with employers for shorter or longer periods of time.

The 1810 census marked the height of those developments. Indeed, Christopher Clark finds that the "demand for household textile production peaked" at the time of that census, and that "between 1815 and 1820 most households abandoned textile production." Put another way, though the early events in the transformation of cloth manufacture heightened some aspects of home production, in time factories would displace home cloth making altogether. Caleb Cook's Hadley accounts, Judd would report, stopped including charges for weaving in about 1819, while Sylvester Smith's family for some reason particularly remembered leaving off the making of woolen cloth specifically in the year 1822.[197] The reminiscences of Elizabeth Porter Phelps's grandson, Theodore Gregson Huntington, of his Hadley childhood in the late 1810s and 1820s, contain vivid descriptions of farm work—the carrying of water to thirsty reapers, the annual apple gathering, summer "chestnutting"—and detailed recollections of his sister spinning, particularly spinning flax in the north kitchen on the eve of her spring 1824 wedding, but through the 1820s, his sisters setting up great wheels in summer in the farm's cornhouse. He described the shearing of the family's sheep, and the fleece in its "entire" being in once piece "carefully rolled up and tied together to be sent to the carding mill or sold"; he recalled the beauty of the flax in the field, the work of pulling it. He also remembered with affection the work of whitening fabric—the cloth being laid in a large tub, covered with lye, and every morning taken out and spread across the grass, as the "homely brown would day by day take on a paler hue until at last the sun would look upon a stainless white and the work would be done."[198] But his "sketches" makes only passing reference to "yarns woven" into various textures, after the spinning, and before whitening. The fact that cloth became the object of attention of the agricultural fairs that blossomed in the second quarter of the century also suggests some effort to revive—one might even say memorialize—a declining domestic industry.[199]

Oddly, Huntington makes no reference to his father's 1830s foray into silk production, which brought some thirty thousand silkworms into the attic, cellar, and ground floor rooms of Forty Acres. As early as 1810, Hampshire County farmers had begun to consider silk production in earnest, producing just over one hundred pounds of sewing and raw silk.[200] Apparently the household at Forty Acres embraced the silk craze when it came to the Connecticut Valley. Theodore's father, Dan Huntington, believed this to be a promising venture for his household and the community more generally, having only minimal start-up costs and demanding little in the way of workload or labor. "As to the labour of setting up and taking down the cradles [shelves for feeding]—gathering and distributing leaves etc.," Huntington writes, "all was done so much at odd spells, and when nothing else would have been done, and which might have been done mostly by children, I can safely make no estimate of it."[201] Huntington carried their output to Samuel Whitmarsh's (short-lived) silk factory in Northampton, where the cocoons were converted into sewing silk for $3.35 per pound.[202] Huntington saw silk production as the obvious next phase for Hadley women's work in cloth production: "When the Piedmontese reel, and the silk loom shall become to our wives and daughters, what the distaff, and the domestic wheel were to their mothers and grandmothers," he (erroneously, it turns out) believed, "then will the culture, and manufacture of silk, through the country, assume its appropriate importance."

If flax in the field, grazing sheep, or mulberry trees no longer offer tangible markers of Hadley's cloth-making past, these calculations among Hadley families are today evidenced, if nowhere else, in the affluence they generated. None of the buildings that housed Hadley's carding mills, or the nearby spinning or weaving operations, are known to survive. What stands today are the impressive brick homes of David Pomeroy and Sumner Gates, partners in the carding and spinning mills along Hadley's Fort River, in the spot known for a time in the early nineteenth century as Mill Hollow. The Pomeroy home stands on a slight rise, overlooking what was once the mill complex that generated the wealth that paid for it, while the elegant fanlight of Sumner and Mary Gates gazes across Bay Road just a third of a mile west of the mill complex. These architectural documents of women's production preferences still stand today, quietly attesting to the goods their mills generated and to the desires those mills reflected.[203]

In the half-century flanking the year 1800, then, cloth making in Hadley saw expansion, contraction, and reconfiguration. Families like the Phelpses of Forty Acres embraced the opportunity represented in carding mills, sheep, and flax, while hired women like Persis Leonard saw another kind of opportunity, and left domestic service for work in a mill. As the women of antebellum Hadley carried their spinning wheels to basements and attics, as looms were dismantled and relegated to barns and outbuildings, and wool combs began the steady march from tool to relic, long-standing relations of work among Hadley families gave way to new associations that were colored more by anonymity and brevity—or, depending on one's point of view, brevity and privacy—than familiarity and continuity.

CHAPTER SIX

Hospitality Work

The inn at the south end of the Hadley Common catered to polite travelers, men and women traveling en route to and from Boston by carriage or coach during the late eighteenth century. The inn at the north end of the Hadley Common, on the other hand, tended to serve a rougher crowd, mainly men who worked on the river. Among other skills, the innkeeper's daughter Tryphena Newton Cook learned to manage the rowdy behavior of the raftsmen. Family tradition in Hadley records her ready response to one man who seemed determined to harass her. Tired of his coarse and constant overtures, she finally took a swing at her tormenter, knocking him down. Startled, he rose to his feet, sputtering and stuttering that "he would only submit to that because she was a woman." To which Cook allegedly retorted that she would not have stood as much as she had unless she *was* a woman.[1]

While the story is surely partly if not wholly apocryphal, there was something about not only the nature of the barroom, but also the character of Tryphena Newton Cook, that her descendants hoped to remember and record in its telling. She was, in Mary Smith Barstow's telling, patient, to a point; shrewd; and strong of will and shoulder. If there is a seed of truth in the family chestnut, then she was also acutely aware of the special burdens of womanhood, especially among women whose work meant they were surrounded by men on the move—lessons she likely learned at the knee of her innkeeping parent, Elizabeth Fairchild Newton.[2]

The pages that follow consider hospitality as a source of livelihood for Hadley women. After reviews of women's work in tavernkeeping as well as the regulatory context for tavernkeeping and innkeeping and its relationship to patterns of marriage and family, the chapter surveys geographies of hospitality and relationships between taverns, neighborhoods, and patterns of travel. A close look at the public house of Mindwell Pomeroy sheds light on the work of provisioning while also revealing patterns of local and regional travel and family labor, while the purpose-built tavern of Elizabeth Newton opens discussion of the cultural work of taverns in postrevolutionary Hadley. Following a brief discussion of work associated with longer-term boarders, attention turns to the challenges presented by alcohol abuse, and the important roles women played in managing alcohol use. Taken together, these subjects suggest the various ways in which women's work in hospitality settings shaped these important centers of community gravity.

Women and the Work of Tavernkeeping

While conventional wisdom in the nineteenth and early twentieth-century community assumed that it was men who kept the so called "Cook Tavern" at the top of the town common, records show that the inn was in fact largely the enterprise of Tryphena's mother, widow Elizabeth Fairchild Newton, who secured innkeeping licenses with little interruption from 1781 to 1810.[3] She is the only Hadley woman to appear with regularity among the several men annually granted tavern licenses by officers of the county courts. Her contemporaries recognized what later generations forgot: when Ephaphrus Hoyt in 1790 traveled from Deerfield to Philadelphia, he recorded in his journal having put up at "Mrs Newton's tavern at the end of Hadley."[4]

Like other working women, tavern- and innkeeping women—those, like Elizabeth Fairchild Newton, at the head of the enterprise, but their children, employees, and enslaved workers even more so—are easily overlooked, especially in rural places.[5] But public houses were significant sites of women's labor in the Massachusetts countryside. As they went about the work of securing provisions; preparing food and drink; washing and maintaining vessels, linens, and tavern spaces; serving customers (effort involving both physical and emotional labor); and other chores associated with this work, tavernkeepers negotiated relations with the outsiders who frequented their establishments; they also—because of where they sat as well as who they served—negotiated relationships and boundaries locally. Taverns were, as we shall see, sites of cultural and social production and policing, spatial dimensions simultaneously reflecting and shaping both inter- and intra-community relations.[6] It seems worth noting, too, the potential intersection of tavern-keeping work and the shaping of collective memory, as among the small number of women Sylvester Judd opted to interview, several were associated with the town's tavern-keeping community, suggesting perhaps their comparatively high profile. For example, Sophia Cook Clark grew up in the orbit of Elisha Cook's tavern, Sarah Graves Amsden and Polly Pomeroy were the daughters of tavernkeepers, and Abigail Dickinson Newton the daughter-in-law of innkeeper Elizabeth Newton.[7] Public houses shaped relationships among women (that is, women at the helm of competing enterprises, women and the workers whose labor they controlled, and women and their female clientele), and between women and men (that is, within families, and between women workers and male customers). Sited as they were at intersections geographic, cultural, social, and economic, such places absorbed and catalyzed change.

To be sure, women were less likely than men to obtain formal licenses in their own names, making it appear that fewer women than men ran taverns (at least with the formal recognition and approval of the courts), but as Sarah Hand Meacham writes in her study of middling Virginia women who kept taverns, "Tavern licenses were assigned to men, but both magistrates and license applicants knew that the tavern itself would be run by the petitioner's wife or daughter."[8] Their reputations and skill were tangible assets to the enterprise. Moreover, numerous women were authorized to keep public houses in Hampshire County in the last half of the eighteenth century and the beginning of the nineteenth. Newton was by no means the only woman at the head of a Hampshire County tavern. In her study of women taverners in the Connecticut Valley, Anne Lanning found some twenty-one women licensed to act as an "innholder, retailer, and common victualler," across fourteen towns.[9] Newton was not alone in her neck of the woods: in the 1770s, Northampton's Jemima Sheldon Lyman continued to operate the tavern once licensed to her now-dead husband, while widow Abigail Smith kept a tavern in neighboring South Hadley, as did widow Mary Pomeroy; residents of nearby Shutesbury enjoyed the hospitality of Joanna Allen, while over the river in Hatfield, townspeople and travelers found refreshment at the tavern kept by Lucy Hubbard. In Sunderland, Jerusha Leonard kept the family tavern running for a decade after the death of her husband Noahdiah before she turned it over to her son Moses.[10]

But official records mislead us about the relative absence or presence of women in the work of tavernkeeping and innkeeping, for whatever name appeared on a license, the wives, daughters, daughters-in-law, and other relatives of license holders, as well as servants and enslaved women and men, prepared meals and beverages; washed glass, ceramic, and metal cooking and serving vessels; laundered bedding; cleaned public areas and lodging rooms; and otherwise provided for guests. They also helped preserve the "good order" on which continued revenue depended. What's more, in addition to the labor of family members, taverns, like large households in general, often required access to the help of domestic servants as well as enslaved women. Persis Morse, we recall, had been the hired woman at an unidentified tavern before joining the Phelps household at Forty Acres; her toddler's "work used to be to go round into all the rooms and chambers, & gather the candlesticks for P. to clean."[11] In Hockanum, Desire Kentfield and Hannah Henry contributed to the success of the White Horse Tavern. Innkeepers Lemuel and Dorothy Phelps Warner seem to have made use of enslaved and free black labor—at least Elizabeth Phelps referenced "Phillis, Mr. Warner's negro woman"—in the management of their enterprise, while Lucy Terry Prince, captured in Africa as an infant, was purchased to work in the Deerfield tavern of Ebenezer Wells.[12] While Tryphena

Newton Cook also worked at tailoring to contribute to her family's income—labor today best documented by her own household's account book—she apparently knew her way around her mother's barroom, too, although no archival evidence survives to confirm her role in that business.[13] And Mary Trainer, as we have seen, may have been keeping an off-the-books tavern in the early years of the nineteenth century.

The work performed by women at the head of a rural public house (whether the license holder or a wife, daughter, or daughter-in-law) is difficult to recover, and that of other women laborers still more so. But taverns and inns provided livelihoods for Hadley women in a range of circumstances; they also placed working women in positions with distinct features and challenges in the social and cultural landscape of the village. Tavernkeeping differs from other occupations undertaken by women considered here in several ways. Unlike women in domestic service, midwifery and health care, and often cloth making, tavernkeeping women did not find themselves working in spaces dominated by other women, but rather in close association with the men who were the vast majority of customers. The surviving ledger associated with the Hockanum public house of Ebenezer and Mindwell Pomeroy contains references to more than two hundred and thirty men in the taproom and lodging rooms, but only a handful of women: Pelham cloth maker Esther Alexander enjoyed the occasional gill of rum, presumably when visiting the tavern in the course of her work as a weaver; Samuel Ayres's account includes charges for his wife's mug of flip and a mess of oats for her horse; and Jemima Parker Brace from time to time charged drinks to the account of her husband, woodworker William Brace.[14] Innkeeping also differed from other kinds of women's work in that it was closely associated with—and regulated by—the state.[15] Licenses to sell liquor drew distinctions based on volume, granting permission to some to sell by the glass and others to sell in bulk. Just as today, when restaurant owners may not sell wine by the case, and liquor store clerks can't sell it by the glass, so too were early American businesses monitored based on the size and intent of their operations.

Regulatory Contexts

The sale and consumption of alcoholic beverages in Massachusetts had been monitored closely since the founding of the colony. As early as 1633, Massachusetts Bay innkeepers were required to obtain licenses from the governor, and display "some inoffensive sign obvious for direction to strangers."[16] A body of law emerged to govern the hours taverns kept, the prices they charged, and the clientele they could serve. In time, the Massachusetts Court of General Sessions regulated liquor sales by establishing two categories of licenses: innholders were to be "furnished with suitable provisions and lodging for the refreshment and entertainment of strangers and travelers," and have pasture, stables, hay and provender for horses, while retailers were allowed to sell spirituous liquor for consumption "out of doors," meaning off premises, and were prohibited from selling wine or strong liquor in quantities less than a quarter cask. In other words, innkeepers sold beverages by the glass; retailers sold liquor in bulk.

Following the Revolution, that body of laws was reasserted. Chapter 68 of the legislation passed in 1786–87 set forth the policies required by the "due regulation of licensed houses." As we've already seen, "no person whosoever, may presume to be a common Victualler, innholder, taverner, or seller of wine, beer, ale, cider, brandy, rum, or any strong liquors, by retail, or in a less quantity than twenty-eight gallons," without a license from the county Justices of the Peace; any person who was found selling "spirituous liquors, or any mixed liquors, part of which is spirituous, without license" duly obtained, would face hefty penalties—twenty pounds for operating without a license, between two pounds and six pounds for other offenses. Vendors had to reapply for the licenses each year, giving their town's selectmen—who provided applicants a certificate attesting to their approval, which the applicant then submitted to the county court—the opportunity to review their ability to run a respectable public house. The law stipulated that "no license be renewed, to any person who shall have been before licensed, against whom any presentment, complaint, or information shall be made for misrule or disorder in such House, or for not being suitably provided as the Law in such case requires, to entertain strangers and travelers at bed and board," before a decision concerning the matter had been rendered by the court.

In part, the licensing process allowed local government to control the amount of alcohol available in the community; they had the authority to determine when and where such an establishment was genuinely wanted and needed, by a neighborhood or along a route of travel, and when an additional tavern would generate unwanted competition, or meant that too much alcohol would flow through too small a place. For tavernkeepers, the licensing process had the effect of regulating competition: when women like Mary Trainer kept taverns off the books, they undercut the market available to licensed innkeepers like Elizabeth Newton, who was trying to earn a living just down the road.

The requirement that applicants be able to "suitably" accommodate their clientele also had the effect of limiting competition, since furnishing the required elements to host travelers and their horses created thresholds not all aspiring innkeepers could easily meet. A "board or sign affixed to his or her house" (note that the law specifically acknowledged female applicants) must be visible at all times in some "conspicuous place near the same, with his or her name at large thereon." Proprietors were not to allow gambling of any kind, including "dice, cards, bowls, billiards, quoits, or any other implements" used in games of chance, and they were not to allow any "dancing, or reveling." Allowing a patron to become drunk commanded a fine of twenty shillings. The law further enabled the justices to assess the number of taverns and inns really needed in a given locality, and to refuse the granting of additional licenses when they judged the number sufficient, "the better to prevent intemperance," and to limit the potential growth of "nurseries of vice and debauchery."

The courts took these provisions seriously. In order to obtain and retain the license that allowed them to operate legally, innkeepers whether male or female had to demonstrate that they could keep good order despite the inevitable effects alcohol would have on their patrons. This made tavernkeepers the first line of enforcement for a variety of laws intended to shape society across the Commonwealth along Protestant preferences. Innkeepers, for instance, could lose their license if they allowed patrons to drink to excess or permit minors or servants to "sit drinking" without permission.[17] Activities that often accompanied inebriated revelry (gaming, backgammon, dice, and so forth) were clearly disallowed; proprietors who allowed these amusements to take place under their roofs risked their licenses. They were also required to turn some patrons away: after 1693, Massachusetts law forbade the serving of enslaved people, and by the mid-eighteenth century, that law had been expanded to include men and women of African descent as well (when selectmen objected to Mary Trainer's house of "ill fame," it may have been at least as much a response to mixed-race sociability as any sort of sexual misconduct, but clearly the town's African and native populations, formally excluded from white establishments, also needed such places to congregate).[18] Of course many of these laws were enforced selectively, but if a crowd got rowdy, it could become an issue for the proprietors of an establishment. When Tryphena Newton Cook took a swing at her aggressive patron, she was demonstrating to any and all observers her ability to meet the expectations the family's license demanded.

Infractions were a real threat, since they could result in the loss of one's livelihood. In 1782, for instance, Hatfield tavernkeeper Lucy Stearns Hubbard (just across the Connecticut River from Hadley, north of Cook's ferry crossing) had been running her tavern for many years, but that fall "did willingly and unlawfully with force and arms" sell "by retail" half a pint of rum (Hubbard of course did not literally force a sale at gunpoint—this phrase was part of the standard language of such documents), which was "then and there contained in one bowl of punch to one Benjamin Prescott" without the appropriate license. The suit further noted that she had also sold privately a bottle of wine to Obediah Dickinson, "the sd wine being a species of strong liquor and a less quantity than a quarter cask, contrary to law of commonwealth." Hubbard did not dispute the charges, and in return the state punished her for only one of the offenses; for her carelessness, Hubbard paid a fine of two pounds as well as her court costs.[19]

But maintaining order was not always easy, particularly when the offenders were men of local influence. In early nineteenth-century Hadley, gaming became a problem, as a gambling club proved irresistible to townsmen. Elizabeth Porter Phelps reported to her daughter that concern over this gambling club—"many of them are married men"—had come to the pulpit, when one husband, who had begun staying out all night, had missed the birth of his child, his wife having suffered a "sore travail" in his absence. When the community of women around her voiced their displeasure, he retreated again to the gambling club for the next day and night. Another mother told Phelps that "she had three sons in the club," but none of them—unsurprisingly—had been in church to hear the sermon in question. "This town has got to be very loose," Phelps opined. But what could be done? Because, as Phelps added, "there was a tavernkeeper said the other day 'how can I prevent gambling in my house . . . they are some of the best men and some of the first characters in town?'"[20]

If tavern-keeping men had difficulty preventing unwelcome conduct, one can imagine that challenge of their female counterparts to be still greater, though women were routinely granted licenses. Several historians have noted the relationship between tavernkeeping and widowhood. David W. Conroy has suggested that granting permission to sell alcohol can be seen as an effort to provide otherwise-needy women, many of them widows, with a source of income. In 1771, he finds, one in five Boston taverns was operated by a woman, while Anne Lanning also notes the preponderance of tavern-keeping women who took over a license awarded to a now dead spouse.[21] In the Hadley village of Hockanum, Zadoc Lyman kept a public house for seven years; the year after his death, his thirty-year-old widow, Sarah Clark Lyman, was subsequently licensed.[22] In Northampton, Jemima Sheldon Lyman continued to operate her family's tavern after the death of her husband William.[23] When Hatfield's Lucy Hubbard obtained a license to be an "innholder and retailer," it was in the "house lately improved for that purpose by her late husband Elisha."[24] After Lucy and Elisha decided to open a public house, Elisha renovated their center-chimney Georgian house to make it more comfortable in its new role. But just a few years later, in 1768, Elisha died at the age of forty-seven, leaving his forty-one-year-old widow and their seven children (ranging in age from four to eighteen) to continue on alone. Lucy Hubbard would go on to operate a highly successful tavern in the 1760s, 1770s, and early 1780s, in the substantial building that still stands along Hatfield's Elm Street.[25]

But Hubbard did not step into a role created or defined by her spouse; rather, it is likelier that he stepped into one informed by his wife. Lucy Stearns Hubbard grew up in the well-known Worcester tavern managed for five decades by her parents, Thomas and Mary Jennison Stearns: the Kings Arms—licensed to Thomas for forty years, and to Mary the dozen following his death.[26] Lucy Hubbard was surely undaunted by the prospect of running the tavern alone after the death of her husband, as she had watched her own mother do before her. Such stories remind us that the relationship between women's work and marriage is complex. The "Hubbard" tavern illustrates how tavernkeeping, like other occupations, was associated with particular families, and was in turn embedded in the identity of any family business, from carpentry to the clergy.[27] Across many communities, local taverns became rooted in sprawling networks of multigenerational kin relations as the daughters of some licensed keepers became the wives of others.

Throughout Hampshire County, taverns were linked by wives, sisters, mothers, and daughters who brought their own skills and experience to new settings. A series of Hampshire County licenses illuminate one family's tavern-keeping tradition. Through most of the 1720s, Mehuman Hinsdale kept the first licensed tavern on the Deerfield Street. Samuel Hinsdale was granted his own licenses in the late 1740s, and Samuel's nephew John Hinsdale (Mehuman Hinsdale's grandson) during the mid-1750s.[28] Samuel's sons Ariel and Samuel II also embraced the family business, and married into another family of tavernkeepers, the Severances. Joseph Severance was a local taverner whose wife and three sisters each headed innkeeping families. Joseph's wife, Mercy Allen, was the daughter of Amos Allen, who moved to Greenfield in 1766 and received tavern licenses for several years. Mercy and Joseph Severance later kept a tavern, also in Greenfield, at the home built by Mercy's parents. In 1771, Samuel Hinsdale had transferred his property to his sons Samuel II and Ariel, a gesture that cleared the men's way to marry: Ariel wed Thankful Severance in 1774, a marriage that allied the Hinsdales with other tavern owners in the Severance, Allen, and Wells families. About 1780, Ebenezer Wells Jr. built a home approximately one-quarter mile south of the Hinsdale property. Wells passed the tavern to his sons Reuban and Elisha in 1795. Elisha married Tirzah Severance (b. 1764), while Reuban married Tirzah's sister Experience (b. 1756). The marriages of three Severance sisters to men in the Wells and Hinsdale families established and affirmed a network of local taverns and tavern-keeping families who served households and travelers across the Greenfield meadows.

Geographies of Hospitality

Between 1760 and 1810, more than a dozen individuals were licensed as Hadley innkeepers, though in some cases these were multigenerational households, as widows, sons, and sons-in-law succeeded parents in the tavern trade. Several families—each serving a distinct neighborhood within the town as well as travelers passing along main transportation routes—had particular staying power, appearing on the rolls of licensed "innkeepers, taverners and common victuallers" for two or three decades, or even longer (figure 6.1).[29] The Lyman family, including Ebenezer and Mindwell Lyman Pomeroy, for many years anchored the hospitality trade in this small settlement across the river from Northampton and just north of the range that separated Hadley from South Hadley. Nathaniel and Sarah Stockwell White kept a tavern on the south side of Bay Road, southeast of Hadley Center, beginning as early as 1770 and persisting into the early nineteenth century.[30] Members of the Kellogg family catered to travelers near the south end of the town common, where Bay Road leads south and east and a ferry to Northampton crossed the Connecticut; Stephen and Joanna Kellogg Goodman would remain at this site into the 1810s.[31] From the early 1780s into the 1810s, Lemuel and Dorothy Phelps Warner also kept an inn at the south end of the town common, not far from the Kellogg/Goodman site.[32] Elisha and Martha Dickinson Cook hosted travelers in their home on the common, about a half-mile north of the Warners, just below where Russell Street would in time cross the common on an increasingly influential east-west road. Oliver Dickinson ran a tavern on the road leading northwest from Amherst, crossing through Hadley on its way to Sunderland.[33] Major John Smith and Ben Smith kept taverns in North Hadley and Hadley Center from the 1790s into the early nineteenth century.[34] Elizabeth Newton and family, situated along the northern bend in the Connecticut River separating Hadley from Hatfield to the north, served travelers heading north by the river road, or to Hatfield via the ferry. And in North Hadley, David and Sarah Allis Stockbridge were longtime licensed innkeepers into the early nineteenth century.[35]

Hadley's public houses—distributed across the landscape as they were—were situated on major circulation routes, but they also served distinct neighborhood clienteles. An advertisement for a tavern in nearby Petersham conveys a sense of a profitable compass when it notes for prospective buyers that that "there is not a Tavern within five miles of said house on way, nor within three miles another."[36] In rural western Massachusetts, whether a customer hailed from the neighborhood mattered: one tavern charged stage travelers 25 percent more for meals than it did locals. Northampton's Polly Pomeroy remembered that her parents charged for a meal one-and-a-half times or even twice what they charged for lodging, and that once the stage began to stop there, the price of a meal went up by another 50 percent.[37] Taverns, then, were places where insiders were distinguished from outsiders, and one could count on running into neighbors, family, and friends. Put another way, public houses and the women who ran them helped construct the social landscape of Hadley, as a place within larger regional and global geographies, and as a town of distinct neighborhoods.

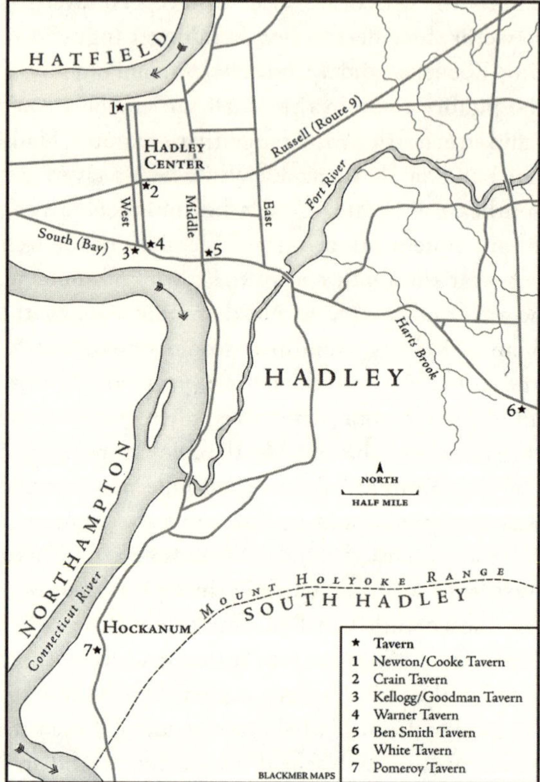

Figure 6.1 Taverns in Hadley. Locations of licensed taverns in Hadley Center and the village of Hockanum suggests the distribution of public houses in and around the town common and in the neighborhoods of Hockanum and Hartsbrook. Other establishments served North Hadley and neighborhoods between Hadley and Sunderland to the north, and Amherst to the east. Map by Kate Blackmer

Because taverns were the scenes of such a wide range of events, from festive entertainments to political assemblies to legal proceedings, the women who worked in them found themselves at the center of public life in ways that set them apart from their counterparts around town.[38] Taverns might shelter town meeting and serve as venues for gatherings of the county court; they were places where the business of political and economic authority was transacted.[39] Taverns were also venues for entertainment, from singing and dancing schools to traveling exhibitions—like the performance on the "slack wire" that visitors to Hadley's Warner tavern were treated to in spring 1784, or the "learned pig," whose apparent ability to read, spell, tell the time of day, and guess playing cards brightened the winter of 1798.[40] Public houses also provided venues for exhibitions like those that sustained itinerant artist Sally Rogers in the face of significant physical challenges. Taverns also proved natural nodes on a large system of outwork, since stagecoaches delivering and receiving materials could easily meet their workforce there.[41]

Taverns were also often the place that newspapers were delivered and read, and the site where both stagecoaches and post riders arrived, making them key junctions in information systems.[42] Generally sited along main arteries of travel—along market roads linking towns, at significant crossroads, and near ferry landings—public houses were points of entry to the communities they served. Their occupants were often the first to see out-of-town papers, the first to hear out-of-town news. Like many small-town watering holes today, conversation at the local public house was how people kept abreast of local events; many years later, Maria Porter Woodward would recall her father Eleazer walking every day to Elisha and Martha Cook's tavern along the town common "to see people and hear the news."[43] While midwives had access to a family's most intimate moments and rooms, and gown makers worked in private spaces to help consumers craft public personas, of the many occupations available to women in eighteenth-century rural New England innkeeping may well have had the highest public profile, as women whose families kept public houses were closer to the pulse of public life than many of their counterparts in other occupations around town.[44] The account book of Mindwell and Ebenezer Pomeroy suggests something of the extent of their enterprise. Some 230 men appear in the pages of their account book, many more than populated the small neighborhood. Of these, about 27 percent are noted as having come from "elsewhere."[45] Occasionally a man is noted as being from "Hadley," but the majority of entries carry no such identifier, suggesting that they are more or less local customers; other men are described as being from nearby Northampton, South Hadley (almost half), Belchertown (known then as Cold Spring), Amherst, Granby, Northfield, Pelham, Springfield, and Sunderland. But customers came, too, from Windsor, Tolland, Hartford, and Lebanon in Connecticut, and from points north too—towns in New Hampshire, New York, and Vermont. From her place behind the bar, Mindwell Pomeroy's view extended some seventy-five miles in any direction.[46]

Over time, new patterns of travel meant that serving travelers and overnight guests became increasingly important. Beginning in the mid-1790s, turnpike development across Massachusetts facilitated overland travel. Towns adjacent to Hadley became connected early on: the Third Massachusetts Turnpike, between Northampton and Pittsfield forty miles west, opened in 1797; the Sixth, linking Amherst to Shrewsbury about sixty miles east, opened in 1799.[47] In Hadley, situated between Amherst and Northampton, pressure on east-west travel would eventually alter the way people moved through the town, changes that would advantage some families and disadvantage others. In 1803, work commenced on a bridge that crossed from Hadley to Northampton, drawing travelers toward the inns at the south end of the town common and Bay Road. What was likely something of a windfall for the Goodmans, Lymans, and Whites was a setback for the Newton/Cook household, and possibly for others north and south as well, as public houses at ferry crossings over time lost out to bridge traffic.[48] Gradually, east-west patterns of circulation would overtake the north-south movement that had characterized Hadley from its founding, bisecting the historic town common and altering the power of place, the relative value and potential of lots rising and falling with their proximity to preferred routes and means of travel.

Mindwell Lyman Pomeroy

Looking closely at two Hadley public houses—those of the Lyman and Pomeroy families in Hockanum, and the Newton/Cook enterprise at the north end of the town common—illuminates differences among rural taverns and the labor women performed to maintain them. The Lymans and Pomeroys quenched the thirst of neighbors and travelers to the south, in the village of Hockanum; the Pomeroys' surviving account book provides a glimpse into the day-to-day, and season-to-season, life in this local public house on the eve of the American Revolution. Nestled between the Holyoke Range and the Connecticut River about three and a half miles south of Hadley Center, Hockanum began to experience European settlement in the mid-eighteenth century when Northampton's John and Abigail Lyman, after a devastating fire that claimed their home and two of their children, decided to rebuild over the river. In exchange for land in Hockanum, the Lymans agreed to build a new road through the meadows. They constructed a home alongside the highway, and brought with them to this new settlement their extended family, including sons Zadoc and Caleb and daughters Mindwell (who would marry Ebenezer Pomeroy III) and Eleanor (who married Stephen Pomeroy, Ebenezer's brother).[49]

The first tavern in the neighborhood was run by Lyman's son Zadoc (1719–1754) and his wife Sarah Clark Lyman (ca. 1724–1795) from the mid-1740s onward; after Zadoc's death in 1754, thirty-year-old Sarah carried on in her widowhood.[50] Son Israel and his wife Rachel would later assume the family business, securing tavern licenses from the early 1780s to the 1810s; Elijah Lyman appears briefly in these rolls as well. A surviving account book yields a glimpse into the tavern of the intervening decades.[51] Zadoc Lyman's sister, Mindwell Lyman Pomeroy (1721–1797), together with her husband Ebenezer, built the two-story center-chimney house, still extant, that in time came to include a single-story ell and a two-story wing that was almost as large as the main house itself.[52] Their establishment, the White Horse Tavern, would thrive for some forty years, serving as the center of gravity for the village. In time, the formal role of innkeeper in that neighborhood changed hands again, shifting sites and proprietors, but remaining a family enterprise in a larger sense: Mindwell and Ebenezer's son's family had managed the tavern for a time as their parents advanced in years, but in 1794, still another generation in this family opened a tavern in the house they built just north of the road that led westward to the ferry.[53] The "focus of much social activity" in the neighborhood throughout the Federal era and through the first quarter of the nineteenth century, that latter inn (no longer extant) was enlarged in 1820 and christened "Hockanum's Tavern."[54]

An examination of the account book that tracked Ebenezer and Mindwell's labors in the last half of the eighteenth century yields glimpses of life in the White Horse Tavern, and suggests ways that the business both shaped and reflected Mindwell's position in the community. If the nucleus of the Hockanum settlement was one extended family, the tavern linked them with families throughout town, across the county, and beyond the colony's boundaries. Like the Cook tavern, the Pomeroy's enterprise benefited from its proximity to a ferry. In the latter half of the eighteenth century, travelers southbound to Hartford, New Haven, and elsewhere, or northbound to Vermont and northern Hampshire County crossed the Connecticut at Hockanum and made their way along the path on the east side of the river, channeling traffic right past the Pomeroy enterprise. But most of the inn's customers were drawn from surrounding towns; the same faces appeared in the taproom week after week, month after month, and year after year.

Archaeologists Diana Rockman and Nan Rothschild, having compared excavations at a range of tavern sites, posit that rural taverns in the eighteenth century were comparatively unspecialized operations; while their urban counterparts focused on their role as public gathering places, rural public houses served as sources of meals and refreshment for local and long-distance travelers as much as or more than they were places of assembly.[55] As we shall see, particularly beginning in the 1790s, some Hadley taverns made significant investments in ballrooms and assembly spaces, building specialized structures to court this kind of business and clientele. But the White Horse Tavern, predating this development by several decades, served men on the move along the river. And so it was primarily labor in and around food preparation and service that occupied women like Mindwell Pomeroy, hired women Desire Kentfield and Hannah Henry, and presumably Mindwell's several daughters, and that work was steady and hard: food and drink had to be produced, acquired, processed; meals were prepared and served; pots, plates, platters, mugs, bowls, and other serving vessels were washed and put away.

The Pomeroy kitchen served breakfast, dinner, and supper as well as "victuals" to both passersby and overnight visitors. Most often, the tavern served "dinner" (that is, the midday meal) and "victuals." Dinner might include meat or fish with vegetables; "victuals" might mean a cold plate.[56] Overnight lodgers needed breakfast (typically bread and milk or cider, though possibly a "hasty pudding" made with milk or molasses) and sometimes supper. The range of beverages that accompanied these meals was fairly wide. At her Hatfield tavern Lucy Hubbard served "sangaree," usually wine that had been sweetened and served garnished with nutmeg.[57] Customers elsewhere ordered egg pop (beer, cider, brandy, or wine mixed with eggs and sugar) or methiglen (wine, honey water, and spices).[58] Far and away the most common charge was for New England or West Indian rum by the quart, pint, half-pint, and gill (that is, around four or five ounces). Flip (a beverage made from beer, sweeteners, and rum, and sometimes eggs, and then heated with a hot iron in order to create the burnt, bitter taste period palettes desired) by the mug and short mug were also among the most popular choices, while many visitors ordered a "dram," "bitter dram," or a "cherry dram."[59] Mugs of cider were not uncommon—though they were less popular, at least at the White Horse in the third quarter of the eighteenth century, than popular historical imagination would suggest. Demand for bowls and short bowls of lemon, cherry, and egg punch was also steady if comparatively modest. The occasional posset and milk toddy (that is, a spiced hot milk curdled with ale, wine, or some other fermented beverage) were on offer as well. The recipes for such offerings, and the ability to source the required ingredients, constituted an important body of knowledge among tavern-keeping women.

The Pomeroy tavern served a wide range of customers—mainly farmers and craftsmen from Hadley and Northampton, as well as their hired men. For instance, Elijah Alvord's account regularly included entries in which he is charged for "a short mug of stif flip" and "lodging him and his man," as well as a "gil of rum and eating some victuals in the morning." On another occasion Alvord paid for his "man Moore and several other hands," including punch and "ten meals of victuals and lodging for five men," while other entries routinely note dinner and drams for Alvord's "log men" and "raft man."[60] John Hunt was billed for "three meals of victuals and lodging one night" (though no alcohol) for his "negro," though Dr. Kellogg paid for a gill of rum "by your negro"; although customers of color were uncommon in the Pomeroy's enterprise, they were apparently served.[61]

The lodging of Alvord's crew underscores the set of tasks associated not with the provision of food and drink, but rather the work of hosting overnight guests. The range of comfort accorded guests in New England's eighteenth-century taverns is well understood—travelers discussed with regularity the sometimes-shocking circumstances endured on the road. And yet, very little is known about the quality of lodging in western Massachusetts in the last half of the eighteenth century, though the Pomeroy account book hints at the work. Charges like that for joiner William Brace's time and talent building a trundle bed suggest how the Pomeroys may have accommodated guests.[62] Usually it was an individual lodger or an account holder together with his hired man who lodged for a night or two, but when as many as four or five men pulled up at the tavern in need of a night's shelter, the Pomeroy women produced sheets, pillows and pillowcases, blankets, and other textiles associated with sleep.[63] To the work of the kitchen, then, the family added the washing of bed linens, and the preparation of beds; implicit as well were the preparation and maintenance of mattresses, pillows, and other necessary objects.

Perhaps Ebenezer Pomeroy himself labored in his family's tavern, but it is likelier that he was out in his fields carrying on the work of the farm while Mindwell and their daughters managed the public house. When the county court granted its first license to Ebenezer and Mindwell Pomeroy, the couple had six daughters eleven years old and younger; all but toddler Mindwell likely contributed to the work of the inn and the farm that supported it. In fact, hired women Desire Kentfield and Hannah Henry appear in the Pomeroy ledger only in accounts dating from the 1750s, suggesting that female hired help became less necessary as the Pomeroy daughters grew older and more capable.

Some small glimpse into the labors of tavern-keeping daughters can be found in the recollections of Polly Pomeroy, whose parents kept a tavern on the Northampton side of the Connecticut River (Polly's father Asahel was Ebenezer's cousin), and in those of Sarah Amsden, whose parents Aaron and Sarah Morton Graves kept a tavern about eighteen miles southeast of Hadley, in Palmer, Massachusetts. Both women, as they looked back years later, remembered snippets of what amounted to girlhood apprenticeships in the family trade—a reminder that children were at work in these spaces. Amsden, for instance, recalled making the flip that her family's tavern served; the flip iron, she added, was "always hot on the coals in cold weather."[64] Polly Pomeroy worked in her family's business from her childhood to her mid-twenties. When asked, forty years later, to reflect on life at the tavern, what leapt to mind were pieces of beef roasting over the fire on a jack. An elaborate system of weights and pulleys turned the meat, and her job was to trot downstairs and wind up the apparatus with a key. She also remembered the white sand brought to cover the tavern floors; swept into appealing patterns, the sand absorbed dirt and grease, and when it was swept away, left a cleaner floor behind.[65] In Sunderland, the daughter of innkeeper Jerusha Smith Leonard—also named Jerusha— sometimes had sole responsibility for the work of the tavern, left to manage when everyone else was called away.[66] But for twenty-two-year-old Jerusha, the constant stream of guests, as well as visits of "young people" and "young fellows" from Sunderland and surrounding towns, "company from Hadley," and area "schollars" seems to have had their pleasures as well.[67]

Provisioning Northampton's Pomeroy tavern (as well as the household), Polly recalled, fell to her mother, Miriam Clapp Pomeroy, who placed orders with men traveling to Boston or Springfield, or sometimes made the trip herself in the family's chaise.[68] Writing about the advent of butchers to Hampshire County, Sylvester Judd records that "meat was occasionally brought to Hadley in panniers or baskets, from Pelham and other towns, and sold to innkeepers and a few others."[69] In Hampshire County, and in Hadley in particular, local shopkeepers courted the business of neighboring innkeepers like these. When Joshua Leonard opened his new bakery at the south end of the Hadley Common, he tapped the advertising columns of the *Hampshire Gazette* to assure "merchants or Tavern keepers" that they "may be supplied with barrels or cases of New Bread, put up in the best order"; moreover, "no payment will be required until it is all sold."[70] Other merchants also underscored goods of interest to area innkeepers. Eleazer Porter, having noted the availability, at his shop, of both St. Croix and New England rum, as well as "Holland, Geneva, Molasses, Loaf, and Brown Sugars," Port, Sherry, London Porter, and wines from Lisbon and Malaga, as well as cod, rice, and salt, added that he offered a "liberal deduction from retail prices" to "tavern-keepers, and others, in proportion to the quantity they may purchase.[71] Chileab Smith & Co. likewise invited "tavern-keepers and other gentlemen" to consider their stock of sweet rum and brandy as well as loaf and brown sugars.[72] Around Hadley, Nathan Seymour, John Hopkins, Windsor and Erastus Smith, and Lewis Williams and Nathaniel Coolidge—each of these Hadley shopkeepers competed specifically for business from the area's tavernkeeping families.[73]

Obtaining provisions also drew innkeeping women into relationships with families across the community. They acquired agricultural products from neighborhood sources, which encompassed local growers as well as importers. Of these more than two hundred names in the Pomeroy tavern's ledger, only a handful are women, and all but a few of the women whose names do appear— hired women Kentfield and Henry, cloth maker Esther Alexander, and neighbor Elizabeth Clark Queen—are members of the Pomeroy family. Kentfield and Henry's contributions were principally their labor, but other women also supplied the public house—and the private house of the innkeeping family. After Hugh Queen died, for instance, Elizabeth Queen continued to trade with the household, supplying winter apples and on at least one occasion twenty "fowl" to offset her debts for both West Indian and New England rum from the Pomeroys—by the quart, half-pint, and gill.[74] Pelham weaver Esther Alexander provided yards of cloth, presumably for both household textiles and apparel. Alexander wove tow cloth as well as checked, streaked, and fine linen, in batches as small as seven yards, but more often closer to twenty. The Pomeroys paid her in bushels of rye and malt; pounds of tobacco, beef, and pork; and rum by the quart, as well as the occasional gill.[75] Jemima Parker Brace—wife of woodworker William Brace—also seems to have woven for the Pomeroy household, producing yards of woolen shirting and also a rag rug.[76] A number of unnamed and unknown women are implicit in the Pomeroy accounts, in columns crediting men like John Hilyard, Stephen Fairfield, and Moses Taylor for spinning.[77]

Much of this cloth making served the needs of the Pomeroy family, but some may also have been prompted by the particular demands of tavernkeeping; for instance, Abigail Fairfield or one of her stepdaughters likely produced the fifteen and a half yards of table linen and other textiles for which Stephen Fairfield was credited in the early 1760s, and Martha Ayres perhaps wove the thirteen yards of bedtick credited to her husband Samuel's account.[78] Given the need to provide beds and bedding for unknown travelers, Mindwell must have had an ample number of sheets and blankets on hand, cleaned, and in good repair—supplies produced by the spinners and weavers responsible for the textile and the domestic labor required for their maintenance.

The Pomeroys apparently produced much of the food they needed right on their farm, and the women of the household are implicated in these transactions, particularly in those surrounding the work of the dairy. Like Elizabeth Porter Phelps, Mindwell Pomeroy and her daughters produced butter and cheese to be consumed by the family and sold by the pound (in fact, by the dozens of pounds), but also to be served with bread in the taproom, and likely as part of other meals as well.[79] The beverages sold also required ingredients that were sourced locally; for instance, the wild cherry found on the slopes of the nearby Holyoke Range may have flavored the punch and rum served by the Pomeroys.[80] Meanwhile, sister Eleanor Pomeroy provided the all-important hops.[81]

Brewing has become an object lesson among students of women's history, one of the early examples of women being boxed out of an occupation that they had once dominated after its profit potential became clear, and the work became centralized and commercialized.[82] James McWilliams has found that women in the Massachusetts Bay Colony retained some control over brewing longer than their counterparts in England; nevertheless, while some 58 percent of households at mid-century owned brewing tools, by the last quarter of the seventeenth century that number had plummeted to 21 percent.[83] In time, brewing joined a number of other occupations that responded to pressure with divided and specialized skills, and gender divisions of labor that over time favored male producers.

Many tavern-keeping households, however, continued to make their own cider from fruit grown locally; some dedicated a corner of land for raising barley for malt beer. The need to process the barley into malt created demand in Hadley for a malthouse, which served local households and taverns from the town's very beginning. Malting, in which grains were specially prepared to release their sugars, was a specialization apart from brewing itself. The earliest Hadley malthouse was owned by John Barnard, who died in 1664; he had had a malthouse in Wethersfield, Connecticut, before moving northward, and he brought his skills and equipment with him. In the long run, more significant were the maltsters of the Warner family. Andrew Warner bought Barnard's malthouse, but was perhaps inexperienced with the kiln: as early as 1665, it was destroyed by fire. Warner then built a second malt-works for himself, and his son Jacob succeeded him in the trade. By the time the Newton and Cook women were learning their way around a barroom, Orange Warner was the fourth generation in that family to run a malthouse, deploying some 130 years of accumulated experience and specialized knowledge with the help of his wife Elizabeth Graves Warner, as well as their several children and laborers.[84]

In the Warner family's malthouse, a vat or cistern at one end held the barley while it soaked for two or three days. Because bacteria in the husk would begin to ferment (and so sour the process) the maltster (or members of his household) had to change the water periodically. After the grain had moistened appropriately, the vat was drained and the grain allowed to sit for six to ten hours. The barley was then moved to the malthouse floor, where it began to germinate. In order to keep oxygen flowing smoothly through the grains, the "piece," at it was known, was turned regularly with wooden shovels. Over the course of six to ten days, the maltster and his helpers moved the barley across to a kiln or oven, where the grains were dried—carefully and incrementally. This curing process determined the eventual color and flavor the resulting beer would take.

Families retrieved the processed barley, or malt, and combined it with their own hops and other ingredients to make beer. About the turn of the nineteenth century, Sylvester Judd learned from his interviews around the community that "beer was generally brewed once a week; malt, hops, dried pumpkin, dried apple parings, and sometimes rye bran, birch twigs and other things, were put into the brewing kettle, and the liquor was strained through a sieve." "This beer was used at home," he added, "and was carried into the meadows by the farmers."[85] Sophia Cook Clark—who grew up in and around the tavern of her uncle and aunt, innkeepers Elisha and Martha Cook—added that from time to time travelers brought jugs full of yeast to Hadley from Warehouse Point in Connecticut. Once or twice a week, she further reported, beer was "carried into the meadow [and] brewed in a great brass kettle, and strained into a large tub," the sieve placed "on a little ladder laid across the tub."[86]

Mindwell Pomeroy, like Sophia Cook Clark and other Hadley women in hospitality work, stood at one intersection (among many) in dense local, regional, and international networks of labor and commerce. Through the meals and beverages served, as well as the bodies (of travelers and of workers) that consumed them, the taproom and lodging spaces of the White Horse Tavern were deeply embedded in complex, overlapping systems that tied together the small neighborhood at Hockanum with regional markets in lumber and other materials passing along the commercial artery that was the Connecticut River, and global markets for rum, sugar, and other commodities. At the same time, the gravitational force of the Pomeroys' enterprise embedded the household in long-standing relationships, both reciprocal and uneven, with local families who provided necessary labor and provisions.

Elizabeth Fairchild Newton

The Newtons were among those families who migrated westward with each generation, ever in search of new opportunities. Francis's father, Phineas, had been born in Marlboro, Massachusetts, as was his mother, Patience Howe. Phineas and Patience moved out to Leicester, where Francis was born, in 1731. When Francis married Elizabeth Fairchild in 1753, the two were living in Belchertown. By about 1760, the couple had moved, first to South Hadley and eventually to Hadley, to a house on the north end of the long town common. But house carpenter, joiner, and wheelwright farmer Francis Newton appears never to have found the success he may have been seeking. In 1770, when he was just shy of his fortieth birthday, his estate was valued at only twenty-nine pounds and eight shillings, notably less than the town median of fifty-two pounds and well beneath the town average of seventy pounds.[87] The family's circumstances over the next several years are difficult to puzzle out, but by the end of the decade the Newtons seem to have been searching for some new ways to augment the meager income derived from Francis's woodworking. Their daughters were in a position to contribute to household fortunes through their sewing skills, and a loom, three flax, and two great wheels allowed the women of the household to gain income from textile production. But with neither the means to purchase farm acreage nor the familial labor to farm it, the Newtons looked to other sources to support the household. In 1778 the family began innkeeping.[88] Elizabeth's oldest daughter, Betty, was about seventeen—old enough to be of real help in the enterprise. The family's three other daughters were younger, but likely old enough to have been of some assistance as well— the youngest, Sally, being about nine years old. Little Francis Jr. was just four years old.[89]

The Newton public house, at least in the 1780s, must have been a fairly modest affair, since their home doesn't appear to have been overly large or supplied beyond the needs of their family of seven. The house contained three beds, and a fourth bedstead; three tables and ten chairs were all that were present through the house. The amount of tableware—slightly more than the Newtons would need for themselves—is the only possible hint that hospitality work may have been occurring: the kitchen held seventeen plates, ten sets of knives and forks, two sets of tea dishes, "sundry items of puter and tin," some woodenware and earthenware, and seven basins, as well as a punch bowl.[90] Yet, in the 1780s and 90s, Hadley residents were attending auctions at "the house of Mrs Newton, Innholder at Hadley," events advertised in the columns of area newspapers.[91]

When Francis Newton died in April 1781, he was insolvent.[92] Elizabeth struggled to settle the debt-ridden estate, petitioning the courts for permission to sell some of the couple's real estate in order to raise funds.[93] Judge Eleazer Porter observed Newton's dower rights, preserving for her use "the south lower room of the great house, and the whole of the kitchen & south half of the cellar, and the whole of the barn"; the lot carved out for her use would contain about three acres.[94] As the estate made its way through probate, Newton appealed to the court to retain some of her household goods, and was allowed beds, linens, a chest of drawers, and the minimum kitchen equipment—as well as a foot wheel and a great wheel, to enable her to continue to spin both flax and wool.[95] That the court did not choose to include the loom that was present in the household is intriguing, since it surely would have been a valuable asset to this household full of women in the wake of Francis's death.

The widow Newton's effort to keep her family afloat reminds us that "occupation" in this place and time is better understood as activity in which one was engaged than a fixed vocation or identity. When the Court of General Sessions of the Peace convened in Springfield four months after Francis's death, Elizabeth was granted the same innholders' license once granted Francis—the only woman among the six innholders and ten retailers listed for the town that year. But the Newton women also continued to sew for the Phelps family at Forty Acres, and likely others as well. Though Newton had been sewing for the Phelps household since at least 1779 (and was sewing for others by 1771, when Josiah Pierce paid her four shillings six pence for making a coat), her work at tailoring increased its pace in the early 1780s, as she adjusted to widowhood, and while she continued to maintain her husband's tavern license.[96] The spring of 1783, for instance, proved an especially hurried season for the Phelpses and the Newtons. In late January, Phelps notes that "Easter" and Betty Newton had come "to taylor" and that they returned again in March and April, and twice in May.[97] In these weeks, Elizabeth Phelps was planning a trip to Boston, while her daughters Betsy and Thankful were preparing to attend school in Amherst, events that could account for the extra attention to their apparel, but more likely it was the spring work of the farm together with the declining health of her slave girl Phillis that kept Phelps from her own sewing. In early April, the household began to make soap, and the following week Lucy Marshall arrived to begin weaving; at the same time, Phelps sent for Phillis's grandmother, Peg, to help care for the weakening child. The same weeks that saw repeated visits of the tailoring Newtons found Elizabeth Porter Phelps anxiously attending to the young girl. Phillis finally died on the last day of April 1783, and was laid to rest at a funeral at Colonel Porter's house on the town common. The Newtons arrived to tailor the next day.[98] The specific nature of their skills or services is rarely described, though a summer reference to Phelps traveling to "Mrs Newtons" to "make a pair of Breeches for my husband" yields some glimpse into the work.[99]

But despite her skills with needles, wheels, and looms, in 1781 Elizabeth Newton also took out the first license in her own name as an innkeeper, and she continued to receive licenses for twenty years, until 1810. Newton, like the others offered licenses, pledged "to keep good rule and order in her house & duly observe the laws made up for the regulation of such houses & also to keep & render the accounts and pay the duties the law requires."[100] But no sooner had Newton gotten her own feet under her than change came to her small family: in 1783, her daughters Betty and Eleanor both married and moved out. That development may have been challenging for Elizabeth, or it may have been a blessing, as Betty married Moses Kellogg Jr., whose father Moses had also received innkeeping licenses for many years. Perhaps mother and daughter were able to support each other in this work, as Betty learned the ins and outs of the trade from this longtime innkeeping family.

For fifteen years Newton appears to have run the tavern out of the home that she had shared with her husband. Couples like the Newtons secured permission and then opened their homes as stopping places, often with little change to the building itself. Families looking to enter this field needed only to acquire some basic items—including perhaps the long tables and benches that were a tavern's hallmarks.[101] Lucy Hubbard's Hatfield tavern was well appointed for its guests. Its rooms contained a wide variety of objects: thirty chairs; a large tavern table; four tables of varying sizes and shapes; seven chests (some with drawers); one gilt mirror and three plain; a variety of earthen and china dishes, knives and forks, wine decanters, pint- and quart-sized bowls; numerous bedsteads; and two sets of bed curtains, one red and white and the other green. A corner cupboard decorated with vine carvings in the parlor offered Hubbard the chance to display imported teaware, especially the "sett of burnt china [Chinese export porcelain] and saucers."[102] Hadley's Kellogg tavern also contained the familiar "long table" as well as some twenty chairs, variously described as "great," "flag bottomed," "skin bottomed," and "bark bottom." The inn's hearth boasted ten meat roasters.[103]

Francis and Elizabeth Newton appear to have begun under modest circumstances, but in time Newton and her family made a significant investment in tavernkeeping. In 1795 Andrew Cooke purchased property on the west side of West Street, and the new house—purpose-built to accommodate tavern life—arose not long thereafter. The substantial, two-story, five-by-four-bay Federal-style house located on the banks of the Connecticut River proved a convenient stopping place for men and women traveling by ferry over the river, often guided by Solomon himself (likely his main contribution).[104] The southeast room housed the bar, a door on the south facade providing direct entry into the taproom; here, the fluted pilasters and broad architrave of the simple but elegant fireplace surround framed the fire by which visitors would be warmed, while an unstructured space on the second floor could be used for assemblies both festive and functional.[105]

Second-floor ballrooms can be considered within other developments that separated women's work and women workers vertically. As Hadley's public houses grew to contain these comparatively large gathering halls, spaces devoted to food preparation and service, laundry, and other necessary labor would be separated from rooms devoted to more elegant activities above. At the same time, these upper-floor rooms were outfitted with movable partitions, creating flexible spaces that could house large assemblies when needed, while still accommodating separate rooms for lodgers when more intimate rooms were required. In this, the tavern on the north end of the common mirrored its counterpart on the south end built by the Warners, who also elected to build a large gathering space divisible by folding panels into three smaller spaces, allowing this enterprise, too, to profit both from large community events and lodgers.[106] The tavern run by Elisha and Martha Cook in these years, also built in the early 1790s not quite a half-mile up the common from the Warners, adopted the same approach, having "folding doors" that allowed the space to be partitioned into two rooms.[107]

Ballrooms convertible into bedrooms and back into assembly spaces provided a versatility absent from most other buildings in the rural village. Movable partitions like these facilitated gendered needs in lodging (separating women lodgers from men, providing space for couples or families apart from rooms occupied by drovers, and so forth). Maintaining these fluid spaces also meant a certain amount of additional labor for women workers, as mattresses, trundle beds, and bedsteads had to be moved, stored, and replaced; chairs and tables carried in and out; and basins and other items of ceramics and glass washed and restored to place.[108]

In rural towns like Hadley, meeting spaces like these served purposes well beyond those associated with the food and drink on offer by innkeepers; in the 1790s, with Hadley's first town hall yet a half-century away, such spaces provided important community services. Though Hadley routinely opted to hold town meetings in the schoolhouse, that space was not available or suitable for all of the residents' various needs.[109] In other Massachusetts towns, for instance, a number of assembly halls were associated with Masonic lodges; in Sunderland, just north of Hadley, the local Freemasons met in an upper-floor double room.[110] A more common use across the Commonwealth was the dancing school.[111] Young women and men in Hadley traveled to area taverns and assembly halls to participate in the dancing schools that became popular in western Massachusetts, as elsewhere, around the turn of the nineteenth century. Beginning in the mid-1790s, Northampton attracted a series of well-known dancing masters in the Northeast: John Griffiths (who had taught from 1788 through 1792 in Boston, but was well traveled across Connecticut and Rhode Island as well), Henry Paul Nugent ("formerly principal dancer at theaters of Philadelphia and Boston"), and Irishman John C. Devero all opened schools in Northampton, meeting at the taverns of Asahel Pomeroy and others.[112] In addition to schools in Northampton and Amherst, local entrepreneur Asaph Stebbins opened a school in Hadley, in the "assembly hall" of the tavern of Elisha Cook Jr.[113] Stebbins's credentials for such an enterprise are unknown—certainly he was not on par with men like Griffiths, Nugent, or Devero—but dancing schools had gained traction, and one had not yet appeared in Hadley. Both he and the Cooks apparently sensed opportunity.

But these schools were more than an additional revenue stream for the taverns that housed them. Catherine E. Kelly, Richard Bushman, and others have linked dancing schools (along with singing schools and literary societies) with the emergence of the rural middle class; as women mastered minuets and cotillion and country dances, and learned to adopt the codes of behaviors such schools promoted, they practiced the grace and ease that would become associated with middle-class bodies, and constructed new identities as middle-class "ladies."[114] Griffiths's pupils, for instance, also learned "good manners, and that ease and politeness of behavior which never fails to please"; he would publish a book compiling some of these lessons, made available at local booksellers.[115] Pupils could then be reminded not to whisper, laugh loudly, point, swing their arms "awkwardly" (especially on the street), and otherwise exhibit "ill manners."[116] These were lessons embraced across Hampshire County. In Hadley Elizabeth Porter Phelps's daughters Betsy and Thankful were—unsurprisingly—on the leading edge of the new development; they availed themselves of the opportunity to attend Griffiths's school when he traveled through the area in

April 1794, traveling to Pomeroy's hall in Northampton to attend the first such school in the area. What's more, Charles and Elizabeth invited the dancing master to take tea at Forty Acres.[117]

The rise of dancing culture entangles the evolution of the architecture and geography of innkeeping as well as innkeeping women like Newton and Cook with other developments in women's dress and deportment.[118] These new postures of gentility—made possible by Tryphena's right hook—became assets that other young women and their dancing school classmates carried with them at all times, and to all places. Hadley's taverns were venues for the cultivation of new sensibilities, and places where they could be performed and perfected, as in the wake of the schools came a wave of "balls"—again, attended by Betsy and Thankful and their peers (Tryphena implicated if not present)— that allowed students to demonstrate their accomplishments.[119]

Over time, Elizabeth Newton became more than just an occasional employee of Charles and Elizabeth Phelps; instead, they termed her "our friend."[120] Members of the Phelps household attended Newton family weddings and funerals, including the burial of Newton's husband Francis.[121] Phelps also cared for Tryphena in her own time of need. In a small community like Hadley, the distance between families like the Newtons and the Phelpses was not always great, and bonds extended over generations. As young Tryphena became a wife and mother with a family of her own to support, for instance, Elizabeth and Charles concerned themselves with the new household as well. Solomon and Tryphena regularly found themselves financially obligated to Charles and Elizabeth, and so Elizabeth hired Tryphena in order to recoup some of those funds, to provide her with the income she needed to sustain her family, and to maintain between the two households a harmonious and ongoing economic relationship.[122]

Elizabeth Newton's last innkeeping license was granted in 1810. She was seventy-four years old. Tryphena had died in 1805, of cancer; the younger woman was the mother of seven children, and it seems likely that Elizabeth stayed on in her daughter's home to help Solomon raise the children, the youngest of whom, Amanda, was just a toddler.[123] When widow Newton died in April 1820, notices appeared in the pages of the *Columbian Centinel,* the *Boston Daily Advertiser,* the *Boston Repertory,* the *Boston Commercial Gazette,* and the *Boston Recorder,* suggesting that readers and travelers in the Boston papers' compass would want to know of her passing.[124] Her family enterprise would survive her, as the tavern continued to serve its local and transitory communities well into the nineteenth century. Tavernkeeping had supported Elizabeth Newton and her family for years, as the Newtons and later the Cooks parlayed the long-standing and profitable feature of their riverbank location into a larger asset as they observed, embraced, and advanced to advantage rising expectations about middle-class deportment.

Keeping Boarders

Taverns also sometimes functioned as boardinghouses, accepting both short- and longer-term lodgers; in summer and fall 1769, for instance, a boarder lodged at the Pomeroy tavern for some sixteen weeks.[125] But taverns and boardinghouses were also distinct enterprises with different features. Boardinghouses would become, especially in the nineteenth century, a significant occupation for women.[126] But women long before then took in boarders to augment their family's income. Boarding was not limited to inns and public houses; anyone with a little extra room could take in lodgers as a means to generate extra income. When in Litchfield, Connecticut, for instance, Elizabeth Phelps Huntington wrote her mother in Hadley that she had begun taking in boarders—students from Tapping Reeve's celebrated law school—to supplement her husband's ministerial salary; after the Huntingtons relocated to Hadley, and Huntington became mistress of Forty Acres, the farm became a boardinghouse for students attending Hopkins Academy, where Dan Huntington became principal.[127] Hadley's Porter family would hit hard times when a lottery to fund the construction of a bridge failed, leaving Samuel Porter responsible for the debts. It seemed likely, even inevitable to some observers, that he would have to sell all his property in order to satisfy the creditors. But his wife, Lucy Hubbard Porter, and their children struggled to stave off desperation by going without the aid of domestic servants and by taking in boarders. Lucy seemed to be "always in motion, and never sits down but at meals until sunset."[128] Thirty-one-year-old Abigail Porter, who never married, was "a mother in the family," to be "consulted on all occasions." (The "strictest economist" Sarah Porter Hillhouse ever knew, Nabby nevertheless was "without meanness.")[129] For the Porters, the ability to take in lodgers bridged the gap when other means of support failed.

Elizabeth Porter Phelps was a regular lodger in a wide range of New England taverns, inns, and boardinghouses, and so understood the hospitality business from both the inside—in the work of Dorothy Phelps Warner—and as a customer. Her memorandum book mentions nearly fifty places in which she lodged, mainly along roads between Hadley and Boston (and of course in Boston), where the family had a good deal of political, commercial, and familial business, and also on roads leading to Litchfield, Connecticut, where daughter Betsy came to reside. In Massachusetts, Phelps was acquainted with the quality of lodging and fare at the Mellen Tavern in Belchertown, George and Tabitha Slocomb's and Farrar's in Shrewsbury (the latter a stopover on the stage line from Hartford to Boston), Austin's in Worcester, Hobart's and Swan's in Leicester, and the Jenks Tavern in Spencer.[130] Trips to Litchfield usually included a stopover to visit Aunt Phelps in Westfield, but inns that proved convenient resting places and points of transfer along that way included Pettibone's in Granby, Connecticut (still extant), and Deodat Woodbridge's in Manchester Green.[131]

In Boston, Elizabeth and Charles visited Bracket's Tavern (also known as Cromwell's Head) on School Street, and Newell's.[132] But Phelps's preferred option came to be the State Street boardinghouse run by Catherine Gray (with the help of two sisters), next door to the American Coffee-House—one of the growing number of boardinghouses operated by widows in the city in these years.[133] Jacqueline Barbara Carr finds that some thirty widows operated such businesses between 1785 and 1795, and that "between 1795 and 1799" that number grew by a full third.[134] Gray advertised "Genteel Boarding & Lodging," which apparently suited the Phelpses better than the options they had previously sampled. Nearly every spring found them at Mrs. Gray's for a night or two.[135] Phelps may have found Gray's establishment quieter and more comfortable than a common tavern, or she may have found Gray's company more appealing (Gray was born about 1739, so she was about eight years Phelps's senior).[136] Gray's operation seems to have been substantial. The 1798 direct tax describes the building as a three-story, eighteen-hundred-square-foot brick house with no fewer than thirty-eight windows, so one can imagine the rooms to have been spacious, well lit, and comfortable.[137] Two stage lines—John Greenleaf's, to Portsmouth, and Jonathan Plummer's, to Newburyport—departed from Gray's boardinghouse; given the nature of her lodgers, Gray's boardinghouse was a routine point of contact for commercial transactions as well.[138]

But taverns were a natural fit with the keeping of boarders, and innkeeping women often also worked to serve this longer-term clientele. At the south end of Hadley Center, the Warner tavern took in boarders.[139] In Hatfield, Miriam and Silas Billings provided regular board for several customers, including Miriam's unmarried sister Rebecca Dickinson, but also local schoolteachers Isaac Curson and "Patte Renalds who lives heere to keep the School the Second Sommer of her living in this town."[140] Curson and Renalds may have lodged at the Billings tavern as well (Rebecca lived in her own home, but walked over to the tavern to dine, "the company" being "more than the provision"), but all three depended on Miriam Billings to provide their meals.[141]

The convivial lunches at the Billings tavern that were so appreciated by Rebecca Dickinson gave way through the afternoon and into the evening to less genteel conversations.[142] One can easily imagine a significant shift in the tone of the taproom after sunset. John Adams's well-known description of a night at a tavern in Weymouth, Massachusetts, helps us envision festive evenings across the Commonwealth: "Negroes with a fiddle, young fellows and girls dancing in the chamber as if they would kick the floor thru . . . fiddling and dancing of both sexes and all ages, in the lower room, singing, dancing fiddling, drinking flip and toddy, and drams."[143]

Sometimes, managing such revelers could be overwhelming. The presence of alcohol could lead to unhappy incidents. On one cold February night in 1803, a group of men from Northampton, anxious to be served after the Warners had closed their doors for the evening, broke into the building and refused to leave. A number of travelers were there, quietly assembled. But the Northampton party remained there for more than two hours, without permission. When Lemuel Warner tried to get them to leave, they roughed him up, making "great noise" and disturbing the peace. This "great error of the citizens" was "in violation of the good rules and order" that the Warners usually kept—indeed, that were essential to retaining Warner's license, and livelihood—and were, the court declared, an "evil example to others."[144]

Such upheaval could prove unsettling, especially to those who had not been exposed to the rougher aspects of tavern life. When the court referred to the "great terror" caused by the threatening and unruly patrons, one can easily imagine that some of that terror was Dorothy Phelps Warner's. Some years later, Warner's third wife confessed that she was not altogether happy in her circumstances as an innkeeper: Elizabeth Porter Phelps confided to her daughter that "brother Warner & Sister made a little, accidental visit she says she is terrible homesick, was never much from home before." Phelps explained to the melancholy bride "how dreadfully you used to feel, & others which I knew of," but to no avail: "she says she must go home next week, & stay at least 3 weeks—has almost entirely done eating—how it will terminate I don't know, brother seems to be kind and attentive—but the tavern, and boarders, are a trouble."[145] Whether Lemuel Warner had access to domestic help or other forms of labor is unknown but seems likely; at least in spring 1775, when Elizabeth Porter Phelps's enslaved woman Rose gave birth to her daughter Phillis, it was "Phillis, Mr. Warner's negro woman," who came to Forty Acres, spending the better part of a month helping out while "Rose had her child to nurse."[146] It would be several years before the Warners would move into the building at the lower end of West Street, but it seems likely that the Warners' tavern deployed the labor of Phillis and other laboring women, white and black.[147] This woman could well be the same "old Phillis" that Elizabeth Porter Phelps would hire to clean and do laundry in her old age. But even with Phillis's assistance, the constant tending to strangers and their various demands was "a trouble."

The "Pernicious Effects of Spirituous Liquors"

Surely the burden of drunken customers was among the most trying aspects of the work, for women and men alike, but perhaps more acutely for women, who had real reason to fear violence from men who had had too much to drink.

The consumption of alcohol happened at crossroads both real and metaphorical, on the physical landscape, but also at the intersection of private and public life, where women's labor was entwined with intimate relations within families, relationships among employers and employees, encounters among strangers, and everyone in between. Women charged with providing inebriating beverages were quietly but constantly negotiating and policing drunken behavior as well as the effects of alcohol on those who drank, and on those who had to contend with those who drank.[148]

Alcoholism was a serious problem in eighteenth-century Hadley, where plenty of evidence could be found of the destructive effects of addiction. In fact, to combat the "pernicious effects of spirituous liquors," in 1798 the Massachusetts General Court passed an "Act to Encourage the Manufacture and Consumption of Strong Beer, Ale and Other Malt Liquors." The legislation, which made brewhouses whose annual output exceeded 131.5 barrels tax-exempt for five years, was good news for maltsters like Hadley's Warner family, and was perhaps greeted warmly by the area's tavernkeepers as well, if it brought the price of beer down for both wholesalers and retailers.[149] It may have been welcome, too, among other members of the community who shared the court's concern that too many townspeople were drinking too much hard liquor.

And apparently some Hadley people did overindulge, at least in the eyes of some: when a movement arose to relocate the Springfield courts to either Northampton, Hadley, or Hatfield, one observer—eager to keep the courts where they were—was said to have remarked, "The people of Hatfield are industrious and thriving, and to have the courts there would injure their industry and thrift. Northampton people are very religious, and the measure would be injurious to their religion. . . ." Hadley, however, "has neither thrift nor morality to be injured," being "then and long after greatly demoralized by hard drinking."[150] While tinged with sarcasm, to be sure, or at the very least with tongue in cheek, the speaker hoped that listeners would find enough truth in his little jibe to support his position, and there is no doubt that some Hadley families indeed knew the effects of hard drinking all too well. Experiences with and attitudes toward drinking were a steady undercurrent affecting all women in Hadley's public houses.

Elizabeth Porter Phelps's memorandum book and correspondence suggest that concern over alcohol abuse and related violence demanded the attention of that household and the neighborhood around it, as Phelps dealt with alcohol abuse both on her farm and in the village of North Hadley. At Forty Acres, the first hint that alcohol was becoming a problem for Phelps involved growing references to its overuse by John Morrison, a Scotsman captured during the Revolution who came to the farm to work. After the war ended Morrison elected to stay on in New England, but the circumstances seem less than happy. In

June 1813, Elizabeth reported to her daughter, "I have had another notable talk with John who is, if possible, worse than ever, drunk perpetually, how can we live so? His store is so large that he abounds in something to fuddle with about all the time, and with the cider which he gets which is about as much as 3 men will drink, he is too troublesome. And what course can or shall we take. Two ladys are coming in."[151] Who the "two ladies" were or what they hoped to accomplish is unknown, but whatever intervention they undertook, it was unsuccessful. In September 1814 she broke the bad news: at the top of the week she'd found Morrison to be "altered greatly," adding that "he has been in a declining state for 2 years . . . Found him dead in his bed about or before 2 o'clock tues morning. Had he lived til November would been sixty-four or five. He was swelled most terribly, and had been a long time. Was buried on Tues, it being judged improper to keep the body."[152]

John Morrison had died, after years of alcoholism. While it was a tragedy for the household, no evidence suggests that Phelps harbored real fear for her safety or felt threatened by her employee's condition, though occasionally it was enough to cause concern: one winter night, while Charles was away on business, she wrote that "this is the second night, two drunken men, have been all the dependence we have had, to take care of the barn and the house. I did fasten my doors last night and intend to tonight."[153] Other women were less fortunate. The violence inflicted by inebriated men on their wives and mothers came to Phelps's attention more than she would have preferred. One fall evening in 1815 Phelps recorded that she and Betsy had

> rode up about 2 or 3 miles to see Eunice Alixander, who was tormented the whole night on the last Thursday night before, by her own son [Paul Wright, named for his father, but apparently born out of wedlock], and only child, who had got very much intoxicated, and threatened to kill her. Tore off her every bit of cloaths she had on, bruised her most shamefully, when he got to sleep she fled to a neighbors, he prevented her before, he took off her gold necklace threw it into the fire . . . Found her comfortable; he is shut in jail.[154]

As the temperance movement gathered steam in the early decades of the nineteenth century, it would articulate the connection between alcohol abuse and domestic violence, but for many families the observation was not a new one.

More than a decade earlier, Phelps had watched this same family wrestle with alcohol-induced violence; Paul Wright's shocking behavior toward his mother Eunice apparently replicated violence he had witnessed as a child, as his father had also lashed out at the women around him. "I have heard strange things today," Phelps wrote to her daughter: "I rather think you have heard us mention Paul Wright, as greatly altered for the worse, for several years past, he has lived a doubel life, drunkenness to a most horrid degree which I suppose has been the occasion of his performing many wicked and awful deeds." From time to time, he heard the voice of God condemning him for his weaknesses; he "got along with" these "strong and sharp convictions" as "well as he could," but "of late," they "seemed to be more forcable." Then, one night "his sins and the wrath of God appeared to him in sich dreadful forms that he was entirely overwhelmed and sunk in the gulph of its pain; he rose out of bed in such agony, thought he would try to pray—but no—not one word or one thot like a prayer—in this situation he felt himself entirely lost, but yealded himself up to God without one reservation to be wholly at his mercy."[155] He was converted. By the next spring, she says of Wright, "we hear good things of him still."[156]

Phelps had heard the above tale not from Wright, but from a Mr. Smith at the mills, suggesting that Wright's behavior and reformation were the talk of the neighborhood.[157] Not long thereafter, there was more discussion of Wright, who apparently had fallen off the wagon. With his wife Deborah in a tough confinement—"lying in and afraid of her life"—he had had a bad turn of drunkenness in the fall.[158] The minister at Sunderland had given him a talking-to, and he resolved to lay off alcohol for six months; in a letter to her daughter, Elizabeth Phelps added that she didn't know if he succeeded, but he "seemed to talk like a Christian" when she saw him.[159] Paul, she said, was "as perfectly raving as a madman." Charles Phelps went to "landlord Stockbridges" and sent two of his young men, who were instructed to "take care that Paul did not hurt anyone and even to bind him if necessary." Finally, Charles himself went to Wright's house "to settle some trouble between him and his wife."[160] "What a dreadful tryal she must have," Elizabeth mused. A few days later, Deborah Sumner Wright wrote Charles Phelps again, begging him to come help her.[161] But things were to get worse before they got better: just a few weeks later, Elizabeth wrote that Wright "carries on higher than ever, his wife has got so well, she has fled to Mr. Stockbridges"—likely the home of her sister-in-law Esther Stockbridge. One neighbor had reported that "there was a number about in that neighborhood who were attentive to the one thing—his wife I had heard off before, her distress he said was great."[162]

Deborah Wright's plea to Charles Phelps fits with larger patterns at the intersection of abuse and assistance: Kelly A. Ryan has found that "between 1790 and 1820 white women and the wives of poorer men were more likely than any other groups of women" to turn to local officials for help in abusive situations.[163] In time, concern about alcohol abuse in Hadley would manifest in larger social action. By 1813, members of the Massachusetts Society for Suppression of Intemperance sought to "discountenance and suppress the too free use of ardent use spirits."[164] Reorganized as the Massachusetts Temperance Society in the 1820s and 30s, their movement spurred the Hibbard family to stop serving liquor in the tavern they operated on the River Road to North

Hadley, and the tavern operated by Major John Smith and his wife Betsy Dickinson Brown Smith would do likewise.[165] The 1830s would witness the founding of the local chapter of the larger "Total Abstinence Temperance Society." More than four hundred residents—some 172 men and 247 women—pledged neither to consume nor to provide intoxicating beverages.[166] Women in these Temperance establishments banked on new patterns of sociability to generate and sustain their livelihood.

Hadley's taverning women, then—whether licensed innkeepers, their sisters and daughters, their hired servants, or enslaved laborers—were proximate to the events of the world in ways that other working women were not. Often the first to hear of developments across the colony, and around the globe, they were also on hand to see and hear the deliberations of the county courts and to witness the vendue sales that shaped neighbors' fortunes.

But their work also proved crucial to the larger web that constituted the social relations of work across the community, and its resonance beyond labor itself. Most obviously, their need to provide refreshment and hospitality to neighbors and strangers made them purchasers of local produce as well as purveyors of imported rum and other goods, and as they hired other women to help meet the everyday demands of a tavern or inn, they were obvious employers. But their work had larger implications as well. Their role as vendors of inebriants meant that they had some influence in the domestic life of families for whom alcohol use became problematic. And as they structured and restructured the physical spaces that sheltered the cultural work that accompanied the articulation of an emerging middle class, they helped to shape social relations across the community. In these ways, women behind the bar played outsized roles in setting the rhythms of life in the places they served.

CHAPTER SEVEN

Healing and Caregiving

"Thursday in the night," Elizabeth Porter Phelps mused one winter day, "Sarah Kellogg and Rhoda Smith both died, next neighbors they lived and died. Rhoda had been in a bad state, tho't consumptive—last Satterday taken with the nervous fever. Sarah taken last Fryday with a sort of cholic—both carried to the grave together a Satterday."[1] Illness and death were familiar to everyone in early America, but the simultaneous death of these two neighbors was particularly poignant to the young Elizabeth Porter Phelps. Sarah Kellogg and Rhoda Smith had lived alongside one another for more than twenty years, and now they were both buried in the Hadley burying ground.

Health was fragile in early America. Consumption and colic were two threats among many in early New England, where illnesses were often hard to diagnose and still harder to cure. Accidents were commonplace as well. Injuries in and around hearths and farmyards impaired working women, and mishaps involving horses and carriages were familiar as well; riders fell from horses, sleighs plunged through ice, and occupants of vehicles were thrown if the horse or wheels met with trouble.[2] In September 1784, as we have seen, Phelps's hired woman Lucy Marshall was driving Peg—formerly enslaved, now free—into town when a team and cart they met on the road hit the horse they were riding; the women were knocked off the horse and run over by the cart's wheels. Peg escaped with only an injured ankle, but Lucy's leg was broken in two places and the cart wheel "went over the lower part of her bowels." A "great number of men" made a stretcher out of a blanket and poles, and carried her home; Lucy was lucky to survive, but with the help of physicians and other caregivers, she did just that.[3] Such unwelcome events, together with the regular course of life, from birth and childbirth through the effects of aging, brought women into contact with women who had cultivated special knowledge of and experience with the body, botanicals, and other practices aimed at restoring health. Such expertise coupled with a set of habits and qualities, including patience and discretion, made healing and health care viable sources of livelihood for women in early Hadley.

Like cloth making and hospitality work, healing professions involved both men and women workers, in ways that became increasingly reconfigured amid shifting gender conventions and that in turned reshaped social relations of labor among women. By the last quarter of the eighteenth century, for instance, men rather than women typically performed bleedings; they also performed most surgeries, and they would soon be encroaching on work traditionally performed by midwives. A hierarchy eventually emerged in which formally trained physicians (of which there were few in early America) trumped doctors trained in apprenticeships, who themselves were increasingly preferred over healers whose training was less structured. Women had long played important roles in preserving the health of their families in communities, in the creation, preservation, and dissemination of "receipts" offering relief for the ailing; in the cultivating of gardens filled with botanicals valued for their restorative properties; and in the delivery of bedside care in moments of need, from sickness to childbirth to death. Through most of the eighteenth century, as today, women acted as specialists in various sorts of caregiving in ways that extended beyond the caring labor that was part and parcel of women's lives as daughters, wives, and mothers. Some women, akin to pediatricians, tended small children in their communities. Others were known by their neighbors to be available to help attend the elderly, disabled, chronically ill, or dying. Still others gained expertise in the delivery of babies. These women, like their counterparts elsewhere across early America, "mobilize[d] their expert healing knowledge as an economic asset."[4] In these occupations, social relations of labor are complicated by the fact that the (healthy) employer or client is also the product, as it were, in an acutely entangled form of exchange.[5]

Following the various sorts of women's work in the fields of caregiving through the life cycle, from birth to death, affords insights into exchanges that were often as embedded in the local economy as any of the others described herein. At the same time, caregiving extended during the most intimate moments of life may or may not have involved a financial transaction. The boundaries of health and healing activities as sources of livelihood are blurrier than many other livelihoods. As economist Nancy Folbre has observed, compassion and compensation are not mutually exclusive; personal relations grounded in love and friendship were not inconsistent with work remunerated in the economy.[6] Susan Brandt's study of healers in the Delaware Valley shows the many ways that the delivery of healing services and sharing of medical acumen, even when no fee was collected, served as "currency to develop economic safety nets: chains of nonmonetary indebtedness and dependency that could be called on in the future to reinforce their social capital or to acquire needed goods and services."[7] And yet some women across early America, in the Connecticut Valley as in the Delaware, did indeed convert medical knowledge to remunerable expertise. And, like other occupations, work involving health and healing ran in families, daughters learning from mothers the skills necessary to earn livings.

Medical Knowledge

The work of healers and caregivers, as with many occupations undertaken by early American women, is largely undocumented, and not well understood.[8] Like both clothing and cloth production, the work of caregiving overlaps with the work women did for and within their own families, blurring lines between women recognized for their special training, experience, or talent and others who were simply attending to their families' everyday needs. And, like domestic service, women's work in health and healing unfolded in domestic settings. In many ways, efforts to group work performed under the broad rubric of health and healing mirror the shortcomings in occupational identity considered in this book's introduction, in that many women moved seamlessly across these roles, offering services simultaneously and over time, as midwives, nurses, and pharmacists. It is more productive, then, to look at the activity (say, nursing), rather than the role (say, nurse). But even those whose practice was extensive remain cloaked in comparative archival obscurity. While we can learn much, for instance, about the work of Hadley physicians Richard Crouch and Giles Crouch Kellogg from their surviving accounts, we know next to nothing about local midwife Elizabeth Parsons Allen, who is believed to have attended more than three thousand Hampshire County births between 1717 and 1800.[9]

Health care was obtained from a wide array of sources, from men whose training was formal, informal, or something in between; from women whose long and often intergenerational experience conferred a degree of expertise; from folk healers; and in time from publications compiling knowledge and experience. Among the earliest formally trained physicians to practice in Hadley was Dr. Richard Crouch, who by 1731 was living with Dr. William Squire, an English or Scottish physician who settled in the town around 1727. Sometime shortly thereafter, perhaps at Squire's invitation, Crouch also emigrated from Great Britain to Hadley. In 1732, he married Mary Kellogg; after the doctor's 1761 death, "Madam Crouch" survived another twenty-seven years. Richard Crouch shared his estate with Mary's nephew, Giles Crouch Kellogg, who succeeded his uncle as the town's primary physician. Born in 1733, Giles was the son of Ezekiel Kellogg, who traded in enslaved workers; he would become a member of the Harvard class of 1751, and a Hadley physician until his own death in 1793. Unsurprisingly, Dr. Kellogg was among the men who in the 1770s claimed possession of enslaved labor, and also among its dozen wealthiest men.[10] In time, he would find colleagues and competitors in Drs. Cutler and Kittredge of Amherst, both of whom began treating Hadley patients at the turn of the nineteenth century.

Both healers and the infirm embraced an array of evolving medical techniques as well as folk practices, superstitions, and supernatural interventions in order to restore a healthy balance. Any combination of therapies was possible: when Phillis, the enslaved girl at Forty Acres, became ill in the 1770s, the Phelpses tried everything to save her, including visits to Hadley's Dr. Kellogg and Northampton's Dr. Mather. But they also took her to see a local man who was the seventh son of a seventh son, in the hope (as it was widely believed in the eighteenth century) that such people possessed special healing abilities.[11] Residents also sometimes turned to the knowledge of Native American healers. Rhoda Rhoades (1751–1841) was an "Indian doctress" of some renown in western Massachusetts.[12] Rhoades and her brother Zebulon attended patients throughout the Connecticut Valley from Hartford to as far north as Northampton, offering to clients generations of accumulated expertise.

Sometimes a cure might be as damaging as the condition it was meant to address, which could put formally trained (male) practitioners in tension with women healers. Certainly this was the case with opium, widely prescribed before its addictive qualities were fully appreciated. Elizabeth Pitkin Porter suffered from a dependence on opiates. The nature of her original ailment is unknown; romantic narratives of her life have posited that it was heartbreak over the death of her husband Moses, killed in the Seven Years' War, that ruined the widow's health, as she was never able to rebound from the trauma. Whatever the issue, she appears to have been ill at least as early as the 1740s, when Dr. Richard Crouch began treating her with doses of both laudanum and "hysteric."[13] In summer 1765, apparently in search of a less pharmaceutical approach, she tried the spring at Cold Spring (today Belchertown, just eighteen miles from her home in Hadley), and even traveled to Stafford Springs (about forty miles southeast of Hadley, in Connecticut) "to go to a Pool there very much famed for cureing disease."[14] The site's "fame" among New England's white residents was only just beginning to spread, but the spring was reportedly well known among the valley's native community, which may be how Porter learned of it.[15] Just six years later, John Adams would travel to sample the benefits of the spring, and he reported that some thirty others were there on the same day—a benefit to the health, too, of the tavern established by the Green family, and the bath house erected by a Mr. Child.[16] The family would rely again on the healing power of Stafford Springs years later, when Phelps's granddaughter Bethia suffered for the better part of a year with a "sore eye."[17]

What relief the sulfur-and-iron-water springs delivered Porter we do not know, but it did not last. Through the years both Drs. Crouch and Kellogg were called in for consultations. At some point she was prescribed opium, and she became addicted. In the 1780s, "Old Mrs. Alixander" (another caregiver in the community, though one more typically called upon to treat children) was called in to help; Alixander pleaded with Porter to give the drug up, but "in vain—she took it before night the next day."[18] At times Porter's addiction confined her to her home, her room in the northeast corner of the family's home, and even her bed. In November 1784, during an especially challenging time, Phelps recorded that her mother "did not get out of bed this day";[19] by August 1795, Phelps would record the fairly momentous occasion of her mother's visit to the Shipman family, noting "she had not been abroad any where for two years."[20]

Porter's travel to Cold Spring and the Stafford pool as well as her eventual confinement remind us that health care and healing had geographies of their own. The business of medicine both compelled patients' travel (for example, to springs for cures) and confined them at home (in pregnancy, in weakness, and in Porter's case, too often in an opium-induced stupor). Meanwhile practitioners, too, crafted and traversed landscapes of healing. Women who offered health care often cultivated gardens attuned to that purpose, growing the botanicals they believed to assist them in their work. Healers traveled near and far in the course of their labors; midwives and doctors were summoned by riders on horseback at every hour, and made rounds through the homes of their clients, while nurses lodged with patients for weeks at a time. It would be a long while before the infirm would be gathered together in hospitals: in the early years of the republic, men and women alike traveled to attend to their patients, though in patterns that responded to other, broader transformations in the social relations of place.

Childbearing and Midwifery

In the eighteenth century as now, women's health was closely tied to their reproductive lives, and the labor of care provided by midwives and nurses entwined with the reproductive labor of motherhood. Concern about the possibility of pregnancy arose as soon as a girl began to menstruate, as we saw earlier, with Betsy Huntington's worry that the family's ward Mitte had become a little too "sociable" in the kitchen with the hired boy Almond.[21] Apart from abstinence from sexual activity, effective birth control methods were largely unknown in eighteenth-century Hadley. Women who wished to terminate a pregnancy turned to a variety of herbs believed to induce abortion, including savin and pennyroyal; some doctors might use instruments to remove a fetus, but the procedure—though legal until "quickening" occurred, when the mother could first feel the fetus move—was difficult and dangerous.[22] Until menopause most women's lives would be dominated by pregnancies, childbirth, nursing, and child-rearing, making midwives, physicians, and nurses among the most important members of their communities, men and women whose knowledge and skills could sustain life or fail to prevent death.

The most familiar of early America's health care occupations is midwifery. On a Wednesday morning in August 1803, an exhausted Elizabeth Porter Phelps sat down to write her daughter with the news: "one more birth has been in this house."[23] At three o'clock in the morning, her son's wife, Sally, had begun feeling "unwell," and by four, Charles Phelps had saddled a horse and ridden out to bring Elizabeth's best friend, Penelope Gaylord, as well as Dorothy Warner, his sister. He also rode to the home of a local midwife, Mrs. Montague, but she was out, attending to another woman in labor, so he headed off to the more distant Northampton for Mrs. Breck. The anxious grandfather-to-be and the midwife returned home at about nine, and just in time; about a half-hour later Sally delivered a healthy nine-pound boy. When Elizabeth sat down later that morning to dash off a note to Betsy with the good news, the exhausted grandmother wrote, "I feel as if my head was turned."

Every community had at least one woman who was called upon to assist with deliveries. In nearby Westhampton, Pliny Pomeroy's wife was the "first and only midwife" in that town, and "supported the family considerably in that way."[24] In Hadley, the Mrs. Montague who had been unavailable to help when Sally Porter delivered in the summer of 1803—possibly Persis Russell Montague (figure 7.1), who as the mother of ten would certainly have known the business of childbirth—was a longtime midwife there, as was the Mrs. Dickinson whom Phelps called when the pregnant spinner Betty Goodrich came time to deliver (though today neither woman's identity is known with more certainty).[25] In Hampshire County, among the most notable midwives was Northampton's Elizabeth Allen, who delivered those three thousand babies over the course of her long career; the Mrs. Breck who attended Sally Phelps's break-of-dawn delivery was Allen's daughter Eunice, the youngest of her own thirteen children.[26]

Midwives in early New England did much more than deliver babies. As historian Laurel Thatcher Ulrich has explained, Maine midwife Martha Ballard "was simultaneously a midwife, nurse, physician, mortician, pharmacist, and attentive wife. Furthermore, in the very act of recording her work, she became a keeper of vital records, a chronicler of the medical history of her town."[27] In Hallowell, Maine, the midwife was called on to assume these many and various roles in part because that comparatively recently settled community contained few others with sufficient expertise to tend to the community's medical needs. In Hadley, almost a century older than Hallowell, midwives likewise cultivated a broad range of knowledge necessary to health and healing from cradle to grave, but in the older town a more complex community of

Figure 7.1 Persis Russell Montague (1765–1851) portrait by Erastus Salisbury Field, ca. 1836. The Mrs. Montague who appears in the memorandum book of Elizabeth Porter Phelps may have been the Persis Russell Montague who in 1786 married William Montague (1760–1839). The couple lived in North Hadley, near the Sunderland line. Courtesy of Pocumtuck Valley Memorial Association, Memorial Hall Museum, Deerfield, MA

practitioners was already thriving, too, in the last half of the eighteenth century and early years of the nineteenth.

No form of women's work was more intimate than midwifery. The midwife might massage the back and belly of the mother-to-be; sometimes she applied butter, fat, or oil to the genitals, or tried to stretch the vagina to ease the birth.[28] She sat with mothers in labor for hours, hearing their hopes and fears, and shared with them the happiness of a successful delivery as well as the pain of a stillbirth. She collected information that could exonerate or damn them in courts of law. Few relationships were as deeply personal.

The risk of death in childbed heightened this already emotionally charged relationship. Pregnancy and childbirth in the eighteenth century were causes for joy as well as concern, but women knew that things could go wrong, and regularly prepared their souls for the trial. When they called the women who would attend them, it was a serious matter. "Thursday," Elizabeth Phelps would write one December afternoon, "daughter and I attended the funeral of Susa Sumner She was taken last Monday night with convulsion fits She expected to have been delivered of a child soon, however her travail was brought on and she lived but a short time after she was delivered, poor foolish girl!"[29] Susa, apparently, was not married, leaving Phelps less than sympathetic when her sins cost her her life. More thoughtful is a reference to the sorrow of "Old Mrs Hubbard," whose "daughter Strong," Phelps learned, "died suddenly this morn in child bed, the ninth day since her delivery, appeared to be comfortable, none thought of any danger till she appeared to be dying."[30]

The stakes were high, and most midwives gained their specialized knowledge through experience, attending dozens of births, observing how to assist both the mother and child, and also how to intervene when something went amiss. Medical treatises and manuals were comparatively uncommon in eighteenth-century Hampshire County, but not unknown. In Northampton as early as the 1740s, books about midwifery were the source of a scandal that rocked the career of Jonathan Edwards, when several young men in their twenties had been reading books and taunting women about menstruation. Elizabeth Pomeroy testified that she had found *The Midwife Rightly Instructed* (a 1736 treatise published in London) hidden in the chimney of their house; Oliver Warner allegedly sold peeks at the book for ten shillings a glance.[31] By the time Elizabeth Allen died at the end of the eighteenth century, she could bequeath to her daughter Eunice Breck, who had followed her in her occupation, her "library on midwifery" together with another important tool of her trade: her sidesaddle.[32] The books Allen owned are not listed on the inventory, but surely included the *Treatise on the Theory and Practice of Midwifery,* published by Britain's leading obstetrician, a man with the unlikely name of William Smellie; Smellie's companion volume *Collections of Cases and Observations in Midwifery*; and Edinburgh University professor Alexander Hamilton's *Outlines of the Theory and Practice of Midwifery,* just published in Northampton in 1797.[33] Many women who became midwives, however, did not acquire their knowledge through volumes like these, but rather through experience, attending dozens of births, usually as an assistant before beginning to direct deliveries on their own.

Difficult deliveries sometimes involved a number and variety of healers. In February 1813, Elizabeth Porter Phelps was called home from church during the first prayer in anticipation of her daughter Betsy delivering her child. Her son-in-law rode on, "brought Mrs Harris and one more," but it turned out to be a false alarm: "Satt better," Phelps wrote. Then, on March 4th, "after meeting

Mr Hunt[ington] carried Mrs Harris home. Ten days later, contractions began again: "tuesday before night daughter unwell, Mr Hunt[ington] brought Mrs Harris jest at dusk, held unwell all day." On Wednesday, Betsy was "very bad"—so distressed that the family called in a male physician. Dr. Tracey came and the family went to bed, only to be awakened in the night when it again seemed delivery was imminent. The various healers "soon came to her help," but "availed nothing"; early in the morning the family sent for yet another physician, Dr. Osborn, who (ominously) "came with instruments of dissection." But both mother and child in the end made it through a safe delivery; Phelps could record that her daughter had a "fine son born." A "Miss Johnson," she added, "nursed."[34]

Though herself a resident of Northampton, Elizabeth Allen ministered to all of Hampshire County, and was regularly called to Hadley. When Elizabeth Porter Phelps delivered her first child in August 1772, she noted in her memorandum book that on Thursday the 6th she had ridden into town in the evening to have tea at her brother-in-law's house. The next day, she "perceived some alteration" in her pregnancy. Charles rode to Northampton and brought Mrs. Allen to the house, and everyone went to bed, waiting to see what would happen. Between three and four in the morning the whole household was roused when it was clear the child was coming, and "just six minutes before six in the morning" she delivered her son.[35] In August 1774, when Mary Bartlett was about to deliver her daughter and namesake Mary, her husband Nicholas stopped in to let the family at Forty Acres know of the impending event as he made his way to the ferry and to Hatfield, to get his mother. Not long afterward he returned, this time to borrow a horse to go and get midwife Allen. Meanwhile, Charles took his wife Elizabeth to the Bartlett home, where she would assist both midwife and mother through the delivery. Allen was the midwife in spring 1775 when fourteen-year-old Rose, the enslaved woman at Forty Acres, delivered her daughter.[36] In August 1775, Charles Phelps's sister Dorothy Warner went into labor while her husband was out of town, "down to the army for a visit." Charles and Elizabeth sent for Mrs. Allen, who stayed with Warner until Saturday morning.[37]

Throughout the region, midwives like Allen were essential members, then, not only of their own, immediate communities, but the larger countryside as well. In Bradford, Vermont, for instance, Lydia Peters Baldwin's midwifery practice encompassed also Corinth and Fairlee, Vermont, as well as Piermont and Orford, New Hampshire.[38] Allen's bequest of her sidesaddle to her daughter and successor Eunice Allen Breck points up the geographic range of any midwife's practice; the sidesaddle and the horse thereby implicated are artifacts both of the need for speed that attended this work, and also the scattered nature of the clientele. The long-serving saddle also reminds us that midwifery, like a range of professions including tavernkeeping, the clergy, and several of the crafts, tended to repeat through families over generations, as children pursued occupations already known to them through the work of their parents. Breck, as we've seen, put her mother's library, and sidesaddle, to good use. Just as Elizabeth Phelps's children had been delivered by Mrs. Allen, her grandchildren were delivered by Mrs. Breck: "This morning before sunrise I was called to my sons they had a fine daughter born about long before I got there, had Mrs Breck from Northampton, Mr Cotton Dickinson's wife [fifty-three-year-old Olive Field Dickinson] nurses."[39]

Some midwives and healers played roles in preventing pregnancy. Given the secrecy in which it was often necessarily veiled, it is very difficult to find historical evidence about the termination of pregnancies in early America. Easier to see are the cases of infanticide, where a mother delivered a child, smothered it, and hoped that she would be able to convince others that the child had died in childbirth. But some strategies for abortion, as well as contraception, were known and shared by some women healers. Long before the advent of any kind of pregnancy test, women could not confirm that they were expecting a child before they began to feel it moving in the womb; therapies to induce menstruation could be embraced long before a woman was at all sure that she was terminating a pregnancy. In other words, the "ambiguity of early pregnancy created an opportunity for women to control fertility, and, for single women, a way to escape the consequences of a fornication charge."[40]

Midwives also played critical roles in systems of public welfare. By obtaining the name of a child's father from the mother during the height of her travail, midwives helped the town government determine the source of the child's future support. These civil matters differed from criminal charges; what historians now recognize as a "sexual double standard"—in which men were no longer prosecuted for fornication, though women continued to be—emerged around the 1740s.[41] But women whose transgression had resulted in a child could turn to the courts in attempts to compel a man to contribute to the child's maintenance. Midwives played a critical role in those suits, since the courts believed that a woman asked to name the father of her child during the pain of childbirth would be unable to lie. In November 1779, for instance, twenty-two-year-old Miriam Pierce of Hadley confessed to having committed fornication "some time November last past."[42] Miriam named Samuel Cooke II as the father of the child she delivered, but he denied responsibility. Miriam, however, was found to be "constant" in her claims, having also named Cooke during her "travail." He was adjudged thirty-five pounds, 13 shillings, and six pence for maintenance of the child to date as well as the costs of prosecution, and directed to provide Miriam forty shillings per week for ongoing support. Cooke continued to support the child for seven years, when he returned to court and successfully argued that, now that "sd child is now seven, healthy, and no longer chargeable," he should be "discharged from expense of further supporting sd child." The court agreed, and Miriam assumed full responsibility for her child's support. Conversely, when Granville's Jemima Munson named Nathaniel Clark Jr. as the father of her son, Clark argued in court that she not be allowed to name him the father now because she *didn't* at time of her travail. The justices agreed, and prevented Munson from charging Clark with the child's support. Not only was her complaint dismissed, but Munson was instructed to cover the costs of Clark's defense.[43]

Perhaps it was apprehension concerning this query that caused Phelps's servant Persis Morse to hold her employer at bay when she delivered her child at Forty Acres. Morse, still unmarried, became pregnant for at least a second time while living in the garret of the Phelps house; when it came time to deliver, she opted not to call her mistress (and perhaps not even a midwife; Phelps's record contains no reference to one being present). On August 11, 1805, Phelps wrote that "Satt: night about 11 o'clock Persis Morse called me to come to her, she had a daughter born before she called me."[44] Perhaps little Dolly arrived in too much haste to assemble the usual number of female attendants, or even to call a midwife; perhaps Morse specifically sought to evade the questions a midwife might feel compelled to ask. Or perhaps Morse called her own women, and simply sought to give birth out of the eye of her employer. In any event, though the two women were living under the same roof, Morse did not involve Phelps in the birth of her child. The following day Phelps could only bring Mrs. Montague—who also seems to have specialized in the care of infants—to look after Persis and the child. The circumstances of the delivery are unknown. The only choice we can today know that she made was the one not to immediately involve her employer; by the time the midwife arrived, the travail—and the opportunity for any paternity quiz—was past.

Caring for Infants and Children

When there was simply not enough time, energy, or good will to go around, families hired others to help provide care, whether it was "watchers" who took nighttime shifts needed to attend to sick relatives, or women who helped out in the days following childbirth. In 1805, Susanna Edwards Porter (as Phelps reported to her daughter) "came home abt 2 wks before her confinement, brought a nurse from Northampton and a midwife when they were wanted."[45] Some years later, when Elizabeth Phelps's daughter-in-law gave birth, Elizabeth noted that the child was born "last week on Thursday"; her "nurse left her, in one fortnight, Patty Sage."[46] For two weeks, Sage hovered about the household caring for mother and child; now, with the mother recovered and ready to take over, she collected her pay and headed home. Likewise, about two hours after Betsy

Huntington went into labor, "Mr Huntington got here with [midwife] Mrs Ransome . . . had a son born about one Monday morning. Monday Mr H carried home Mrs Ransome—fetch'd a nurse Lydia Hodgekiss—thanks be to the god of providence."[47] In each of these instances, once the midwife's duties—Mrs Breck's, or Mrs. Ransome's—were over, a nurse's began.

In some cases these were attendants to help care for the routine needs of a newborn; in other cases women were routinely engaged to breastfeed another woman's child as a wet nurse, another way that the employment of some women contributed to reproductive labor more generally.[48] Like midwifery, few relationships between employers and employees were as intimate as this one. And so it is unsurprising that much attention was given to the selection of wet nurses in the eighteenth-century Atlantic World. Among the well-to-do in seventeenth-century England, it had been usual for women to hire a wet nurse rather than nurse infants themselves, and the fashion traveled to the New England colonies with the migrants. Although community clergymen saw the occasional need to criticize elite women who simply preferred not to nurse, no stigma was attached to nursing itself and women nursed openly, their breasts exposed even in the meetinghouse.[49] But new mothers sometimes needed help feeding their infants, particularly when fatigue or illness interfered with the mother's ability to make or release milk.[50] Some families hired a wet nurse for that window of time before the arrival of the mother's milk, a period of up to five days for first-time mothers and two or three for others. Before the purpose of colostrum, the first breast secretions containing nutrients and anti-allergens that protect infants from infection until their own immune systems develop, was understood, people believed that colostrum was not only inferior to milk, but actively harmful to newborns, and so hired wet nurses to feed the baby.[51] Fathers sometimes needed to hire a nurse when mothers died in childbirth, leaving a hungry infant behind. Conversely, a woman who had delivered a child only to lose it might nurse someone else's infant, reminding us of the acute pain and loss behind some women's availability to serve in this role.[52]

Many times, such exchanges were made in the context of neighborly compassion rather than the marketplace; as Janet Golden writes, "in a society with a high birth rate and probably frequent instances of postpartum ailments, brief, informal assistance was part of a patchwork of reciprocal relations that knit communities together. Its casual and spontaneous nature rendered it largely invisible; woven into the fabric of everyday life, it remained beyond the gaze of critics, ministers and doctors."[53] In 1776 Elizabeth Porter Phelps's second son died within a week of his birth. At the same time, a woman who had given birth to twins had died following her labor. The infant's relatives probably tried to feed her animal milk or a mixture of flour, water, and mile (pap) from spoons, pap boats, or bottles, but these foods could be hard for babies to digest, difficult for them to take in from the vessels available, and not as nutritious as their mother's milk would have been. These relatives sought another alternative, and approached Elizabeth as a possible substitute for one of the infants, the other having gone to another Hadley woman. For her part, Elizabeth was unsure; word got back to her that the mother of the child had had scabies, and since Elizabeth was still weak from her delivery, the risk seemed unwise. But in the end Elizabeth changed her mind, and she nursed and in fact kept the child: Thankful Richmond would remain a member of the family through her marriage, raised like a daughter.[54]

For some households, wet nursing provided some much-needed income, "perhaps," as Karin Wulf has noted, "at a critical moment when a woman was prevented from income-earning activities by virtue of recent childbirth."[55] As Nora Doyle, too, has observed, "economic necessity drove women to seek employment as wet nurses, which usually paid them more than they could earn for other kinds of domestic labor."[56] Women recognized their milk as an asset that could be of value to other families: "Any Family that wants a wet nurse to suckle a Child," an ad might read, "may hear of one with a good breast of milk, by enquiring . . ."[57] Ads concerning the hire of wet nurses were the first notices related to women's income-seeking activities to enter the pages of the *Hampshire Gazette* (alongside notices published for "cash given for long human hair," another bodily product with commercial value in paper's advertising columns).[58] In August 1789, a family placed an advertisement seeking "a wet nurse, with a breast of young milk, to go into a family to suckle. N.B. the highest wages will be given in cash."[59] In this case, the notice was repeated twice more, suggesting perhaps that the family did not immediately find someone; in the winter of 1790, another family repeated a similar notice over a period of just over a month before they found someone or quit trying.[60] Another household anticipated their coming needs, it seems, publishing a notice in late November to alert readers that "a wet nurse, is wanted during the ensuing winter," and repeating the notice another five times over the same number of weeks.[61] Another published notice traveled in the opposite direction: in the summer of 1810, "any person having a young child that they wish to put out to nurse" was invited to contact Obadiah Frary in nearby Southampton for information.[62] Had someone in Frary's household recently lost a child? Perhaps so.

Because so few traces of these exchanges survive in period account books it is difficult to discover much about the relative compensation this service afforded. Janet Golden calls the question "open": high wages might have been used to "induce women to wean their own children," or perhaps "the value of the board and lodging given to domestics meant that the wet nurses were not well compensated." She also suggests there might be a difference between private hiring and the hiring of women to nurse infants "under the public charge," by town or church authorities to feed motherless children in their care.[63] References in the *Hampshire Gazette* to the "highest wages" offered wet nurses—and the further assurance that compensation would be "given in cash" (a feature that was perhaps particularly attractive as Massachusetts weathered a volatile postrevolutionary economy)—suggest the value placed on these workers in Hampshire County.[64]

A short step from midwifery and wet nursing was medical care for infants and young children. As the role of male physicians expanded (and the role of midwives contracted) one space that remained open for women was in the care of young children as early America's pediatricians. In Revolutionary Northampton, Lewis Tappan recalled hearing that when his father requested that a male physician by the name of Mather attend to his young daughter, Mather refused, insisting, "I don't visit little children; go and get Granny Hodge."[65] Like Olive Field Dickinson, who arrived as the first nurse to attend Phelps's newborn granddaughter, some women seemed to have specialized in the care of infants and young children, and gained authority for their expertise. In Hadley, a Mrs. Montague as well as a Mrs. Alixander tended to the Phelps children when they were sick. "Our baby came down worse than ever it did before," Phelps wrote one March, "but god was gracious. Wednesday I brought Mrs Alixander here to do for him."[66] Childhood was a dangerous time in early New England, and women like Alixander were essential to larger systems of reproductive labor. Not only were illnesses and diseases rampant and not well understood, but the opportunities for accidents around houses, shops, and farms were ample. Phelps's memorandum book teems with entries in which children were injured around houses and farms: she notes one child scalded with boiling fat and another in a tub of wort, and yet another burned "extreme bad": another child drowned in a tub of water, while Simon Baker, a "little boy" who lived and worked at Forty Acres, broke his toes at the saw mill.[67] In July 1773, Phelps's son "was left alone in the room, crept to a tea kettle of scalding water turned it over scalded one hand very bad the other a little." Once again, Mrs. Alixander was called to the scene.[68]

Nursing the Sick and Infirm

When Mary ("Madam") Crouch (the wife of the Hadley physician and aunt of his successor) died in 1781, among the expenses settled by the estate were eight shillings "paid to Josiah Pierce's wife for tending [Crouch] in her last sickness."[69] Because Pierce was present over the course of these final days, she could also testify that the curtains appraised in the inventory had been given by Crouch to Mary Kellogg and so were "inventoried by mistake."[70] "Nursing," the historian Karin Wulf observes, "seems to have been a specialized skill, but it also commingled with midwifery and laying out the dead."[71] As was true with many occupations, more specialization emerged in urban areas, but even in comparatively rural settings some women's particular abilities as caregivers were recognized, and their time and skill both "nursing" and "watching" was compensated.[72] Account books of the period hint at the cost of nursing; Robert Breck's 1760s accounts, for instance, suggest that he paid eight pence per day for his washing, two shillings eight pence per week for general domestic help, and three shillings per week for nursing.[73] Bills submitted to the estates of the deceased note expenses associated with nurses and nursing in the time of the decedent's "final sickness." In 1777, Enos Smith hired Anne Cook to nurse for three weeks; she charged three shillings four pence for her services.[74] Twenty-five years later, after the death of Thankful Coates, her estate was billed for every twenty-four hours of nursing care, over the forty-five days of her final illness; the sum was among the estate's largest debts, constituting almost 20 percent of the total bill from her last caregivers.[75]

Indeed, arrangements like these abound in early Hampshire County accounts. When Juliana Dickinson died, widow Lucy Dickinson charged the estate fifty cents per week for some thirty-two weeks—the better part of a year—for "keeping, nursing and boarding" her; Hosea Shaw likewise charged for "nursing said child when sick."[76] In Northampton, the wife of a William Miller cared for a "lame" young man for close to ninety weeks—almost two years—charging twenty pounds for her time and effort and another seventeen pounds for the more general expenses of boarding him.[77] While two years of care is unusual in these records, the work of nursing often extended over comparatively long periods of time. Widow Ruth White, for instance, boarded Jonathan Atherton for some sixteen weeks. She provided for "watchers" as well as washing for him over those four months. She kept two horses for his physicians for nearly a week, and cut up sheets and cloths for his bandages. Atherton survived his illness, and lived nearly forty years more. When he died in the winter of 1781, White remembered every minute of that care, billing his estate for the provisions, laundry, stabling, and cloth. What's more, she added an additional charge of six shillings for "extraordinary wear of bed & bedding."[78] Ruth White's palpable resentment survived Atherton's illness by some forty years, and in the end survived Atherton as well.

Indeed, White's frustration reminds us that nursing could tax the patience of caregivers every bit as much then as it does today. For women struggling to attend to ailing family members while meeting their existing obligations in the home or workplace, caregiving could easily drain their good will. Hatfield gown maker Rebecca Dickinson captured some of that frustration when she confided to the pages of her diary how annoyed she was that her seventy-five-year-old mother had "in a Pusseling fit" broken the glasses she so depended on: "a great loss to me for tha Suted me so well that i ginny should not have bought them out of my hand."[79] When Susanna Pierce cared for her brother-in-law Reuban Belden, she struggled to cope with his emotions as he faced his final illness. "He was very childish," she remembered, "and would cry for little matters." He asked Pierce to bear with him, and she did, but not without strain, for he was so often "as a child." "At sundry times he would take nothing but what [she] gave him"—that is, he wanted her to feed him—and sometimes he insisted that she taste anything he was to eat or drink.[80]

Another area of health care bears mention, though it is also a subject that is comparatively difficult to recover historically. While there was not yet any such thing as mental health care in this era, there was of course mental illness.[81] Hadley families, like their counterparts across the region, struggled to care for family members who suffered from a range of disorders. Some conditions caused erratic, frightening behavior. Elizabeth Porter Phelps's family well knew the consequences of mental illness and behavior Phelps typically described as "crazy." In fall 1784, for instance, she noted that her aunt Catherine Parsons was visiting together with "her sister [Lydia Phelps] Pomeroy crazy"; the pair borrowed the chaise to return Pomeroy home safely.[82] Closer to home, Phelps's brother-in-law Solomon suffered for some fifteen years from an ailment that caused violent outbursts that were alarming enough to cause his family to chain him from time to time in the nearby barn or another outbuilding. What Phelps meant when she wrote that Sol was "crazy," or "raving," is unclear, but for years, the Phelps household lived with the uncertainty of his mental status, never knowing when another incident might occur. During these episodes, Phelps feared for the safety of herself and her family. In the end, Solomon's illness drove him to cut his own throat.[83]

Anxiety and depression were also known to early Hadley. Charlotte Williams Porter, for instance, apparently struggled to manage emotions apparently associated with concern about the state of her soul. Her father after one visit reported to another daughter that Charlotte "appeared much like what I have conceived to be meant by being possessed of the devil; but I am not sure that I have conceived rightly of that matter. A partial derangement only appeared at times, at other times it seemed almost complete, and when this was not the case there was a degree of reason and some propriety of thought with absurdities interspersed; but a constant impression of the idea that her doom to wretchedness was inverably [*sic*] fixed."[84] He hoped that these "melancholy apprehensions respecting divine forgiveness would by degrees leave her." They feared suicide, or at best "loss . . . of her usefulness in the family."

Families in the last half of the eighteenth century were sadly ill equipped to handle members who were suffering from various disorders ranging from depression to psychosis. No matter where a person sat on the continuum of behavior understood to be acceptable and healthy, very little in the way of support was available to families grappling with any sort of cognitive, emotional, or behavioral disorder. Hadley's Charlotte Porter was married to physician William Porter, but the family seems to have relied on prayer and companionship to help restore Charlotte's health.[85] The suggestion by historian Mary Ann Jimenez that "the majority of distracted Massachusetts residents . . . were probably cared for by their own families" resonates with evidence from Hadley; indeed, there were few alternatives, as institutional care was only just emerging. But families often hired help to soften the burden, if they could afford it.[86] For instance, the effects of dementia associated with aging challenged caregivers then as it does now. In Springfield, Sarah Ball's behavior was so erratic that she would be found to be non compos mentis; in a statement concerning this determination, town selectmen noted that she was both forgetful and belligerent. She often failed to recognize neighbors, and frequently ordered work done only to promptly forget about it, and then berate the person in question or refuse to pay. Ball was largely confined to her bed, but "the task of tending her is so disagreeable," officials stated, "that it is very difficult to procure necessary attendance," yet Ball refused to pay her nurses beyond supplying their meals.[87] The courts stepped in to appoint a guardian to make sure, at the very least, that the necessary caregivers were justly compensated. In October 1780, Northampton's Overseers of the Poor addressed both illness associated with aging and some other sort of disorder when they asked probate judge Eleazer Porter to appoint a guardian for both Mrs. Bethia Hawley ("an aged person upwards of eighty years old and by reason of her age and infirmities" unable to manage her affairs) and Ann Bartlett, a member of Bethia's household ("a Lunatick or distracted person," "wholly incapable of ordering herself or providing her own subsistence").[88]

In Hadley, in order to attempt to address what appears to have been the depression and associated addiction of Elizabeth Pitkin Porter, the household at Forty Acres engaged "Old Mrs Alixander"—probably the same woman routinely called to help care for the family's children—to assist. Mrs. Porter was in the midst of "one of her low turns," her daughter noted. Mrs. Alixander "came here with a view to persuade my mother to leave off taking opium but in vain—she took it before night the next day."[89] Alixander stayed until Saturday, but it was all to no avail. In November, Phelps recorded that her mother was "very low," and "did not get out of her bed" all day; she prayed that God would calm her mother's "distressed mind."[90] The following week they summoned a Dr. Wells to come see her, who concluded that she was no danger to herself, but she did not improve.[91] A week later, Phelps sighed that her mother was "not Dangerous but must be diverted," but continued to be "quite lost. . . . I am afraid she will not hold it long."[92]

Elizabeth Pitkin Porter surprised her daughter, and "held it" another fourteen years, before she passed away at the age of seventy-nine, in September

1798. Family friends Submit Gaylord and Sally Parsons laid out the body; Lucretia Gaylord arrived later to help.[93] But such assistance was not always possible, and it is those rare instances that afford us some glimpse into women's roles in the business of dying. In the spring of 1786, for example, an unidentified body was found in Hadley. The tavern-keeping widow and sometime tailoress Elizabeth Newton was asked to help prepare the remains for burial, probably making the grave clothes (given her needle skills), for which the town's selectmen authorized payment of five shillings.[94]

Whatever the state of an eighteenth-century body—fit or infirm—all deaths invoked the labors of one final set of caregivers, whose charge it was to perform the "last kind office," that is, to prepare the body for burial. This too, involved a series of tasks that, like other aspects of care, could lay at an intersection of emotion and economics, but it was also understood as work that could and should be compensated (as Karin Wulf has observed, "women's responsibility for attending the dead was both social custom and economic opportunity.")[95] Very little is known about the work of preparing bodies for burial in rural western Massachusetts, or really anyplace in early America, in part because this labor was most often provided by a family member.[96] The body was washed, sometimes shaved, and laid out on a sheet or shroud, which could be made of linen, muslin, wool, or of cere-cloth, a linen impregnated with wax. A winding sheet might be wrapped around the body, beginning with the feet and then secured at the head, while a more structured shroud could be "shaped like a long dress or skirt, bound up with pins or knotted at the feet." Shrouds sometimes "resembled a long, backless nightshirt" and could be ornamented with ruffles.[97] The woman preparing the body for burial often stitched the shroud or winding sheet together along its edges, though the copper shroud pins often recovered archaeologically document another way bodies were secured for interment.[98] As these hands passed one final time over the deceased, the work of caregiving was complete.

Toward Professionalization

As the eighteenth century gave way to the nineteenth, new systems of belief and new technologies of health care changed the practice of medicine in New England, and along with those changes, women's labor in health care also transformed. Sometimes, emerging fields initially had room for female practitioners; for instance, dentistry was in its infancy in the eighteenth century, but the need for dentists was ongoing, and early on, before the work was formalized, female practitioners could be found in Hampshire County. Elizabeth Phelps regularly reported "violent toothaches," unsurprising in an era before the importance of dental hygiene was widely understood.[99] In 1796, she and the many men and women who also suffered through dental problems may have found some relief in the visit to Northampton of an itinerant dentist, Jenny Dodge.[100] In early America, dentistry began as largely a side job for men who perhaps sold wigs or kept occupations as silversmiths. By the second half of the eighteenth century advertisements for toothbrushes had begun appearing in the American press.[101] Dodge had taken her training in New York: "Jenny Dodge respectfully informs the public, that she carries on the business of a DENTIST in Northampton. Having taken great pains to procure instruction from the most approved Dentists in New York, and having furnished herself with the finest of Ivory, she flatters herself she shall be able to give satisfaction to any who shall employ her. She resides at present at Dr Porters, in the south part of the town."[102] The reference to ivory suggests that false teeth were part of Dodge's trade, a service wanted in Hampshire County; whether or not she availed herself of Dodge's skills, in 1811 Elizabeth—who had lifelong problems with her own teeth—recorded that her daughter and son-in-law were both "getting teeth put in."[103]

Dodge was of course quite rare in the nascent health care field: of some sixty-five itinerant surgeon-dentists found by Peter Benes in his study of itinerant physicians, healers, and surgeon-dentists in eighteenth-century New England and New York, only one—Dodge—was clearly female.[104] After her tenure in western Massachusetts, she moved to Boston, where she advertised in 1797.[105] No more is known of her or her work, but women would not become a significant presence in dentistry as it expanded during the nineteenth century. Meanwhile, the next dentist to advertise in the pages of the *Hampshire Gazette* does not appear until 1808, when a man named Bradley, also from New York, advertised that he was passing through town. Bradley added that "ladies who wished to be waited on at their houses" could be accommodated.[106] Jenny Dodge, as she traveled through New England, tested the waters of medical entrepreneurship. Her only slight imprint on the public record suggests that she perhaps never found traction as an itinerant dental practitioner, though it also seems true that, in the same years she attempted to carve out space for herself as a traveling oral health provider, the field of dentistry was beginning to see itinerancy supplanted by permanence, as practitioners shifted toward stable offices.[107]

More familiar in the history of medicine are transformations in the fields of midwifery and obstetrics, which were dramatic as male physicians made increasing inroads into territory once the preserve of women. As early as 1768, discussions emerged about the treatment of women, presumably by male physicians; at least one diarist that year recorded "a dispute in the chambers concerning the manner of healing women. Memorandum: women are treated without the least modesty nowadays."[108] But nevertheless, more and more births came to be attended by male physicians equipped with formal training, texts, and tools. In Springfield, Joseph Lumbard March's 1792 probate inventory contained a pair of forceps worth two shillings six pence and "a complete set of obstetric instruments" valued at two pounds ten shillings. Among the first glimpses of these developments in Hadley is the January 1798 birth of Thankful Richmond Hitchcock's child, assisted not by a midwife but by Amherst's Dr. Isaac Gurnsey Cutler, who would record some 1,336 births of children in Amherst and its environs from about 1805 through 1833—102 of them in Hadley.[109] The household at Forty Acres owned William Buchan's 1797 treatise *Domestic Medicine,* which among other things condemns the traditional gatherings of women around mothers in labor as a "ridiculous custom" that did nothing but introduce noise, crowding, and suspect advice into an already risky situation.[110]

In part, the rise of male physicians over their less formally trained female counterparts reflected changes in relationships between institutions and professions, a growing interest in credentials, and other artifacts of an economy and society increasingly detached from face-to-face familiarities. It can also be linked to the growing interest in gentility among men and women of a nascent middle class. As historian Richard Bushman has explained, part and parcel of the "refinement of America" was a fashionable discomfort with the body: "The delicate person flushed with shame at the mere mention of the grosser bodily processes that civilization had driven from the conversation of polite people."[111] Over time, the familiarity with bodily functions that women across communities shared became untoward for aspirants to gentility, creating new distances between women who tended to and cleaned up after the sick and women whose delicacy discouraged experience in such matters. The emerging class of trained physicians sequestered that experience within the appropriate domain of professionals; women who were willing and able to confront the least attractive moments of human life in the course of nursing and other forms of caretaking found their work accorded low status. Even the laying out of the dead succumbed to those new logics, as the commercialization of the funeral industry deployed new ideas about feminine sensibilities to redefine dead bodies as inappropriate objects of women's gaze.[112]

Occupations in caregiving proved particularly susceptible to the changes reconfiguring women's place in local economies. Midwifery would fall to the margins of obstetrical practice, and the counterparts of Jenny Dodge would not be seen for more than a century. In her excellent study of "Gifted Women and Skilled Practitioners" in the eighteenth- and early nineteenth-century Delaware Valley, Susan Hanket Brandt wisely urges historians to abandon the "declension narrative" that has shaped understanding of how women healers fared amid the "emergence of a consumer society, a culture of domesticity, the professionalization of medicine, and the rise of enlightened science, which generated discourses of women's innate irrationality."[113] She argues that some women drew on long-standing associations between women and healing to develop new sources of authority as authors and as students educated in the sciences, and other opportunities, while others created space for themselves as herbalists, apothecaries, and druggists in an "increasingly commercialized and consumer-driven marketplace."[114]

Some sense of those negotiations and adaptations can be spotted in the Connecticut Valley. The year 1811, for instance, saw the publication of the first American book on the care of children authored by a woman, Mary Palmer Tyler's *The Maternal Physician; A Treatise on the Nurture and Management of Infants, from the Birth until Age Two Years Old.*[115] Born in 1775, Vermont housewife Tyler was midway through her thirties and the mother of eight at the time she penned her treatise, embracing opportunity inherent in the print revolution to claim and share expertise. As she described how best to care for infants, Tyler deployed emerging cultural and political ideals surrounding motherhoods real and metaphorical to claim a place for herself among authors of health care manuals.[116] More immediately, she deployed knowledge gained through the career of her husband (lawyer, novelist, and playwright Royall Tyler) to turn her expertise—as a mother, and as close reader of existing health care literature—to profit in the world of publishing.[117] Tyler's pocket-sized publication and others like it would reshape landscapes of care in the Connecticut Valley and across New England. Kathleen Brown has correctly suggested that Tyler's work reflects the "opportunities republican motherhood" opened up for women, but such publications had implications too for the informal work of neighborhood healers.[118] If Tyler's aim was to spare mothers the need to consult male physicians, the pages of self-help treatises like this one also enabled women to find answers to their questions without consulting, whether formally or casually, local women who had established themselves as experts in the care of young children.

The issue here, then, is less how women whose livelihoods involved health care fared alongside men working in the same arena than how these developments altered relations among women, though the former necessarily affected the latter. Indeed, once the ideal of republican motherhood entered the print revolution, a flood of publications advised middle-class white women on matters related to caregiving, among many other domestic concerns. Information once the province of specialists became more widely available, though unlike the field of gown making, the upshot was not a larger number of practitioners who bought primers and opened practices.[119] Instead, informal practitioners like Hadley's Mrs. Alixander became less necessary as books published their collected advice while the gulf between households and professionally educated physicians widened. Along with these developments came various and new forms of bias. Wet nursing, for instance, became vaguely suspicious, as it was perceived to violate the integrity of the increasingly important nuclear family. Texts on child-rearing separated middle-class mothers and the poor or working-class women who had traditionally worked as wet nurses, now increasingly seen as "medically threatening and morally lax."[120] In time, publications that encouraged readers to acquire knowledge necessary to provide their own health care were succeeded by others that framed their female readers' contribution to health principally in terms of their roles as keepers of clean homes, deferring to the formal expertise of physicians for any medical needs of substance.[121] Hadley's place at the epicenter of broom production, which drew some women into production and many into consumption, while generating significant wealth for a handful of households, presents one way that the town was entangled in larger trajectories of cleanliness, though these new standards would resonate across domestic landscapes and the workers therein.

These developments had consequences for healing landscapes, and the ways in which the social relations of women's health were shaped and reshaped in the early republic. Some aspects of care, as we have seen, involved significant travel. Elizabeth Pitkin Porter and other affluent women traveled to what were literally therapeutic places, seeking out healing waters—pools and spas—to remedy a range of ailments, effort that brought them into the orbit of hospitality workers at those destinations, and at sites along the way. Meanwhile, native healers like Rhoda Rhoades ranged widely, sharing their skill and knowledge across a wide swath of western New England. Midwives like Elizabeth Allen also traveled across and between communities, though their sites of work—spaces of a woman's "confinement," to use the period term—were microgeographies of privacy and intimacy. In the early nineteenth century, practitioners like Northampton's itinerant dentist would mention attending to "ladies" in their own homes as a feature of genteel care, though of course medical caregiving already largely unfolded in the home. Physicians and healers as well as nurses like Lydia Hodgekiss or Ruth White, whether dealing with short-term circumstances or chronic illness, also labored in intimate spaces (in their own homes or in the homes of those in their care), the presence of caregivers and caregiving reordering, for varying lengths of time, physical and social spaces. For women in health and healing roles, providing such care could be a mainstay of one's livelihood and identity—as it appears to have been for Hadley's midwives—or an occasional, but significant, activity performed by women with aptitude, inclination, availability, and experience.

Women's work in health care and healing knit together households around Hampshire County and beyond, in relationships inflected by both care and commerce. Then as now, those responsible for providing care assumed positions of unusual power in the lives of their clients. Relationships grounded in exchange, like domestic service and cloth making, suggest certain braided and interdependent lines of authority and autonomy, but relationships grounded in health care and healing were steeped as well in vulnerability and dependence, fear and frustration, gratitude and appreciation. Boundaries of the work both literal and metaphorical were porous, as caregivers' roles and those of domestic servants could become ill-defined. Moreover, caregiving invoked the needs of (concerned, sometimes desperate) family members beyond those directly involved in provision or receipt of attention. And lastly, health care and healing work demanded the emotional labor of compassion and the cultivation of patience, alongside more specialized medical knowledge as well as long experience.

Yet, alongside continuity is change, and alongside entanglement is untangling. New social relations of labor in and around caring work are perhaps most visible in the work of wet nursing. Historian Nora Doyle has convincingly argued that, as motherhood became increasingly sentimentalized after the turn of the nineteenth century, relationships among women changed. "Whereas the women who employed wet nurses in the eighteenth century tended to see their nurses as part of their community of friends and acquaintances," she writes, "by the early decades of the nineteenth century women were more likely to define their wet nurses as troublesome laboring bodies, exposing the race and class biases that played an increasingly important role in the way women defined themselves as mothers and how they viewed other women."[122] As Hadley entered the nineteenth century, new attitudes toward breastfeeding allowed some women to "[fulfill] the ideals of sentimental motherhood," while for others breastfeeding "was a bodily function that could be bought and sold"—developments that, Doyle continues, "allowed women to fracture the community of mothers along lines of race and class."[123] The print revolution, too, facilitated separation among households, as women who once might have called in a neighbor to advise and assist with the care of children could now seek remedies in the burgeoning world of advice literature, preserving their family's privacy while sparing themselves the small bit of commercial and social exchange such consultations involved.

As caring occupations in Hadley shifted over time, women like Jenny Dodge and Mary Palmer Tyler, possessed of some entrepreneurial demeanor and positioned to embrace new opportunities, created new roles for themselves in the medical marketplace. Other women healers and care providers fielded other kinds of change; midwife Betty Allen may have bequeathed her practice to her daughter, but the latter woman's practice would unfold amid the robust competition of male physicians. Along the way, the work of nursing—long stints at bedsides, waiting and watching; the laundering of sheets and bedclothes; the bathing and soothing of patients, and others acts of care—persisted in many ways unaltered.

TOPOGRAPHIES OF CHANGE

Working Women and the Domestic Landscapes of Forty Acres

Mrs. Lord is "coming," wrote Elizabeth Porter Phelps one April morning, though "I have felt almost afraid to have her, for my situation has been a great deal farther distant from gentility than ever—& you surely remember that was far eno." If in 1803 Elizabeth Porter Phelps perceived herself to be "far distant" from gentility, of the women in Hampshire County she was far nearer than most.[1] Rather, Charles and Elizabeth's household was among Hadley's wealthiest, and the couple had accrued a good deal of the town's political, social, and cultural authority. Indeed, in late eighteenth-century Hadley, the Porter and the Phelps families *defined* gentility. Elizabeth's reference that morning was not to any real or metaphorical separation from polite society. Instead, the nagging sense of inelegance of which she complained was the result of her temporary but chronic lack of household help. The quest for gentility, over the course of the eighteenth century, had swelled gaps among aspirants, some of whom were necessarily more successful than others. But at the same time, through the effort to distinguish themselves from their neighbors, people like Charles and Elizabeth Porter Phelps in fact cultivated close ties with those same neighbors.[2]

But if Elizabeth Phelps conceived of social position as a place, a spot on a mental geography from which she herself was "far distant," other distances, other, nearer spaces, also shaped and reflected her family's refinement. In the early republic, as ever larger numbers of men and women strove toward a standard of living that historians have termed "refinement," ultimately creating what we now see as a middle-class sensibility, domestic workspaces were altered to reflect the shifting position of household workers in the evolving social and economic order. Themes of labor and liberty run through these decades, and through this study.[3] Elizabeth Phelps regularly wrote of finding herself more "at liberty" upon the return of a hired woman who freed her hands for less onerous labors. Meanwhile, Peg, the enslaved woman who lived in the household, "went off free" in 1783, her place filled by other servants as well as African American women, freed from other households, who took in washing. Finally, other Anglo-American workers themselves harnessed the rhetoric of Revolution and pressed for the "liberty" to move freely through the homes of their employers.[4] These pages opened with an imaginary tour around the town common, inviting readers to picture the houses clustered around the community's center of social, cultural, and economic gravity. In this final section we begin by peering inside the Phelps farm, Forty Acres, to see women in the more intimate physical setting of home, and contemplate how interior topographies and landscapes both shaped and reflected shifting social relations of labor.

Both the longing for gentility and the confluence and conflation of physical environments with social identity have attracted significant scholarly attention.[5] The arrangement and alteration of domestic landscapes and the constellations of objects upon and within them also yield important clues to how different sorts of women's work functioned within households. There can be no doubt that access to domestic spaces was carefully and critically controlled by and among men and women in early New England: one need only look at the language of legal instruments establishing the dower rights of widows to see how the right to inhabit, pass through, and utilize spaces was jealously guarded. For example, after the death of her husband Quartus, Deerfield's Lucy Barnard Wells was granted use of the south half of the family home, but the judge further specified her right to "go in and out of the front door and up and down the front stairs," to "pass in and out of the south door, to pass to and from the oven in the middle room" (she had also been granted the use of the south half of that room), and to use the oven. In addition, Wells had rights to "the south half of the chamber over the middle room, the right to pass to and from the south chamber in the front house to the chamber over the middle room," and finally, to use the east half of the kitchen, and the "Buttery in the passway leading from the said Middle room to the kitchen," as well as the right to "use the passway from the middle room to the kitchen and to the wood house."[6] While this document might be notable in its detail, it is not unusual in its form or intent. In 1794 Susanna Bartlett Catlin (whose sister Patience sewed at Forty Acres before she married and moved to Deerfield) was granted use of the lower room in the southeast parlor of her house, the south half of the southwest chamber, and one-third of the cellar at the house's south end. She also was assured access to the kitchen, the right to store her flour in the kitchen chamber, and to keep her clothes in the "east part of a press in the south entry." Access to space could be closely monitored and controlled. Objects and spaces helped to define relationships not only of widows and children (or, perhaps more to the point, daughters-in-law), but also between clients and craftswomen, employers and employees, and women workers in a variety of positions in the household.

This analysis brings into focus one of those sites of consumption—and production—by looking at how those spaces that sheltered work processes wove together disparate forces and perspectives while at the same time altering them.[7] To do so, it examines spaces in which women worked, as well as elements of the built environment that suggest the values of both employers and employees. Sometimes, those artifacts are all but ephemeral, and yet powerful even in their ephemerality. For instance, the most poignant physical evidence of working women left at Forty Acres is surely the dark stain that rings the baseboards in one of the pantries—a faint trace of some hundreds of good scrubbings that bodies forth the "invisible hand" of capitalism imagined by Adam Smith in these same years.[8] There is a good deal of evidence of that labor contained not only in Phelps's lifelong memorandum book and extensive correspondence, but in the spaces of the house itself, a domestic landscape that both resisted and accommodated the rural workforce she oversaw. Rethinking domestic structures like the Phelps house from the perspective of the working women who crossed their thresholds affords an opportunity to reconsider the social relations of women's work as they shifted and reconfigured across domestic terrains of the early republic.[9]

Landscapes of Refinement

Scholars interested in material culture have tracked long and gradual changes in the relationship between individuals and their communities that are particularly visible in the artifacts of domestic life. A seventeenth-century world of benches and shared serving vessels slowly gave way to sets of individual chairs and dishes; multi-use spaces gave way to separate rooms dedicated to sleeping, entertaining, or dining. Such innovations were slower to come to some families than others. In Hampshire County, Hannah Judd Lyman remembered that when her family sat down to their morning meal in the late eighteenth century, a single plate or platter of meat together with bread and butter was offered, sometimes with potatoes that were cut into mouthfuls. She married in 1802, and believed that before that time there were never plates on her family's breakfast table, while at dinner, too, meat, pudding, and other things were "cut up and handed round on plates. Sometimes the vegetables also; & sometimes each helped himself to potatoe."[10] As late as 1800, her family was still eating from shared vessels passed around; separate place settings were not yet part of her everyday world, though the tabletop manifestations of new ideas about individuals, identity, family, and community already afoot would soon arrive.

Lyman's breakfast reminds us that changes experienced across American society in the early years of the republic came in fits and starts, reaching some communities and some families well before others. Such developments can be viewed, too, through alterations to the architecture that sheltered the Hadley household of Charles and Elizabeth Porter Phelps. During their nearly fifty-year tenure, from 1770 to 1817, the house underwent three major transformations in three separate remodeling campaigns: in 1771; between 1775 and 1786; and at the end of the century, around 1797 to 1799, when the house assumed its present appearance.[11] Each renovation served to expand and elaborate the formal spaces of the house, while removing its work spaces farther from view, enabling work itself—whether performed by the mistress of the house or others who worked for her—and also enlarging both spatial and social distances between employers and employees.

Even when first constructed in 1752, Moses Porter's house was a striking departure from local precedent. The pitched roof of this large and imposing building sheltered what would become (but was not yet) the familiar two-story, double-pile, central-passage house of New England's rural gentry, but Porter made choices that set his home well apart from the majority of his neighbors, and even from most of his peers. Most noticeable, and visible to all passersby, was the decision to use rusticated siding to suggest the appearance of a large stone mansion. The three presentational facades of the house—the north, south, and east sides—were covered with wooden boards that had been scored and beveled to resemble stone coursing, an effect enhanced with reddish-brown paint mixed with sand (simulating Longmeadow sandstone) on the faux "stones," and white trim in the grooves between, to imitate mortar. The effect was continued in flat arches that marked the building's entrances. While Moses Porter's house was not the only eighteenth-century building in New England that was so covered, it was among the earliest. In fact, no other houses with rusticated siding are known to have been built in the Connecticut Valley in the eighteenth century.[12] Moreover, houses even of brick were rare. As William Hosley notes in a discussion of the brick "manor house" erected in 1659 by western Massachusetts' unrivaled power magnate Colonel John Pynchon of Springfield, "more than a century later, brick architecture was still practically unknown in the Connecticut Valley and even wooden houses with double chimneys and central halls"—features also employed by Porter—"were few in number and owned only by the wealthiest of the Valley's inhabitants."[13]

Perhaps Porter consciously sought to allude to the Pynchon dynasty when he chose this appearance for his new home. Certainly his house was among the most distinctive in Hadley. Arrivals at the Phelps home, then, were initially impressed with the sheer size of the building, and then with the striking materials in which the large frame was sheathed. Then they proceeded through the series of barriers that defined the Georgian style while also regulating movement through the home. First they encountered the presentational spaces of the Phelps dooryard and portico—outdoor space separating residents from passersby—before proceeding to the doorway and the central hall. Once there, visitors were directed to spaces appropriate to their needs and status.[14] Through the central hall the Porter and later Phelps families were more equipped than most to control access to spaces within their home, protecting their growing desire for privacy while directing and controlling the movements of workers and guests in the house.

These architectural hurdles confronted all the women who arrived at Forty Acres, though it affected them differently, depending on the purpose of their visit and their points of departure. "Doorways," writes Robert Blair St. George, "were fragile membranes separating the outside world of the locally made and the inner world of elite fashion. They were portals through which only the chosen few, the socially elect, could pass."[15] The women of Phelps's kinship and social networks who left equally well-appointed and fashionable homes, who traveled in fashionable forms of conveyance to Phelps's house to participate in group quilting activities, or to join the family for tea, were indeed members of that "elect" group. Though subjected to the rigor of the processional entrance, they passed easily through it, and gained entry to spaces throughout the house. What's more, they were familiar with this arrangement. Indeed, far from being intimidated, these women found movement through those hierarchically arranged spaces reassuring tokens of other hierarchies, welcome signs of commonality, of their shared and sure membership in the social and cultural groups to which they aspired.[16] Their easy movement through this house was well practiced in houses throughout the region, spaces to which they gained entry as guests of their friends and relatives, men and women who wielded power and influence in other communities just as their families wielded power and influence in Hadley. Their familiarity with landscapes well beyond Hampshire County made this one more legible: the floorplan was familiar, the architecture familiar, the objects housed here had familiar forms and styles. It was a recognizable territory, one that they, as Phelps's peers and guests, could easily negotiate.

Other women arrived at rear doors, membranes of another sort, and experienced the house's spaces of refinement very differently. The first landscape experienced by Hampshire County workers employed at Forty Acres was the most literal one: the ground between their own homes and the site of their labors. Many of the women arrived not by carriage, but on foot. Hampshire County women were well used to walking great distances when necessary, and smaller ones almost daily. Women used other means of conveyance as well, from horses, to wagons, to chairs, to carriages. Though most Hampshire County working women were by no means itinerant in the usual sense of the word, travel to and from worksites was an integral part of their experience. In that commute, women traversed more than measures of rods and miles as they entered the homes of others and encountered there new material environments.

Perception of distance in early America was largely determined by one's ease of movement and access to technologies of mobility. Elvira Casal has described the shifting significance of distance in the past: "While measurement of distance in miles may be objective, the perception of distance is subjective, determined by the individual's experience, personality and position in this world."[17] Therefore, she concludes, the two major categories most relevant to the experience of distance are those that most influenced mobility: wealth and gender. In the eighteenth century as today, greater wealth made travel more convenient, more comfortable, more readily accessible, and more reliable, for all that possessed it. But even among women of some means, travel posed more difficulties for women than it did for men. What might have been an unremarkable distance for men could present complications for women (especially women concerned with gentility), if it was sufficient to require a traveling companion, or if the distance or destination discouraged travel on horseback, demanding a more appropriate means of conveyance. Wealth and gender shaped the experience of distance among Hampshire County working women, too. Access to horses, carriages, and sleighs, the types of tools they required for the work they intended to perform, and the potential and means for those tools' conveyance, were all products of intersections between wealth, gender, and mobility.

Even Elizabeth Porter Phelps, though she was better traveled than the majority of her Hadley neighbors, and certainly her employees, navigated a closer circumference than did her husband Charles. Typical is a journal entry of August, 1779: "Tuesday my husband set out for Concord to a convention i went into town of errands . . ."[18] Charles's political duties, as selectman (twenty-one terms) and representative (seven terms), took him on trips throughout the state—the same trips that brought him into contact with potential servants.[19] Elizabeth meanwhile records hundreds of such "errands" into Hadley and back. While he traveled far, she traveled near: "Satt Morning Mr Phelps set out for Boston (he sent his cattle on Tuesday) just at night I rode as far as the Mills of errands."[20] While he went to the city to take his beef to market, she rode around town to get cloth fulled, milk pans mended, and broken crockery replaced.[21] Indeed, Charles himself, as a surveyor, helped to create the very roads on which he and his wife would travel: "Thurs morn [Charles] went out to Ware with others as a committee to lay roads. Fryday afternoon returned. I rode out did some errands."[22] Charles's trips to Boston took the better part of three days on horseback; Elizabeth's trips into town required much briefer absences.

In their access to various means of conveyance, Charles and Elizabeth joined a handful of Hadley families able to travel in relative comfort. In 1791, that meant the families of Eleazer and Elisha Porter (who each owned fall-back chaises); Azariah Dickinson (who also owned a fall-back chaise); Enos Smith (whose stand-top chaise was most like the Phelps's); and William Shipman (whose family enjoyed a riding chair).[23] In 1795, Dorothy Ashley Williams described the "handsome coachee" of Pierpont Edwards and family, who arrived for a visit in "high style," "the harness heavy with silver and other things in proportion."[24] Elizabeth's father Moses had been one of only two carriage owners in all of Hampshire County.[25] In time, Elizabeth Phelps would enjoy so many options that at the close of the century she and Charles built a dedicated building, a "carriage house," to store them. She generally records having "rode" into town to complete her errands, although she occasionally distinguishes when she was on foot: for example, "Thursday I up to the mill on foot for a reed."[26] When she rode, did she travel in a chair or carriage, or on horseback? She also records many occasions on which she "rode out" with her husband to survey their property, visit neighbors, seek out shops, and so on. Were they riding together on a horse? Before the end of the eighteenth century, Sylvester Judd records, Hampshire County women commonly traveled by horseback, often on "pillions" (that is, a cushion attached behind the saddle, for a second rider). Elizabeth Porter Phelps records having "made the Pillion clothes," suggesting something of her means of travel and her sewing responsibilities as well.[27] But the mud-hemmed skirts of the working women who walked to Forty Acres tell another story. Coupled with the carpets on the Phelps's floor, they suggest ways that hired and artisanal women experienced the domestic landscape here differently than Phelps's own circle of family and friends.

Geographies of Gentility

Like the carriages and saddles that waited in the family's barns, objects and spaces within Forty Acres signaled the family's privilege, cultural leadership, and membership among the gentry.[28] For instance, although the quilters who came to help Phelps create the distinctive petticoats worn by fashionable women were subjected to the formal barriers of the processional entrance, they moved smoothly through them, encountering throughout the house a recognizable landscape, one that they could easily navigate. The material appointments of quiltings enabled members of the rural gentry to share the accoutrements of gentility between them, to enhance their sense of commonality, and to distinguish themselves from neighbors who were unable to acquire these goods, and were unfamiliar with the rituals associated with their proper use.[29] In the words of the historian Ann Smart Martin, "the tilt of the head, the turn of a phrase, the grasp of a glass—all combined to create a gentry language that knit together the elite and excluded the commoner."[30]

Those "commoners" who may well have found Forty Acres exclusionary included women who labored there. For some, the interior rooms of the Phelps home were what we might today call "aspirational"—whether or not women who passed through these spaces were able to afford many of its accoutrements, the material environment—the comfortable textiles, writing and reading equipage, fine china, and other luxury goods—was familiar. For others, much of this environment must have appeared at best unfamiliar, and at worst intimidating. The scale of the house itself may have proved daunting, and the interior settings unfamiliar to those visitors to the house who were less well traveled.[31] The furnishings of Hadley houses varied widely, but a cursory comparison between the probate inventories of the fathers and husbands of women employed at Forty Acres with those in the Porter families (unfortunately, none survive for Elizabeth and Charles Phelps's household) suggests a widening gap in the number and quality of the objects surrounding them. Picturing these women negotiating spaces at Forty Acres helps us to imagine the different ways in which workwomen entered this environment. Around 1788, for instance, Charles and Elizabeth Phelps purchased the first carpet in Hadley. As many as thirty years later, there were still only "very few" carpets in Hadley, while Northampton's Olive Clark recalled that, as late as 1809, "there was not a carpet in the town of Williamsburg or Chesterfield and there were not many carpets in Northampton. I never saw a carpet until I was eighteen years old."[32]

Such differences were surely not lost on Hampshire County's working women. For example, the home of wheelwright Francis Newton, tavernkeeper Elizabeth Newton, and their two daughters, Betty (among Forty Acres' weavers and needlewomen) and Tryphena (who also sewed for the Phelps family, and worked in the family tavern), was quite spartan in comparison to the home where these women traveled to sew. In addition to an assortment of bedsteads, underbeds, and bed linens, the Newton house held just three chests (one with drawers), three tables, and ten chairs. A mirror helped light one room, reflecting the flame of four candlesticks. Around the hearth lay two teakettles, an iron pot and basin, a frying pan and a brass skillet, as well as the ubiquitous peal, tongs, and skimmer. Serving dishes were of wood, tin, and pewter, though the Newtons did enjoy two sets of tea dishes, as well as a few scattered pieces of earthenware, woodenware, and glassware. Of interest too is what is not listed in Newton's inventory, which mentions no silver canns or spoons on Newton's shelves, nor a single book. No carpets warmed and softened any floor. When Betty and Tryphena walked to the Phelps house to work, how did they register the gap between their own material circumstances and the Phelps family's?[33] Put another way, if part of the currency of the shared work of quilting, or more gatherings both social and strategic, was the use and exchange of familiar forms of gentility, then conversely, part of the transactions between workers and their employers was the heightened awareness of the gaps forming between some families able to employ help and other families seeking employment.

In some rooms of Forty Acres, the objects encountered were just like those in their own homes; in other rooms, they were both unfamiliar and unattainable. While Phelps's practical furniture was probably made by local craftsmen such as Ansel Goodrich and Samuel Gaylord, the parlor furniture likely came from urban centers like Boston, distances between sites of production and consumption themselves creating distances among neighbors as they distinguished who could afford such goods and who could not.[34] The desk and bookcase that stood in the Phelpses' parlor may have served as a singular symbol of one of the main differences between Elizabeth Phelps and themselves. "You must know I have got all my writing apparatus into the long room, my letters and papers make the table and room look like a writing office almost," Elizabeth on one occasion wrote to her daughter.[35] Writing apparatus, letters, and papers—a source of genuine pleasure for Elizabeth Phelps—might have been somewhat intimidating to women who marked their name, when public documents required it, with an *X*. For women unfamiliar with legal processes, or for whom contact with "professionals" usually meant trouble, the appearance of a "writing office" may have been discomforting. These large, imposing pieces of furniture must indeed have been "powerful statements of economic status, learning, and possible commercial pursuits."[36] Observers well knew that behind the hinged doors (themselves suggesting concealment and inaccessibility) lay published books and pamphlets (that could also remind them of their own limited facility with texts, and lack of formal education) and account records (perhaps containing the very records of their own indebtedness, or at least signaling by comparison the smaller scale of their own financial prospects). Books furthermore marked a different order of affluence: they indicated ample expenditures not only of wealth but of time.

The writing surface may have cued other concerns, suggesting to the observer not only the wider horizons that prompted a large correspondence, but the likely recipients of that correspondence, powerful men and women throughout the region. The Phelpses' desk would have been recognized as a site of literacy, of correspondence, a symbol of the Phelpses' easy movement in a wider social and economic universe. The parlor was a space in which Elizabeth Porter Phelps felt especially comfortable, but which might have been fairly intimidating to a working woman whose access to literacy was comparatively circumscribed.

How people employed at the farm handled these and other minutiae of daily intercourse is impossible to know: shades of meaning passed perhaps imperceptibly, with little notice of naivete. Or perhaps the Phelps women knew how discreetly to initiate the uninitiated. Did the craftswomen who entered the Phelps household know the proper way to hold a teacup or how to signal when they were finished? Perhaps so, and perhaps not. Whether the family politely overlooked these differences, it seems as if at least one inhabitant of Forty Acres occasionally blanched at the lack of refinement among her neighbors. While in Brimfield, Massachusetts, a young Betsy Phelps wrote her brother Charles that while she found the town's inhabitants to be honest, industrious, and clever, they are "rather more rustical (if possible) than those of Hadley."[37] The nineteen-year-old was largely just teasing her older brother, then a more cosmopolitan resident of Boston, and perhaps poking a little fun at herself, as one of those rustical residents. But her mirth also hints that at least one of them had indeed at some time past chuckled at the "rusticity" of their Hadley neighbors.

Knowing how to handle the plenitude of imported goods was not the sole mark of refinement. Alongside the mastery of the tangible accoutrements of gentility lay mastery of intangibles as well—Martin's "tilt of the head." Posture was an integral part of genteel appearance, and young gentlewomen were well tutored in carriage, gestures, and positioning. Learning to hold one's head and shoulders properly, how to enter and leave a room, how to sit, or how to strike an appealing pose, as we have seen, became the province of dancing masters who cultivated among their rural pupils the appropriate demeanors. Taking the example of needlework, the link between posture and sewing was neither subtle nor indirect. The gulf between elite and working women was pronounced in silhouette, in women seated, for example, at tambour or embroidery frames versus seamstresses hunched over their sewing. Gentlewomen were noted for their upright, though not stiff, posture. "The proper posture of one that sits," according to one courtesy book, "is to have that part of his Body from the Waste upwards, upright, tho' free and moveable, and the lower part firm, close to his Seat, and motionless, without crossing his Legs."[38] In his 1792 play, *The School for Scandal*, Richard Sheridan describes Sir Richard Teazle's first glimpse of the woman he would marry: "Recollect, Lady Teazle, when I saw you first, sitting at your tambour, in a pretty figured linen gown, with a bunch of keys at your side, your hair combed smooth over a roll, and your apartment hung round with fruits in worsted of your working."[39]

Notice the elements required of a gentlewoman that Sheridan selects: her upright posture, sitting at the tambour frame, the tambour work itself, and the other "fruits in worsted" hung about the room, demonstrating her education, her family's wealth and leisure, the figured linen gown, indicating both wealth and style, and the keys hanging at her side, signs of her authority over the spaces of her household. Lady Teazle's cultured demeanor was exactly the effect to which gentlewomen aspired. Sheridan's fictional figure found living counterparts in parlors throughout New England, including Forty Acres. In a letter to her daughter, Elizabeth Phelps described how Deacon Williams surprised her with a "fore-noon visit," but she hastened to add that Betsy need not "be feared," for "my head was combed and cap on and set down to sewing in very decent order."[40] Phelps assured her daughter that by the time the unexpected company had arrived, she had, luckily, finished her work, taken off her "morning clothes," and had achieved an appearance (her hair, like Teazle's, "combed smooth") and work ("set down to sewing") that would render her "decent" in the eyes of the Deacon.

In contrast, needleworkers whether male or female have long been noted for their peculiar posture, cross-legged and bent over their work. Tailors in shops sat in this pose on surfaces raised up above the floor and near windows, to take advantage of the light.[41] Tailors like Mary Trainer's husband Francis probably did likewise. Sewing women most likely approximated this posture seated in chairs, with one leg crossed over another to form a temporary work surface in their lap. Observers worried that sustaining this position—and the generally sedentary nature of the work itself, in contrast to most other occupations of the time—could be hazardous to one's health. Historian Madeleine Ginsburg has noted that the rounded backs demanded by sewing was believed to be injurious; the folk phrase "nine tailors make a man," some sources suggest, may have arisen in part from the notion that the occupation was not "conducive to sound physical development."[42] Even Campbell's mid-eighteenth-century guide to trades advised parents that, while tailoring was by no means an arduous or dangerous occupation for their children, the demands of the work were not always especially healthful: "The custom of sitting cross-legged, always in one posture, bending their body, makes them liable to coughs and consumptions, more than any trade I know. You rarely see a Taylor live to a great Age; therefore I think a sickly tender Constitution, or a Habit the least inclinable to a Consumption, is very unfit for a Taylor."[43]

Historian and poet Dolores Hayden has written of what she calls "body memory"; she suggests that, when groups of people linked by a common gender, race, or class share dwellings, public spaces, workplaces, or the means of travel between home and work, they reflect that social position in the position of their own forms. "The experience of physical labor," Hayden adds, "is also part of body memory. In a dusty vineyard, a crowded sweatshop, or an oil field, people acquire the characteristic postures of certain occupations—picking grapes, sewing dresses, pumping gas," and so on.[44] One Hampshire County diarist captured something of the unseemly postures involved in women's labor as he described women cooking: "In they come one a hunching one way and another the other way and after while the breakfast is ready."[45] Hadley's working women too, whether bent over sewing or mending, or washtubs and hearths, possessed body memory of their labor.

Gentility in domestic landscapes and work spaces required both the possession of certain objects and a certain poise regarding their use. Laboring women's movement through those spaces and positions, literally and figuratively, was determined at least in part by the demands of their work. Conversely, when

Deacon Williams arrived unexpectedly on that spring morning in 1801, Phelps had successfully hidden the evidence of her own effort. She had altered her appearance, exchanging a set of work clothes for more formal attire. She had altered her location, leaving the kitchen and settling down in the parlor. And she had altered her activity, from the hard work of starting the day on a large farm to the more subdued work of sewing. To be a proper lady she had to hide the evidence that in reality she *did* work in the morning, that the house wasn't always what it appeared. In those alterations, Elizabeth Phelps sought to close the gap between herself and gentility.

Renovating the Social Relations of Work

Forms of transportation and postures might have been the first hints of enlarging disparities between women, but more substantial were those taking place within those domestic spaces themselves—developments that altered spaces according to the desires and preferences of the homeowners, and the workloads and perceptions of the working women who encountered them as well. Much of that reconfiguration reflected and helped drive changing relationships with other kinds of domestic workers at the close of the eighteenth century, but all of these alterations—physical, social, and cultural—were embedded in an economy that was straining toward something new, in shifting relationships between employers and employees, and emerging attitudes toward women's domestic work that affected hirers and hired alike. The significant renovations to the Phelps house in the last quarter of the eighteenth century throw at least a slanting light on the evolution of women's work relationships in early New England.

When Elizabeth Porter married Charles Phelps in 1770, her home had remained unchanged from the dwelling that her father constructed in 1752. Four rooms downstairs were separated, two on each side, by a central hall. The second story largely repeated that arrangement. Chimney stacks on either end of the house provided corner hearths to these rooms. The unusual faux stone facade of the house conveyed a sense of grandeur that surely affected working women traveling from their own single- or one-and-a-half-story more plainly constructed wooden houses. The floorplan of the house was equally unfamiliar, central-hall plans being the exception throughout most of eighteenth-century rural western Massachusetts (figure 8.1).[46]

The effect of the central hall in its day must indeed have been dramatic, even daunting.[47] Houses oriented around a central chimney—the vast majority of houses in Hampshire County in this period—were entered via a small vestibule made shallow by the winding narrow staircase placed directly in front of the entrance. Visitors to Moses Porter's home, by contrast, would see the door swing open to reveal a spacious central hall, opening to the visible

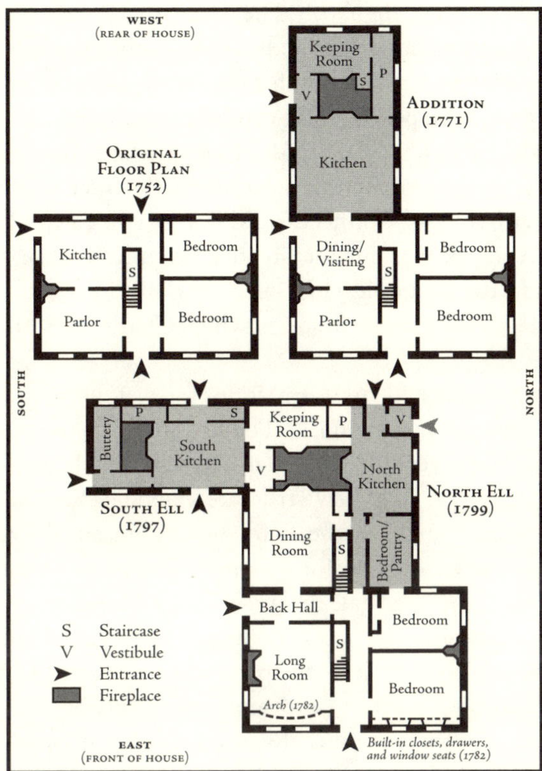

Figure 8.1 Forty Acres floorplans, 1752–1820. Over the course of Forty Acres' first seven decades, the extent, use, and arrangement of rooms for living and working at the farm evolved. As the family made alterations that increased their privacy and ability to control movement through spaces, labor and laborers drifted from easy view. Those same changes, however, also increased privacy and autonomy for the farm's working women. Drawing by Kate Blackmer

second story and extending to the rear wall. The narrow winding staircase that in most houses clung to the chimney stack immediately beyond the threshold was replaced in this house by a spacious hall, and a broad set of stairs straight ahead, ornamented by airy balusters and anchored by newel posts. This staircase itself carried an aura of grandeur, and was certainly intended to be impressive, if not intimidating. Though a larger number of homes in Hatfield and Hadley contained a second story, most of them were central-chimney, one- or one-and-a-half-story houses that permitted no such expansive vista. At a time when three-fourths of the houses of Colrain, and two-thirds of the houses in Pelham—communities from which many of the town's domestic servants were drawn—were still just a single story, the effect of this ornate, open hall must have been singular.[48] The innovative floorplan and distinctive exterior made a special statement to all comers—that the family within was culturally and socially positioned both to inherit features of residential architecture long aligned with power, and to embrace new trends in domestic architecture, and that it was financially positioned to adopt them. The house's external appearance was not matched, however, by the interior finishing of these rooms; like other homes of Connecticut Valley gentry, Moses Porter preferred to invest the greater part of his architectural resources in features visible to observers outside the home, leaving interior walls either unfinished or only plainly finished. These were the rooms in which Charles and Elizabeth courted and then married.

But the young couple had larger ambitions for their home, and immediately embarked on a series of renovations.[49] The first major change to the structure, undertaken less than a year after Charles's arrival, was the construction of an ell, raised in April 1771. The new structure extended behind the southwest chamber (then functioning as the main hearth for meal preparation) and housed a new kitchen and "keeping" room.[50] The latter kitchen contained a much larger cooking hearth than the previous corner hearth, and a large pantry.[51] A winding stair provided access to the ell's attic. A built-in or "press" bed provided additional, ad hoc sleeping space when it was required. Access between the kitchen and the farmyard and woodpile was directly through a south-facing doorway; visitors using this entrance passed into a small vestibule from which one could continue on to either the keeping room on the left (west) or the kitchen to the right (east).

The immediate effect of this addition was simply to provide more space for what was already one additional member of the family, and to prepare for the others the couple hoped would arrive in the ensuing years. Moses Porter could not of course have known when he built it that his life would be cut so short, but the modest corner hearth he designed satisfied his widow and only child for almost twenty years. The new ell perhaps embodied the optimism of newlyweds who hoped soon to outgrow that small kitchen; indeed, Elizabeth occupied the new keeping room, adjacent to the kitchen, following the births of her children.[52] But as a workspace, the new kitchen offered significant improvements over its predecessor, including a larger and more functional hearth, more storage, and more light, thanks to the south- and north-facing windows as well as a plastered ceiling, if not also walls.[53] The new chimney stack accommodated a new, larger hearth and bake oven for this ground-floor kitchen, as well as a smoke oven above and perhaps basement fireplace or oven as well.[54]

If the new ell reflected Charles and Elizabeth's hopes for their eventual family, it may have reflected other aspirations as well. The larger kitchen, for example, helped accommodate the feeding of Charles Phelps's growing number of farmhands. It also seems possible that the new garret may have provided additional space to lodge servants or laborers, perhaps even Peg, Cesar, Phillis, and Rose, the enslaved African Americans whose labor the family claimed in the 1770s (Zebulon Prutt having been sold from the farm by this date).[55] It is worth pausing here to consider their distinct experience of this architecture. In his pathbreaking study of race and plantation architecture, Dell Upton suggests that circumventing the formal barriers of the processional entrance "[could] undercut the social statement made by the formal approach. In this kind of landscape, blacks could pass almost at will, while whites from outside had to observe the formalities."[56] Alexandra Chan likewise posits, in her discussion of the enslaved inhabitants of the Royall House in Medford, Massachusetts, that these laborers were "probably more intimate with the house than any of the Royall's visitors could be and more privy to the intimacy of the Royall family than even the Royalls themselves could imagine."[57] Peg, her daughters, and granddaughter knew Forty Acres as the site of their labor and their enslavement. Cesar, as a male laborer whose workday took him around the farm's vast acreage, found a wider compass; for him, the barn and other outbuildings formed a larger part of his everyday landscapes.

The shifts in room use introduced in the 1771 renovation were formalized in a second, longer, and more extensive remodeling campaign, which stretched from 1775 to 1786.[58] Over the course of this decade, the functions of the house's older rooms were altered and upgraded via refinishing. Unlike the first renovation (and the third, yet to come), which altered the external appearance of the house in ways that signaled wealth and gentility, this round of renovations was almost wholly interior, visible only to people who gained entry to the home, and not those more casually acquainted with the house. Indeed, some of these alterations, in spaces largely devoted to the entertaining of visitors to whom Elizabeth Phelps referred as "smart folk" were not visible even to everyone who gained entrance to the house, like farm help whose responsibilities never led them, for example, to the house's second-floor bedchambers.[59]

More elaborate wood trim and finishes ("Georgian" moldings, raised-panel wainscoting and baseboards) were added to the central entrance hall, the northeast first-floor bedroom, and three bedchambers on the second floor,[60] while Northampton painters updated the finishes of several interior spaces.[61] The addition of new woodwork, the concealing of the house's heavy frame behind newly plastered walls, paint and trim applied to previously undecorated wooden surfaces, the installation of new window glass—all of these things together gave the house the lighter, brighter feel appropriate for the home of fashionable Federalists.[62] As Charles and Elizabeth gained affluence and influence, they brought their home into closer correspondence with their notions of gentility, at least as they had observed it in homes of their peers throughout the region.

The third round of renovations began after February 1794, when Charles Phelps Jr. purchased the property from his mother-in-law, Elizabeth Pitkin Porter. Soon after, more construction was underway, partly in anticipation of the marriage and impending return to Hadley of Charles and Elizabeth's son, Charles Porter Phelps.[63] The Phelps household was growing, not only in terms of the return of son Porter, his wife, and their hoped-for children, but also in the numbers of hired help that the large farm—now occupying some six hundred prosperous acres—required and serviced. Their solution was to enlarge the home considerably. The appearance of the house changed greatly when, around 1800, Phelps replaced the pitched roof with an imposing gambrel roof intended to shelter new third-story apartments for the young couple (though when Charles Porter Phelps and his wife Sarah Parsons Phelps decided instead to construct a separate house across the street, the work of finishing this space was abandoned).[64] In addition, Charles and Elizabeth had already constructed two additional kitchens, one north of the 1771 ell that would be devoted to the needs of the growing family, and an enormous kitchen in a new ell south of the 1771 ell, to serve the growing needs of the farm.

The new north kitchen looked much like the other additions of the 1790s: planed board wainscoting, thin chair rails, and Federal-style mantel and surrounds, indicating that some trouble was taken to make the space both fashionable and functional. The former oblong pantry was dismantled in order to create the new kitchen's large hearth and bake oven, but what appears to have been another pantry or kitchen-related space was constructed east of the kitchen, adjacent to the original 1752 house. At least this room (converted into a bedroom by 1820) appears to have begun life as a space freely accessed by hired help, since its doors, unlike those in the other bedchambers, were never secured with locks. Moreover, the doors—recycled from the original double doors at the house's 1752 entrance—held panes of glass that would have afforded little privacy to this space's occupants, and perhaps intentionally permitted their observation.[65]

The new kitchen on the south side of the 1771 ell was also erected about 1797. This new structure created additional space devoted to Elizabeth's thriving "making-cheese business" and to feeding the growing number of field hands necessary to farm their vast acreage: the ten hands Phelps provided dinner for in August 1802 constituted just one of many such gatherings Phelps fed through the years.[66] In particular, as we have seen, this addition may have been yet more encouragement from Charles to Elizabeth to expand the dairying business, an effort she warily—and wearily—resisted.[67] Indeed, Elizabeth's letters to her daughter, many of which appear to have been written from the cheese room or adjacent kitchen, capture something of the constant drudgery of her "making-cheese business," describing the "churning and cheese and a great deal to do in the cheese room."[68] For Elizabeth, this room became a center of household production, and a place for stolen moments of leisure: "Here I am in the ketchen waiting for the cheese to drain of the whey I will improve the time to fill up the paper."[69]

The size of this kitchen and its relationship to the adjacent rear (west-facing) stoop also reflected the growing agricultural labor force on the Phelps farm. The fireplace opening in this kitchen is larger than any other in the house—nearly eight feet across and more than four feet high, with a firebox and bake oven housed beneath the lintel. Unlike the north kitchen, constructed at approximately the same time, the south kitchen had almost no ornamental woodwork, and this fireplace was the only one in the house without any sort of surround. Only the multipaned door with sidelights that connects this space with the dooryard nods to the prevailing neoclassical style. It was here that Phelps placed the large chest that served as Mary Andries's 1809 bed (which they placed "against the outward east door in the kitchen, put straw at the bottom then a bed—that is her night accommodation"[70]). This is also the kitchen, "full of talk and brawl," to which Elizabeth Phelps Huntington would object that same year. Finally, this latter building effort also involved the construction of several new structures around the farmyard, including the carriage barn (1795)[71] and a woodhouse (1797).[72] Two other barn or shed sections were erected on the south end of the new woodshed as well.[73] Other outbuildings included a number of barns, and a cider house.[74] This constellation of spaces—service kitchen, milkroom / washroom / buttery, woodhouse, and carriage house—would become a standard feature of "progressive" New England farmhouses by the mid-nineteenth century.[75]

While the creation of the north and south ell additions pushed the cooking spaces farther from the parlor, they also facilitated the creation of a truly stylish formal room at the front of the house. The house's original southeast and southwest chambers were combined into a single large parlor—termed the "Long Room" in family parlance—that became the "most thoroughgoing Federal-style space" at Forty Acres.[76] That the phrase "Long Room"—a term associated in this era with spaces in taverns or coffee houses dedicated to assemblies, entertainments, dancing, and other activities, as well as spaces in commercial settings (custom houses, exchanges, and so forth) dedicated to meetings, or recordkeeping—is itself telling; though some affluent households, like the Phelpses, enjoyed Long Rooms in residential settings, the phrase is more often associated with political and commercial transaction.[77] While surely tongue in cheek, the family's long-standing preference for "Long Room" over "parlor" nevertheless hints at the way they understood the room and its principle uses, as well as how they perceived themselves in the context of other leading families whose dwelling contained (and required) such a space. Accordingly, brass hardware on the door from the entry hall to the parlor contrasted with the more crudely wrought iron hardware seen throughout the rest of the hall, alerting visitors to the importance of this space. Concealing the framing of the house (by building out the plaster walls beyond the face of the beams) further enhanced the sophistication of the room. This renovation also created the room's most impressive feature, the "broad, graceful arch" that sections off the east end of the room, framing the front windows and helping to create an illusion of symmetry. The arch was completed just in time to shelter Betsy's marriage to the Reverend Daniel Huntington on New Year's Day, 1801.[78]

Finally, in much the same way as the first addition to the house (the construction of that 1771 kitchen) had transformed what had been working rooms into more intermediate spaces, so too did this round of renovations. With additional kitchens now flanking each side of the 1771 kitchen, that space too, through the reduction in the size of the hearth and the addition of a Federal-style mantel and surround, was transformed into something of an informal space or sitting room for the family. At some point, the press bed that had once occupied the east wall of this room was removed, further narrowing the uses of a formerly multifunctional space.[79] The construction of the Long Room also resulted in the creation of a back hall that further mediated between this sitting room and the formal parlor of the Long Room. The woodwork that ornaments the west wall of the back hallway was recycled from the west wall of the original parlor (where it had been added in the second remodeling campaign that updated older spaces), dismantled at that same time to create a large room, and reused in the back hall. Woodwork once appropriate for the house's formal spaces was downgraded to use in spaces only temporarily occupied, and then most often by servants and other workers. Passageways are by definition intermediate and transitory; not surprisingly, they are also most closely associated with peripheral or transitory members of the household.[80] The offhand appearance of these spaces matched the position of the workers who passed through them, the individuals and the architectural elements sharing a peripheral relationship to the family and the core spaces of the family's life.

Meanwhile, on the other end of the house's physical and social continuum, when friends and guests of the Phelpses arrived, they confronted a new facade. The faux stonework so carefully created by Moses Porter more than forty years earlier was now covered by more fashionable clapboarding. The third-story rooms created under a new gambrel roof, though never finished, nevertheless made the already-large home seem still more impressive. The processional path was elaborated by the addition of a new door surround and fashionable Federal-style portico. New purchases updated interior spaces as well. For example, if the architectural transformation was intended to refashion the Phelpses' public image, then so too was the new mirror—a large oval affair encircled with leaves and topped with an urn—that Charles Phelps purchased from a Boston merchant to ornament his increasingly formal parlor. The height of neoclassical style of the day, the new mirror reflected, in both form and function, the progress of their own self-fashioning.[81]

Taken together, this twenty-plus-year series of alterations largely repeated and elaborated on earlier priorities. Moses Porter's 1752 preference for a central hall had simply been the start of a long-standing, multigenerational effort to secure greater privacy for members of the family, and to separate more effectively the Phelpses' peers from the working men and women who crossed their threshold, and perhaps from the servants and slaves who crossed their threshold and also lived under their roof. The final result of these transformations was the concealing of work spaces, workers, and work itself. Throughout, the Phelpses' main concern was the expansion of the house's work- and service-related areas, while at the same time pushing them to the rear of the building, reifying the growing dichotomy between work and leisure while rendering servants' work physically more difficult by increasing the distances between cooking hearths and dining tables, or dining tables and wash basins. Moreover, guests in the parlor would no longer see their hostess bent over a hearth; family members more rarely met servants on the stairs. In keeping with what Richard Bushman and others have observed to be a trend through the century, "every practical function" had finally been removed from the parlor, and now confined strictly to rear service areas or upper chambers.[82] From the time that the house was built in 1752, the house had had a side door on a south elevation that permitted direct entry into the kitchen area, without use of the front door, but while that entry was once just around the corner from the main entrance, now it had moved significantly farther. In 1752, 74 feet separated the formal and service entrances of the house; after 1771, that distance increased to 96 feet; by 1800, fully 132 feet divided the two entrances. Both the north kitchen addition and the south kitchen addition contained pump, sink, or washrooms easily accessed from the west side of the house, the unornamented facade that faced the Connecticut River, the approach that hired hands probably used when coming in from the barns, the farmyard, river, or fields. It is the facade approached by the working women and hired help who ferried across the Connecticut to the Phelpses' rear stoop. The farm's primary kitchen was now far removed from the refinement of the parlor.[83] Along with the kitchen went the heaviest, dirtiest part of clothing care and maintenance—carrying heavy buckets of water, building and tending fires, making soap, scrubbing clothes, heating and lifting cumbersome irons. All this work steadily receded from the parlor's view, along with the women Phelps secured to perform it.[84]

These renovations might have erected only intangible barriers, simply by discouraging unnecessary traffic between the house's work and formal spaces. But the notion of barriers was not merely metaphorical in the Phelps household, for access to spaces in the house was carefully regulated by Elizabeth and Charles Phelps. Charles on more than one occasion wrote Elizabeth, away visiting their children, to find out where she kept the keys to various chambers and cabinets. Her replies tell us a good deal about the degree to which space could be controlled in the household: "The key of the South west chamber door is in my locking drawer at the south west corner . . . —the key of the parlour chamber door is in the same place—if you want the keys of the other chambers you may find them in the parlour chamber." Elizabeth Phelps here took advantage of her home's central-hall plan, which allowed her to close off these two rooms—one of which was the bedchamber reserved for important guests—without disrupting the flow of traffic or tasks to be accomplished in her absence. Her work in supervising the hired help was to some degree indicated by her decision to close these two rooms while she was away, despite the fact that her husband Charles remained behind. That this control of access was noticed and resisted by at least one employee of the household is evidenced in a complaint lodged by a parent, annoyed that his child had been "denied liberty" of the house.[85] For other members of the household, the denial of liberty was never metaphorical. Wherever they slept, the close quarters of the house allowed the family to keep a constant eye on their enslaved workers.[86]

If much care was taken by Elizabeth Porter and Charles Phelps to create and maintain distances between themselves and their servants, women who arrived at Forty Acres to sew, spin, or weave also may have been increasingly segregated from the family. While little direct evidence survives to document which spaces at Forty Acres were most often employed for these tasks, contextual and archaeological evidence suggests which spaces were most frequently inhabited by various sorts of craftswomen. Eighteenth-century novels, for example, occasionally locate the activity of sewing within specific spaces of a house.[87] Novelists regularly presumed that women hired to do plain sewing for a family would normally be shown to spaces in the backs of houses, often small chambers off the kitchen, though generally not *in* the kitchen, perhaps because they might be in the way, or, depending on what they were working on, because they might soil the fabric, but they do seem to have been separated from the family, and at least somewhat from other servants. Most commonly they occupied "little rear chambers" apart from, but connected or adjacent to, some space occupied by the mistress of the house, in order to facilitate communication, but to avoid constant contact.

At Forty Acres, a likely space for this purpose might have been the "keeping room" erected at the rear of the 1771 ell. Of course, lighting is also extremely important to needlework and may well have drawn sewing women outdoors when at all possible. Period artwork often depicts women doing handwork near the light admitted by windows, and archaeologists at the Spencer-Pierce-Little farm in Newbury, Massachusetts, for example, found a "high proportion of pins and a thimble" just west of the house's front porch, suggesting that the porch—as it offered bright light and clean air—was a preferred site for needle chores.[88] After 1799, the house's newly constructed rear veranda probably afforded the best light.[89] At least Phelps herself spent a good deal of time there, referring to this space as "the stoop where you know I live."[90] The better light may not have been the only reason Phelps liked to stake out a spot on that long porch, next to the new dairy kitchen and overlooking the field between the house and river. Interestingly, there is a slight hint in Phelps's diary that she recognized a risk when help worked out of her sight: in January 1796, we recall, she wrote her daughter, anxious that one hired man was not trustworthy: "I really feel concern'd for he has all the chance any one can desire, threshing and dressing flax, tis easy for him to pay himself . . ."[91] Perhaps Phelps, well aware of the temptation among spinners to shorten a skein, or among sewers to help themselves to an extra twist of thread, liked to keep her workers in plain view.[92]

Liberty and Privacy

The elaboration of workspaces clearly afforded greater privacy and control to family members while increasing the labors of working women. But these changes may have had positive consequences, too, for the women who both lived and worked at Forty Acres, most notably because it gave them an area of the house in which they were relatively free from supervision. That separation of spaces appears to have given servants a degree of sexual liberty too, judging from the number of women who became pregnant while working there. The newly designed workspaces would prove to be an asset for working mothers, whose children—as we've seen—were increasingly alongside them. When Betsy Huntington, writing to her mother from their home in Connecticut, struggled over whether to hire a servant who came with a child in tow, desperation in the end trumped convenience: she finally offered the woman the job, concluding that, as they have a "lower kitchen" the child won't make "much trouble." Like Persis and Dolly, the mother with her child could be accommodated because the spaces they occupied were distanced from the family. Elaboration of workspaces allowed working women to raise children in their place of employment.

As workers who visited clients for brief stints (one or two days at most, if they lodged at all), more skilled women—mainly gown makers and health care providers—had different relationships to their domestic workspaces than domestic servants. In part, the special requirements of the work contributed to heightened levels of intimacy and perhaps permitted some women artisans to enjoy more of that "liberty of the house." Paul Gilje has noted that, among men who worked in maritime settings, "liberty" was grounded in skill: the more skill a man possessed, the greater his liberty.[93] The same can be said for artisanal women. The most accurate measuring of a client for a gown, for example, took place over her shifts and stays, and occasionally required as many as sixteen separate measurements.[94] Often gown makers came into the women's homes to cut and baste a dress, and then the two women worked together stitching the seams and hems. These time-consuming processes required access to the interior, even intimate rooms of the community's most respected families, with access to goods and spaces that might otherwise have been closed. Indeed, there was an opposite side to the gown maker's access to the house during an extended visit: often the craftswoman's arrival—and those time-consuming chores of measuring and making—required the mistress of a house to stay at home during the two or three days that an artisan lodged there. As one Massachusetts woman wrote, "I felt as if I could write volumes but I had a mantua maker here and did not expect her to stay long enough to finish my work. I was obliged to work with her every moment."[95]

Hatfield gown maker Rebecca Dickinson gained entry, for instance, to the home of the "Monarch of Hampshire County" when she worked for the wives and daughters of Hatfield's Israel Williams. Williams and his family occupied a "mansion house" appropriate to their station at the pinnacle of local political, social, and cultural authority.[96] This large, gambrel-roofed house (extant until 1852, when it was razed to make room for another structure of authority, Hatfield's new town hall) boasted front rooms trimmed with high wainscoting, paneled and carved by hand, as well as rich papers covering the walls. The Williams parlor was swathed in deep crimson velvet. Immense fireplaces heated every room, and elaborate hand-carved mantels and beautifully designed corner cupboards "abounded."[97] Acquisition of such notable clientele proved advantageous beyond simple economic gain; additional occupational perquisites included entry, both literally and figuratively, into elite circles. As Witold Rybczynski has observed, "activities in the home were separated vertically; public below, private above. 'Going upstairs' or 'coming downstairs,' means not just changing floors but leaving or joining the company of others."[98]

If gown making afforded craftswomen access to otherwise closed spaces, and "confined" employers to their homes, other sorts of confinements also brought employers and employees together in the house's most intimate spaces. "Confinement" was of course also a euphemism for childbirth, reminding us that other workers also had steady access to a home's most private spaces. Midwives and nurses occupied bedchambers, and they needed free access as well to the kitchen and perhaps gardens; they were also exempt from architectural efforts to protect a family's privacy. Their arrival was often abrupt and might occur at any time of the day or night: no efforts could be made to present any artificial front to these workers, who would necessarily see the household as it functioned out of view. For both midwives and gown makers, then, their employer's real and metaphorical confinements provided access to interior spaces that were otherwise closed. When these working women passed into the hall of Forty Acres, and were then directed not into one of the several downstairs adjoining spaces, but ascended the stairs to a more private chamber, they joined the company of other women in spaces that were among the house's least public.

Admission to the innermost spaces of the home conferred other related benefits. And here, too, we see a certain correspondence between highly skilled and comparatively high-status enterprises like midwifery and gown making. No one was more privy to sensitive information than midwives, charged by the courts with the gathering of evidence during unsanctioned births. The temptation to gossip about the deliveries they witnessed—whether clearly of "illegitimate" children born out of wedlock or simply curiously "large" children (as Phelps would note) born just a little too soon to escape notice—must have been strong indeed. Midwives were thus keepers of powerful information. Court testimony from nurses, too, about deathbed declarations or changes to legal documents, shows these women clearly in a position to obtain significant, sensitive information in a home's most private chambers, testing their own discretion.[99]

If skilled workers like gown maker Rebecca Dickinson and midwives like Elizabeth Allen were able to subvert, at least to a degree, formal spatial hierarchies, the attenuation of workspaces had advantages for other occupants of the house as well. As servants' spaces became more separate from their employers, servants' liberty within those spaces expanded. The construction of the south kitchen in 1797 created new spaces primarily inhabited by the working men and women of Forty Acres. In addition to the kitchen itself, the ell afforded direct access to the long veranda across the rear of the house, where hired men congregated and were fed. The kitchen also housed the only access to the garret space above, where hired help slept. Elizabeth Phelps's memorandum book makes clear that she was a full participant in the work of the farm, making her a regular presence in the kitchen and on the rear veranda, if not in the garret above, and she instructed her newly married daughter that when it comes to servants, it is important to "take hold right sharp."[100] Still, her correspondence also makes plain that she felt a certain lack of control over these spaces and the servants' behavior in them.

Once the south kitchen became the province of the farm's workers, Phelps knew less and less about what went on there. In February 1801, Phelps walked into the ell and "was sure" she "smelt brimstone," a sulfur used to cure "scabies." An infection of the skin caused by mites, scabies was a contagious disease that would spread easily and quickly through the household—obviously a cause for alarm. She "finally came to search onto the matter we found that Reuban has been ointing for the itch." "Judge dear child my feeling," she wrote: "not one intimation did I ever have til then of the matter . . . Judith says it was the talk among the boys before you left us."[101] Phelps had been entirely excluded from the development, while Judith was well aware of the problem, which had been "the talk among" the hired men. Phelps's words reflect not just her frustration at the potential disaster only nearly averted, but also dismay at having been so easily kept out of the loop.

The seclusion of the rear workspaces, as we have seen, gave Phelps occasion to worry about theft (and she well remembered when Sarah Bartlett willfully burned Moses Marsh's house to the ground to conceal "false ties" in her spinning); still, she mainly complained of the kitchen's "talk and brawl," which she was apparently unable to squelch.[102] One wonders what Phelps thought when Hadley's Overseers of the Poor sent transients like the idle and intemperate Timothy Booge to work on her farm rather than place them in the local house of correction.[103] Indeed, sometimes her hired men got so drunk that Phelps worried about her own safety.[104] But while the hired men would sober up in the morning, Phelps's hired women's unwelcome behavior carried more ominous consequences: as we have seen, a striking number became pregnant while working at Forty Acres, complicating issues of dependence and dependents, and undermining the household's gentility in more ways than one.[105] The conduct of Mitte West, Persis Morse, and other employees suggests that "liberty of the house" may well have had another meaning for the men and women who worked at Forty Acres: as workspaces migrated to the rear of the house, laboring men and women gained some freedom, at least to a degree, from the supervision of Charles and Elizabeth Phelps. Certainly the laborers who regularly worked and lived in the kitchen and its garret spaces enjoyed a good deal of privacy offered therein. Court records from the turn of the nineteenth century make plain that sexual behavior among servants was a matter of rising concern. Indentures once required only that servants and apprentices "gladly obey, and in all things behave . . . as a good and faithful apprentice ought to do"; because both parties knew what was expected, a few words were all that were needed. Over time, however, as that understanding collapsed, indentures came to include clauses making explicit reference to fornication as a breach of contract. But servants nonetheless exercised their preferences in this regard. When Clarissa Foster, a servant in the home of Deerfield farmer Aaron Rand, named Caleb Allen Jr. as the father of her illegitimate child, she reported to her selectmen that the child was conceived "between the hours of eight and nine in the evening of said Day, upon a Bed in the north room of the Dwelling House of Aaron Rand of sd Deerfield."[106] Sally Pitt of Greenfield, a servant in the employ of Deerfield tavernkeeper Erastus Barnard, confessed to having sex with stage driver James Leonard "between the hours of three and four o'clock in the morning of said Day, upon a bed in a bed Room in the northeast corner of said house."[107]

Clearly, servants found the time, place, and privacy to engage in their own intimacies, whatever the preferences, admonishments, and requirements of their employers. And indeed, even members of the rural gentry recognized the privacy offered by rear workspaces, and they too took advantage of it. When Deerfield's Elihu Ashley was boarding as an apprentice with Dr. Williams's family in 1774, he kept his courtship with Williams's daughter Polly private by using a room that was primarily associated with daytime activities and by choosing a time when, presumably, no one in the household was awake to hear the lovers' conversation: Ashley courted Williams by "talking in the back kitchen—often until dawn."[108] The kitchen could also serve as a private space for other sorts of confidential conversations; when a company of men visited Belchertown's Reverend Justus Forward in the winter of 1799 to discuss a deeply divisive quarrel between Forward and a Dr. Phelps, Forward left the company in his study and led Phelps to the kitchen. Forward's hired woman, Eunice Shaw, was evidently out of earshot at the time, allowing the antagonists to speak frankly, without witnesses. In this case, the kitchen proved a space more private than even the minister's personal study.[109]

In any event, the autonomy that servants enjoyed, and the activities they embraced, proved increasingly distressing for Elizabeth Porter Phelps and other members of the rural gentry. We have already observed Phelps breathlessly reporting to her daughter in 1807 that "there was said to be 9 girls pregnant in Northampton, that they principally were of the lowest class, Mary Wire, &c, that two of the new converts were tho't to be of that number, & that they had not behaved with that solemnity as others had done." This news—the number of girls pregnant, that two of them professed to have experienced religious conversion, and that one of them was Mary Wire, no doubt a relative of their own former hired girl, Meriam Wire—was shocking enough. But equally alarming was the fact that "about 3 weeks ago the man who was courting [one girl], took her & went off, came back married—he has above one year of his apprenticeship yet to serve, [and] she had gone to a friend in Greenfield to reside till he should at least be his own man."[110] Clearly neither the doctrines of the church nor the demands of the law had proved sufficient tools to police laborers' behavior.

The culture of the south kitchen, then, made Phelps uncomfortable, but there appeared to be little she could do about it. And she was not alone; while the church and the courts responded in their own ways, women of the rural gentry also observed a widening gulf between the behavior they deemed appropriate for respectable women and the behavior they observed around them.

After a ride on the local stage in the summer of 1799, Julia Cowles, a young woman from Farmington, Connecticut, confided to her diary: "I was shocked to see the indelicacy with which some of my sex appeared in. One, perhaps a woman of 40, went far enough to use very vulgar expressions and even to strike a gentleman who sat upon his horse, with whom she was an entire stranger. It wounded my delicacy to see girls of 17 encircled in the arms of lads; what a pity that their reason could not have taught them better! Why could reason dictate thus!" Cowles's reaction is perhaps more extreme than young Betsy Huntington's, but both women were dismayed—or at the very least understood that it was necessary to express dismay—by the public behavior of women of other social spheres. In 1797, when she herself was eighteen years old, Betsy too found herself traveling by stage. Anxious to preserve some social distance even in these close quarters, she reported afterward to her mother that she didn't speak to anyone during the trip to Boston: "I did not wish to be too sociable, for fear they would be too familiar."[111] Perhaps Huntington would have shared Cowles's conclusion: "Girls who would have made (with a little education) fine women, good mothers, and happy wives, will now make neither, entirely destitute of the common rules of decency."[112]

Gentlewomen like Cowles, Huntington, and Phelps had plenty of opportunity to observe whether such women made good mothers, as the segmentation of domestic spaces made it easier for both members of the rural gentry and the women they employed to accommodate the results of these liaisons, especially when the employing family was loath to tolerate a hired woman's child, but reluctant too to lose good help if they had it. Recall how in 1801, for example, Betsy's husband Dan Huntington "obtained a girl, for a week," who lived with her mother while going out for "days works." Her "boy about 2 years old," Huntington assured her mother, is "not troublesome," and "she is an excellent girl for business—and there is no objection against her but the child." Two weeks later, when Betsy reported that she and her husband had begun supplementing Dan's meager ministerial salary by taking in boarders, she wrote that "we should not have undertaken this business had we not the prospect of good help—a black girl in town, by the name of Chloe, who has formerly kept a family is coming to live with us—she has a child, too, about three years old—a girl . . . She is coming this week to agree upon the terms. If we can get her, we should be highly favoured."[113] The fact that servants came with a child in tow was naturally undesirable, but they were desperate, and Chloe was said to be the "best help in town." Fortunately, the prospective employer observed, "as we have a lower kitchen, she will not make much trouble."[114] In Litchfield, as in Hadley, kitchens placed at a distance from other living spaces enabled employers to adapt to the changing nature of the rural workforce. Women like Chloe, already gaining some leverage in a tight labor market, were able not only to demand higher wages, but also to turn architectural changes implemented by the rural gentry to their own particular advantage, and even to require their employers to house additional family members. In this case, however, the servant elected not to stay. Chloe came for two weeks on trial, at the close of which Huntington observed that the toddler was a "pretty little girl, not troublesome." However, with a child to support and good skills to offer, Chloe, as we have seen, required higher wages than the family could muster, and the two families parted ways.[115]

Nor was it easy for women running households to surveil their servants and enslaved workers around the clock, especially as architectural changes intended to protect privacy also facilitated secrecy and deception. At Forty Acres, for example, not long after completion of their large south kitchen, Elizabeth and Charles Phelps faced their "suspicion" in February 1805, confirmed in March, that Persis Morse was pregnant, and that the father, Reuban Debell, was long gone.[116] Given Persis's dilemma, Elizabeth wrote that "I do now feel, as if I hardly dare go to bed." Phelps's surveillance of the help simply could not extend around the clock: "What could, what should, we do, if (as you know is many times the case) an early muster should take place—but it must not be entertained in tho't—if it does actually take place the Lord will direct, I hope and pray."[117] There were no easy solutions. For her part, Persis suggested that her child could prove an asset to the household, and Elizabeth was inclined to agree. In the end Persis stayed and had her daughter Dolly in the house, remaining with the family for two years more—four years in all—after which Elizabeth wished her and her child well. But from the start, as we've also seen, Persis strove to secure a modicum of privacy for herself and her child, not alerting Elizabeth Phelps that she'd gone into labor—she called her only after the child had safely arrived.

By the turn of the nineteenth century, the accommodation of servants' sexual behavior had become an issue for both Phelps and her daughter—one that architecture both mitigated and made possible. For women like Persis Morse, architecture, too, both facilitated new liberties, and made possible a wider variety of domestic arrangements. Susanna Whipple spent more than two years living at Forty Acres, working for the Phelps family and raising her daughter Mitte there. Persis Morse and her daughter Dolly remained for two years. When Persis left, the woman who filled her place was a Mrs. Hancock, a widow who herself brought along two young children. She stayed for some seven months, from March until September, before moving on to another household. Elizabeth's daughter Betsy likewise housed a series of hired women with children, including Candace and her young son, and Chloe and her three-year-old daughter. For hired women like these, single mothers raising their children in their workplaces, rear ells may have afforded some small measure of privacy as they sought to act simultaneously as employees and as parents. These rear additions bespeak a certain tension between dependence and dependents, as Elizabeth Phelps's need for domestic labor collided with the consequences of her servants' differing moral compass and divergent rules of sexual behavior. The labor shortages that accompanied democratization gave working women more power, requiring the gentry to accede as laborers pressed their own social and economic agendas, developments that were both facilitated by and reflected in the built environment.

Houses like Forty Acres, then, are not simply documents of early American refinement; instead, they open a view on a world of laboring women and their families, and afford unusual insight into the social relations of work among women during the forging of a new republic.[118] Taken together, as central halls and rear ells give evidence of new class hierarchies working to assert themselves, protestations regarding the liberty of the house and sitting at table, as well as the desire to reconcile conceptions of work and family that departed from those of their employers, point up working women's efforts to resist those changes. In *Home and Work*, Jeanne Boydston traced what she termed the "pastoralization of housework"—a largely rhetorical process in which middle-class white women's household activities were distinguished from actual "work"; more recently, Nora Doyle has observed how, over the course of the late eighteenth and early nineteenth century, visions of white middle-class motherhood came to emphasize "spiritual and emotional work" over the necessary physical labor.[119] At Forty Acres as elsewhere, renovations to the family home gave that pastoralization physical form, but the effort to cloak the labors of the mistress of the house also kept paid laborers hidden from view: kitchens drifted farther from parlors, while the expansion of rear service areas channeled working women away from the processional entrance entirely. The initiative launched at Forty Acres in the 1770s five decades later had gained real purchase: as early as the 1810s, Connecticut Valley houses rose with ells incorporated into the original plan, and by the 1830s, the integrated ell was "well established."[120]

But this pastoralization of hired labor was not inevitable; though it did indeed proceed, it proceeded in a haphazard and uneven fashion that reflected both the presence of multiple and competing hierarchies among early American women and the instability of those hierarchies. As some women worked to erect, both literally and figuratively, more explicit class boundaries, others sought to subvert them. As a result, these "refined" dwellings at the turn of the nineteenth century were multiple, fluid spaces in which complex constellations of factors—including race, skill, social and economic status, and stage in the life cycle—shaped the ways in which working women experienced these spaces.

Women like Elizabeth Porter Phelps harnessed constructions of both space and gentility to secure their position in the new republic; women like Persis Morse forged their own "republic of labor" as they asserted their own value, and values.[121] Places like Forty Acres, no less than workingmen's halls and factory floors, became testing grounds in which competing conceptions of liberty were advanced and refined. As Timothy Cresswell has astutely observed, "the inertia of the everyday softens the intrusion of capitalism into life,"[122] but these changes in the domestic landscape nevertheless alert us to broader changes in the configuration of women's work and their position vis à vis a rapidly changing American society.

CHAPTER NINE

New Labor, New Landscapes

On the occasion of her sixtieth birthday, Hadley gentlewoman Elizabeth Porter Phelps paused to reflect in the pages of her journal that her life, though long, seemed "so short when past—a tale, a vapour, a shadow, yet big with everlasting consequences."[1] Indeed, Elizabeth Phelps's life, and the life of her community, is today but a "shadow, yet big with everlasting consequences." As Phelps and women both like and unlike her moved through the trajectories of their own lives, so too did a larger transatlantic world move along another trajectory, one that would usher in new relationships between individuals and their communities, reconfigure the local, regional, national, and international networks that linked workers, employers, and consumers, and enlarge a yawning gap between the haves and the have-nots—all broad and far-reaching changes big with everlasting consequences for her, for them, and for us.

Phelps died in 1817. By then, her daughter Betsy Huntington had assumed responsibility for the house at Forty Acres; her own large family, eleven children in all, would come to call Forty Acres home, and their own travels and experiences would transform the place from a large working farm to a rustic summer home. Huntington lived until 1847. The town that mourned her passing was very different from the one that had witnessed her birth more than six decades earlier. Historians have drawn in detail the contours of middle-class womanhood that emerged in New England in the first decades of the nineteenth century.[2] Looking more carefully at how those ideas took hold on the ground as class, gender, and race entwined to help establish the single (male) breadwinner model suggests the subtle ways in which alterations in physical place and social "place" both shaped and reflected those developments.

Moreover, that story is inextricable from other changes to relations among women. Most immediately apparent are the ways in which the labors of some women constructed and reconfigured the gentility of others. At the same time, however, we also see ways that the transition that Richard Bushman has described, in which the "gentility" of some gave way to "refinement" of many, was also shaped by labor. In fact, looking so closely at the work undertaken by a variety of women in these years reminds us that even in communities that at first glance appear relatively homogeneous, subtle but substantive distinctions shaped experiences and opportunities for the town's wives and daughters, distinctions that would widen in the radiating forces that both drove and were accelerated by industrialization. These forces taken together added momentum to the social centrifuge that was the market revolution, even in rural western Massachusetts, as opportunities for and relationships among women changed shape in the context of an emerging, identifiable middle-class culture.

A Community in Transition

Historian Mary Babson Fuhrer has written compellingly about the "unremitting turmoil" that rocked New England towns between 1815 and 1848, and if this study continued its close investigation of Hadley into the decades of the 1830s and 40s, Hadley would look very much like Fuhrer's Boylston some sixty miles to the east.[3] In Hadley as in Boylston, a "community of necessity and custom became a community—or communities—of choice and interest," as "residents felt empowered to choose their own social relations. Where once identity had been centered in town belonging, now people turned inward to self-reliant or intimate connections, or outward to unions with distant strangers who shared selective causes. Relations shifted from neighbors to networks, from compulsory to voluntary, from corporate to divergent."[4]

Hadley residents would have recognized those developments, part of the larger emergence across the region of new constellations around social class. Historians have observed the advent and evolution of the middle class in a variety of forms. Some examine, for example, the appearance of new occupations, while others stress organizational innovation—voluntary societies, self-improvement initiatives, and reform groups—associated with middle-class life; others point to less formal examples, but likewise emphasize gatherings that drew together, and developed, men and women of like sensibilities, values, postures (real and metaphorical) and demeanors.[5] Other researchers argue that evidence of "how the middle class treats the working class"—in the creation of new institutions, and in the deployment of goods and spaces—is key to understanding class formation.[6] Still others observe expressions of distinct sets of shared cultural and material values, captured in housewares, apparel, and other artifactual gestures. One might incorporate, too, new spatial patterns and material goods that served to articulate emerging sensibilities of difference in households, farmsteads, and communities.[7] Certainly all of these developments can be observed in nineteenth-century Hadley, from the emergence of the Seamen's Friend Society (1834) to the pelerines that graced the town's most fashionable shoulders. Richard Bushman has explained how, beginning in the 1790s, more and more middling Americans adopted and transformed elements of a comparatively exclusive genteel culture toward their own ends, creating codes of refinement that selected certain attributes—restraint, industry, frugality, temperance, among others—as most desirable, setting themselves apart from both their more- and less-privileged neighbors.[8] Middle-class society gained stability, C. Dallett Hemphill proposed, as the young men and women from these families were urged to "choose their company from among their social equals rather than their superiors or inferiors. One writer advised middle-class parents to 'habituate' their daughters 'to regard distinctions of wealth and rank as circumstances wholly unconnected with personal worth; let her companions be in general, neither much above her own level, nor much below it.'"[9]

The forces were of course at work in Hadley, too. We have already seen Betsy Huntington's embrace of dancing schools and other elements of an emerging middle-class culture as well as her effort to keep fellow passengers on the Boston stage at arm's length, when in 1797, at the age of eighteen, she attempted to preserve some social distance from women who did not meet her expectations by maintaining her reserve throughout the trip ("I did not wish to be too sociable, for fear they would be too familiar")—as well as her dismay at the sexual and economic choices of the laboring women around her.[10] By the time she had married and was establishing a household of her own, she plainly saw herself as someone who shared little in common with the women whose labors she supervised. Jeanne Boydston likewise argued that the "response of elite women to the political and economic turmoil of the late eighteenth century was to separate themselves emotionally and rhetorically from working women."[11] "For prosperous women," she continues, "the process of withdrawing from bonds of familiarity (not equality, which had not existed) with working women was part of a process of moving toward an identification with the new social order, and particularly with the civic culture of the men of their class."[12]

That withdrawal wasn't merely metaphorical; even in small communities like Hadley, women were increasingly separated physically as the routines of their lives drifted apart. Farmyards, gardens, and other outdoor domestic spaces ceased to be used as areas of female productivity; women of comparative privilege retreated indoors while their husbands and sons found other uses for these landscapes, while working women continued to traverse public roads and private spaces in the course of their labors.[13] This final chapter selects and surveys a number of changes across Hadley's tangible and metaphorical landscapes in the first decades of the nineteenth century, and considers how these developments both reflected and helped propel these larger alterations to less tangible topographies of culture and class.

The Whitening of the Town

The most dramatic transformations in labor relationships between women in the decades following the American Revolution were surely the elimination of slavery in the Commonwealth, the ensuing relocation of Hadley's people of color, and Yankee womens' postrevolutionary flight from domestic service. Some free women of color, as we have seen, remained in service as white women moved toward other occupations; as labor became increasingly scarce, both Elizabeth Porter Phelps and her daughter Betsy understood what it meant when, due to some woman's departure, she must "be her own negro now."[14] Although racial prejudice continued to circumscribe the options available to women of color, the fundamental change in legal status gave black women a modicum of autonomy for the first time. Some evidence of that increased autonomy is suggested in rising birth rates; in the colonial era, black families had an average of 2.0 children, but after 1783, that number rose dramatically, to 3.45. As women gained greater control over the paths of their lives, they were more able to embrace the pleasures of family life.[15] But whatever their reproductive choices, most women (and men) of color remained in poverty, with few options in the labor market.

Emancipation sparked an internal migration as women and men of color tried to resettle themselves as free blacks, only to find their efforts directed, misdirected, and hampered by warning-out systems that kept them on the move. Joanne Pope Melish finds that freed people routinely ignored efforts to control their movements, but also that they were highly motivated to leave the scenes of their enslavement, often heading to the region's cities. As she writes, "The presence of free people of color was merely the most visible and, to whites, irritating symptom of the growing disjuncture between the traditional New England community—organized around such concepts as legal settlement—and the ever more mobile and fractured, commercially oriented society of 1800 and after . . . Free people of color constituted an element of disorder merely by virtue of being a new category in a system with no space to accommodate it."[16] Catherine Adams and Elizabeth Pleck likewise track the disentangling of black and white as black families strove to form their own households, and the number of blacks who lived among whites "plummeted" across New England.[17] The number of African Americans in Hadley was never large, though the decades following Independence saw the percentage dip, from about 2 percent in 1790 to 0.5 percent in 1810 (when the census identified just 7 of Hadley's 1,247 residents as people of color). That number in the decades before the Civil War would grow slightly, but it reached just 1 percent (22 of 2,104) in 1860.

In affluent households across Hadley, women and men once enslaved grew older and eventually passed away, while their sons and daughters looked elsewhere for opportunity. Some of that migration was involuntary. As the eighteenth century drew to a close, the town took steps to remove structures associated with households of color. In April 1797, Levi Prutt was "ordered to remove his house and effects" within thirty days; in April 1800, selectmen ordered the removal of the "house built on the town land by Cato Robinson, at the upper end of the back street."[18] Robinson had been warned out in 1795, as had Caesar Prutt, possibly a brother of Levi.[19] The motive behind these removals is unclear, and may have been environmental; in these same years, the selectmen began allocating funds and attention to what would be a never-ending battle to contain the Connecticut River along its northern bend, and the constellation of dwellings occupied by families of color in that area perhaps were deemed unsafe, or inconvenient to steps being taken to shore up the riverbank. Whatever the reasons, as these homes were dismantled, the town's physical and demographic landscape was altered. Levi remained in the community, as did Cato, the latter assisted by the Overseers of the Poor; by the fall of 1809 he was lodging in the nearby household of Solomon Cook, who furnished him with "victuals, drink and cloathing in a comfortable manner" for a dollar per week. When Cato died at the end of that year, Ralph Way Jr. earned about that same amount for digging his grave in the cold winter earth.[20]

No mention is made in these records of the home occupied by the household of Joshua Boston, which also stood in this neighborhood, but Boston's family persisted in Hadley into the 1820s. In 1800 Boston's home sustained four free blacks—Boston and his wife Pits Boston, as well as town "pauper" Phillis Aberdeen, and an unknown individual.[21] Unlike many free blacks in Hampshire County, Joshua Boston had become a vehicle of public support rather than the recipient of it. The town selectmen reimbursed Boston for his costs in keeping Aberdeen at least as early as 1800, and as late as 1813 (and likely until Aberdeen's death in May 1816).[22] Elizabeth Porter Phelps attended the 1806 funeral of Pits Boston; Joshua Boston, having reached the grand age of eighty, died in December 1819, though Nancy Boston remained in Hadley into the 1820s.[23]

The descendants of Ralph Way also remained an important presence in Hadley into the nineteenth century. Ralph Sr. would be remembered years later as a "shrewd calculator" with "considerable" property—assets that would be lost over the lifetime of his son, Ralph Jr. In his 1778 will, Ralph Way Sr. left just five shillings to his namesake and five shillings to another son, Hermon. To his granddaughter Nancy and grandson Philip, Way bequeathed half the residue of real and personal estate in the hands of his executor, Edmund Hubbard, to be managed for Nancy's support while she was a minor and delivered to her in full when she came of age. But Hubbard found that the value of the estate was less than its total debts; the court granted him permission to sell one hundred pounds' worth of real estate in order to meet the demands of the family's various creditors. By November 1790, the men appointed by the court to distribute Way's estate set off to Nancy Way "four acres on the North side of the Homelot in the back street, the whole of the mill plain lot, and the whole of the lot in the 2nd division and the lot in the sheep pasture as her part of sd.

estate." Philip got the rest of the home lot.[24] Seventy-six-year-old Ralph Way Jr. died in December 1821, and his wife Margaret followed just a month later, but Nancy Way, like Nancy Boston, remained present in Hadley's community of color—seventeen men, women, and children in 1820.[25]

While Hadley's families of color continued to carve out lives on the margins of the community, attention turned to captive Africans beyond the region. Responses in Hadley to abolitionist sentiment were decidedly mixed. Betsy Huntington had little memory of growing up around the people enslaved in her childhood home; Cesar left and Rose died before Betsy was born, and she would have been only three when Phillis died and Peg left for freedom (born in 1779, Betsy may have had some dim memory of Peg's 1783 return to nurse her dying granddaughter Phillis). But she was twenty in 1799, when her family observed the death of Maria, a woman once enslaved by the Porter family, and certainly knew most if not all of the women and men who survived to see slavery made illegal in Massachusetts.[26] As an adult, Betsy Huntington became deeply concerned about slavery—she would declare in 1840 that the "abominations of slavery" are "at the bottom of all our national trouble"—and initially supported efforts to transplant formerly enslaved workers to colonies in Africa. Colonization of course represented the most ambitious effort to whiten New England, and towns like Hadley.[27] Hadley's Reverend John Woodbridge was a lifetime member of the American Colonization Society, Charlotte and Dr. William Porter were donors, and in the 1830s Huntington was persuaded of this course as well, though she would change her mind about that strategy in time.[28] She read antislavery tracts, and she distributed antislavery pamphlets to her North Hadley neighbors. She subscribed to the *Liberator*, and her family attended meetings of Hatfield's Anti-Slavery society. At least three of her children—Charles, William, and Frederic Dan—would take up the cause as well (like her, they initially embraced and then rejected colonization).[29] Across town, Alfred and Drusilla Johnson are remembered as having been vocal abolitionists; acquaintances of William Lloyd Garrison and Wendell Phillips, in the 1840s they named a son Liberty.[30]

Meanwhile, Hadley's color line remained firmly in place. This was nowhere more visible than from the pulpit of the congregational church. The town's third meetinghouse, built in 1808, was segregated by race. Language drafted for the deeds to the pews stipulated that purchasers were forbidden to rent "the said pew, or any part thereof, to any negro or mulatto, or in any way admit any negro or mulatto to the possession or occupancy of the same"; any violations meant that the property would revert to the town.[31] The town also voted that parts of the north gallery would be retained by the town for women, and the south for men; lastly, the town "voted that the North arched pew be appropriated to the use of the Black females and the South to that of Black males."[32] As late as 1836, pew owners in the First Church still forfeited their property if they permitted a "negro or mulatto" to sit in seats not reserved for people of color.[33] "The pews for the Negroes," one resident later recalled, "were in the tower, and were reached from the rear, and were open in front & a balustrade which prevented any communication with the other seats in the gallery. The black men (B.M.) sat on the south side and the black females on the north. . . . These negro pews are arched over the top."[34] These "arched" pews (probably meaning covered), "separated from the rest of the gallery by a balustrade, or barrier," prevented African Americans present from communicating with other worshippers.[35]

The policy aimed to maintain long-standing barriers that separated Hadley's few congregants of color. Though opinion in town was not unified—Theodore Gregson Huntington recorded with pride that his grandfather once sat in the so-called "negro" pew to protest segregation in the meetinghouse—these patterns persisted.[36] Across Massachusetts in the first half of the nineteenth century, congregants of color pushed back against racial geographies that segregated meetinghouses, but white resistance remained; for instance, while the first integrated free church in Boston dated from 1839, the meetinghouse in Brockton would remain segregated as late as the 1870s.[37] It is not clear how long Hadley's meetinghouse retained these segregated spaces, by policy or custom, but certainly well into the second quarter of the nineteenth century the ecclesiastical terrain reflected these secular biases.

The women of color who worked in Hadley in the early nineteenth century carved out niches in the local labor market that conformed to entrenched patterns of work—in particular, associations between women of color and work in the laundry. For instance, one "large and vigorous and very black colored woman" named Mrs. Jackson was known more commonly around town as "Mrs. Jack"; Hockanum's Hannah Johnson remembered her standing in the doorway of her small house with a white turban on her head.[38] Like generations of women of color before her, including Hadley's "old Phillis" and Lucinda Till, Jackson took in laundry, helping middling white families achieve ever-rising standards of cleanliness.

Laundry and landscape are not as distinct as they might at first seem. As expectations about cleanliness intensified in the early nineteenth century, a growing preference for whiter and whiter goods simultaneously permeated exterior and interior landscapes. A decades-long search for ever-whiter ceramics was advanced by technological innovation, and white and marble supplanted granite and schist as the preferred materials to mark the burial sites of loved ones.[39] Meanwhile, the empire-style gowns that clothed fashionable Hadley women lightened sartorial landscapes as well, as white cottons and muslins supplanted the more colorful fabrics favored by the Revolutionary generation.

The neat town common of popular historical imagination, lined with white houses, emerged from these decades, as white paint supplanted the darker exteriors of earlier generations ("We have gone thro' with a great white washing," Charlotte Porter wrote in 1813, "& it had caused a pleasing change in the looks of the house.").[40] By 1835, a traveler from Northampton to Boston would observe, "The villages through which we passed presented the same characters— white wooden houses with green Venetian blinds, and everything wearing the appearance of cleanliness, order, and comfort."[41] "White things radiated refinement, order, discipline," Bridget Heneghan has proposed, "but in doing so, they also radiated race."[42] The changing population of people of color, their continued segregation in the meetinghouse, the congregation of African American women around the work of laundering, and perhaps even in the general affinity for things white—in these ways, towns like Hadley rewrote and affirmed their color lines.

Other less tangible steps also had the effect of whitening the landscape metaphorically, as antebellum Hadley contemplated whether "the town will change the name of school district 7 from Hockanum"—the Nolwotogg name for the neighborhood south of town center—"to Holyoke Village" (gesturing toward Mount Holyoke, which rose above it, named for Elizur Holyoke, a 1630s settler of Springfield). Proponents of the alteration prevailed; in 1840, Hadley "voted that Hockanum Village be, and is hereby changed to the name of Holyoke Village."[43] The reasons they contemplated such a change just at that moment are unknown. Memory of the area's native past had not long since been stirred by the 1838 visit to Northampton of a group of more than two dozen natives, among them a woman descended from the celebrated Eunice Williams, taken to Canada as a child in the celebrated 1704 raid on Deerfield. She and her descendants were members of both Abenaki and Mohawk communities.[44] The Abenaki group had visited Deerfield the year before and received a warm reception, but the Northampton *Courier* described the travelers as "slothful, ragged, dirty, squalid."[45] The *Hampshire Gazette*, likewise, while observing that "visitors have enthronged their encampment from all quarters," groused that "a more squalid, filthy looking pack, can hardly be imagined."[46] Curiosity seekers—including Betsy Huntington's family—had gone to see the group, having "taken up their residence in the woods between Northampton and Hatfield."[47] Later that summer, residents in South Deerfield dedicated the "Bloody Brook" monument, commemorating the 1675 clash between English militia and Nipmuc forces during King Philip's War.

Perhaps the proposers of this change in nomenclature—and identity— meant to put some distance between the village's past and its present and future, and between Native American policy then and now. The alteration never took hold—the neighborhood is known as Hockanum yet today—but the impulse to replace native place names with English references reflects broader desires to put the town's multicultural past firmly behind them. Hadley residents still collectively remembered the spellbinding stories of their neighbor Rebecca Crow, who once "delighted the young by her great fund of anecdotes and stories." Her best material included the "barbarities" of the Indians, but by the second quarter of the nineteenth century, those old tales seemed like safe stories.[48] In those years, Sylvester Judd observed in his notebooks that a native named Joseph Sampson had once "had a hut near Smith's mills," further noting that "his was the last family of Indians in Hadley."[49] Polly Sampson, too, was a member of this family; before her death in 1814, as we have seen, she lived with Joshua Boston.[50] Judd was of course wrong about the demise of the Sampson family—he himself added that Joseph's daughter, Anne, married Levi Prutt, and that Anne also had a sister and two brothers (John and Tom)—but the notion that the native nations had all but vanished was alive and well.[51] Hadley consistently included, then as now, both African and Native American residents, but the attempted renaming of Hockanum points up a desire to close, rhetorically at least, that particular chapter in local history.

Women of Hadley's nascent middle class meanwhile expressed and created their emerging status by focusing their interest on native people farther afield. In 1819, the American Board of Commissioners for Foreign Missions received from the young ladies of Hopkins Academy—likely, as we shall see, at the urging of preceptress Sophia Moseley, whose sister Sybil Bingham would become an influential missionary in the Hawaiian islands—a "box and package containing various articles of clothing" designated for their mission in the Sandwich Islands (Hawaii); Charlotte Williams Porter likewise gathered seventy-one "articles" for the Choctaw of Elliot, Mississippi.[52] In that same year, women in Hadley's First Church formed the Onondaga Missionary Society, opening their purses and sewing kits.[53]

The Social Centrifuge

Among working-class women of English descent, onetime domestic servants seized the rhetoric of independence, liberty, and equality to abandon residential employment for occupations that allowed them greater control over their time and space. Domestic servants became harder to come by as young white women found other means of employment more suited to their sense of themselves as working citizens of a new republic. The women willing to work as hired help were more and more often "poor stick, down at the heel" (and increasingly the daughters of New England's fast-growing Irish population), while women who had once performed the common work of the household now chose to work at selected tasks—knitting caps, sewing, laundry, ironing, and so on—in their own homes.[54] No longer would women like Elizabeth Phelps and Persis Morse negotiate their different value systems within shared domestic spaces; as the eighteenth century gave way to the nineteenth, Persis simply moved out.

At the turn of the nineteenth century, New England women witnessed the start of this transition. As early as 1802, Betsy Huntington wrote her mother: "Your letter gave me sensations both of pleasure and pain—I lament that you should thus toil as you say—when you live in the midst of plenty—surely for some price help might be obtained, and any sacrifice of property ought to be made, rather than health. I hope you have now got through the worst, and will not again be so worn out."[55] Betsy's own situation was little better; her newly hired domestic help, a girl named Betty, turned out to be pregnant—"the business was done before she came here"—and her parents arrived to take her home and force the man to marry her. Huntington would have liked to ask her mother to find her a girl in Hadley, but knew full well that "there is as much want among you as there is here."[56] When, several months later, a black girl finally arrived and offered her services, Betsy was so relieved that she nearly burst into tears.[57] In her first nine months of marriage, Betsy would churn through no fewer than ten different domestic servants.[58]

In August 1802, fifty-five-year-old Elizabeth Phelps found herself more and more often "fatigued at the burden of caring for this great house and farm." She wondered "why it is so, that now in the decline of life we are so embarrassed . . . all the skill I have and can but jest get the necessary mending done—and there is now more than 15 or 20 pair of stockings more to mend. . . ."[59] For her part, Betsy knew that her mother missed her terribly, and wanted to relieve some of her burden, just as she always had. "I feel for you very sensibly this summer," she wrote, adding that "if we lived together, I am sure we could assist each other, and even now if you could send me some sewing I could do it as well as not."[60] It would be several more years before Elizabeth Phelps would once again enjoy the companionship and aid of her daughter, and eventually that of her granddaughters as well. In the interim, she struggled to manage, and her daughter only too plainly knew it: "I wonder how you could contrive to send the boys cloathes home in such good order—it must have been quite a task for you."[61]

But domestic service had reached its nadir, at least among the daughters of New England's Anglo-American families. As Huntington complained to her mother when her present hired helper quit, the puzzling girl was a "homebody": she would rather stay at home, "in rags and poverty," than "live out, and earn something for herself." To Huntington's astonishment, therefore, she planned to leave the family's employ.[62] Huntington could not believe that any woman would decline the wages offered by domestic service in order to preserve her own privacy and autonomy, but this woman was by no means alone in her preference: the number of advertisements seeking young women to "live in a family" that began to appear after 1805 in the columns of the *Hampshire Gazette* alone attest to the declining practice. Meanwhile, a series of 1809 notices in the *Hampshire Gazette* seeking an "industrious girl" for work in a paper mill—probably the enterprise active in Springfield, the first to open in this part of the Commonwealth—suggests the growing alternatives available for women eager to avoid service.[63] As a consequence, Elizabeth Phelps and her daughter Betsy Huntington more and more often found themselves performing chores they once hired other women to do. One spring day in 1805, Betsy was somewhat astonished and more than a little amused to find herself—given her age and station in life—at a task she had not had cause to undertake in a good long while: "You cannot guess my employment . . . why it was spinning—only think of it—I have spun 10 skeins already, and intend to spin 5 or 10 more, and then shall go sewing with Mary as fast as possible that we may finish what is necessary before May."[64]

Persis Leonard, Persis Morse, and hundreds of other young white women in Massachusetts left work in proximity to their middle-class employers and sought out instead the company of others like themselves. As Christopher Clark has explained, from time to time women in the Connecticut River Valley were attracted to the large mills in Lowell and Lawrence, but they were the exception rather than the rule: "In areas such as this," Clark adds, "where farming remained prosperous, they were more likely to find livelihoods in or near their homes than were women from the poorer hill towns."[65] In other words, Persis Leonard went to a spinning mill that was comparatively local. Neither the Yankee servant girl nor the mill operative of popular historical imagination, Leonard escaped the scrutiny of her employers yet still remained close to home.

The opening decades of the nineteenth century also witnessed changes in the organization of clothes making that were as significant as, and bound up with, that shortage of domestic help. As was the case with other kinds of labor, for example, fewer needlewomen sustained long-term relationships with their employers. During the final years of Phelps's memorandum book, no new names appear with the regularity or longevity that women like Persis Leonard, Tabitha Smith, or the Newtons once had. Young women like Fanny Dickinson, Hannah Bucknum, and Lucinda Noble are mentioned sporadically as having arrived to tailor for a day, and then they disappear from Phelps's journal. Though it is difficult to speculate as to why Phelps failed to replace her regular tailoresses, it is worth noting that during these years she also journeyed with greater frequency to the shops of Northampton to acquire various clothing-related goods. It seems likely that Phelps had begun to leave the highly personalized world of Hampshire County clothing production and embrace the commercial world of Northampton merchants.[66]

Persis Leonard, Hannah Bucknum, Eunice Breck, the Phelps and Huntington women—as the eighteenth century gave way to the nineteenth, the lives of these women and others like them were gradually disentangled, at least in immediately identifiable ways grounded in day-to-day lives and landscapes. Relationships among women were reconfiguring themselves. For the community's comparatively privileged members, transformations in the economy would alter the ways they dealt not only with their employees, but with each other as well. As Catherine Kelly has observed, "the hierarchical obligations of kinship and community that dictated so many aspects of provincial women's lives" were also transformed in these years, "freeing them to develop voluntary bonds with one another."[67] For women of some modest privilege, the emerging social order gave them a chance to form richer and deeper friendships. Sociologist Karen V. Hansen also sees more opportunity for affective relationships among middling women—relationships that, it would appear, were more difficult to achieve among their less fortunate counterparts. Having tracked the rising sphere of sociability among New England women, Hansen finds that the nature of friendship itself diverged in the nineteenth century as middle-class women were able to establish enduring relationships with peers, while working women's friendships were more transitory, unable to persist within the constraints of marriage.[68]

Education, Culture, and Class

Historian Mary Kelley has shown how transformations in the education of women in the early decades of the American republic helped forge new roles for women in civil society.[69] As women in the postrevolutionary United States made claims grounded in implications of female citizenship, the significance and influence of education—and educators—expanded. The proliferation of academies and seminaries, together with changes in public education, created new platforms for women as consumers and producers of knowledge; at the same time, new opportunities appeared for women—especially younger women—who were newly able to secure livelihoods in this thriving economic and cultural arena.

The trajectory of female education in Hadley was not unlike that of other towns around the Commonwealth. Since the seventeenth century, white children in Massachusetts had attended schools that the colonial government compelled towns to provide. Men were hired by town selectmen to run schools during the winter months, while women offered summer classes in reading to younger children.[70] Boys typically continued their winter schooling as they got older, but girls did not advance into these classes, remaining instead under the tutelage of female instructors. By the 1760s, Hadley routinely hired Josiah Pierce to teach school, though there was some ambivalence over whether he would offer separate sessions for boys and girls. At the time he was engaged in January 1760, for instance, he was to offer a five-month session for boys, and a four-month one for girls. But for some reason by June plans had changed, and an equal sum was voted to fund a school for "boys & girls . . . to be instructed together."[71]

With the founding of the Commonwealth, new policies concerning education were asserted and implemented. The 1780 Massachusetts Constitution clearly stated the need for an educated populace in a young republic, noting that as "wisdom and knowledge, as well as virtue" were "necessary for the preservation of [a people's] rights and liberties," access to education was therefore essential "among the different orders of the people"; "legislatures and magistrates," then, had the "duty . . . to cherish the interests of literature and the sciences, and all seminaries of them," including public schools, town grammar schools, private societies, and public institutions. In addition to the "promotion of agriculture, arts, sciences, commerce, trades, manufactures, and a natural history of the country," these places would also "countenance and inculcate the principles of humanity and general benevolence, public and private charity, industry and frugality, honesty and punctuality in their dealings; sincerity, and good humor, and all social affections and generous sentiments, among the people."[72]

Hadley quickly fell behind on this civic obligation. In February 1781, the justices seated on the Court of General Sessions heard the case of the Commonwealth v. Hadley. "Since 1 April last," the court observed, Hadley "has not had a school master to teach the children and youths . . . to read and write (and meets requirement of 50 householders and upwards) has neglected and still neglects to provide a school master to teach and instruct the children and youth . . . contrary to law." The facts of the case were undisputed; the town had little choice but to pay the fine.[73] Perhaps Pierce, now in his seventies, had retired from the work, and the town was slow to replace him.

In time, demand was sufficient that towns paid women teachers out of public funds, and some of these women gradually offered instruction in writing as well as reading. In August 1787, for instance, across the river in Hatfield diarist Rebecca Dickinson mentions "Patte Renalds who lives heere to keep the School [boarding in the home of Dickinson's sister, innkeeper Miriam Billings] the Second Sommer of her living in this town," while a Betty Reynolds—perhaps Patty's relative—occasionally taught in Hadley.[74] For one summer and perhaps two in the 1790s, Jerusha Leonard (the daughter of Sunderland innkeeper Jerusha Leonard, whom we met in chapter 6), taught school in Hadley; she lodged with Penelope and Samuel Gaylord one summer, and may have boarded at the Warner tavern another.[75] Keeping school was a common undertaking among

Jerusha's set of acquaintances; her sister Tabitha had also been engaged that spring to keep school in nearby Whately.[76] Jerusha "began school" on Monday, May 2, and "dismist [her] school" on October 22.[77] But just what sort of school this was, and where it was located, is not entirely clear, because at this time Hadley began allocating funds for schools serving the town's several outlying neighborhoods. In 1791, Hadley voted funds for the purpose of "hiring schools in several parts of the town, in proportion to the number of scholars, male and female."[78] The village of North Hadley, about two miles north of town center, almost surely received separate attention at this time, and likely Hockanum to the south as well. As the town began funding schools across the community, more opportunities emerged for women like Jerusha Leonard.

Daughters of a town's more affluent families could opt to attend private schools. Northampton's "Mrs Ashmun" used the pages of the local paper to announce her own school "for the instruction of Misses in reading, writing and needlework."[79] The first notice for what would become the well-regarded South Hadley school of Abby Wright appeared in the April 25, 1804, edition of the *Gazette,* noting that the "subscription school" would train "young misses, in the several branches of reading, writing, grammar and geography" as well as "plain needle work, embroidery, &c &c."[80] In Hadley, as early as 1805 a recovered Charlotte Williams Porter (the same Charlotte whom we met as she struggled with depression)—the second wife of physician and merchant William Porter— also opened a school for girls, in the substantial 1780s home her husband had built on the Hadley Common, just steps from the meetinghouse. Porter elected to give his substantial dwelling a gambrel roof, a choice that, as historian Kevin Sweeney has argued, suggested (as this form was common in institutional buildings of the period) its association with authority. "The use of a gambrel roof on a two-story house," Sweeney observes, also "readily conveyed the size and roominess of the entire structure. It articulated at the gable ends a third and, occasionally, even a fourth floor"; three tall pedimented dormer windows across the front of the house likewise reported a third story.[81] The capacious three-story building was certainly a good venue for an academic enterprise. But Porter's school seems not to have thrived.[82] Perhaps Porter was just not up to the demands of life as an educator, or perhaps she was too late in entering the competition for local students, as it was "not so large a school" as her father "wished and expected," having "only 4 from Williamstown" and one of those apparently dropping out after the death of her mother.[83] Porter's school was probably not unlike another opened by a Pollina Sellon some years later. Sellon offered girls instruction in ornamental needlework, and likely other subjects as well (figure 9.1).[84] But her enterprise, too, left but slight imprint on the historical record.

Twelve-year-old Betsy Phelps and fourteen-year-old Thankful Richmond started school in Amherst in July 1791, under the tutelage of a male schoolmaster,

Figure 9.1 Abigail Cook (b. 1815), Pollina Sellon sampler. The inscription on this sampler reads "Wrought by Abigail F. Cook at Miss Pollina Sellon's School, Hadley, Mass AD. 1825 Aet 10." While little is known about Sellon, she and women like her found opportunity in the flourishing interest in women's education that emerged in the early republic. Hall and Kate Peterson Fund for Minor Antiques. Reproduced by permission of Historic Deerfield (HD 96.002). Photo by Penny Leveritt

Mr. Harris.[85] They had been taught to read and write at home by their grandmother, Elizabeth Pitkin Porter, and at least for a time a six-year-old Thankful attended school in town. But as they entered their teens, the girls were placed in this Amherst school, boarding with the family of Amherst physician Robert Cutler. Years later, Thankful would recall for Sylvester Judd only that they were educated in "various branches."[86]

As Mary Kelley, Jason Opal, Catherine Kelly, and others have shown, interest in women's education exploded in postrevolutionary New England. "Independence," Opal writes, "had sparked fresh interest in formal education, and while state governments proved unwilling or unable to form tax-supported school systems, they eagerly incorporated any boosters who offered to build an academy."[87]

Notions of republican virtue and womanhood led to new expectations for white women as wives and mothers, which in turn placed new importance on female education.[88] Academies in which women would master the intellectual, religious, social, and aesthetic content necessary to build a virtuous nation proliferated. In 1802, Westfield Academy (incorporated in 1793 and opened in 1800 to "youths of both sexes" who could "read and write in a decent manner") alerted the "young ladies" who read the *Hampshire Gazette* that the trustees of the academy had hired a "young lady to assist the proprietor in the instruction of youth"; the following year, they announced that they had engaged Miss Elizabeth Sumner of Middletown ("a young lady of distinguished reputation and abilities") to teach in the spring and summer quarters, when she would instruct "young ladies" in "common branches of literature" as well as "all kinds of useful needlework."[89] Emma Hart Willard joined the faculty of Westfield Academy in 1807 (she would later found the influential Troy Female Seminary, attended by several of the Huntington daughters). Undaunted by her competition, that same year a Mrs. Tuckett together with her husband threw her own chalk into the ring when she opened a "Young Ladies Academy" in Northampton.[90]

The daughters of Charles and Elizabeth Phelps had attended a private school in Amherst, but their grandchildren would attend (and later teach at) Hopkins Academy in Hadley.[91] Founded in the 1660s as a public grammar school, Hopkins Academy was reimagined and incorporated in 1816—opened to "youth of both sexes, who can read decently, in a common English book without spelling and write a joined hand and are of good moral character."[92] A history of the school asserts that, after incorporation, "more young women than young men have enjoyed the advantages of the school."[93] The plain painted brick structure, sited between West and Middle Streets along the road to Amherst, rose three stories, its ground floor devoted to two schoolrooms that flanked a center hall. Second-floor spaces housed a library, scientific apparatus, and rooms for recitation, while the top story held "Academy Hall." On Wednesday afternoons, students stepped on the stage there, and performed "rhetorical exercises"; the space also accommodated exhibitions and public lectures.

Elizabeth Phelps's son-in-law, the Reverend Dan Huntington, was hired as the academy's preceptor, and its first preceptress was Sally Williston, daughter of the Easthampton minister, who assumed this position though she must have been only in her teens.[94] She was succeeded by Westfield native Sophia Moseley, who was almost certainly a graduate of Westfield Academy.[95] She and her sister Sybil (who had also been educated at Westfield Academy) were left without parents in 1811, and in 1813 Sybil launched her own school for women in Canandaigua, New York; Sybil Moseley would go on to marry Hiram Bingham and establish an important mission in the Hawaiian islands.[96] Twenty-year-old Sophia likely found this opportunity to work as an educator in Hadley most welcome in the wake of her parents' death and her sister's departure. Her position paid twelve dollars per month plus her board; at the same time, it gave her a position of authority and influence in the town.[97]

Catherine E. Kelly has considered the role of these academies in constructing what she terms a *Republic of Taste;* as Sophia Moseley guided young women from Hadley and elsewhere in their intellectual and aesthetic pursuits, she cultivated the technical skills and visual literacy necessary to convey and create the material environment that constituted middle-class homes. Moseley parlayed her own training at Westfield Academy into a position of authority in this new enterprise, and new community, helping her charges (and their parents and siblings) absorb the values and priorities associated with what Kelly calls the "early Republic's Janus-faced culture of class, which simultaneously promised opportunity and reinforced distinction."[98] As a teacher Moseley guided students in academic studies as well as demeanor and appearance. A member of a generation and network of young educators in motion, she also served as a conduit to larger developments; it seems certain, for instance, that the charitable work taken up on behalf of the American Board of Commissioners for Foreign Missions in Hawaii was prompted by Sophia's desire to assist her sister's work there.

Moseley's female charges came from twenty-six communities in five states, studying painting and embroidery as well as "the higher branches of education"— perhaps history, geography, philosophy, and mathematics, subjects Moseley would have encountered at Westfield Academy after they were introduced by instructor Emma Hart Willard.[99] An early catalogue shows the 126 students divided about evenly, with as many young women as men. While the majority (33) of young women came from Hadley, and several other students hailed from neighboring towns, others traveled from as far afield as Spencertown, New York (just west of the Massachusetts border); Windsor, Vermont (90 miles north); Haverhill, New Hampshire (some 130 miles northeast); and Enfield, Connecticut (30 miles south). The composition and distribution of the male student body was similar; the school's incorporation and growth must have been a boon for families positioned to take in students, as well as instructors like Williston and Moseley, as boarders.

Unlike many of the occupations considered here, teaching was a growth industry for Massachusetts women. As more families sent daughters to school, gender constructions were rethought, and women's alleged capacity for nurturing was articulated as a strength that made them natural teachers. If discipline in the classroom had once been perceived to be a product of force and harsh authority (stories of strict, even cruel teachers abound), it was gradually replaced—in a culture that would romanticize childhood in new ways—by an ethic of persuasion, and supportive encouragement. That women could be paid one-half to one-third of men's wages provided silent support for this ideological argument. Whatever its sources, the assemblage of rationales transformed teaching, at least at the lower levels, to a largely female enterprise. As Catherine Kelly has observed, by the 1820s "provincial centers" like Northampton saw rising numbers of women in search of positions as teachers, with "competition for students" reaching "comic proportions."[100] In 1829, just over half of all Massachusetts teachers (summer and winter sessions combined) were women; by 1841, fully a third of winter-session teachers were female, and by 1860, close to 80 percent of all teachers were women.[101]

For young women like Jerusha Leonard, Patty and Betty Reynolds, Sally Williston, and Sophia Moseley, new opportunities in classroom settings offered broader horizons. Like Massachusetts and Vermont schoolteacher Charity Bryant, whose thirst for intellectual stimulation and (social and sexual) independence has been so beautifully envisioned by historian Rachel Hope Cleves, these young women—coming of age together at the turn of the nineteenth century—embraced the opportunity to travel to new communities and deploy newly gained knowledge and expertise. As Cleves suggests, working as a teacher allowed middling women "a window of time in which to earn wages, live apart from their families, pursue intellectual interests, and still preserve their good name"; unlike tavernkeeping or tailoring, she adds, teaching conformed to emerging gender and class prescriptions that would become increasingly intolerant of work that put men and women in close proximity.[102] The transformation in the gendered logics of education is reminiscent of another centuries earlier that allowed women to enter and then control the trades involving women's apparel: when economic and social conditions created a demand for female employment, gender conventions not only bent to accommodate it, but were overtly deployed to effect the change. At the same time, events in other arenas facilitated this development, too. As cloth manufacture gradually entered the factory, ever-larger numbers of young women from middling families found themselves free to pursue more education, and to share their new skills and knowledge with others. For a time, some young women alternated between teaching and factory work, but eventually prospective teachers and prospective operatives would be sorted more firmly by class position.[103]

New Landscapes

Hadley as a landscape, too, had grown and changed, influenced by impulses of nostalgia and romance even as it was transformed by industry and commerce. The gristmill and sawmill around the pond in North Hadley were gradually joined by other enterprises—a linseed oil mill in 1795, and the carding mill. At the turn of the century some twenty taxpaying heads of household were gathered around the mills here, with a new dam (built in 1818) supporting yet more new enterprises.[104] By 1832, the firm Gates & Pomroy had launched a Fort River mill in which seven people labored to produce woolen cloths and satinet.

But in Hadley, the big story was the booming broom corn industry, and the new economy that accompanied it. Between the end of the Revolution and 1830 the town's population doubled, and while the local economy remained grounded in agriculture, crops like corn, rye, wheat, and flax "gave way to the commercial production of broom corn, and, as that subsided, tobacco."[105] Gloria L. Main, in a study of inequality as measured in Massachusetts probate records, has found that, "measured in terms of its distribution of probate wealth, society in eighteenth-century New England appears positively egalitarian compared to the degree of inequality which one encounters in Massachusetts in the following century"; by 1830, the Commonwealth had undergone a "transformation in its distribution of wealth," an upshot in part due to the growth of manufacturing.[106] Hampshire County was slower to join those developments, but broom corn production, which spurred manufacturing, would alter significantly economic, social, and natural landscapes. Between 1810 and 1831, the acreage devoted to broom corn rose while the number of brooms produced in western Massachusetts increased tenfold, to over a million brooms each year.[107]

In Hadley, by 1832 some sixty people were employed in the broom industry; a wireworks sprung up in North Hadley to help support production.[108] Louis McLane's report published that year found a half-million pounds of "brush" converted into brooms.[109] The household at Forty Acres, like others around town, embraced the opportunity, growing broom corn and selling brooms for ten cents each; Dan Huntington, who waxed poetic about how just as the "sun, in the pride of his strength, sends forth his rays in all directions, [so] Old Hadley, in the pride of its commerce, sends forth its broom carts, to all the wards of heaven," would write his daughter Elizabeth, away at Emma Willard's Troy Female Seminary, that "whenever you see a load of brooms in your street take courage and believe that you have friends near."[110] Hadley merchant William Porter was purchasing wooden handles to supply manufactories, while notices appeared in the *Hampshire Gazette* from stores as far south as Hartford, eager to supply tacks, twine, and copal varnish.[111] In time, C. D. Dickinson launched a broom tool manufacturing business from the North Hadley dam, producing "scrapers" (used to scrape the corn), "pounders" (which separated corn from their stalks), metal needles, and sewing cuffs.[112] Hadley's broom corn, Dan Huntington would assert, "contributes to the making of neat housewives, when otherwise we should look for them in vain" (adding that he had just sold to a "shaking Quaker" some sixty dollars' worth of broom corn, "without the trouble of manufacturing it."[113]

Hadley women like Mary Trainer, as we have seen, embraced the broom corn phenomenon almost immediately, though the evidence involving Trainer finds her mainly in the field, rather than in the fabrication of brooms. Interestingly, historian Gregory Nobles found "no evidence of women broommakers in Hadley"; he concludes that, though it is "entirely possible" that women participated in some aspects of this industry, women were unlikely to have been significantly involved in broom production.[114] In this regard, broom production differed from another local enterprise, palm-leaf hat making, which engaged a significant number of women, especially in and around Amherst.[115] As Christopher Clark explains, in the 1820s "families split the leaf by hand, braided it, and dewed and fashioned it into hats, returning them to the store for credit or payment." In North Hadley, shopkeeper Edward P. Huntington—one of Elizabeth Phelps Huntington's several sons—was shipping hats by traders in nearby Sunderland and North Amherst; in 1839 some sixteen outworkers were fabricating goods for his enterprise.[116] By the mid-1840s, Hadley merchants William and James Porter were receiving palm leaf from Leonard M. Hills, "one of the leading Amherst suppliers"; by 1850, 41 percent of the households beyond Amherst who braided for Sweetser, Cutler and Company lived in Hadley.[117]

Hat braiding, broom making, and even wireworks, requiring fairly little in the way of infrastructure, made only modest impressions on the landscape; for instance, the ell behind the 1835 Philo and Irene Hibbard Clark house once sheltered a broom shop.[118] Farmers built freestanding shops for broom production, and set up shops in their barns as well as the ells and attics of their homes.[119] Francis Smith turned his barns into broom shops; Cotton Marsh likewise devoted space in his outbuildings and ells to that enterprise, as did the households of the Breckenridge family, Joseph Spear, and Oliver Marsh.[120] Even as late as 1850, when brooms were leaving Hadley by the tens of thousands, there was still no building that could be construed as a "factory." The village at North Hadley became known as the "upper mills," and the Fort River mill site on the road to Hockanum "Mill Hollow," but Hadley did not come to possess any "factory hollow," the way Amherst and other surrounding towns did. As J. Ritchie Garrison has explained, "in terms of work discipline," broom-making operations "shared characteristics with industrialized production"; "the equipment and the process used in manufacture were designed to reduce variation . . . and to turn out thousands of brooms that all had more or less the same qualities." Yet, he continues, this was not factory production: most shops employed only a handful of workers, some working only seasonally, during gaps in the agricultural calendar.[121] Gregory Nobles confirms that, as late as 1850, of forty-one businesses listed in the federal census, most (with one exception) employed six or fewer workers, and "a dozen or so were one-man shops"; thirty of the forty-one shops were run by men whose primary occupation was something else—mostly farming—while only eleven identified themselves as broom makers.[122]

The industry's impact on the landscape was perhaps more visible in the residential architecture it financed, like the stately Greek Revival home (1838) of broom manufacturer Albert and Mary Hibbard Jones, its gable front resting on three massive fluted Doric columns.[123] The even more elaborate home of Nathan and Polly Clark (1836)—its own full-height entry porch likewise ornamented by two-story, paneled corner pilasters, with an eight-paned oculus ornamenting a broad triangular pediment—was equally monumental, and paid for by the piano wire and wire cards manufactured at Clark's mill across the street.[124] Today, a dozen Greek Revival homes built between 1834 and 1840 stand to document the village's growth in this decade. This burst of development converted the neighborhood around Hadley's upper mills into a proper village in its own right, including the establishment of a second Congregational Church (organized in 1831), its sanctuary constructed in 1834—the same year as the wireworks.[125] The gable of the elegant, restrained church building, with its four tall pilasters framing three bays beneath broad entablature, and its entire facade sheathed with flush boarding, lent an air of sophistication to Hadley's mill village.[126]

Elsewhere in Hadley, townscapes were becoming more groomed. For instance, until 1800, cattle and cows were allowed to run at large on the common; in that year the town's governance determined that only cows would be allowed to roam free, and in 1801, they, too, were banned.[127] Lombardy poplars were planted along the seventeenth-century common, some of Hadley's earliest conscious landscaping for ornamental purposes.[128] Introduced into the United States in the 1780s outside Philadelphia, the poplars had become one of the country's first horticultural fads. Both George Washington and Thomas Jefferson grew them on their Virginia estates, and when the nation's capital was developed, Washington insisted that Lombardy poplars be planted along the streets of the District of Columbia. Soon, the residents of Salem, Massachusetts, leveled their common and planted rows of poplars all around it, and the same year the city of Boston planted poplars on the common there.[129] Hadley, not to be outdone, planted poplars lining the common in a gesture that suggests their desire to conform to cultural preferences thriving well beyond the Holyoke Range or the Pelham hills. By the 1810s and 20s, an older, "ruder and less orderly" landscape was well on its way to being replaced as new priorities took hold.[130]

In part, that grooming also meant a certain formalizing across town institutions and the buildings that housed them. Once, some spaces in any given community sheltered both sacred and secular functions: the same building that housed worship services also accommodated town meeting and court sessions. As the eighteenth century gave way to the nineteenth, parlors, taverns, and meetinghouses were increasingly excised from judicial landscapes as legal proceedings relocated to dedicated courthouses (and ever-larger jails).[131] The succession was more direct in Hatfield, where the Williams family's large, gambrel-roofed house was razed in 1852 to make room for a new town hall. As church and state were disentangled in the Commonwealth (Massachusetts being among the last states to relinquish an established church), so too did towns witness a "process that transformed the New England meetinghouse into a church and gave birth to the meetinghouse's less-well-known offspring, the town house." Hadley embraced that trend comparatively late, but in 1841 townspeople also began to gather in a new, two-story hall in the Greek Revival style, its generous Doric portico assuring visitors of the community's embrace of the classical style that had become de rigueur for public buildings.[132] With the simultaneous removal of the town's 1808 meetinghouse from the common to Middle Street, next door to the new town hall, Hadley marked a significant change, its center of gravity no longer the 1659 town common and all that it represented, but rather a new town center just to the east—on Middle Street, the successor to the onetime Back Street—that was created as new forces, and new families, gained power in the mid-nineteenth century village.[133]

As Hadley residents reshaped the townscape, they groomed domestic environments as well. David Jaffee has shown how rural and small-town Massachusetts producers, propelled by the "Village Enlightenment," helped create a "new nation of goods" as they reinterpreted genteel taste for the widening audience of middle-class consumers.[134] Not only were residential landscapes becoming whiter; they also became more polished. Sophia Buck Smith remembered making her first carpet from yarn in 1831, and she also recalled the arrival of the first piano in town, in the parlor of Erastus and Lydia Smith. The number of pianos in Hadley soon grew to five.[135] Such indulgences were made possible by other, more mundane developments that transformed domestic spaces. Cookstoves, for instance, appeared in Hadley kitchens by the 1810s, and as prices dropped, more and more families incorporated this innovation into their homes, until by the 1840s they were relatively common.[136] The introduction of sinks and water systems also altered the shape of household labor, freeing some women to embrace new opportunities in the outwork system (while at the same time helping drive upward standards of cleanliness).[137] Sophia Cook Clark would later recall for Sylvester Judd that the wells she remembered from her own Hadley youth in the early nineteenth century had begun to acquire pumps, easing the burden for some West Street housewives. But nevertheless, the ever-larger wardrobes of antebellum Hadley, coupled with rising expectations about hygiene and personal grooming, had made washing a bigger chore than she remembered it having been in 1800, when a "family . . . had not more than half the washing that a family of the same property & numbers have now."[138]

Domestic architecture and the evolving layouts of farmsteads affirmed and advanced these changes. Multipurpose spaces that once witnessed a range of tasks and laborers slowly gave way to more dedicated spaces that segregated work and workers; architecture articulated new values surrounding the construction of both gender and class.[139] Houses throughout the village, following the lead of earlier efforts by the Phelpses and other affluent families, gained rear ells and refined farmyards. The architectural historian Nora Pat Small has explained how, elsewhere in Massachusetts at the turn of the nineteenth century, the design and arrangement of rural farmsteads and farmhouses became associated with the virtue of the family within. Mantels, chair rails, cornices, and entablatures all afforded opportunities for rural households to demonstrate their embrace of classical decorations, with all of their political and cultural implications. While excess in ornament was always frowned upon, "tidy, economical" farms and farm buildings beautifully symbolized the ideal of the enlightened farmer whose virtue, hard work, and proximity to the land anchored the fledgling republic.[140] Meanwhile, other choices reflected the turning-inward of family life; houses whose main entrances were once oriented to the street were increasingly supplanted by new configurations in which the entrance was positioned to the side yard, creating a sort of virtual anteroom that further sheltered the family from public life.[141] Small, subtle distances increasingly set apart individual households from the larger community. By the 1830s, fences—once the province only of those wealthy families who could afford the expense of sawn pickets and milled rails—enclosed most front yards.[142]

In time, these new social relations between women and men and among women produced an affinity for what has come to be called the Gothic Revival style. Homes infused in both floor plan and ornament by Christian aesthetics embedded new gender and class relations in Christian beliefs and values.[143] The middle-class home, at least among families poised to achieve one, was increasingly defined not simply as apart from any economic sphere, but in fact the antidote to it. Rural families differed from their urban counterparts in the degree and manner of their response to these larger cultural impulses, but even in Hadley, tablewares, furniture, architecture, and clothing would come to reflect the spread of these notions in society writ large. When in 1831 mason David William Cook built his brick cottage in the Gothic style on the west side of the Hadley Common, its pointed arches proved a distinct departure from its neighbors. Soon, other cross-gabled, board-and-batten houses with ecclesiastical windows would be cropping up around town. And soon Hadley's middling housewives found themselves keepers of homes whose domestic and religious implications mirrored their own emerging role as the so-called Angel of the House, a role for which they would also find themselves appropriately costumed as the pelerine infiltrated Hadley wardrobes, the reference to the apparel of medieval pilgrims likewise infusing their middle-class white womanhood with domesticity, piety, and romantic nostalgia (figure 9.2).[144]

Figure 9.2 Mary Jones (1817–1865) portrait by Erastus Salisbury Field, 1836 (*top*); pelerine (*bottom*). This oil portrait affirms that women in Hadley fully embraced the fashions of nineteenth-century romantic revivals. The pelerine that cascades over Jones's shoulders—a sartorial allusion to religious pilgrims of medieval Europe— allowed Jones to tangibly don evidence of a timeless faith, domesticity, and sentimentality. Reproduced by permission of Historic Deerfield (HD 2001.28.1 and HD 2001.28.2). Photo by Penny Leveritt

The Hadley of the 1830s was a different village than the Hadley of the 1780s, though only a few short decades divided those moments, and many residents watched that gradual evolution over the course of a lifetime. The matrons of the town's middling families no longer rose before dawn to churn in the cool of the day. As the daughters of antebellum Hadley carried their mother's spinning wheels to basements and attics, as looms were dismantled and relegated to barns and outbuildings, and wool combs began the steady march from tool to relic, long-standing relations of work among Hadley families gave way to new associations that were colored more by anonymity and brevity—or, depending on one's point of view, brevity and privacy—than familiarity and continuity. As more young women found employment in factories and mills, fewer willing to work as domestics could be found easily by word of mouth. Despite Phelps's willingness to pay "almost any rate" to keep good help, women simply left service for better employment opportunities elsewhere. Persis Leonard quit domestic service and embraced spinning, while a hired girl from nearby Pelham, burdened with the care of her elderly aunt and illegitimate child, "could not support a family . . . and half-cloath herself," on her wages at Forty Acres, so she exchanged service for outwork, and, along with many Hampshire County women, began braiding straw hats.[145] Newly minted teachers like Sophia Moseley arrived to cultivate the next generation among Hadley's families of relative privilege. The landscape of women's labor was being reconfigured, transforming relationships among households both nearby and at a distance. Through it all, division and unity, assertion and accommodation, set the pulse of community life, as it had from the beginning.

Remembering Women and Work

As we leave Hadley, let us walk once again down the town common, picturing it now as Hadley entered the second quarter of the nineteenth century (figure coda.1). The weathered dwellings of the first period of settlement have been largely supplanted by new architectural styles and new generations of residents. At the corner where the road leads west into the Great Meadow, the broad plain saltbox built around 1700 by Andrew Cooke is more and more an outlier among the crisp Federal and Greek Revival farmhouses that have replaced the town's first-period dwellings. Across the common, the stately outline of Nathaniel Coolidge's new home—Hadley's first to embrace the fashionable three-bay, side-hall plan—makes the old Cooke house seem all the more antiquated (Coolidge was all-in on the new fashion, instructing his builders to install an elliptical fan so large that it dominates the closed triangular pediment, its broad entablature supported by four colossal pilasters).[1] Alongside such additions are found equally telling absences. Only a handful of the home lots along the common are still occupied by descendants of the seventeenth-century families who settled them.[2] The constellation of houses along the north bend of the Connecticut River, once a gathering of Hadley's families of color, is gone. The only remnants of Mary Andries's onetime home on the south edge of the Phelps family's farm are two lush beds of mint that mark the spot where her dwelling once stood.[3]

In the two centuries since this imagined walk along the common in the early nineteenth century, other choices have together shaped community memory of the town's complex past, and particularly how residents came to understand histories of women, work, and the early American economy. In many cases, these are stories of erasure. The name of the street on which the last "poor house" once stood—Town Farm Lane—was altered in the 1990s to simply "Farm Lane," a small edit that, with the dropping of that single word, elided on the landscape of common understanding the memory of this local institution, supplying in its stead a notion of rural production, and for some, a notion of idyll.[4] Of the many hundreds of baskets produced by the valley's native women in these years, only a handful are preserved in area collections; while eager nineteenth-century collectors gathered up literally hundreds of skeletal remains,

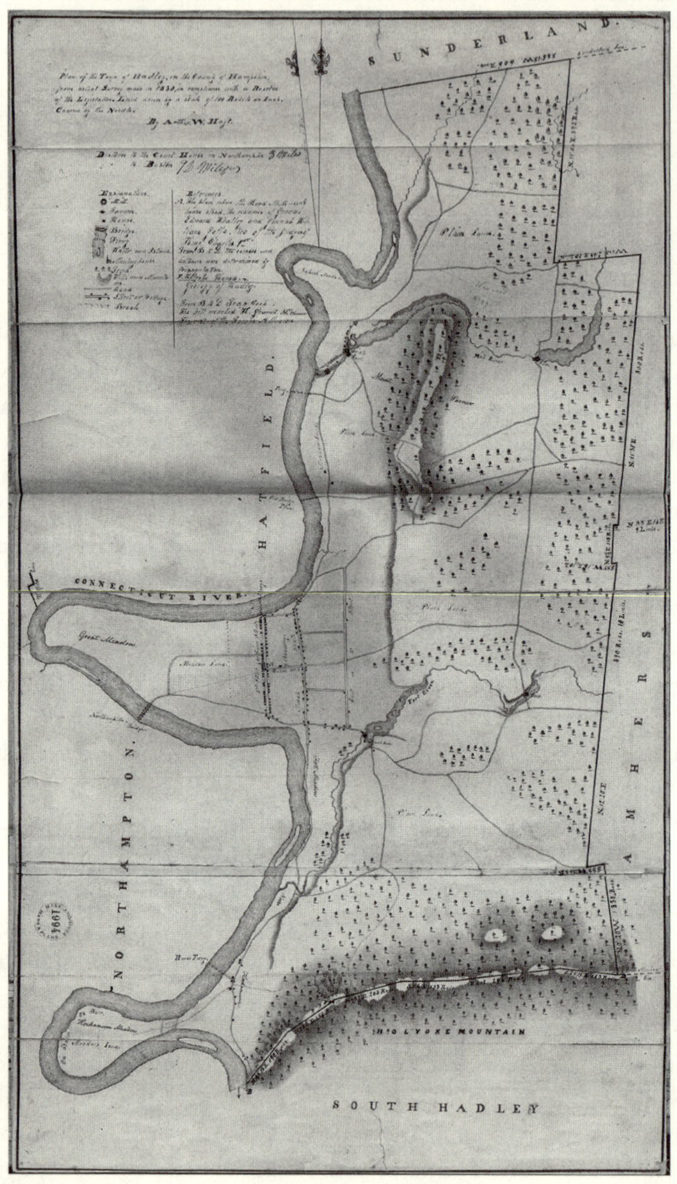

Coda.1 Hadley, Massachusetts, in 1830. Hadley in 1830 encompassed several neighborhoods anchored by mills and was connected to the region via various highways, ferries, and bridges; surveyor Arthur W. Hoyt also marked prominently the site of the town's academy. He also nodded to local history and memory, indicating the site where in the seventeenth century the regicides Whalley and Goffe were harbored. Map of Hadley, v. 2, p. 7, 1830 Map Series (SC1/series 48x), courtesy of Massachusetts Archives, Boston, MA

"they made virtually no attempt to record ethnographic information on living Native peoples in the valley."[5] Though dozens of African American dead have been interred in Hadley, only a single grave of any of the people confined by enslavement is known to be marked: a stone post in the Old Hadley Cemetery honors the life and death of Ishmael Prutt, son of Joan and Abner, who died in 1809 at the age of eighty-eight.[6] With this lone exception, Hadley's enslaved men and women rest in obscurity.[7]

Attending to the history of pastkeeping in Hadley and places like it helps us see how contemporary understanding of the history of women's work found its shape—a subject of significance as deeply held misapprehensions about women's work in the American past continue to shape attitudes about labor policy today.[8] Hadley's sense of its own history and identity evolved, beginning in the second quarter of the nineteenth century, both in response to the ongoing development of the town's economy and declining political and cultural influence, and in contradistinction to events elsewhere. In these decades, the community's agricultural past became a source of both authority and nostalgia. As the historian David Danbom has argued, in the nineteenth century farmers commanded particular cultural appeal, in that they helped reconcile tensions between luxury and necessity exacerbated by an expanding market. Their lives close to nature, secured by an admirable access to property ownership—all of this contributed to the growing sense of "rural superiority" that has also been observed by historians Catherine Kelly, Richard Bushman, and others.[9] As Kelly writes, in the 1820s, 30s, and 40s, "provincial New Englanders manipulated an increasingly hollow notion of the household economy to position themselves uneasily between their poorer neighbors and their urban counterparts." She continues on, "Men and women whose lives were shaped by the imperatives of a market society continued to hold the homely virtues of their households and towns against the fashion and show they associated with bourgeois society. In the process, they obscured the growing distance that separated even members of a provincial middle class from their poorer farming and laboring neighbors."[10]

Thanks to the pathbreaking work of historian Laurel Ulrich, too, we now have a better appreciation of how the mythical "Age of Homespun" was constructed by early national families and bequeathed to the generations to follow. In the second quarter of the nineteenth century, as households and communities absorbed ever-larger numbers of factory-produced goods, the objects made by the hands of their forebears became increasingly venerated. A distorted view of eighteenth-century household production emerged that gave something to everyone: "For sentimentalists, spinning and weaving represented the centrality of home and family, for evolutionists the triumph of civilization over savagery, for craft revivalists the harmony of labor and art." "New England women moved into the industrial age," Ulrich writes, "with trunks full of stockings and a heavy weight of history." Conventional wisdom insisted that they had it far easier than their forebears. But "in reality, there was plenty of work, some of it created by the labor-saving devices that had supposedly liberated them. An abundance of factory-made cloth expanded the standard of clothing a family required; new concepts of cleanliness required a greater investment in laundry, mopping and cleaning; more varied foodstuffs, condiments, and table accessories encouraged more complex meals and entertainments; cookstoves, oil lamps, indoor pumps, and iceboxes added additional forms of maintenance."[11] The idealization of childhood, motherhood, and education transformed parenting while also removing (white, middling) children and their labor from the household.[12] Meanwhile, increasing numbers of local women went off to work in Massachusetts factories, migrations that proved nourishing for romantic fantasies of homes in which middle-class housewives were not, at least visibly, workers.

When Sylvester Judd began his studies as the Revolutionary era drifted beyond the reach of memory, his generation—as is often the case—romanticized the world that was lost almost beyond recognition. Then as now, the "good old days" are usually those that were just barely past—a sunnier time that seemed, at least in memory, less complicated, less fraught with tension. Judd lived in a world in flux. The county's Congregational community had been divided, not only by the challenges of Methodism, Baptism, and Unitarianism, but also competition among multiplying Congregational gatherings. Meanwhile, "growing inequality" in Judd's Northampton "opened a social gulf that left fully half of the town without taxable or real property."[13] Judd "lamented the widening distance between social classes" and invited his informants to lament alongside him, and share his longing for what he believed to be the "rough equality of preindustrial New England."[14] In the second quarter of the nineteenth century, a "Mr. West" (b. 1766), Judd wrote, "is confident that there was more happiness and contentment among people formerly than now. The spinning girl spun barefoot and sung merrily and was ready to dance at night and was very happy." Another of Judd's informants, Sarah Graves Amsden—the daughter of tavernkeepers and "a woman qualified to judge," he noted, for reasons unknown—"is confident that there was more happiness and enjoyment and neighborly feeling among people formerly than now." Amsden in particular stressed that there was "not so much striving to get above one another, or to get up equal to another, as now." People endeavored less to obtain "showy and fashionable things."[15] Indeed, he continued, "all elderly people with whom I converse, or almost all, make the same comparison; I mean those of the working classes. . . ." There is, Judd further assessed, "doubtless more strife for preeminence"; borrowing Amsden's phrase, he confirmed that he perceived "more attempts to out do each other in what is showy and fashionable than formerly."[16]

Amsden and Judd's nostalgia, again, tells us more about the anxieties of their age than the past they sought to describe. Whether the shoeless spinning girl of Judd's historical imagination would have told the same story seems doubtful. She may have been one of the women who, like Persis Leonard, rejected domestic labor as soon as possible for the privacy afforded by palm-leaf hat production, or the relative autonomy conferred by outwork in its earliest incarnations. But over time, memory of the working women whose lives constructed eighteenth-century Hadley faded, in part simply as new layers supplanted old. Some historical memory among selected Hadley women was captured by Sylvester Judd, in the people he chose to interview and the topics they covered. Other gestures of pastkeeping were simultaneously more material and more metaphorical, as women selected artifacts for preservation, for purposes both practical and sentimental (opting to save, for instance, the pelerine pictured in figure 9.2b). In some instances, they created new objects that tapped remnants of earlier women's work while reinventing them for the present, a new generation selecting elements of the past to advance, while placing them in new material, social, and cultural contexts (figure coda.2).

Memory shifted too in the wake of active attempts, over the course of the nineteenth century, to shape and reshape historical understanding. In 1891, Arria Sargent Huntington, a great-granddaughter of Elizabeth Porter Phelps, published *Under a Colonial Rooftree: Fireside Chronicles of Early New England*.[17] Huntington devoted a chapter of the family history to her great-grandmother's diary. While she reveled in the picture of rural gentility captured in those pages, she did not entirely overlook labor and laborers, pausing to note the "itinerant workwomen who were such a feature of life of those days," and devoting several lines to the presence of enslaved women. In these passages, Huntington's text emphasizes Phelps's qualities as a caring and thoughtful mistress. The author, for instance, observes the importance to Phelps of young Mitte West, but in her version of these events, Mitte was not the unsanctioned daughter of a domestic servant, but rather "a young woman whom Phelps befriended and brought up"; in Huntington's telling, "in the end, after several lapses, Mitty [*sic*] made a respectable marriage and lived to old age", though it is difficult to confirm Huntington's assertion.[18] "Of the other hired help," Huntington concludes, "Mrs Phelps was always most considerate. She praised them for their faithfulness, was solicitous for their welfare, and took unwearied pains in the training of the young."[19] Huntington's own life experience was less sheltered than the pages of this volume might suggest. Like many women of her class, region, and generation, she was committed to social reform; over the course of her life, she was active (in and around her home in Syracuse, New

Coda.2 Pieced quilt, ca. 1825, unidentified maker, attributed to Hadley area. This quilt, probably made from recycled pieces of eighteenth-century bedhangings alongside more contemporary cotton fabrics, in the patchwork configuration popular in the nineteenth century, captures in its materials and design the changing nature—and incremental, gradual aspects of those changes—of women's lives. Old Sturbridge Village, MA

York) on behalf of homeless women, sex workers, women in carceral systems, and child laborers. Perhaps those interests help explain her need for a past that was less problematic. Whatever the reason, there is nothing particularly surprising about Huntington's treatment of her family history, which is fully consistent with how other women of her class envisioned New England's history. Nevertheless, accounts like this one, which glossed over the power held by employers like Elizabeth Porter Phelps, as well as the conflicting interests of enslaved women like Peg and hired workers like Submit West, blurred distinctions among women in early Massachusetts.[20]

While Huntington's text gently elided the working women of Forty Acres, another generation's reverence for the past produced the active removal of barns, outbuildings, and other physical evidence at odds with the memory of the family as effortless members of the rural gentry. In the early twentieth century, Phelps's descendant James Lincoln Huntington—who was fascinated, like his aunt Arria, by his family's history—acquired full ownership of Forty Acres. By this date, "Forty Acres" was a much more accurate name for the property, which had dwindled from the six-hundred-acre farm it had been in its heyday to a family summer home encompassing less than a tenth of its onetime acreage. In the 1940s Huntington retired from his medical practice and relocated from Boston to Hadley to devote his full attention to pastkeeping. He gave tours of the house and researched its history, publishing that work in his 1949 book *Forty Acres: The Story of the Bishop Huntington House*—emphasizing the celebrity of his grandfather, Frederic Dan Huntington, the Episcopal bishop of central New York, rather than the property's origins as a large farm of the late colonial period.[21] As historian Daniel Horowitz would observe, Huntington's book "defined the borders of this house" in ways that place commercialism beyond the property's boundaries, helping to prevent visitors from seeing the role of work in the history of the site, and to "minimize the contributions of women, African Americans, and Native Americans."[22]

Huntington's decision making sheds light on the particular history he sought to celebrate in the creation of the historic house museum. The farm's grounds had once included a tan house, cider house, and other facilities, but Huntington dismantled and removed small outbuildings and service structures, and in 1929 he sold the large, timber-framed 1782 barn, which was then moved to Hadley Center; the foundations on which the barn once stood became a fashionable "sunken garden." Shortly thereafter, the carriage barn, built in 1795 to house the family's stylish means of conveyance, was renovated into comfortable, modern living quarters.[23] The once-bustling farmyard, without the substantial structures that had defined its southern perimeter, became largely illegible (figure coda.3).[24]

The Phelpses' barn had been purchased by other Hadley pastkeepers—bookseller Henry Johnson and his brother, author and photographer Clifton Johnson, collectors who specifically eschewed preserving "furniture, costumes, and the indoor household life," items that they believed were already well attended to in the region's cultural institutions. The Johnsons preferred to begin their work "at the back door."[25] They had been looking for a venue to house their enterprise, approaching James Lincoln Huntington about building a replica of the barn at Forty Acres. Huntington offered to sell the structure itself, and in 1930 the Hadley Farm Museum opened in the Phelps barn, removed

Coda.3 Forty Acres farmyard. The farmyard as it appeared before James Lincoln Huntington sold the 1782 barn to the Johnson family and the house to the Hadley Farm Museum. With the large barn and also the carriage barn gone, the farmyard is no longer legible as a working space, presenting a challenge to the interpretation of farmwork for the present-day museum. The Porter-Phelps-Huntington Family Papers, on deposit at Amherst College Archives and Special Collections, Amherst, MA, Box 144 folder 9

from its original location and moved to its new site in the town center. The Johnson family traced its Hadley story back to the eighteenth century, when Stephen Johnson wed Sarah Lyman, daughter of the Hadley innkeeper. Generations later, Henry Johnson became interested in antiques, amassing a collection that over time outgrew his home, the dedicated space within his Springfield bookstore, and the Johnson family farm at Hockanum.[26] He and Clifton—as well as Clifton's wife Anna McQueston Johnson—became museum makers. The Johnsons' remembrance work would become a key venue for the preservation of the material culture of women's work in Hadley, in "innumerable baskets and buckets, dairy equipment, including butter and cheesemaking utensils," as well as quilt frames and cookware. While the Porter-Phelps-Huntington museum celebrated gentility and refinement, the collections of the Farm Museum elevated "Antiquities of Agriculture" (which Clifton Johnson, incidentally, hoped might "serve as a counteracting influence to the age of jazz").[27] Interestingly, however, and somewhat in contradistinction to this collecting impulse, once it was moved, the building was clapboarded and windows were installed to make it more consistent with the 1808 meeting-house sited next door (moved to this location in the 1840s as part of general revolution in the town's geography), while a new door surround in the iconic Connecticut River Valley style, modeled after the Porter house on the town common, would give the building a more residential feel.[28]

But the Johnson family's commitment to documenting the history of work in rural New England was significant. In fact, when the Johnsons acquired the Phelps barn, they brought with it various tools of women's work Huntington also felt no need to preserve: an apple parer inscribed with the initials of Elizabeth Whiting Phelps is likely just one of many tools of everyday labor that left Forty Acres for the nascent Farm Museum (and is now on display there). As a relatively early effort in Massachusetts museum making, few records were generated or preserved that link particular objects with the Hadley women who once used them, but the constellation of objects was aimed at memorializing and celebrating the everyday labors on which the town was built.[29] A well sweep, its squeak once announcing the break of day for so many Hadley women, stood in the yard by the museum's entrance; cheese ladders and churns, flax brakes and hetchels, spinning wheels and tape looms—the collection teemed (then as it does now) with artifacts that documented early American women's labor history.

In the 1950s, as James Lincoln Huntington continued to develop his memorial to family affluence and influence, other elements of Hadley's physical fabric were likewise serving as cultural commodities in the mnemonic work of others.[30] In 1955, a 1773 home in the "Dickinson family" was purchased by Electra Havemeyer Webb and moved to the grounds of Vermont's Shelburne Museum, to serve as a setting for the stunning assemblage of decorative arts gathered by Webb as well as collector Katherine Prentis Murphy, for whom the house is now named.[31] Another early house left the landscape when Mount Holyoke College alumna Irene Gillette Steiner purchased the ca. 1710 saltbox house built and occupied for generations by the Cooke family. Henry and Helen Geier Flynt had been contemplating the acquisition of the house for the colonial village they were then creating in Deerfield, but for whatever reason, they had opted not to pursue this property. They referred Steiner to the opportunity, and the Flynts' restoration carpenter, William E. Gass, supervised the dismantling of the saltbox and its reconstruction in Greenwich, Connecticut (where it stands today). Gass assigned the construction date based in part on the use of flax fibers as insulation between boards of the north wall, a welcome if small reminder of some of the work that once unfolded within those rooms.[32]

Hadley's twentieth-century pastkeeping mirrored the trajectory of communities around the region. Around the turn of the twentieth century, a chapter of the Daughters of the American Revolution formed, generating papers and collecting artifacts; around the time of the US Bicentennial, the newly established Hadley Historical Society assumed stewardship of the DAR's collections and gathered together other town papers, records, and objects, while the Hadley Historical Commission, also convened in these years, began attending to the town's historic buildings and landscapes.[33] As is often the case, such organizations represent both preservation and erasure, as choices were made about which stories, objects, and buildings to document and steward, and which to let go. Hundreds of Hadley homes are now documented, for instance, in local, state, and national registries, but—as preservation professionals now recognize—most are identified only by the name of the male head of household, concealing from easy view the names of the wives, mothers, and daughters whose labors made those structures possible.

Today, the Hadley Farm Museum continues to welcome visitors, sharing collections that document women's labor alongside men's. It is entirely possible that the cheese ladders, tape looms, cheese and laundry baskets, wool cards, and spinning wheels are the very tools once used by women considered in these pages, gathered up alongside Elizabeth Whiting Phelps's apple parer and carried to this new home. But most recently it is the Porter-Phelps-Huntington Foundation that has become most active in the preservation and interpretation of Hadley's working women in the eighteenth and early nineteenth century. In the mid-twentieth century the efforts of James Lincoln Huntington to create a historic site gained increasing traction. Forty Acres received an Award of Merit from the American Association of State and Local History in 1955.[34] In the 1960s, Huntington brought most of the "diary" of Elizabeth Porter Phelps into print in the pages of the *New England Historic and Genealogical Register,* which in turn allowed historians to begin to tap this rich resource.[35] The museum—responding to the late twentieth-century flowering of scholarship on women, work, and the early American economy—pursued a reinterpretation initiative in the 1990s.[36] My own 1997 dissertation and 2006 book *The Needle's Eye* both informed and were informed by museum-based and academic research at the site, and in 2004, art historian and museum board member Elizabeth Pendergast Carlisle published a biography of Elizabeth Porter Phelps, *Earthbound and Heavenbent,* which explored Phelps's life as a woman of the rural gentry, with particular attention to spiritual, family, and social life.[37] This scholarly activity proved influential, and the historic house museum continues to incorporate content about enslaved and employed women in the household, alongside members of the family.

Today, historic sites like the Porter-Phelps-Huntington Museum and the towns in which they stand—their houses, landscapes, and artifactual and archival records—help us see how, in the last decades of the eighteenth century, capitalism's centrifugal force set in motion changing social relations of labor that had long-lasting repercussions among the women of rural Massachusetts. These reconfigurations, these shifts in social and economic power, could be seismic, fortunes rising and falling suddenly along a community's fault lines. But alteration also came more gradually, as incremental change accumulated over decades. The ways in which these new patterns took hold often seem elusive. To map them, we investigate instead the substances that cast those shadows: letters anxiously seeking news of women whose labors might be available for hire; posthumous lists of goods bought and used over a lifetime; ledgered traces of production, consumption, and exchange; the tools and spaces of production, from baskets woven by indigenous hands to the dairies, taverns, and kitchens they occupied; and the buildings and landscapes themselves, from rear ells and ballrooms to mill villages and place names. Taken together, these traces of the past witness larger developments in the lives of rural Massachusetts women, and forces that both reflected and reshaped labor and livelihood in early New England.

Repositories

BPL	Boston Public Library
CHS	Connecticut Historical Society, Hartford, Connecticut
CSL	Connecticut State Library, Hartford, Connecticut
FL	Forbes Library, Northampton, Massachusetts
HCMRP	Hampshire County Massachusetts Registry of Probate
HCRD	Hampshire County Register of Deeds
HD	Historic Deerfield
HHS	Hadley Historical Society, Hadley, Massachusetts
HN	Historic Northampton, Northampton, Massachusetts
MACRIS	Massachusetts Cultural Resources Information System
MHC	Massachusetts Historical Commission
MHS	Massachusetts Historical Society, Boston, Massachusetts
OSV	Old Sturbridge Village
PPHFP	Porter-Phelps-Huntington Family Papers, on deposit at Amherst College Archives and Special Collections, Amherst, Massachusetts
PVMA	Pocumtuck Valley Memorial Association, Deerfield, Massachusetts

Publications

CC	*Connecticut Courant*
HG	*Hampshire Gazette*
JER	*Journal of the Early Republic*
NEHGR	*New England Historical and Genealogical Register.* The diary of Elizabeth Porter Phelps was published sequentially as follows: 1766–1769 (January 1964); 1770–1773 (April 1964); 1774–1776 (July 1964); 1777–1778 (December 1964); 1779–1781 (January 1965); 1782–1783 (April 1965); 1784–1786 (July 1965); 1787–1789 (October 1965); 1790 (January 1966); 1791–1792 (April 1966); 1793–1794 (July 1966); 1795–October 23, 1796 (October 1966); October 30, 1796–1798 (January 1967); 1799 (April 1967); 1800 (October 1967); 1801 (January 1968); 1802–1803 (April 1968); 1804 (July 1968); 1805 (October 1968).
NEQ	*New England Quarterly*
WMQ	*William and Mary Quarterly*

Proper Names

CP	Charles Phelps Jr.
CP Sr.	Charles Phelps Sr.
EPP	Elizabeth Porter Phelps
EWPH	Elizabeth Whiting Phelps Huntington
RD	Rebecca Dickinson

Preface

Epigraph: Edgar Lee Masters, *Spoon River Anthology* (New York: Macmillan, 1915).

1. For dates of houses, see the Massachusetts Historical Commission's database, Massachusetts Cultural Resource Information System (MACRIS), accessible at http://mhc-macris .net/index.htm. On the footpaths, see Patricia Laurice Ellsworth, "Hadley West Street Common and Great Meadow: A Cultural Landscape Study" (MA thesis, University of Massachusetts Department of Landscape Architecture and Regional Planning, 2007), 38.

2. See the World Monuments Fund Watch List page at http://www.wmf.org/project /cultural-landscape-hadley-massachusetts. According to Ellsworth, "Hadley West Street Common and Great Meadow," 9–10, the contemporary common very nearly retains its original dimensions; its width was decreased by 60 feet sometime before 1851 when the land transferred to home lots, and its length reduced approximately 280 feet by erosion where the Connecticut River passes to the north.

3. Also, more than 120 buildings constructed before 1840 are documented on the state register of historic places; see MACRIS.

4. The Porter-Phelps-Huntington Family Papers, 1698–1968, are owned by the Porter-Phelps-Huntington Foundation and housed in the Amherst College Archives and Special Collections.

5. Marla R. Miller, *The Needle's Eye: Women and Work in the Age of Revolution* (Amherst: University of Massachusetts Press, 2006).

6. Miller, *Needle's Eye,* 22.

7. Marla R. Miller, *Rebecca Dickinson: Independence for a New England Woman,* Lives of American Women (Boulder, CO: Westview Press, 2013). This book also drew on my first published work on Dickinson, "'My Part Alone': The World of Rebecca Dickinson, 1787–1802," *NEQ* 71, no. 3 (1998): 341–71. Along the way, my understanding of gender, artisanry, and revolution beyond New England was also expanded through my study of that much-misunderstood craftswoman Betsy Ross; see *Betsy Ross and the Making of America* (New York: Holt, 2010).

8. My thinking on this issue was informed and energized by the June 2018 symposium, "The Role of Historians in Public Life" (organized by Tammy Gordon of North Carolina State University and Jaroslav Ira of Charles University, at the North Carolina State European Center in Prague), which confronted the many ways in which local history, public history, and professional historical scholarship both support and challenge one another. Particularly valuable to my own thinking were Jakub Jareš, "Contemporary History in Czech Local Museums"; and Jaroslav Ira, "The Social Functions of Local History in Small Towns." I am grateful to Professors Gordon and Ira for including me in those provocative conversations.

9. Elsa Barkley Brown, "Polyrhythms and Improvisations: Lessons for Women's History," *History Workshop* 31 (Spring 1991): 85–90. Brown urges us (p. 86), in prose as compelling today as it was in 1991, "to recognize not only differences but also the relational nature of those differences. Middle-class white women's lives are not just different from working-class white, black, and Latina women's lives, it is important to recognize that middle-class women live the lives they do precisely because working-class women live the lives they do.

White women and women of colour not only live different lives but white women live the lives they do in large part because women of colour live the ones they do."

Introduction • Placings

1. See, e.g., Tim Cresswell, *In Place/Out of Place: Geography, Ideology, and Transgression* (Minneapolis: University of Minnesota Press, 1996), 11; Christopher Tomlins, "Afterward: Constellations of Class in Early North America and the Atlantic World," in Simon Middleton and Billy G. Smith, eds., *Class Matters: Early North America and the Atlantic World* (Philadelphia: University of Pennsylvania Press, 2008), 214; and Michael Frisch, "De-, Re-, and Post-Industrialization: Industrial Heritage as Contested Memorial Terrain" (paper at the conference Toward a Common Ground, annual meeting of the American Studies Association, Pittsburgh, November 10, 1995); see also entries in the *Oxford English Dictionary and the Oxford American Writer's Thesaurus* (New York: Oxford University Press, 2004). Note that this use of place does not emphasize the hierarchical in the same way as metaphors emphasizing verticality (e.g., rungs on a ladder, or social "strata"); see Oliver Fisher, S. Casey O'Donnell, and Daphna Oyserman, "Social Class and Identity-Based Motivation," special issue on inequality and social class, *Current Opinion in Psychology* 18 (2017): 61–66.

2. Judd notes that the records that do survive from "daughter" towns Amherst and South Hadley used "age, estate and qualifications"; Hatfield, which separated from Hadley in the seventeenth century, used "age, estate and places of trust." See Sylvester Judd, *History of Hadley: Including the Early History of Hatfield, South Hadley, Amherst and Granby, Massachusetts* (Springfield, MA: H. R. Huntting, 1905), 320. The original edition of the *History of Hadley* was published in 1863 by Northampton printers Metcalf & Co. These notes will cite the 1905 edition. Judd's research notes for the *History of Hadley*, and his studies on many other subjects in local and state history, are contained in a set of volumes known locally as the Judd Manuscript—sixty-four bound volumes arranged in several series, from those like the three volumes pertaining to Northampton or five volumes pertaining to Hadley to the larger "Miscellaneous" series of nineteen, all in the collections of the Forbes Library (FL) in Northampton, MA. In order to distinguish Judd's manuscript notes on Hadley history from his published work, the former will appear as Judd, "Hadley," and the latter as Judd, *Hadley.*

3. Laurel Thatcher Ulrich, *Good Wives: Image and Reality in the Lives of Women in Northern New England, 1650–1750* (New York: Knopf, 1982; New York: Vintage, 1991), 66.

4. Judd, *Hadley,* 312. See also Robert J. Dinkin, "Seating the Meetinghouse in Early Massachusetts," *NEQ* 43 (1970): 450–64; and Kevin M. Sweeney, "Meetinghouses, Town Houses, and Churches: Changing Perceptions of Sacred and Secular Space in Southern New England, 1720–1850," *Winterthur Portfolio* 28, no. 1 (1993): 59–93.

5. Town meeting records, May 5, 1760, Hadley Town Records, 1659–1805, 257, Hadley Town Hall; Judd, *Hadley,* 312; and Judd, "Hadley," vol. 3, 344 (Judd Manuscript), FL, citing Town meeting records, February 1, 1764, Hadley Town Records, 1659–1805, 272, Hadley Town Hall.

6. See Town meeting records, March 9, 1772–April 13, 1772, Hadley Town Records, 1659–1805, 297–301, Hadley Town Hall.

7. In 2004, Gary Nash noted with surprise that early Americanists "have not come farther" in our understanding of "women's history as it relates to class analysis and class

consciousness." See Nash, "Class in Early American History: A Personal Journey," in Simon Middleton and Billy G. Smith, "Class Analysis and the Atlantic World: Foundations and Future," special issue of *Labor: Studies in Working-Class History of the Americas* 1, no. 4 (Winter 2004): 25.

8. In 2008, Simon Middleton and Billy G. Smith surveyed the histories of both the term and the concept of class and the ways that they have operated in historical inquiry. In his own essay, Middleton also suggests that "class as a social relationship . . . exists whenever individuals share structural positions in relation to the opportunities and constraints that develop in response to production and accumulation. In this sense class is concerned with inequalities in material conditions and social power and with the maintenance of these inequalities, either consciously or unconsciously, by dominant groups, ideas, and cultural arrangements." See the introduction, and essays gathered together, in Middleton and Smith, eds., *Class Matters*; for quotations here, see Simon Middleton, "A Class Struggle in New York?," in Middleton and Smith, eds., *Class Matters*, 90. See also the essays on "Class in the Early Republic," *JER* 24, no. 4 (Winter 2005): 523–64; and Seth Rockman, "What Makes the History of Capitalism Newsworthy?," *JER* 34, no. 3 (Fall 2014): 439–66.

9. In many respects this book responds to such calls. Seth Rockman has made several important interventions in these discussions, including his prizewinning book *Scraping By: Wage Labor, Slavery, and Survival in Early Baltimore* (Baltimore: Johns Hopkins University Press, 2008); especially influential to this project was his July 2004 paper, "Class: A Useful Category of Analysis for the Early Republic?," at the annual meeting of the Society for Historians of the Early American Republic in Providence, RI. For Rockman, see also "The Contours of Class in the Early Republic City," *Labor: Studies in Working-Class History of the Americas* 1, no. 4 (Winter 2004): 91–107, as well as his remarks in "Where Is Labor History of the Early Republic? A Roundtable," Society for Historians of the Early American Republic, Philadelphia, 2008. Maria Ågren, too, in the important recent study of early modern women and work in Scandinavia and Europe, asserts that "what historians really need today is information about actual work practices." See Maria Ågren, ed., *Making a Living, Making a Difference: Gender and Work in Early Modern Society* (New York: Oxford University Press, 2016), 8.

10. Mary Babson Fuhrer, *A Crisis of Community: The Trials and Transformation of a New England Town, 1815–1848* (Chapel Hill: University of North Carolina Press, 2014), 17.

11. This is the top tenth per annual worth of the whole real estate according to *The Massachusetts Tax Valuation List of 1771* (Boston: G. K. Hall, 1978). For comparison with other Hampshire County communities, see Christopher Clark, *The Roots of Rural Capitalism: Western Massachusetts, 1780–1860* (Ithaca, NY: Cornell University Press, 1990), 22. The value of estate by taxpayer for Hadley (£7.30) was the highest in Hampshire County, followed by Northampton (£6.32), Amherst (£.6.17), and South Hadley (£5.34).

12. Clark offers these figures in *Roots of Rural Capitalism,* 61. Also helpful on this point, on Connecticut before the Revolution, is Gloria L. Main, "The Standard of Living in Southern New England, 1640–1773," *WMQ,* 3rd ser., 45, no. 1 (January 1988): 124–34.

13. The helpful phrase and concept "culture of appraisal" (and its equally valuable companion, "calculus of esteem") appears in Alexandra Shepard, *Accounting for Oneself: Worth, Status, and the Social Order in Early Modern England* (New York: Oxford University Press, 2015), 31–32.

14. Christopher Clark, "The View from the Farmhouse: Rural Lives in the Early Republic," in John Lauritz Larson and Michael A. Morrison, eds., *Whither the Early Republic: A Forum on the Future of the Field* (Philadelphia: University of Pennsylvania Press, 2005), 56.

15. Jeanne Boydston, "Gender as a Question of Historical Analysis," *Gender & History* 20, no. 3 (2008): 558–83.

16. Boydston, "Gender as a Question of Historical Analysis," 576.

17. Ågren, *Making a Living, Making a Difference*, 9.

18. Alexandra Shepard and others explored this point during the workshop "Women's Work across Time and Place: Foundations for Comparison in Pre-census Europe," University of Glasgow, September 11–12, 2014. My deep thanks to Margaret Hunt, Alexandra Shepard, Maria Ågren, and the other organizers for inviting me to participate in that lively and productive discussion, which has been influential in my thinking here.

19. Nancy Folbre and Julie A. Nelson, "For Love or Money—or Both?," *The Journal of Economic Perspectives* 14, no. 4 (Autumn 2000): 123–40, 131.

20. Martin Bruegel, *Farm, Shop, Landing: The Rise of a Market Society in the Hudson Valley, 1780–1860* (Durham, NC: Duke University Press, 2002); and also his essay "The Social Relations of Farming in the Early American Republic: A Microhistorical Approach," *JER* 26, no. 4 (Winter 2006): 523–53. The project, then, also concurs with Daniel Vickers's observation that "it was the co-existence of individualism *and* reciprocity that defined relationships between free households before the age of capital." Vickers, "Errors Expected: The Culture of Credit in Rural New England, 1750–1800," *The Economic History Review* 63 (November 2010): 1032–57.

21. Boydston, "Gender as a Question of Historical Analysis." More recently, Michael Zakin and Gary Kornblith have likewise urged scholars to transcend the "categorical division between materiality and mentality." See Zakim and Kornblith, eds., *Capitalism Takes Command: The Social Transformation of Nineteenth-Century America* (Chicago: University of Chicago Press, 2012), 5–6.

22. Massey is quoted in Daphne Spain, *Gendered Spaces* (Chapel Hill: University of North Carolina Press, 1992), 4. A number of other scholars are members of this chorus. Camille Wells, a social historian of architecture, put it another way when she wrote that the built environment "can be understood in terms of power or authority—as efforts to assume, extend, resist or accommodate it." Landscapes, as well as the constellations of objects contained therein, were certainly, as Robert Blair St. George has further suggested, "extensions of ideological processes, mediators of social relations." See Wells, "Old Claims and New Demands: Vernacular Architecture Studies Today," in Wells, ed., *Perspectives in Vernacular Architecture,* vol. 2 (Columbia: University of Missouri Press, 1986), 1–10; quotation, 9; and Robert Blair St. George, ed., *Material Life in America, 1620–1860* (Boston: Northeastern University Press, 1988), 357. See also Michael Ann Williams, "Inside and Out: Vernacular Dwellings as Artifacts of the Lives of Southern Appalachian Women" (conference paper, Women and Historic Preservation, Bryn Mawr, June 1993).

23. Cresswell makes this observation in *In Place/Out of Place*, 11. The project is also informed by the scholarship of labor geographers, including Andrew Herod, *Labor Geographies: Workers and the Landscapes of Capitalism* (New York: Guilford, 2001), 5. A good point of entry to that literature is the January 2008 special issue of *Antipode*, vol. 40, no. 1, "Geography and New Working Class Studies," including Jane Wills, "Mapping Class and Its Political Possibilities," Linda McDowell, "Thinking Through Class and Gender in the

Context of Working Class Studies," and Alison Stenning's "For Working Class Geographies." Andrew Herod has written extensively on these subjects; see his "Workers, Space and Labor Geography," *International Labor and Working Class History* 63 (Fall 2003): 112–38; and Herod, *Labor Geographies,* which calls for studies that consider "how space and spatial relations may serve as sources of power and objects of struggle," 2. On women, work, and space in England and New England, see also Amanda Flather, *Gender and Space in Early Modern England,* Royal Historical Society Studies in History (Rochester, NY: Boydell & Brewer, 2007); John Styles and Amanda Vickery, eds., *Gender, Taste, and Material Culture in Britain and North America, 1700–1830* (New Haven, CT: Yale University Press, 2006); and Deborah Rotman, *Historical Archaeology of Gendered Lives* (London: Springer, 2009).

24. My thanks to Margo Shea, as well as one of the book's readers (anonymous), for helping articulate this theme.

25. Clark, *Roots of Rural Capitalism,* 15–16.

26. There is a large and still-growing literature here, but I am thinking particularly of David Jaffee, *A New Nation of Goods: The Material Culture of Early America* (Philadelphia: University of Pennsylvania Press, 2010); Catherine E. Kelly, *In the New England Fashion: Reshaping Women's Lives in the Nineteenth Century* (Ithaca, NY: Cornell University Press, 2002) and *Republic of Taste: Art, Politics, and Everyday Life in Early America* (Philadelphia: University of Pennsylvania Press, 2016); Richard Bushman, *The Refinement of America: Persons, Houses, Cities* (New York: Knopf, 1992).

27. Particularly valuable here in contemplating the nature of change in the social relations of labor of the early US republic is Cathy Matson, ed., "Connection, Contingency, and Class in the Early Republic's Economy," special issue of *JER* 26, no. 4 (2006): 515–21.

28. Joseph A. Amato, *Rethinking Home*: *A Case for Writing Local History* (Berkeley: University of California Press, 2002), 3; see also Robert Archibald, *A Place to Remember: Using History to Build Community* (Walnut Creek, CA: AltaMira, 1999) and *The New Town Square: Museums and Communities in Transition* (Walnut Creek, CA: AltaMira, 2004); Carol Kammen, *On Doing Local History,* 3rd ed. (Lanham, MD: Rowman & Littlefield, 2014).

29. See Clark, *Roots of Rural Capitalism,* 63, n. 10, citing Lucius M. Boltwood's "Genealogies of Hadley Families," in Judd, *Hadley.*

30. Historians of European women and work—most notably Marilyn Boxer, Jean Quataert, and Judith Bennett—have articulated the importance of taking the long view when it comes to understanding the history of women and work, a position I embrace as well. See Boxer and Quataert's observations concerning the need to consider change over long spans of time in *Connecting Spheres: European Women in a Globalizing World, 1500 to the Present,* 2nd ed. (New York: Oxford University Press, 2000), 9; and Judith M. Bennett, *History Matters: Patriarchy and the Challenge of Feminism* (Philadelphia: University of Pennsylvania Press, 2006). An important reconsideration of traditional periodization as it pertains to Anglo women's and gender history is Alexandra Shepard and Garthine Walker, eds., *Gender and Change: Agency, Chronology and Periodisation* (Oxford: Wiley-Blackwell, 2009). See also Stephen W. Silliman's helpful article, "Change and Continuity, Practice and Memory: Native American Persistence in Colonial New England," *American Antiquity* 74, no. 2 (April 2009): 211–30; though Silliman discusses continuity and change in native culture, his observations about the measure and pace of intergenerational change are relevant here as well.

31. Examples include Mary Beth Norton, "A Cherished Spirit of Independence: The Life of an Eighteenth-Century Boston Businesswoman," in *Women of America: A History* (Boston: Houghton Mifflin, 1979), 48–67; Mary H. Blewett, *Men, Women, and Work: Class, Gender, and Protest in the New England Shoe Industry, 1780–1910* (Urbana: University of Illinois, 1988); Laurel Thatcher Ulrich, *A Midwife's Tale: The Life of Martha Ballard, Based on Her Diary, 1785–1812* (New York: Knopf, 1990); Susan L. Porter, "Victorian Values in the Marketplace: Single Women and Work in Boston, 1800–1850," *Social Science History* 17, no. 1 (Spring 1993): 109–33; Jacqueline Barbara Carr, "Marketing Gentility: Boston's Businesswomen, 1780–1830," *NEQ* 82, no. 1 (March 2009): 25–55; Ruth Wallis Herndon, "Poor Women and the Boston Almshouse in the Early Republic," *JER* 32, no. 3 (Fall 2012): 349–81; Ellen Hartigan O'Connor, *The Ties That Buy: Women and Commerce in Revolutionary America* (Philadelphia: University of Pennsylvania Press, 2009); Cornelia H. Dayton and Sharon V. Salinger, *Robert Love's Warnings: Searching for Strangers in Colonial Boston* (Philadelphia: University of Pennsylvania Press, 2014); and Fuhrer, *A Crisis of Community*. See also Thomas Dublin, *Transforming Women's Work: New England Lives in the Industrial Revolution* (Ithaca, NY: Cornell University Press, 1994); Elaine Forman Crane, *Ebb Tide in New England: Women, Seaports, and Social Change, 1630–1800* (Boston: Northeastern University Press, 1998); Patricia Cleary, *Elizabeth Murray: A Woman's Pursuit of Independence in Eighteenth-Century America* (Amherst: University of Massachusetts Press, 2000). See also my own "The Last Mantuamaker: Craft Tradition and Commercial Change in Boston, 1760–1845," *Early American Studies* 4, no. 2 (Fall 2006): 372–424.

32. Good places to begin include Margaret R. Hunt, *The Middling Sort: Commerce, Gender, and the Family in England, 1680–1780* (Berkeley: University of California Press, 1996) and *Women in Eighteenth-Century Europe* (New York: Longman, 2009); Jane Whittle, "Housewives and Servants in Rural England, 1440–1650: Evidence of Women's Work from Probate Documents," *Royal Historical Society Transactions* 15, no. 1 (2005): 51–74; Jane Humphries and Carmen Sarasúa, "Off the Record: Reconstructing Women's Labor Force Participation in the European Past," *Feminist Economics* 18, no. 4 (2012): 39–67; Amy Erickson, "Eleanor Mosley and Other Milliners in the City of London Companies 1700–1750," *History Workshop Journal* 71 no. 1 (2011): 147–72; John Styles, "Spinners and the Law: Regulating Yarn Standards in the English Worsted Industries, 1550–1800," *Textile History* 44, no. 2 (November 2013): 145–70, and *The Dress of the People: Everyday Fashion in Eighteenth-Century England* (New Haven, CT: Yale University Press, 2008); Amanda Vickery, *Behind Closed Doors: At Home in Georgian England* (New Haven, CT: Yale University Press, 2009); and Vickery and Styles, *Gender, Taste, and Material Culture*. The list of other relevant work is long, but encompasses Gay L. Gullickson, *Spinners and Weavers of Auffay: Rural Industry and the Sexual Division of Labor in a French Village, 1750–1850* (New York: Cambridge University Press, 1986); Elizabeth C. Sanderson, *Women and Work in Eighteenth-Century Edinburgh* (New York: St. Martin's, 1996); Clare Haru Crowston, *Fabricating Women: The Seamstresses of Old Regime France, 1675–1791* (Durham, NC: Duke University Press, 2001); Marjorie Keniston McIntosh, *Working Women in English Society, 1300–1620* (Cambridge: Cambridge University Press, 2005); Nancy Locklin, *Women's Work and Identity in Eighteenth-Century Brittany* (Aldershot, UK: Ashgate, 2007); Natasha Korda, *Labor's Lost: Women's Work and the Early Modern English Stage* (Philadelphia: University of Pennsylvania Press, 2011); Tim Reinke-Williams, *Women, Work and Sociability in Early Modern London* (Basingstoke, UK: Palgrave Macmillan, 2014); and Daryl Hafter and Nina

Kushner, eds., *Women and Work in Eighteenth-Century France* (Baton Rouge: Louisiana State University Press, 2014).

33. Ågren, *Making a Living, Making a Difference*, 3; Ågren cites here Hunt, *Women in Eighteenth-Century Europe*, and Boxer and Quataert, *Connecting Spheres*.

34. Ågren, *Making a Living, Making a Difference*, 4.

35. Other studies that have depended heavily on this collection include Clark, *Roots of Rural Capitalism*; Jane C. Nylander, *Our Own Snug Fireside: Images of the New England Home, 1760–1860* (New York: Knopf, 1993); Bruce Laurie, *Beyond Garrison: Antislavery and Social Reform* (New York: Cambridge University Press, 2007); Elizabeth Pendergast Carlisle, *Earthbound and Heavenbent: Elizabeth Porter Phelps and Life at Forty Acres* (New York: Scribner, 2004); and Kelly, *In the New England Fashion*.

36. Often referred to in other scholarship as the diary of Elizabeth Porter Phelps, the volume is termed a "memorandum book" by Phelps herself in an entry dated January 12, 1777. I prefer this nomenclature, which underscores the record's various purposes. The memorandum book (1766–1812) of Elizabeth Porter Phelps (1747–1817) is preserved among the Porter-Phelps-Huntington Family Papers housed at the Amherst College Library, and it was published in segments through several consecutive issues of the *New England Historical and Genealogical Register* (*NEHGR*), vols. 118–122 (January 1964–October 1968). Citations from this source will usually provide the date of Phelps's diary entry, which readers can consult in print in the pages of the *NEHGR*, but because the *New England Historical and Genealogical Register* omits the final years of Phelps's text (1806–1812), citations from entries after 1805 note the box and folder number for the unpublished manuscript housed in the Porter-Phelps-Huntington Family Papers (hereafter PPHFP). (Abbreviations and acronyms used in these notes are explained in "Abbreviations" in the back of the book.)

37. Phelps's record is not unlike the narrative accounts described by Vickers in "Errors Expected." On women's recording practices, see also Ulrich, *A Midwife's Tale*, 8; Ellen Hartigan O'Connor, "Abigail's Account: Economy and Affection in the Early Republic," *Journal of Women's History* 17, no. 3 (2005): 35–58; and Nancy Grey Osterud, *Bonds of Community: The Lives of Farm Women in Nineteenth-Century New York* (Ithaca, NY: Cornell University Press, 1991), 220–21.

38. EPP to CP, June 2, 1780, Box 5 folder 13, PPHFP.

39. Carlisle, *Earthbound and Heavenbent*, 108.

40. EPP memorandum book, August 18, 1788, *NEHGR*.

41. Hadley women who served as Judd's informants include Sophia Cook Clark (b. 1793), Permelia Westood Crane (b. 1792), Thankful Richmond Hitchcock (b. 1777), Martha Richmond Smith (b. 1802), Abigail Dickinson Newton (b. 1776), Ruth (Mrs. Ephraim) Smith (probably b. 1788), and Maria Porter Woodward (b. 1797).

42. Johnson, "Witchcraft," Clifton Johnson papers, Ser. 1 Writings, Box 4 folder 13, Special Collections, Jones Library, Amherst, MA.

43. Judd, "Hadley," vol. 3, 354.

44. See Judd, "Hadley," vol. 3, 39. For a thoughtful consideration of "pastkeepers" like Crow, Judd, and Johnson, see Michael Batinksi, *Pastkeepers in a Small Place: Five Centuries in Deerfield, Massachusetts* (Amherst: University of Massachusetts Press, 2004). An important conversation unfolded during the roundtable "New Intellectual Histories of Early American Women" at the 2018 meeting of the Society for Historians of the Early American Republic, on storytelling as a form of women's intellectual history.

45. Altina Waller, "Sylvester Judd: Historian of the Connecticut River Valley," *Historical Journal of Massachusetts* 10, no. 2 (June 1982): 48–49. Waller does not probe the nature of the history that Judd went on to practice, though these same issues certainly colored his version of the past. Moreover, Judd's politics embraced the Workingmen's Party, through which he enjoyed close association with the historian George Bancroft.

46. See the Judd Manuscript, FL; and Judd, *Hadley*; also Waller, "Sylvester Judd," 43–56; Gregory H. Nobles and Herbert L. Zarov, *Selected Papers from the Sylvester Judd Manuscript* (Northampton, MA: Forbes Library, 1976); and Bruce Laurie, *Rebels in Paradise: Sketches of Northampton Abolitionists* (Amherst: University of Massachusetts Press, 2015), which contains a chapter on Judd. On Clifton Johnson's project, variously also referred to as "Old Town in New England," "Oldtown Chronicles," and "Oldtown Folks," see Clifton Johnson papers, Ser. 1 Writings, Box 4, 5, Special Collections, Jones Library, Amherst, MA. The family work referenced here includes Theodore Gregson Huntington, "Sketches of Family and Life in Hadley," Box 21 folder 5, PPHFP; Arria Sargent Huntington, *Under a Colonial Rooftree: Fireside Chronicles of Early New England* (Syracuse, NY: Wolcott's Bookshop, 1905); and James Lincoln Huntington, *Forty Acres: The Story of the Bishop Huntington House* (New York: Hastings House, 1949). On memory, nostalgia, and place-making, relevant scholarship here includes Kelly, *In the New England Fashion*; Jean M. O'Brien, *Firsting and Lasting: Writing Indians out of Existence in New England* (Minneapolis: University of Minnesota Press, 2010); and Laurel Thatcher Ulrich, *The Age of Homespun: Objects and Stories in the Creation of an American Myth* (New York: Knopf, 2001).

47. Judd, "Northampton," vol. 1, 332.

48. There is a robust literature on the history of slavery and freedom in Massachusetts and New England; classic and recent points of entry include Lorenzo Johnston Greene, *The Negro in Colonial New England* (New York: Columbia University Press, 1942); William D. Piersen, *Black Yankees: The Development of an Afro-American Subculture in Eighteenth-Century New England* (Amherst: University of Massachusetts Press, 1988); Joanne Pope Melish, *Disowning Slavery: Gradual Emancipation and "Race" in New England, 1780–1860* (Ithaca, NY: Cornell University Press, 1998); Robert K. Fitts, *Inventing New England's Slave Paradise: Master/Slave Relations in Eighteenth-Century Narragansett, Rhode Island* (New York: Garland, 1998); John Wood Sweet, *Bodies Politic: Negotiating Race in the American North, 1730–1830* (Baltimore: Johns Hopkins University Press, 2003); Wendy Warren, *New England Bound: Slavery and Colonization in Early America* (New York: Liveright, 2016); Gretchen Holbrook Gerzina, *Mr. and Mrs. Prince: How an Extraordinary Eighteenth-Century Family Moved Out of Slavery and Into Legend* (New York: Amistad, 2008); Catherine Adams and Elizabeth H. Pleck, *Love of Freedom: Black Women in Colonial New England* (New York: Oxford University Press, 2010); C. S. Manegold, *Ten Hills Farm: The Forgotten History of Slavery in the North* (Princeton, NJ: Princeton University Press, 2010); Margot Minardi, *Making Slavery History: Abolitionism and the Politics of Memory in Massachusetts* (New York: Oxford University Press, 2010); Richard Bailey, *Race and Redemption in Puritan New England* (New York: Oxford University Press, 2011); Allegra di Bonaventura, *For Adam's Sake: A Family Saga in Colonial New England* (New York: Norton, 2013); and Jared Ross Hardesty, *Unfreedom: Slavery and Dependence in Eighteenth-Century Boston* (New York: New York University Press, 2016). For an overview of Massachusetts slavery and freedom in the archaeological record, see Anthony Martin, "On the Landscape for a Very, Very Long Time: African American Resistance and Resilience in

19th and Early 20th Century Massachusetts" (PhD diss., University of Massachusetts Amherst, 2016).

49. Ruth Herndon and Ella Sekatau, "Pauper Apprenticeship in Narragansett Country: A Different Name for Slavery in Early New England," in Peter Benes and Jane Montague Benes, eds., *Slavery/Antislavery in New England*, Proceedings of the 2003 Dublin Seminar for New England Folklife (Boston: Boston University, 2005), 56–70. More recently, Hardesty also emphasizes this approach in *Unfreedom*.

50. Representative and valuable work in the early American context includes Philippa Glanville and Jennifer Faulds Goldsborough's *Women Silversmiths, 1685–1845: Works from the Collection of the National Museum of Women in the Arts* (Washington, DC: Thames and Hudson, 1990); Patricia Cleary, "'She Will Be in the Shop': Women's Sphere of Trade in Eighteenth-Century Philadelphia and New York," *The Pennsylvania Magazine of History and Biography* 119, no. 3 (July 1995): 181–202; Glendyne R. Werglund, "Designing Women: Massachusetts Milliners in the Nineteenth Century," in Peter Benes and Jane Montague Benes, eds., *Textiles in Early New England: Design, Production and Consumption*, Proceedings of the 1997 Dublin Seminar for New England Folklife (Boston: Boston University, 1999), 203–11; Sarah Hand Meacham, "Keeping the Trade: The Persistence of Tavernkeeping among Middling Women in Colonial Virginia," *Early American Studies* 3, no. 1 (Spring 2005): 140–63, and *Every Home a Distillery: Alcohol, Gender, and Technology in the Colonial Chesapeake* (Baltimore: Johns Hopkins University Press, 2013); and my own *The Needle's Eye: Women and Work in the Age of Revolution* (Amherst: University of Massachusetts Press, 2006); "Gownmaking as a Trade for Women in Eighteenth-Century Rural New England," *Dress* 30, no. 1 (January 2003): 21–37; and "The Last Mantuamaker."

51. See Ågren, *Making a Living, Making a Difference*, for a "verb-based" approach that works to offset these problems. For a study that tracks comparable activity in a Massachusetts context, see Winifred B. Rothenberg, "Structural Change in the Farm Labor Force: Contract Labor in Massachusetts Agriculture, 1750–1865," in Claudia Goldin and Hugh Rockoff, eds., *Strategic Factors in Nineteenth Century American Economic History: A Volume to Honor Robert W. Fogel* (Chicago: University of Chicago Press, 1992), 105–34.

52. These ideas were developed in the discussion that constituted the workshop "Women's Work across Time and Place."

53. There has been much excellent scholarship on women's work in Revolutionary America, and New England in particular. The best places to begin are Ulrich, *A Midwife's Tale* and *Age of Homespun*; Jeanne Boydston, *Home and Work: Housework, Wages, and the Ideology of Labor in the Early Republic* (New York: Oxford University Press, 1990); Jane C. Nylander, *Our Own Snug Fireside*; Ellen Hartigan-O'Connor, *The Ties That Buy: Women and Commerce in Revolutionary America* (Philadelphia: University of Pennsylvania Press, 2009). Thomas Dublin, *Transforming Women's Work: New England Lives in the Industrial Revolution* (Ithaca, NY: Cornell University Press, 1994); and Peter Benes and Jane Montague Benes, eds., *Women's Work in New England, 1620–1920*, Proceedings of the 2001 Dublin Seminar for New England Folklife (Boston: Boston University, 2003).

54. See, e.g., Joan Gunderson, *To Be Useful to the World* (New York: Twayne, 1996), especially 59–60; Pamela J. Snow, "Increase and Vantage: Women, Cows, and the Agricultural Economy of Colonial New England," in Benes and Benes, *Women's Work in New England*; and Margaret Ellen Newel, *From Dependency to Independence: Economic Revolution in Colonial New England* (Ithaca, NY: Cornell University Press, 1999).

55. Martin Bruegel, "Work, Gender, and Authority on the Farm: The Hudson Valley Countryside, 1790s–1850s," *Agricultural History* 76 (Winter 2002): 1–27; and Bruegel, "The Social Relations of Farming in the Early American Republic: A Microhistorical Approach," *JER* 26, no. 4 (Winter 2006): 523–53.

56. See, e.g., EPP memorandum book, June 12 and September 4, 1785, *NEHGR*. The subject of women and financial services in early Massachusetts could use further scrutiny. The Hampshire County probate inventories that include among a female decedent's list of assets a number of "notes" could provide a point of departure. See, e.g., the inventory of West Springfield's Elizabeth Lankton, October 26, 1802, Box 86 no. 28, HCMRP, which includes seventeen notes, their "interest with principle" worth over $500, or about one-third the estate's total value. For an entry into this emerging field, see Anne Laurence, Josephine Maltby, and Janette Rutterford, eds., *Women and Their Money 1700–1950: Essays on Women and Finance* (Abingdon, UK: Routledge, 2009); and Amy Froide, *Silent Partners: Women as Public Investors during Britain's Financial Revolution, 1690–1750* (New York: Oxford University Press, 2016).

57. Hadley in this period had about four shops; see Clark, *Roots of Rural Capitalism,* 29. We know that women sometimes staffed these counters, certainly by the 1820s, when the "widow Jones" managed the Huntington store in Hadley's upper mill village; see Dan Huntington to John Whiting Huntington, July 8, 1825, Box 15 folder 11, PPHFP.

58. On Massachusetts women and shopkeeping, see Patricia Cleary's study, *Elizabeth Murray: A Woman's Pursuit of Independence*; and Jacqueline Carr, "Marketing Gentility: Boston's Businesswomen, 1780–1830," *NEQ* 82, no. 1 (March 2009): 25–55. On the complexity of interactions among shopkeepers, shoppers, and proxy shoppers and the creation of consumer values, see also Ann Smart Martin, *Buying into the World of Goods: Early Consumers in Backcountry Virginia*, Studies in Early American Economy and Society from the Library Company of Philadelphia (Baltimore: Johns Hopkins University Press, 2008); and the essays gathered by Styles and Vickery, in *Gender, Taste, and Material Culture.*

Chapter 1 • From Nolwotogg to Hadley

1. The best discussions of the topography of Hadley and environs are found in J. Ritchie Garrison, *Landscape and Material Life in Franklin County* (Knoxville: University of Tennessee Press, 1991), 8–17, and Thomas R. Lewis, "The Landscape and Environment of the Connecticut River Valley," in Gerald W. R. Ward and William N. Hosley, eds., *The Great River: Art & Society of the Connecticut Valley, 1635–1820* (Hartford, CT: Wadsworth Atheneum, 1985), 3–15. In addition to Sylvester Judd's *History of Hadley: Including the Early History of Hatfield, South Hadley, Amherst and Granby, Massachusetts* (Springfield, MA: H. R. Huntting, 1905), scholarship includes Marla R. Miller, ed., *Cultivating a Past: Essays on the History of Hadley, Massachusetts* (Amherst: University of Massachusetts Press, 2009).

2. See Douglas C. Wilson, "Web of Secrecy: Goffe, Whalley and the Legend of Hadley," in Miller, ed., *Cultivating a Past,* 91–120; also Carl Hammer, *Pugnacious Puritans: Seventeenth-Century Hadley and New England* (Lanham, MD: Lexington Books, 2018).

3. Indigenous peoples had been present in this area for some nine thousand years prior to English settlement; by the early seventeenth century, scholars estimate a native population of about five thousand in this section of the Connecticut Valley. For narratives of native history in the middle Connecticut Valley, see Margaret M. Bruchac's important dissertation, "Historical Erasure and Cultural Recovery: Indigenous People in the Connecticut

River Valley" (PhD diss., University of Massachusetts Amherst, 2007); and Siobhan M. Hart, Elizabeth S. Chilton, and Christopher Donta, "Before Hadley: Archaeology and Native History, 10,000 BC to 1700 AD," in Miller, ed., *Cultivating a Past*, 43–67. See also Peter A. Thomas, *In the Maelstrom of Change: The Indian Trade and Cultural Process in the Middle Connecticut River Valley, 1635–1665* (New York: Garland, 1990); Lisa Brooks, "'Every Swamp Is a Castle': Navigating Native Spaces in the Connecticut River Valley, Winter 1675–1677 and 2005–2015," *Northeastern Naturalist* 24, no. 1 (Special Issue on Winter Ecology: Insights from Biology and History, ed. Scott Smedley and Thomas Wickman, March 2017): 45–80; and Brooks, *Our Beloved Kin: A New History of King Philip's War* (New Haven, CT: Yale University Press, 2018).

4. See Alice Nash, "Quanquan's Mortgage of 1663," in Miller, ed., *Cultivating a Past*, 31.

5. Judd, *Hadley*, 104.

6. Patricia Laurice Ellsworth, "Hadley West Street Common and Great Meadow: A Cultural Landscape Study" (MA thesis, University of Massachusetts Department of Landscape Architecture and Regional Planning, 2007), 8.

7. As quoted in J. Edward Hood and Rita Reinke in "The Fortification of Hadley in the Seventeenth Century," in Miller, ed., *Cultivating a Past*, 73. See also Brooks, *Our Beloved Kin;* and Christine M. DeLucia, *Memory Lands: King Philip's War and the Place of Violence in the Northeast* (New Haven, CT: Yale University Press, 2018).

8. Hood and Reinke, "The Fortification of Hadley," 72.

9. See Ellsworth, "Hadley West Street Common and Great Meadow", 22; and Judd, *Hadley*, 190–91.

10. Judd, *Hadley*, 423.

11. See the 1765 census as reproduced in J. H. Benton Jr., *Early Census Making in Massachusetts* (Boston: Charles E. Goodspeed, 1905).

12. Judd, *Hadley*, 424.

13. Bettye Hobbs Pruitt, *The Massachusetts Tax Valuation List of 1771* (Boston: G. K. Hall, 1978), 394–97.

14. See, e.g., Susan Geib, "Changing Works: Agriculture and Society in Brookfield, Massachusetts, 1785–1820" (PhD diss., Boston University, 1981), 115–20, 128–29.

15. Christopher Clark, *The Roots of Rural Capitalism: Western Massachusetts, 1780–1860* (Ithaca, NY: Cornell University Press, 1990), 33–38.

16. See George Sheldon, *History of Deerfield: Massachusetts* (Greenfield, MA: E. A. Hall & Co., 1895–96) as cited in Marla R. Miller, *The Needle's Eye: Women and Work in the Age of Revolution* (Amherst: University of Massachusetts Press, 2006), 9.

17. Clark, *The Roots of Rural Capitalism*, 33–38.

18. During the eighteenth century there were generally about four stores in Hadley, and as many as nine in Northampton. See Clark, *Roots of Rural Capitalism*, 28–29.

19. Judd, "Massachusetts," vol. 5, 292–95 (Judd Manuscript), FL. For below, see Judd, *Hadley*, 393.

20. EPP memorandum book, July 28, 1771, *NEHGR*.

21. See Judd's transcriptions in "Miscellaneous," vol. 17, 152, FL.

22. Judd, *Hadley*, 89.

23. James Avery Smith, *History of the Black Population of Amherst* (Boston: New England Historic Genealogical Society, 1999), 59.

24. On slave ownership in Hampshire County, see Kevin M. Sweeney, "River Gods and Related Minor Deities: The Williams Family and the Connecticut River Valley, 1637–1790" (PhD diss., Yale University, 1986); Gretchen Holbrook Gerzina, *Mr. and Mrs. Prince: How an Extraordinary Eighteenth-Century Family Moved Out of Slavery and Into Legend* (New York: Amistad, 2008); Robert H. Romer, *Slavery in the Connecticut Valley of Massachusetts* (Amherst, MA: Levellers Press, 2009).

25. Jonathan Edwards told his congregation that slavery was acceptable, as long as masters did not abuse their authority. Richard Bailey, "Naming Slaves and Redeeming Masters," in Peter Benes and Jane Montague Benes, eds., *Slavery/Antislavery in New England*, Proceedings of the 2003 Dublin Seminar for New England Folklife (Boston: Boston University, 2005), 44–55. See also Kenneth P. Minkema, "Jonathan Edwards' Defense of Slavery," *Massachusetts Historical Review* 2 (2002); and "Jonathan Edwards on Slavery and the Slave Trade," *WMQ* 54 no. 4 (October 1997): 823–30. On Hadley's slaveowning ministers, see Romer, *Slavery in the Connecticut Valley*, 173–74. See also EPP memorandum book, February 7 and October 4, 1768, *NEHGR*.

26. Eleazer Porter estate inventory, 1757, Box 117 no. 10, HCMRP.

27. Alexander Ormound Boulton, "New England's Slave Quarters," *Journal of Regional Cultures* 5 (1985): 6–12.

28. Judd, "Hadley," vol. 3, 32. Ezekiel Kellogg's grandfather was the Farmington, Connecticut, weaver Joseph Kellogg; he moved to Hadley about 1662. The family had links to Windsor, Colchester, Hartford, and other Connecticut towns, which may have helped support Kellogg's work as a trader. On the Kellogg family genealogy, see Boltwood, "Genealogies of Hadley Families," in Judd, *Hadley*, 81–87. Ellen Hartigan-O'Connor's discussion of women and commerce in Newport sheds important light on enslavement there; see *The Ties That Buy: Women and Commerce in Revolutionary America* (Philadelphia: University of Pennsylvania Press, 2009).

29. Peter Hinks, "The Internal Slave Trade of Connecticut," paper presented at the conference *Slavery/Antislavery in New England*, Dublin Seminar for New England Folklife, 2003.

30. See Lorenzo J. Greene, *The Negro in Colonial New England* (New York: Columbia University Press, 1942); William D. Piersen, *Black Yankees: The Development of an Afro-American Subculture in Eighteenth-Century New England* (Amherst: University of Massachusetts Press, 1988); and Joanne Pope Melish, *Disowning Slavery: Gradual Emancipation and "Race" in New England, 1780–1860* (Ithaca, NY: Cornell University Press, 1998). By comparison, in Boston, about 35 percent of enslaved people lived alone, as members of a white household; 30 percent lived as part of a pair; 17 percent in a group of three; 8 percent as one of four; and 10 percent in groups of five or more. See Catherine Adams and Elizabeth H. Pleck, *Love of Freedom: Black Women in Colonial and Revolutionary New England* (New York: Oxford University Press, 2010), 105.

31. EPP memorandum book, October 4, 1768, *NEHGR*.

32. EPP memorandum book, May 7, 1775, *NEHGR*.

33. Bernard L. Herman, *Town House: Architecture and Material Life in the Early American City, 1780–1830* (Chapel Hill: University of North Carolina Press, 2005), 134.

34. Dell Upton, "White and Black Landscapes in Eighteenth-Century Virginia," *Places* 2, no. 2 (1984): 59–72; and *Another City: Urban Life and Urban Spaces in the New American Republic* (New Haven, CT: Yale University Press, 2008).

35. Hinks, "The Internal Slave Trade."

36. Diane Cameron discussed the cosmograms found in Wethersfield in "Enslavement, Freedom, Possibility, and Poverty: Four Generations of Quash Gomer's Family," in Benes and Benes, eds., *Slavery/Antislavery in New England*, 102–13 ; see also Alexandra A. Chan, *Slavery in the Age of Reason: Archaeology at a New England Farm* (Knoxville: University of Tennessee Press, 2007); James C. Garman, "Rethinking 'Resistant Accommodation': Toward an Archaeology of African-American Lives in Southern New England, 1638–1800," *International Journal of Historical Archaeology* 2, no. 2 (June 1998): 133–60.

37. Robert E Desrochers Jr., "Slave-for-Sale Advertisements and Slavery in Massachusetts, 1704–1781," *WMQ*, 3rd ser., 59 (July 2002): 623–64. Michael A. Gomez cautions that "Guinea" was an imprecise term and could mean the west coast of Africa, or simply Africa; see *Exchanging Our Country Marks: The Transformation of African Identities in the Colonial and Antebellum South* (Chapel Hill: University of North Carolina Press, 2009), 103.

38. Sheldon, *History of Deerfield*, vol. 2, 897–98.

39. Chan, *Slavery in the Age of Reason*, 163. On cultural survivals among Africans and African Americans in New England, see also Piersen, *Black Yankees*, 74–86.

40. Lorenzo Greene, "The New England Negro as Seen in Advertisements for Runaway Slaves," *Journal of Negro History* 29 (April 1944): 136; see also Sharon Block, *Colonial Complexions: Race and Bodies in Eighteenth-Century America* (Philadelphia: University of Pennsylvania Press, 2018).

41. Dr. Richard Crouch ledger, vol. 2, January 19, February 20, and May 7, 1748, Hadley, MA, FL.

42. The injury could be related to frostbite; Phelps recorded "Last Tuesday Cesar froze his finger" in her memorandum book, December 22, 1771, *NEHGR*; some years later (June 4, 1775) she recorded being "much surprized with Cesar's hand . . . has had a terrible swelled hand this month," though by then it was "thought to be the rhumatizm." Phelps assured his son that he would urge Cesar to return to his usual labors with "gentleness and persuasion"—what's more, he would offer him the opportunity to make sugar (one of the products of Charles Phelps's Vermont enterprise) for himself as a further motivation for recovery. CP Sr. to CP Jr., February 15, 1776, Box 2 folder 2, PPHFP.

43. Adams and Pleck, *Love of Freedom*, 38–40. Worth noting too, in thinking about the risks of servitude, are the early deaths of the enslaved women and girls who lived at Forty Acres, which together might suggest an elevated incidence of certain diseases among the enslaved population. Peg's daughter Phillis died of tuberculosis. The cause of Rose's death is unknown, but Rose's own child, named Phillis for her sister (who died the same week that Rose gave birth to her daughter), would suffer from what the family believed might be rickets (see EPP memorandum book, May 11, 1776, *NEHGR*)—defined as the softening and weakening of bones in children, usually due to an extreme and prolonged vitamin D deficiency—and in time would die of scrofula, another form of tuberculosis. The pattern raises questions about the early deaths of other enslaved women in the area, like Smardin, a child and a member of the Porter household in town, whose death EPP records April 14, 1771, *NEHGR*.

44. Adams and Pleck, *Love of Freedom*, 14.

45. *CC*, August 13, 1770.

46. *CC*, May 12, 1778, March 2, 1779.

47. See Adams and Pleck, *Love of Freedom*, 129.

48. See Emily Blanck, *Tyrannicide: Forging an American Law of Slavery in Revolutionary South Carolina and Massachusetts* (Athens: University of Georgia Press, 2014), 118–22.

49. Desrochers, "Slave-for-Sale Advertisements."

50. See Thomas J. Davis, "Emancipation Rhetoric, Natural Rights and Revolutionary New England: A Note on Four Petitions in Massachusetts, 1773–1777," *NEQ* 62 (June 1989): 248–63; and Blanck, *Tyrannicide.*

51. Philip S. Foner in *Blacks in the American Revolution* (Westport, CT: Greenwood Press, 1976), 68, estimates five hundred; another report estimates just over eight hundred: see Eric G. Grundset, ed., *Forgotten Patriots: African American and American Indian Patriots of the Revolutionary War* (Washington, DC: National Society of the Daughters of the American Revolution, 2001), 27.

52. Sylvia Frey, *Water from the Rock: Black Resistance in a Revolutionary Age* (Princeton, NJ: Princeton University Press, 1991), 78.

53. EPP memorandum book, February 25, 1776, *NEHGR.* Other Hadley blacks who served in the Revolution include Ralph Way and Joshua Boston, as well as "mulatto" Levi Prutt.

54. Cesar [Sezor] Phelps to CP Jr., September 30, 1776, Box 4 folder 12, PPHFP.

55. Margot Minardi, "Freedom in the Archives: The Pension Case of Primus Hall," in Benes and Benes, eds., *Slavery/Antislavery,* 128–40.

56. Minardi, "Freedom in the Archives"; and also Jared Ross Hardesty, *Unfreedom: Slavery and Dependence in Eighteenth-Century Boston* (New York: New York University Press, 2016); Herndon and Sekatau, "Pauper Apprenticeship."

57. See John Adams diary, June 8, 1771, in Charles Francis Adams, *The Works of John Adams, Second President of the United States,* vol. 2 (Boston: Little, Brown, 1850–1856), 272; and Phelps's memorandum book, May 3, 1772, *NEHGR.* Plainville, Russellville, and Hartsbrook would emerge later as other identifiable neighborhoods in Hadley.

58. For a detailed account of the Porter family in Massachusetts, see Andrew Raymond, "A New England Colonial Family: Four Generations of the Porters of Hadley, Massachusetts," *NEHGR* 129 (1975): 198–220; and Clifford K. Shipton, *Sibley's Harvard Graduates,* vol. 8 (Boston: Massachusetts Historical Society, 1879–1919), 769, in Raymond, "A New England Colonial Family," 207. Family reminiscences regarding the estate include John Phelps, *Family Memoirs* (Brattleboro, VT: Selleck and Davis, 1886); Arria S. Huntington, *Under a Colonial Rooftree: Fireside Chronicles of Early New England* (Boston: Houghton Mifflin, 1891); Ruth Huntington Sessions, *Sixty-Odd: A Personal History* (Brattleboro, VT: Stephen Daye Press, 1936); and James Lincoln Huntington, *Forty Acres: The Story of the Bishop Huntington House* (New York: Hastings House, 1949).

59. Robert Blair St. George, "Artifacts of Regional Consciousness in the Connecticut River Valley, 1700–1780," in Ward and Hosley, eds., *The Great River,* especially 29.

60. Raymond, "A New England Colonial Family," 212.

61. This and the following are based on Kevin M. Sweeney, "Mansion People: Kinship, Class, and Architecture in Western Massachusetts in the Mid Eighteenth Century," *Winterthur Portfolio* 19 (1984): 231–56.

62. Sweeney, "Mansion People," 240.

63. Sweeney, "Mansion People," 242.

64. Elizabeth Pendergast Carlisle, *Earthbound and Heavenbent: Elizabeth Porter Phelps and Life at Forty Acres (1747–1817)* (New York: Scribner, 2004), 10.

65. In 1993, Gregory Farmer and Bonnie Parsons found that all nineteen extant Federal-era structures in North Hadley shared five-bay, center-hall plan construction, with

central chimneys and one-story rear ells. See Gregory Farmer and Bonnie Parsons, "North Hadley Historic District," National Register of Historic Places Nomination, 1993.

66. See Carlisle, *Earthbound and Heavenbent,* 19–21, and chapter 7 herein.

67. On the Phelps family, see especially John Phelps, *Family Memoirs*; James Lincoln Huntington, "The Honorable Charles Phelps," Colonial Society of Massachusetts, *Publications* 32 (1933–1937): 441–60; Kevin Graffagnino, "Vermonters Unmasked: Charles Phelps and the Patterns of Dissent in Revolutionary Vermont," *Vermont History* 57 (1989): 133–61; and Peter E. Dow, "Bucking the Tide: Charles Phelps and the Vermont Land Grant Controversies, 1750–1789" (MA thesis, University of Massachusetts Amherst, 1990). The 1730–1747 account book of Phelps's father, Northampton bricklayer Nathaniel Phelps, can be found in the collections of the Pocumtuck Valley Memorial Association, Deerfield, MA.

68. See Charles Porter Phelps's Autobiography, 1857, Box 10 folder 21, PPHFP.

69. It is possible that Charles was hired to help run the estate after the departure of Daniel Worthington, who had managed Forty Acres from April of 1761 to May of 1767. On the opposition to this marriage, Charles and Elizabeth Porter Phelps's grandson, Theodore Gregson Huntington, reported family tradition that the Porters had identified a member of the influential Williams family as a suitable spouse for Elizabeth; Charles Phelps "was without title civil or military and probably had not even the advantage of wealth to recommend him and it was quite shocking that he should aspire to the heart and hand and estate of one so much above him." See "Sketches of Family and Life in Hadley," Box 21 folder 5, 36, PPHFP.

70. In 1799, Charles Phelps and his son were assessed $535 in taxes. The next closest was Enos Smith at $298. Judd, "Hadley," vol. 3, 302.

71. Hadley 1770 tax valuation, published in Judd, *Hadley,* 423.

72. See Beth Terhune, "A Study of the Porter-Phelps-Huntington House Land and Structures, Hadley, Massachusetts, 1652–1830," unpublished manuscript, 1995, Porter-Phelps-Huntington House.

73. Regina S. Leonard, "The Porter-Phelps-Huntington Property, 1659–1955: History of the Vernacular Landscape in Context" (MA thesis, University of Massachusetts Amherst 2000), 51–52, 45.

74. Timothy Dwight, *Travels in New England and New York,* vol. 1, Barbara Miller Solomon, ed. ([New Haven, CT: S. Converse, 1821] Cambridge: Belknap Press of Harvard University Press, 1969), letter 35, 259–60.

75. Judd, *Hadley,* 445–51.

76. A sketch of the interior plan of the meetinghouse ca. 1788–1800 can be found in Judd, *Hadley,* 317.

77. Robert Blair St. George discusses the role these "calculated acts of largesse" played in the perpetuation of a rural aristocracy in "Artifacts of Regional Consciousness," in Ward and Hosley, eds., *The Great River,* 35; for an alternative view, see Karen Parsons, "We Owe Something More Than Prayers," in Falino and Ward, eds., *New England Silver and Silversmithing, 1620–1815* (Boston: Colonial Society of Massachusetts, 2001), 89–112. Phelps's role in mending division in Hadley's first church is considered in my own "The Feud of the Streets: The 1841 Move of Hadley's 1808 Meetinghouse," in Peter Benes and Jane Montague Benes, eds., *Our Vanishing Landmarks,* Proceedings of the 2018 Dublin Seminar for New England Folklife (Deerfield, MA: Historic Deerfield, forthcoming).

78. Likewise, the several additions and renovations undertaken by Charles Phelps updated the house to reflect recent architectural fashion, using the finest materials. The 1790s

addition of a stylish neoclassical facade reaffirmed the Phelpses' status as arbiters of regional taste, consumers of imported goods and employers of local labor. For a discussion of this house and others like it, see Sweeney, "Mansion People," and chapter 8 herein.

Chapter 2 • *Women, Work, and the Business of Gentility*

Epigraph: In Sylvester Judd, "Hadley," vol. 3, 189 (Judd Manuscript), FL.

1. Perhaps Clark was nostalgic too: the house in which she was raised had been torn down twenty years earlier. Judd was curious about that as well and Clark was no doubt only too happy to recall its nooks and crannies for him; see Sylvester Judd, "Hadley," vol. 3, 3 (Judd Manuscript), FL.

2. Bruce Laurie, *Rebels in Paradise: Sketches of Northampton Abolitionists* (Amherst: University of Massachusetts Press, 2015), 14–15.

3. Judd, "Miscellaneous," vol. 19, 353. On nineteenth-century nostalgia regarding women's work, see also Jeanne Boydston, "The Woman Who Wasn't There: Women's Market Labor and the Transition to Capitalism in the United States," *JER* 16, no. 2 (1996): 183–206.

4. I have written elsewhere about the ways that needlework—and quilting in particular—worked to create and sustain community among women of the rural gentry. See *The Needle's Eye: Women and Work in the Age of Revolution* (Amherst: University of Massachusetts Press, 2006), chapter 3; see also my essay, "'. . . Others of Our Own People': Needlework and Women of the Rural Gentry," in Lynne Bassett, ed., *What's New England about New England Quilts?* (Sturbridge, MA: Old Sturbridge Village, 1999), 19–33. On visiting as a form of work, see Karen V. Hansen, "Rediscovering the Social: Visiting Practices in Antebellum New England and the Limits of the Public/Private Dichotomy," in Krishan Kumar and Jeff Weintraub, eds., *Public and Private in Thought and Practice: Perspectives on a Grand Dichotomy* (Chicago: University of Chicago Press, 1997), 268–302.

5. Interview with Sophia Cook [Mrs. Allen] Clark (b. 1793), in Judd, "Hadley," vol. 3, 189.

6. EPP memorandum book, May 6, 1792, *NEHGR*.

7. EPP to EWPH, February 26, 1801, Box 6 folder 1, PPHFP.

8. See Deborah Valenze, "The Art of Women and the Business of Men: Women's Work and the Dairy Industry, c. 1740–1840," *Past and Present* 130 (February 1991): 142–69; Elinor Oakes, "A Ticklish Business: Dairying in New England and Pennsylvania, 1750–1812," *Pennsylvania History* 47 (1980): 195–212. See also Anne Poubeau, "'You Did Not Mention Whether You Had a Cow . . .': Cheese Making at the Porter Phelps Farm, Hadley, MA, 1770–1815" (unpublished seminar paper, Fall 1999, University of Massachusetts Amherst); and Kristina M. Nies, "Chore, Craft & Business: Cheesemaking in 18th-Century Massachusetts" (MA thesis, Boston University, 2008).

9. Carole Shammas, in "How Self-Sufficient Was Early America?," *Journal of Interdisciplinary History* 13 no. 2 (Autumn 1982): 247–72, especially 261.

10. Sylvester Judd, *History of Hadley: Including the Early History of Hatfield, South Hadley, Amherst and Granby, Massachusetts* (Springfield, MA: H. R. Huntting, 1905), 385, 393, and 431–32; and Bettye Hobbs Pruitt, ed., *The Massachusetts Tax Valuation List of 1771* (Boston: G. K. Hall, 1978), 394–97. The cows noted were those three years old or older.

11. On dairying in Hampshire County, see Christopher Clark, *The Roots of Rural Capitalism: Western Massachusetts, 1780–1860* (Ithaca, NY: Cornell University Press, 1990), 77, 145.

12. Sarah F. McMahon, "A Comfortable Subsistence: The Changing Composition of Diet in Rural New England, 1620–1840," *WMQ*, 3rd ser., 42, no. 1 (January 1985): 26–65; especially 38–39. Shammas, in "How Self-Sufficient Was Early America?," 260, also notes the rise in dairy production across the board.

13. Judd, *Hadley*, 377.

14. EPP to EWPH, November 15, 1805, Box 5 folder 7, PPHFP.

15. Invoice, December 1793, William Porter Papers, 1785–1850, Box A folder 1.

16. EPP to EWPH, September 13, 1802, Box 5 folder 4, PPHFP.

17. Bettye Hobbs Pruitt, "Self-Sufficiency and the Agricultural Economy of Eighteenth-Century Massachusetts," *WMQ* 41, no. 3 (July 1984): 33; Shammas, "How Self-Sufficient Was Early America?," 260–61.

18. Moses Porter, March 8, 1756, Box 117 no. 19, HCMRP.

19. EPP to EWPH, November 15, 1805, Box 5 folder 7, PPHFP; and Daphne L. Derven, "Wholesome, Toothsome, and Diverse: Eighteenth-Century Foodways in Deerfield, Massachusetts," in Peter Benes and Jane Montague Benes, eds., *Foodways in the Northeast*, Proceedings of the 1982 Dublin Seminar for New England Folklife (Boston: Boston University, 1984), 51.

20. EPP to EWPH, July 10, 1807, Box 5 folder 9, PPHFP.

21. Judd, "Miscellaneous," vol. 18, 99.

22. EPP to EWPH, October 14, 1813, Box 5 folder 11, PPHFP.

23. EPP to EWPH, November 13, 1810, Box 5 folder 10, PPHFP.

24. Fortunately for the Jacksons, no one ever appeared to attempt to retrieve Peter. How she and Peter met and when they married is not known, but by the 1790s they were living in western Massachusetts. Their son and two daughters had been born there by 1800. Always living on the margin, by the 1830s the Jacksons had moved down the hill and into Amherst, a farming community and now a budding college town. By 1832, the Jacksons are listed among Amherst's paupers. See James Avery Smith, *History of the Black Population of Amherst* (Boston: New England Historic Genealogical Society, 1999), 81.

25. CP to EPP, May 15, 1803, Box 4 folder 4, PPHFP.

26. See EPP memorandum book, August 8 and 10, October 17, 1802, *NEHGR*.

27. EPP memorandum book, October 17 (Zerviah's departure) and October 24 (Assinah's arrival), 1802, and January 2, 1803, *NEHGR*. On native women and domestic service, see Daniel R. Mandell's excellent study *Tribe, Race, History: Native Americans in Southern New England, 1780–1880* (Baltimore: Johns Hopkins University Press, 2010), 8.

28. EPP memorandum book, January 2, 1803, *NEHGR*; and EPP to EWPH, December 1802. As Margaret M. Bruchac points out in "Historical Erasure and Cultural Recovery: Indigenous People in the Connecticut River Valley" (PhD diss., University of Massachusetts Amherst, 2007), 2, "It has been difficult for historians to document, let alone track, the valley's Native peoples during the 1700s (Temple and Sheldon 1875), a time when many families relocated (for a few years, or a few generations) to refuge villages like Schaghticoke in New York (Calloway 1990), Christian Indian missions like St. Francis in Canada (Day 1974), or Abenaki communities in northern New England (Stewart Smith 1998), to escape conflicts in the valley."

29. EPP to EWPH, December 20, 1802, Box 5 folder 4, PPHFP.

30. EPP to EWPH, January 29, 1803, Box 5 folder 5, PPHFP.

31. CP to EPP, May 15, 1803, Box 4 folder 4, PPHFP.

32. See, e.g., cheese basket, Memorial Hall Museum, K.751, American Centuries Digital Collection. Examples in the collection of Historic New England include two hexagonal-weave hickory-splint cheese baskets associated with Middlesex County (1927.2165 and 1927.2138); and two reed baskets (1934.2951 and 1955.220). Mandell discusses "traveling Indian craftswomen" in *Tribe, Race, History*, 31–32.

33. See Nan Wolverton, "A Precarious Living: Basket Making and Related Crafts among New England Indians," in Colin G. Calloway and Neal Salisbury, eds., *Reinterpreting New England Indians and the Colonial Experience* (Boston: Colonial Society of Massachusetts, 2003), 341–68; and Laurel Thatcher Ulrich, "A Woodsplint Basket," in *The Age of Homespun: Objects and Stories in the Creation of an American Myth* (New York: Knopf, 2001), 340–73. Also Jean M. O'Brien, "'Divorced' from the Land: Resistance and Survival of Indian Women in Eighteenth-Century New England," in Colin G. Calloway, ed., *After King Philip's War: Presence and Persistence in Indian New England* (Hanover, NH: University Press of New England, 1997), 144–61; and Ruth B. Philips, *Trading Identities: The Souvenir in Native American Art from the Northeast, 1700–1900* (Seattle: University of Washington Press, 1998).

34. Judd, "Miscellaneous," vol. 19, 141, and vol. 15, 159.

35. Theodore Gregson Huntington, "Sketches of the Family and Life in Hadley," Box 21 folder 5, PPHFP, 6. On Shutesbury and the Nipmuc lands on which it sits, see the Indian Land Archives of Springfield (1660–1835), housed at Cornell University.

36. Based on a review of inventories preserved in the HCMRP, vols. 8–23; see "The probate records for Hampshire County, 1660–1820, in the Hampshire County Registry of Probate, Northampton, Mass" [microform] (Holyoke, MA: New England Archives Center for the Connecticut Valley Historical Museum, Springfield, MA, n.d.).

37. For bread baskets, see the probate inventories of, e.g., Eliakim Smith (Hadley) February 4, 1777, Box 134 no. 19; and John Sexton (Deerfield) March 21, 1785, Box 129 no. 37; for cutlery baskets, see, e.g., David Smith (Hadley) March 3, 1772, Box 134 no. 2; and Elihu White (Hatfield) April 1, 1794, Box 158 no. 24; and for corn, flax, and strawberry baskets, see Samuel Colton (Longmeadow) October 20, 1785, Box 36 no. 14, HCMRP.

38. See the probate inventories of Jedediah Bliss (Springfield) February 27, 1778, Box 16 no. 17; Jonathan Strong (Northampton) April 7, 1767, Box 144 no. 18. For hanging baskets, see, e.g., John Pomeroy (Northampton) April 13, 1762, Box 116 no. 13, or Abraham Adams (Springfield) April 13, 1762, Box 1 no. 30, HCMRP.

39. For clothes baskets, see, e.g., Frederic Chapin (Hatfield) July 26, 1802, Box 27 no. 7; for cheese baskets, see, e.g., Samuel Colton (Longmeadow) October 20, 1785, Box 36 no. 14, HCMRP.

40. Hadley inventories containing baskets include Frances Spear, December 17, 1770, Box 139 no. 11; Josiah Dickinson, January 27, 1774, Box 47 no. 54; Eliakim Smith (Hadley) February 4, 1777, Box 134 no. 19; Oliver White, January 6, 1790, Box 159 no. 30; and Paul Wright, October 4, 1808, Box 165 no. 32, HCMRP.

41. For an intriguing discussion of "memory and practice" as key to interpreting material evidence with both Native and European resonance, see Stephen W. Silliman, "Change and Continuity, Practice and Memory: Native American Persistence in Colonial New England," *American Antiquity* 74, no. 2 (August 2009): 211–30, especially p. 215.

42. Silliman, "Change and Continuity, Practice and Memory," 215.

43. EPP to EWPH, April 4, 1807, Box 5 folder 9, PPHFP.

44. EPP to EWPH, February 7, 1803, Box 5 folder 5, PPHFP. It is probably not coincidental that the export trade in the products of American dairies had recently reached its peak, in 1801; see Oakes, "Ticklish Business," 211.

45. Gregory Clancey, "Historic Structures Report," Adams and Roy Consultants, Inc., Box 178, PPHFP, 65.

46. In central Massachusetts, Sutton's Malachi Marble built a lean-to shed against his house to enclose a well room that supported his wife's work in her dairy. This "significant innovation" improved workflow without disrupting life in the main house—although Mrs. Marble already captured some of that space for production, using an upper chamber (the "cheese chamber") for curing and storing cheeses, while milk was stored and processed "in the buttery on the first floor to which the well room was attached." See Nora Pat Small, "The Search for a New Rural Order: Farmhouses in Sutton, Massachusetts, 1790–1830," *WMQ*, 3rd ser., 53, no. 1 (January 1996): 73–75.

47. *HG*, July 7, 1802.

48. EPP to EWPH, June 1805, Box 5 folder 7, PPHFP.

49. My thanks to Kristina Nies for help understanding this passage.

50. CP to EPP, May 16, 1803, Box 4 folder 4, PPHFP.

51. EPP to CP, May 22, 1803, Box 5 folder 13, PPHFP.

52. EPP to EWPH, February 7, 1803, and May 21, 1807, Box 5 folder 5, and Box 5 folder 9, PPHFP.

53. EPP to EWPH, May 21, 1807, Box 5 folder 9, PPHFP.

54. CP account book, 1805–1815, Phelps Family account books, 1805–1858, Baker Library, Harvard Business School; and Carlisle, *Earthbound and Heavenbent*, 60.

55. EPP to EWPH, December 17, 1804, Box 5 folder 6, PPHFP.

56. EPP memorandum book, March 10, 1810, Box 7 folder 3, PPHFP. Winifred Rothenberg cites Till's varied seasonal wages—reflecting the comparatively lesser/greater difficulty in farm labor over the course of the agricultural year, earning $6 per month between January and April 2011 and $11.50 from May to November. See Winifred B. Rothenberg, "Structural Change in the Farm Labor Force: Contract Labor in Massachusetts Agriculture, 1750–1865," in Claudia Goldin and Hugh Rockoff, eds., *Strategic Factors in Nineteenth Century American Economic History: A Volume to Honor Robert W. Fogel* (Chicago: University of Chicago Press, 1992), 105–34, 121. The labor (carrying the cheese to Boston) falls in the former category.

57. On Phelps and the Massachusetts Society for Promoting Agriculture, see *Laws and Regulations of the Massachusetts Society for Promoting Agriculture* (Boston: Isaiah Thomas and Ebenezer T. Andrews, 1793). By the 1840s, journals such as the *New Genesee Farmer* would observe that "thirty years ago it would have been almost as difficult to find a man milking as to find women mowing"; now, however, they noted that dairy chores had become more lucrative, and, at the same time, increasingly the province of men. See *New Genesee Farmer*, May 1840, quoted in Poubeau, "'You Did Not Mention Whether You Had a Cow . . . ,'" 6.

58. EPP memorandum book, May 23, 1813, Box 7 folder 4, PPHFP.

59. EPP to EWPH, June 13, 1813, Box 5 folder 11, PPHFP.

60. EPP to EWPH, July 27, 1813, Box 5 folder 11, PPHFP.

61. EPP to EWPH, October 13, 1813, Box 5 folder 11, PPHFP.

62. EPP to EWPH, August 6, 1802, Box 5 folder 4, PPHFP.

63. EPP to EWPH, August 6, 1802, Box 5 folder 4, PPHFP.

64. EPP to EWPH, June 17, 1803, Box 6 folder 1, PPHFP.

65. An excellent description of the processes behind milking and cheese making is found in Oakes, "Ticklish Business"; on the evolution of dairying and gender divisions of labor, see Sally McMurray, *Transforming Rural Life: Dairying Families and Agricultural Change, 1820–1885* (Baltimore: Johns Hopkins University Press, 1995); and also McMurray, "Women's Work in Agriculture: Divergent Trends in England and America, 1800 to 1930," *Comparative Studies in Society and History* 34, no. 2 (April 1992): 248–70; Joan M. Jensen, *Loosening the Bonds: Mid-Atlantic Farm Women* (New Haven, CT: Yale University Press, 1986). On women in England in this period, see Valenze, "The Art of Women."

66. Clark, *Roots of Rural Capitalism*, 145.

67. Betsy and her husband Dan in 1816 inherited half of her parents' estate; they and their eleven children lived in the family home, Forty Acres. Little evidence survives to document dairy operations at Forty Acres during the tenure of Betsy Huntington as mistress of the house, though Dan Huntington would cover the rent he owed upland farmers for pasturing cattle on their land by allowing them to retain all or part of the cheese produced from cows milked during their stay. See Clark, *The Roots of Rural Capitalism*, 83 (n. 44). Betsy's brother Charles Porter Phelps inherited the balance of the estate and, after a career in Boston, returned to Hadley to farm across the road from his sister. See Phelps Family account books, 1805–1858, Baker Library, Harvard Business School.

68. Dairy operations would persist into the early twentieth century, long after Forty Acres had become a summer retreat for the descendants of Elizabeth Porter Phelps. See Henry Barrett Huntington, "Hadley Farm Material," Box 60 folder 47; see also Box 82 folder 50 and Box 163 folder 8, PPHFP.

Chapter 3 • Women, Work, and "Economies of Makeshifts"

1. Laurel Ulrich has also pointed toward the importance of gender balance in the family, as households were in need of both daughters and sons to do the work of the farm. A shortage of either would increase the need to hire help of that gender. See "Martha Ballard and Her Girls: Women's Work in Eighteenth Century Maine," in Stephen Innes, ed., *Work and Labor in Early America* (Chapel Hill: University of North Carolina Press for the Institute of Early American History and Culture, 1988), 70–105; see also Gloria Main, "Gender, Work and Wages in Colonial New England," *WMQ* 51 (1994): 39–66, especially 55–56.

2. On this term, see Olwen H. Hufton, *The Poor of Eighteenth-Century France, 1750–1789* (Oxford: Clarenden Press, 1974).

3. Dr. Richard Crouch ledger, June 28, 1754, Hadley, MA, FL.

4. Chester Williams's will, October 1, 1753, Box 161 no. 8, HCMRP. See also Sylvester Judd, *History of Hadley: Including the Early History of Hatfield, South Hadley, Amherst and Granby, Massachusetts* (Springfield, MA: H. R. Huntting, 1905), 393.

5. See, e.g., *CC*, February 16, 1773; January 9 and 23, 1775; April 3, 1783.

6. *CC*, February 16, 1773.

7. On northern women, motherhood, family, and enslavement, see Catherine Adams and Elizabeth Pleck, *Love of Freedom: Black Women in Colonial and Revolutionary New England* (New York: Oxford University Press, 2010), 103–25; Nora Doyle, *Maternal Bodies: Redefining Motherhood in Early America* (Chapel Hill: University of North Carolina Press,

2018), 131–32; Allegra di Bonaventura, *For Adam's Sake: A Family Saga in Colonial New England* (New York: Liveright, 2003); James H. Sweet, "Defying Social Death: The Multiple Configurations of African Slave Family in the Atlantic World," *WMQ* 70 (April 2013): 251–72; and the valuable essays on "the everyday experience of caring for children in a context of coercion" gathered in a special issue of *Slavery and Abolition: A Journal of Slave and Post-Slave Studies* 38, no. 2 (2017). An important study of a Connecticut Valley family in enslavement and freedom is Gretchen Holbrook Gerzina, *Mr. and Mrs. Prince: How an Extraordinary Eighteenth-Century Family Moved Out of Slavery and Into Legend* (New York: Amistad, 2008). For particular consideration of fatherhood among enslaved men, see Gloria McCahon Whiting, "Power, Patriarchy, and Provision: African Families Negotiate Gender and Slavery in New England," *Journal of American History* 103, no. 3 (December 2016): 583–605.

8. "Those present witness that Jerusha Chauncy of Hadley in the county of Hampshire and province of the Massachusetts Bay in New England for and in consideration of £150 old tenor . . . to be paid by Moses Porter of Hadley have sold to him the said Moses my negro boy Zeb about 14 years of age . . . 26 July 1745. Signed by Jerusha, Josiah Chauncy and Mary Chauncey, witnesses." See receipt, PPHFP Box 3 folder 4. Zebulon's brother Caesar by 1770 was claimed by Josiah Chauncey, and valued at twenty-five pounds. James Avery Smith, *History of the Black Population of Amherst, 1728–1879* (Boston: New England Historic Genealogical Society, 1999), 110–11.

9. *Hartford Courant*, September 15, 1766.

10. EPP memorandum book, February 7, 1768, *NEHGR*.

11. By 1800, Caesar and Zebulon had drifted east to Amherst, where they became paupers dependent on town support. On this family, see Smith, *History of the Black Population of Amherst*, 110–11; on patriarchal naming patterns among families in enslavement, see Whiting, "Power, Patriarchy, and Provision," 599–601.

12. According to Judd, *Hadley*, 313, Boston was about seventy-nine when he died in 1819.

13. Smith, *History of the Black Population of Amherst*, 6.

14. EPP, "Births and Deaths" *NEHGR* (January 1969), 18; *HG*, June 3, 1904; and Sylvester Judd, "Hadley," vol. 3, 32 and 305 (Judd Manuscript), FL. A glimpse of Joshua Boston as a young man is captured in enlistment records created during the American Revolution: when he joined up for a six-month term of service in 1781, he was thirty-five years old and six feet tall; he reported his occupation to be a farmer. Massachusetts Office of the Secretary of State, *Massachusetts Soldiers and Sailors of the Revolutionary War*, vol. 2 (Boston: Wright and Potter Printing Co., State Printers, 1896–1908), 294. Other surviving descriptions likewise note his remarkable "dignity and majesty," and recall him being particularly well dressed; it seems likely that Boston may have regularly acquired the castoff clothing of the Porter men. For an intriguing discussion of appearance among enslaved New Englanders, see Antonio J. Bly, "Pretty, Sassy, Cool: Slave Resistance, Agency and Culture in Eighteenth-Century New England," *NEQ* 89, no. 3 (September 2016): 457–92. Boston's economic activities are well documented in the day and account book (1767–1806) of Samuel Hopkins in the collections of the Pocumtuck Valley Memorial Association, in the Memorial Libraries of Deerfield, MA.

15. Theodore Gregson Huntington, "Sketches of Family and Life in Hadley," 18, Box 21 folder 5 PPHFP. Her mother would attend the January 1806 funeral of Boston's wife, Pits; Boston himself died in Hadley in December 1819; see EPP memorandum book, January 19, 1806, Box 7 folder 3 PPHFP; Judd, *Hadley*, 321.

16. Samuel Hopkins, "Baptisms since the Burning of My House," 240, First Church, Hadley, MA.

17. Phelps, *Phelps Family*, 133. See also Tera W. Hunter, *Bound in Wedlock: Slave and Free Black Marriage in the Nineteenth Century* (Cambridge: Belknap Press of Harvard University Press, 2017).

18. Peter Benes, "Slavery in Boston Households, 1647–1770," in Peter Benes and Jane Montague Benes, eds., *Slavery/Antislavery in New England*, Proceedings of the 2003 Dublin Seminar for New England Folklife (Boston: Boston University, 2005), 12–30.

19. Adams and Pleck, *Love of Freedom*, 103–24.

20. Bill of Sale, March 13, 1770, Box 4 folder 15, PPHFP.

21. CP Sr. to CP Jr., February 15, 1776, Box 2 folder 2, PPHFP.

22. Josiah Pierce almanac, May 4, 1771, as transcribed in Judd, "Hadley," vol. 3, 245.

23. EPP memorandum book, April 3, 1772, *NEHGR*.

24. An enslaved man and woman could marry, but masters retained their rights to sell their human property. See Adams and Pleck, *Love of Freedom*, 104; Jared Ross Hardesty also discusses marriage between enslaved people in *Unfreedom: Slavery and Dependence in Eighteenth-Century Boston* (New York: New York University Press, 2016), 85–92, reporting 223 marriages of people of African descent, and 162 unions of enslaved men and women, between 1700 and 1775. On tensions between marriage and property law, see Adams and Pleck, *Love of Freedom*, 171. On the significance of marriage prohibitions as a tool to control labor, see Whiting, "Power, Patriarchy, and Provision," 603–4.

25. Hardesty notes (*Unfreedom*, 87) that, in unions between enslaved partners, "a slave would now have a second master to contend with—that of his or her spouse. Having two white men with tremendous power over slaves' lives and marriages was certainly an added layer of stress on already tenuous relationships."

26. Whiting, "Power, Patriarchy, and Provision," 595, 602.

27. Bill of Sale, March 13, 1778, PPHFP Box 4 folder 15.

28. EPP memorandum book, June 9, 1782, *NEHGR*.

29. EPP memorandum book, August 25, 1771, *NEHGR*.

30. EPP memorandum book, April 20, 1783, *NEHGR*.

31. EPP memorandum book, April 9, 1792, *NEHGR*.

32. EPP to EWPH, November 13, 1810, Box 5 folder 10, PPHFP. Another woman, Maria, described as "Colonel [Elisha] Porter's negro woman," like Phillis seems to have remained in the Porter household after the demise of slavery as an institution, although Porter himself had died three years earlier, and his wife Abigail Phillips Porter several years before that; see Henry Bond, *Family Memorials: Genealogies of Families and Descendants of the Early Settlers of Watertown, Massachusetts, including Waltham and Weston* (Boston: Little, Brown, 1855), 903; and EPP memorandum book, October 27, 1799, *NEHGR*.

33. E.g., Hadley Overseers of the Poor treasurer's ledger, 1807–1852, January 1, 1812, HHS. Too little is known about Aberdeen (d. 1816) to understand the course of her own life. In a note concerning "Negroes of Hadley," Sylvester Judd referenced a Caesar Aberdeen, who was "not a slave in Hadley, but a pious church member and conscientious man," but we cannot know today whether this man was Phillis's father, husband, son, or brother; whether Phillis had ever been enslaved; and, if so, how she came to be free. Judd, "Hadley," vol. 3, 32.

34. Clifton Johnson papers, ser. 2, Miscellaneous Writings, "Gossip and Odds," Jones Library Special Collections, Amherst, MA.

35. Barry Levy, *Town Born: The Political Economy of New England from Its Founding to the Revolution* (Philadelphia: University of Pennsylvania Press, 2009).

36. James Russell Trumbull, *History of Northampton, Massachusetts, from its Settlement in 1654*, vol. 2 (Northampton: Press of Gazette Printing Co., 1902), 337.

37. Trumbull, *Northampton*, 338; see also EPP memorandum book, May 18, 1800, *NEHGR*.

38. "Two-in-One Book," Hampshire County House of Correction, 1784–1830, FL. On women and theft, see Serena R. Zabin, *Dangerous Economies: Status and Commerce in British New York* (University of Pennsylvania Press, 2009).

39. The literature on charity and poor relief in early New England is large. Most relevant here are Ruth Wallis Herndon, *Unwelcome Americans: Living on the Margin in Early New England* (Philadelphia: University of Pennsylvania Press, 2001); Cornelia H. Dayton and Sharon V. Salinger, *Robert Love's Warnings: Searching for Strangers in Colonial Boston* (Philadelphia: University of Pennsylvania Press, 2014); Carla Gardina Pestana and Sharon V. Salinger, *Inequality in Early America* (Hanover, NH: University Press of New England, 1999); Allan Kulikoff, "The Progress of Inequality in Revolutionary Boston," *WMQ* 28, no. 3 (1971): 375–412; Billy G. Smith, "Poverty and Economic Marginality in Eighteenth-Century America," *Proceedings of the American Philosophical Society* 132, no. 1 (1988): 85–118; Charles R Lee, "Public Poor Relief and the Massachusetts Community, 1620–1715," *NEQ* 55, no. 4 (1982): 564–85.

40. Deerfield Overseers of the Poor, Deerfield Town Manuscripts, Box 9 folder 1, PVMA, Memorial Libraries, Deerfield, MA.

41. RD diary, June 14, 1795, PVMA.

42. Deerfield Town Records. On warning out in Massachusetts, see Dayton and Salinger, *Robert Love's Warnings*, 8–21, 57–59.

43. EPP memorandum book, February 29, 1784, *NEHGR*.

44. Kulikoff, "Progress of Inequality"; and Dayton and Salinger, *Robert Love's Warnings*.

45. Emerging scholarship on women's employment services will enrich our understanding of these patterns. See, e.g., April Haynes, "Female Intelligence Offices and Domestic Labor Markets, 1810–1850," paper presented at the 2018 meeting of the Society for Historians of the Early American Republic, Cleveland OH, part of her larger project, *Tender Traffic: Intimate Labors in the Early American Republic*.

46. Warning out, February 18, 1788, Hadley Old Records, 1700–, Box 1 folder 6, HHS. Adams and Pleck discuss the warning out of women of color in *Love of Freedom*, 160–63; see also Dayton and Salinger, *Robert Love's Warnings*, 82–84, 125–28.

47. As quoted in Christopher Clark, *The Roots of Rural Capitalism: Western Massachusetts, 1780–1860* (Ithaca, NY: Cornell University Press, 1990), 57.

48. Judd, *Hadley*, 414.

49. Hadley Overseers of the Poor treasurer's ledger, 1807–1852, January 1, 1808, HHS.

50. Hadley Overseers of the Poor treasurer's ledger, 1807–1852, April 1, 1813, HHS.

51. Hufton, *The Poor of Eighteenth-Century France*; see also Seth Rockman on "The Hard Work of Being Poor," in *Scraping By: Wage Labor, Slavery and Survival in Early Baltimore* (Baltimore: Johns Hopkins University Press, 2009), 158–93.

52. On women who served in the military, the best place to begin is Alfred F. Young, *Masquerade: The Life and Times of Deborah Sampson, Continental Soldier* (New York:

Knopf, 2004). On women in the theater, see Faye Dudden, *Women in the American Theatre: Actresses and Audiences 1790–1870* (New Haven, CT: Yale University Press, 1994).

53. See Laurel Daen, "Martha Ann Honeywell: Art, Performance and Disability in the Early Republic," *JER* 37, no. 2 (Summer 2017): 225–50.

54. Daen, "Martha Ann Honeywell," 225, 229.

55. *HG,* February 18, 1807. My deep thanks to Anne Lanning for sharing information from her own work on Rogers. See Lanning's article, "Sally Rogers: The Celebrated Paintress," in *Historic Deerfield* magazine (Summer 2012), 2–7. On public painters and other traveling performers, see Peter Benes, *For a Short Time Only: Itinerants and the Resurgence of Popular Culture in Early America* (Amherst: University of Massachusetts Press, 2016).

56. *A Real Object of Charity, at Once Surprisingly Curious, Beautiful, and Astonishing . . ."* (Walpole, NH: The Press of the Political Observatory, 1806).

57. Penelope Lane, "Women on the Margins: Poor Women and the Informal Economy of Eighteenth and Early Nineteenth-Century Leicestershire," *Midlands History* 22 (1997): 85–99.

58. The quote is from Serena R. Zabin, "Places of Exchange: New York: 1700–1763" (PhD diss., Rutgers University, 2000), 144; see also her book *Dangerous Economies: Status and Commerce in Imperial New York* (Philadelphia: University of Pennsylvania Press, 2009).

59. Forty-two-year-old Lucy Trask was described in the jail's record book as "dark," as was Polly Morgan, a four-foot-one, twenty-year-old woman confined for six months in August 1820. See the "Two-in-One Book," Hampshire County House of Correction, 1784–1830, FL.

60. *Massachusetts Vital Records to 1850,* "Hadley," 199, indicates that marriage of Francis Trainer and Mary Clark or Clarke took place on February 25, 1768. The spelling of Clark (with and without an *e*) varies across these records.

61. Military records list Francis as twenty-nine years old in 1780, putting his birthdate around 1751. See *Massachusetts Soldiers and Sailors*, vol. 16, 15–16. He is also described as being five foot eight with a complexion described as both "reddish" and "dark."

62. Judd, *Hadley*, 424.

63. Judd suggests that this was a Scotch Irish family; John Clark Sr. and his sons John Clark Jr. and William Clark were in Hadley as early as 1758, when they served in the Seven Years' War. See Judd, *Hadley*, 339.

64. *Massachusetts Soldiers and Sailors*, vol. 16, 15.

65. Revolutionary War Rolls, 1775–1783 (National Archives microfilm M246, 138 rolls); War Department Collection of Revolutionary War Records, Record Group 93; National Archives, Washington, DC, Ancestry.com.

66. Revolutionary War Rolls, 1775–1783 (National Archives microfilm M246, 138 rolls); War Department Collection of Revolutionary War Records, Record Group 93; National Archives, Washington, DC, Ancestry.com.

67. *Massachusetts Soldiers and Sailors*, vol. 16, 32.

68. Francis Trainer to William Tobin, April 19, 1786, vol. 1, 455, HCRD.

69. Hadley Town Records, HHS: Town Treasurer's receipts, 1784.

70. Francis Trainer to William Tobin, April 19, 1786, vol. 1, 455, HCRD.

71. Execution of Judgment, May 1788, vol. Ex1, 55, HCRD.

72. Execution of Judgment, May 1788, vol. Ex1, 55, HCRD.

73. Hampshire County Court Records, Inferior Court of Common Pleas, General Sessions of the Peace, University of Massachusetts Special Collections and Archives, May 1792, vol. 19 (1790–99), 56, 65.

74. Execution of Judgment, July 2, 1792, vol. Ex1, 201, HCRD.

75. Execution of Judgment, July 2, 1792, vol. Ex1, 201, HCRD.

76. US Census Bureau (1800 United States Federal Census), Hadley, p. 479.

77. Hampshire County Court Records, Inferior Court of Common Pleas, General Sessions of the Peace, University of Massachusetts Special Collections and Archives, May 20–24, 1794, vol. 19 (1790–99), 114; and Judd, "Miscellaneous," vo. 19. 141.

78. Solomon and Tryphena Newton Cook account book, 1789–1807, HHS, 88–89; the federal census of 1800 (see n. 76 above) indicates that the Cook family lived just a few doors away from the Trainers.

79. Cook account book, HHS, 114.

80. Cook account book, HHS, 114, 131–32.

81. EPP memorandum book, January 28, 1798, *NEHGR*; and December 22, 1811, February 16, 1812, PPHFP.

82. For Elihu Warner and John Cook (below), see Judd, "Hadley," vol. 3, 13. Christopher Clark discusses Hadley's broom-corn industry in *Roots of Rural Capitalism,* 83.

83. Judd, "Hadley," vol. 3, 13, and "Miscellaneous," vol. 19, 159.

84. Judd, "Hadley," vol. 3, 13. Heber "tied one end of the string to a door handle and something on the side of the room and then stood on the opposite side and, as he wound it round the corn, he advanced toward the door handle, & reached it, & used up the string. The string was tarred in the early days. Levi Dickinson contrived to sit in his chair, had the strong round a roll under his feet & then the handle and forming broom on his knees, & so wound the string round the corn." Sylvester Smith, quoted in Judd, "Hadley," vol. 3, 188.

85. Judd, "Hadley," vol. 3, 13. By 1810, the census return of corn brooms made in Hampshire County was seventy thousand; by 1850, some three-quarters of a million brooms shipped out from more than forty Hadley workshops. Judd, "Hadley," vol. 1, 222; "Hadley," vol. 3, 13; and *Hadley,* 360–61. Dickinson peddled the brooms locally, and then in Boston and Albany, until his new enterprise resulted in a major Hampshire County industry; at the time of Dickinson's death, forty-one sites in Hadley were converting nearly five hundred tons of broom brush into over seven hundred thousand brooms per year; Judd, "Hadley," vol. 3, 186–87. See also Gregory H. Nobles, "Commerce and Community: A Case Study of the Rural Broommaking Business in Antebellum Massachusetts," *JER* 4, no. 3 (Autumn 1984): 287–308. Winifred Rothenberg reports that "broomcorn cultivation apparently required two to three times as much labor as corn," in Winifred B. Rothenberg, "Structural Change in the Farm Labor Force: Contract Labor in Massachusetts Agriculture, 1750–1865," in Claudia Goldin and Hugh Rockoff, eds., *Strategic Factors in Nineteenth Century American Economic History: A Volume to Honor Robert W. Fogel* (Chicago, University of Chicago Press, 1992), 119, n. 26, citing Percy W. Bidwell and John I. Falconer, *History of Agriculture in the Northern United States, 1620–1860* (Washington, DC: Carnegie Institution of Washington, 1925), 245.

86. *CC,* September 8, 1766. My thanks to local historian Robert H. Romer for bringing this ad to my attention. His own research on slavery in the region is published in *Slavery in the Connecticut Valley of Massachusetts* (Amherst, MA: Levellers Press, 2009).

87. Clifton Johnson, Notebooks, "Old Town in New England," ser. 1, Clifton Johnson Papers, Jones Library, Amherst, MA. The "shanty" may have been a home specifically constructed by the town in the early nineteenth century to house indigent residents. On unions among Native Americans, African Americans, and poor whites in New England,

see Daniel R. Mandell, *Tribe, Race, History: Native Americans in Southern New England, 1780–1880* (Baltimore: Johns Hopkins University Press, 2010). The genealogical tangle here is a bit unclear, but this woman appears to be the granddaughter of Francis and Mary Trainer. Johnson's notes on this family are unfortunately inflected by racial prejudice; his biases must be acknowledged, though his assertion that the family was multiracial resonates with other archival material.

88. Cook account book, December 1805, 114, HHS.

89. Cook account book, December 1805, 114, HHS. Cook earned two shillings for a day's work and a shilling for a half day; she was paid eighteen shillings for cutting the acre of corn.

90. Cook account book, February 1812, 132, HHS.

91. Mary Trainer to Eli P. Ashman, February 27, 1808, vol. 27, 389, HCRD.

92. Overseers of the Poor receipts, 1809, Box 1 folder 5, Hadley Town Records, HHS.

93. EPP memorandum book, March 23, 1806, Box 7 folder 3, PPHFP.

94. See *The Acts and Resolves, Public and Private, of the Province of the Massachusetts Bay,* vol. 1 (Boston: Wright and Potter, 1869), 538. On 1720, see also Judd, "Miscellaneous," vol. 14, 34. For more on meanings of "ill fame," see Kelly A. Ryan, *Regulating Passion: Sexuality and Patriarchal Rule in Massachusetts, 1700–1830* (New York: Oxford, 2014), 26–27.

95. *Acts and Resolves,* vol. 2, 580, 1054.

96. As quoted in Sharon V. Salinger, *Taverns and Drinking in Early America* (Baltimore: Johns Hopkins University Press, 2002), 159.

97. David W. Conroy, *In Public Houses: Drink and the Revolution of Authority in Colonial Massachusetts* (Chapel Hill: University of North Carolina Press, 1995).

98. Salinger found that rural women were less likely than their urban counterparts to secure a license; see her valuable study *Taverns and Drinking,* especially 115, 170–71, and 181.

99. *An Act for the Due Regulation of Licensed Houses, 1786 Mass.* Stat., ch. 68, § I (Act of February 28, 1787), in Theron Metcalf, ed., *General Laws of Massachusetts* (Boston: Wells & Lilly and Cummings & Hilliard, 1823), 297–304.

100. On mixed-race gatherings in unlicensed taverns, see Hardesty, *Unfreedom,* 94–95.

101. Sally Williams was incarcerated beginning December 3, 1811, for just under six months for "lascivious behavior," while Sarah Smith was confined for "lewdness." See "Two-in-One Book," Hampshire County House of Correction, FL.

102. See Ryan, *Regulating Passion,* 134–35. Though Barbara Meil Hobson in *Uneasy Virtue: The Politics of Prostitution in the American Reform Tradition* (New York: Basic, 1987) suggests that Boston's first "full municipal campaign" against sex workers emerged in the 1820s, Ryan finds evidence of civic attention to these matters as early as the 1790s. On general anxiety about crime in Revolutionary Boston, see Jacqueline Barbara Carr, *After the Siege: A Social History of Boston, 1775–1800* (Boston: Northeastern University Press, 2005), 130–33.

103. Ryan, *Regulating Passion,* 135–39.

104. Ryan, *Regulating Passion,* 125.

105. Hadley Overseers of the Poor treasurer's ledger, 1807–1852, January 24, 1811, HHS.

106. For their arrival, see EPP memorandum book, December 15, 1782, and November 16, 1783. The pair are discussed in Elizabeth Pendergast Carlisle, *Earthbound and*

Heavenbent: Elizabeth Porter Phelps and Life at Forty Acres (1747–1817) (New York: Scribner, 2004), 253; and Karen Parsons, "We Owe Something More Than Prayers," in Jeannine Falino and Gerald R. Ward, eds., *New England Silver and Silversmithing, 1620–1815* (Boston: Colonial Society of Massachusetts, 2001), 89–112. In a letter dated March 4, 1805, Elizabeth Porter Phelps indicates that Charles Phelps was collecting money in Boston, probably from the state's poor accounts—for "A & Mary's support," likely Andries and Mary. See also December 6, 1805, for an account of Andries's illness and the family's care, Box 5 folder 7, PPHFP. They also received support from the town, including $31.50 for keeping Mary from January to May 1810. See Hadley Overseers of the Poor treasurer's ledger, 1807–1852, June 3, 1811, HHS.

107. EPP to EWPH, December 15, 1809, Box 5 folder 9, PPHFP. Mr. Hair is Robert Hair, present at Forty Acres as early as 1807, when he witnessed the indenture of Robert Frasier; see Box 4 folder 32, PPHFP. The Hadley Overseers of the Poor treasurer's ledger, 1807–1852, HHS, on April 1, 1810, indicates that the town assumed over $110 for the cost of Andries's support, far and away more than any other charge.

108. Charles Phelps's account book, vol. 1 (1805–1815), in Phelps Family account books, 1805–1858, Baker Library, Harvard Business School; see Carlisle, *Earthbound and Heavenbent*, 254.

109. Trainer received some forty dollars for her costs; see Hadley Overseers of the Poor treasurer's ledger, 1807–1852, January 24, 1811, and June 3, 1811, HHS. Mary Andries died October 24, 1810; the church record book speculates that she was somewhere between "85–100 years" and noted that she was "a pauper" (see "Records of the Church of Christ in Hadley, Kept by John Woodbridge, Pastor," First Congregational Church of Hadley) For Elizabeth Phelps's account of Mary Andries's death at the home of Mary Trainer, see EPP, October 21, 1810, PPHFP.

110. See Hadley Overseers of the Poor treasurer's ledger, 1807–1852, HHS; on June 30, 1817, for instance, she received $19.50, and in October 1817, $23.41 (of a total of $107.50). On December 31, 1817, she received $20.17 (of $107.22). The last entry in this series (March 30, 1820) awards "Mary Trainer for Mrs Black," $5.90.

111. Clark, *Roots of Rural Capitalism*, 135; Clark's analysis of Boltwood's "Genealogies of Hadley Families" found that women wed in the 1780s had on average 7.22 recorded live births, which in the 1790s dropped to 6.52.

Chapter 4 • Domestic Service

1. Excellent descriptions of the relentless rounds of household chores include Holly Izard, "The Ward Family and their 'Helps': Domestic Work, Workers, and Relationships on a New England Farm," *Proceeding of the American Antiquarian Society* 103 (1993): 61–90; Elisabeth Donaghy Garrett, *At Home, The American Family, 1750–1850* (New York: Abrams, 1989); Barbara Clark Smith, *After the Revolution: The Smithsonian History of Everyday Life in the Eighteenth Century* (New York: Pantheon, 1985); and especially Jane C. Nylander, *Our Own Snug Fireside: Images of the New England Home, 1760–1860* (New York: Knopf, 1993).

2. EPP memorandum book, November 13, 1810, Box 7 folder 3, PPHFP.

3. Pamela Sharpe, *Adapting to Capitalism: Working Women in the English Economy, 1700–1850* (New York: St. Martin's, 1996), 104.

4. Sharpe, *Adapting to Capitalism*, 102.

5. Samuel Hopkins (1729–1811) day and account book, 1767–1806, Memorial Libraries, Deerfield, MA.

6. EPP to EWPH, September 15, 1814, Box 5 folder 12, PPHFP. I am grateful to Ruth Herndon for pointing out the gendered element here as well, that even a man at the bottom of the socioeconomic hierarchy could get a woman to do this labor for him.

7. Izard, "The Ward Family," especially 67.

8. Cornelia H. Dayton and Sharon V. Salinger, *Robert Love's Warnings: Searching for Strangers in Colonial Boston* (Philadelphia: University of Pennsylvania Press, 2014), 80, 120–22; also Ruth Wallis Herndon, "Poor Women and the Boston Almshouse in the Early Republic," *JER* 32, no. 3 (Fall 2012): 349–81.

9. Izard, "The Ward Family," 75; and Ross W. Beales Jr., "'Slavish' and Other Female Work in the Parkman Household, Westborough, Massachusetts, 1724–1782," in Peter Benes and Jane Montague Benes, eds., *House and Home*, Proceedings of the 1988 Dublin Seminar for New England Folklife Annual Proceedings (Boston: Boston University, 1990), 48–57.

10. While no study has yet been undertaken focused on Hadley's farmhands, they too seem to have come from a wide range of places. Just over a dozen boys and men appear in the pages of Phelps's memorandum book and in family papers; their lives would make for a useful study. See EPP memorandum book, e.g., January 9 and May 20, 1767; January 21 and November 5, 1770; April 3, 1774; October 22, 1776; August 17, 1777; April 4, 1779; June 15, 1783; January 21, 1787; January 28, 1790; April 3, 1791, *NEHGR*.

11. As Cornelia Hughes Dayton has observed, historians interested in a family's decision to "put out" daughters "have focused on the issues of discipline and education, not on the fluctuating labor needs of farming households." See Dayton, *Women before the Bar: Gender, Law, and Society in Connecticut, 1639–1789* (Chapel Hill: University of North Carolina Press for the Institute of Early American History and Culture, 1995), 79; and Laurel Thatcher Ulrich, "Martha Ballard and Her Girls: Women's Work in Eighteenth-Century Maine," in Stephen S. Innes, ed., *Work and Labor in Early America* (Chapel Hill: University of North Carolina Press, 1988), 70–105. Elizabeth Whiting Phelps Huntington's correspondence provides a good example of the way in which one family might decide to let a girl go, and another might come to take one in: "Mr H attended a wedding in a family who are in low circumstance, and the woman offered him a girl—she has several daughters, and we might take one—eleven—or fourteen—she did not want wages—but to have them brought up steadily and taught to work—and have us keep her til she was eighteen—I shall think of it . . ." EWHP to EPP, November 11, 1815, Box 13 folder 13, PPHFP.

12. EPP memorandum book, August 10, 1788, *NEHGR*. On the placing of young people by Boston's Overseers of the Poor, see Ruth Wallis Herndon and John E. Murray, eds., *Children Bound to Labor: The Pauper Apprentice System in Early America* (Ithaca, NY: Cornell University Press, 2009); Ruth Wallis Herndon and Amilcar Challú, "Mapping the Boston Poor: Inmates of the Boston Almshouse, 1795–1801," *Journal of Interdisciplinary History* 44, no. 1 (Summer 2013): 63–83; and Herndon's work-in-progress, tentatively titled *Children of Misfortune: Growing Up Poor in Early New England*.

13. On England, see Sharpe, *Adapting to Capitalism*, 102.

14. Kevin M. Sweeney, "River Gods and Related Minor Deities: The Williams Family and the Connecticut River Valley, 1637–1790" (PhD diss., Yale University, 1986), 655.

15. On Sally Maminash (1765–1853), see Sylvester Judd, "Northampton with Westfield," vol. 2, 372 (Judd Manuscript), FL; and also Margaret Bruchac, "The True History of Sally Maminash, 'The Last Indian' in Northampton," unpublished paper, 1996; see also Bruchac, "Native Presence in Nonotuck and Northampton," in Kerry Buckley, ed., *A Place Called Paradise: Culture and Community in Northampton, Massachusetts, 1654–2004* (Amherst: Historic Northampton Museum and Education Center, in association with University of Massachusetts Press, 2004), 18–38. My deep thanks to Marge for sharing her research.

16. EPP memorandum book, October 24 (Assinah's arrival), 1802, and February 7, 1803, *NEHGR*.

17. On Rachel, see EPP memorandum book, March 6, 1808, Box 7 folder 3, PPHFP.

18. EPP memorandum book, April 16, 1815, Box 7 folder 4, PPHFP.

19. EPP to EWPH, April 20, 1815, Box 5 folder 12, PPHFP.

20. EPP to EWPH, April 20, 1815, Box 5 folder 12, PPHFP.

21. EPP memorandum book, April 23, 1815, Box 7 folder 4, PPHFP.

22. EPP to EWPH, May 4, 1815, Box 5 folder 12, PPHFP.

23. Hampshire County Court Records, Inferior Court of Common Pleas, General Sessions of the Peace, May 21, 1771, vol. 10 (1766–1771), 175; and May 15–19, 1787, vol. 14 (1776–1790), 233, Special Collections and University Archives, University of Massachusetts Amherst; and p. 178 herein.

24. Indenture, John Davis to Oliver Smith, May 2, 1759; and Mark Noble to Moses Marsh, February 14, 1760, Boston Overseers of the Poor. My deep thanks to Ruth Herndon for sharing these and other documents from her own research on Boston's poor relief systems.

25. Indenture, Mary Craigie to Nathaniel Phelps, September 19, 1759, Boston Overseers of the Poor.

26. See, e.g., the December 14, 1808, *HG*, which included a notice seeking "a little girl, from eight to twelve years of age. The services expected of her will be light, and her situation will be such as to afford her opportunities for instruction."

27. Indenture between the Overseers of the Poor of the Town of Northampton in the County of Hampshire [and] Elisha Allis of Hatfield, FL. On March 17, 1802, Elizabeth Porter Phelps wrote her daughter-in-law that young Mitte "has spun one run of yarn, two thirds of a days work for a maid." See EPP to EWPH, March 14, 1802, Box 5 folder 4, PPHFP.

28. See EPP memorandum book, March 26, 1769; March 17, 1771; July 10, 1773; May 6, 1787, and November 30, 1794, *NEHGR*; also September 26, 1808, Box 7 folder 3, PPHFP.

29. Izard, "The Ward Family," 72.

30. See Lucius M. Boltwood, "Genealogies of Hadley Families," 7, in Sylvester Judd, *History of Hadley: Including the Early History of Hatfield, South Hadley, Amherst and Granby, Massachusetts* (Springfield, MA: H. R. Huntting, 1905). Ayres remained in the Phelps household until 1773, when she moved to the household of Charles Phelps's tenant, Francis Trainer.

31. CP to EPP, November 7, 1796; and EPP, November 7 and December 4, 1796, and September 16, 1798, Box 4 folder 3, PPHFP; on Pelham, see EPP memorandum book, April 17, 1802, *NEHGR*.

32. Reverend Daniel Huntington, likewise, on a trip "found a girl at humphrey's tavern in Simsbury." When recounting this to her mother, EWPH inserted "white" above, suggesting that she believed she would need to clarify the point, that her mother could be expected to assume otherwise. EWPH to EPP, June 21, 1805, Box 13 folder 9, PPHFP.

33. EPP to EWPH, March 27, 1805, Box 5 folder 7; April 4, 1807, Box 5 folder 9; May 4, 1815, Box 5 folder 12; and November 13, 1810, Box 5 folder 10, PPHFP.

34. EPP to EWPH, January 28, 1796, Box 5 folder 3, PPHFP.

35. The problem of theft was of course a transnational one. See, e.g., Amanda Vickery, "An Englishman's Home Is His Castle? Thresholds, Boundaries and Privacies in the Eighteenth-Century London House," *Past and Present* 199 no. 1 (2008): 147–73; and the work of John Styles, including in particular *The Dress of the People: Everyday Fashion in Eighteenth-Century England* (New Haven, CT: Yale University Press, 2007); and "'Intended as a Terror to the Idle and Profligate': Embezzlement and the Origins of Policing in the Yorkshire Worsted Industry, c. 1750–1777," *Journal of Social History* 31, no. 3 (Spring 1998): 647–69.

36. In time, Marshall married Nathaniel Briggs Jr. and moved to nearby Shutesbury. See EPP memorandum book, September 29, 1793, *NEHGR*; and Massachusetts, Town and Vital Records, 1620–1988, Ancestry.com. She remained friendly with the family and returned for visits in later years.

37. EPP to Sally Parsons Phelps, March 17, 1802, Box 5 folder 15, PPHFP.

38. EPP to EWPH, February 26, 1801, Box 6 folder 1, PPHFP.

39. Dorothy Williams (Hadley) to Mrs. Dorothy Williams (Dalton), June 25, 1795, Williams Family Papers, Box 7 folder 9, Williams Family Papers, PVMA.

40. EPP to EWPH, March 2, 1801, Box 6 folder 1, PPHFP.

41. EWPH to EPP, January 11, 1801, and February 14, 1801, Box 13 folder 5, PPHFP.

42. EPP to Sally Phelps, March 17, 1802, Box 5 folder 15, PPHFP.

43. May 16, 1791, Thaddeus Leavitt diary, 1784–1794, typescript, Kent Memorial Library, Suffield, CT.

44. April 18 and May 17, 1791, Thaddeus Leavitt diary, 1784–1794, typescript, Kent Memorial Library, Suffield, CT.

45. EPP to EWPH, November 4, 1797, Box 5 folder 3, PPHFP.

46. EPP memorandum book, May 18, 1783, and July 13, 1783, *NEHGR*.

47. EWPH to EPP, November 16, 1804, Box 13 folder 8, PPHFP.

48. EWPH to EPP, June 20, 1801, Box 13 folder 5, PPHFP.

49. EWPH to EPP, January 11 and February 14, 1801, Box 13 folder 5, PPHFP.

50. EWPH to EPP, May 27, 1804, Box 13 folder 8, PPHFP.

51. EWPH to EPP, February 17, 1802, Box 13 folder 6, and March 7, 1803, Box 5 folder 5, PPHFP. Here we are reminded too of the balance that determined when she would hire more skilled help: "Today I am making new sleeves to my habit—having worn the old ones entirely out—I shall not go to a mantu maker, for I have sufficient time to do many such things." EWPH to EPP, October 26, 1797, Box 13 folder 4, PPHFP.

52. EWPH to EPP, January 23, 1813, Box 13 folder 12, PPHFP.

53. EWPH to EPP, November 1, 1805, Box 13 folder 9, PPHFP. When Hotchkiss left, they engaged Lucy Palmer, a twelve-year-old whom they paid one shilling six pence per week (EWPH to EPP, December 9, 1805, Box 13 folder 9, PPHFP). This wage seems unusually low, perhaps due to her age and lack of experience. Later Hotchkiss returned, and in March 1807, Huntington again wrote that Hotchkiss was leaving—they needed another woman, and they got one by a "singular Providence": "Barzilla & I took the cutter and started between 9 and 10 in pursuit of a girl, we had heard of several, one very good one." The "very good one" they missed out on hiring by just minutes, and the rest said no. Betsy

and Barzilla returned disheartened at two p.m., and "there I left it." But then, on "Saturday between sundown and dark," to Huntington's enormous surprise and relief, a twenty-year-old African American girl from Milton named Clara, with experience, came and offered her services at spinning or house work. See EWPH to EPP, March 24, 1807, Box 13 folder 11, PPHFP.

54. Sarah Parsons Phelps to EPP, December 23, 1802, Box 11 folder 4, PPHFP.

55. Indeed, some labor agreements at about this time attempted to address the problem of unwanted pregnancies directly. Indentures drafted by Northampton's Overseers of the Poor contain language like that directed at sixteen-year-old Lucretia Clark in 1804: "*Fornication* she shall *not* commit." That this word is underlined, and the only point so emphasized, suggests the urgency of the matter, and perhaps something of Clark's past as well. See the Northampton Town Papers, Overseers of the Poor, "Indentures, 1795–1865," FL.

56. See Laurel Thatcher Ulrich, *A Midwife's Tale: The Life of Martha. Ballard, Based on Her Diary, 1785–1812* (New York: Knopf, 1990); and Sandra Slater, "Sex and Sin: The Historiography of Women, Gender, and Sexuality in Colonial Massachusetts," *Historical Journal of Massachusetts* 41 no. 1 (Winter 2014), 105–35.

57. Cornelia Hughes Dayton, "Taking the Trade: Abortion and Gender Relations in an Eighteenth-Century New England Village, *WMQ*, 3rd ser., 48, no. 1 (January 1991): 19–49.

58. On 1785, see EPP memorandum book, July 17, 1785, *NEHGR*. For more on Converse, see Marla R. Miller, *Rebecca Dickinson: The Independence of a New England Woman* (Boulder, CO: Westview, 2013), 103–8. On capital punishment in Massachusetts, see Alan Rogers, *Murder and the Death Penalty in Massachusetts* (Amherst: University of Massachusetts Press, 2008); and Brian J. Rizzo, "'Certainly a Man May Quibble For His Life': Public Execution and Capital Punishment in Massachusetts," *Historical Journal of Massachusetts* 38, no. 2 (Fall 2010): 120–33.

59. Daniel Scott Smith and Michael S. Hindus, noting the sharp rise in premarital pregnancy in the late eighteenth century, suggest that young men and women used pregnancy as a strategy to force parents to consent to early marriages; see "Premarital Pregnancy in America, 1640–1971: An Overview and Interpretation," *Journal of Interdisciplinary History* 5 (1974–1975): 537–70. Another good possibility is that different values prevailed among the working classes.

60. EPP to EWPH, November 12, 1807, Box 5 folder 9, PPHFP.

61. EPP memorandum book, December 11, 1791, *NEHGR*. If West was the name of her father, then it seems likely that he was one of the sons of Daniel and Mary Cook West, probably Dan Jr. (b. 1772), who lived near the Boston road on Hadley's south end. Dan Jr. was nineteen and Susanna seventeen when the baby was born. Interestingly, this was not the first time that an unexpected pregnancy shaped circumstances for the family; when Dan Jr. himself was born, Elizabeth Porter Phelps recorded in her memorandum book that "Dan West and his wife [Mary Cook West] made public confession for the sin of fornication—she went hardly seven months . . ." See EPP memorandum book, May 10, 1772, *NEHGR*.

62. EPP memorandum book, March 30, 1793, and September 14, 1794, *NEHGR*.

63. EPP September 28, 1794, *NEHGR*; see also Hopkins, "Baptisms since the Burning of My House," which records on that date the baptism of "Submit West in the right of Charles Phelps and his wife," First Church, Hadley, MA.

64. EPP to EWPH, August 20, 1794, Box 5 folder 3, PPHFP.

65. EPP to EWPH, August 29, 1802, Box 5 folder 4, PPHFP.

66. EPP memorandum book, June 20, 1801, *NEHGR*.

67. EPP to EWPH, December 20, 1802, Box 5 folder 4, PPHFP.

68. EPP memorandum book, November 25, 1804, *NEHGR*.

69. See also Kirsten Fischer, *Suspect Relations: Sex, Race and Resistance in Colonial North America* (Ithaca, NY: Cornell University Press, 2002), chapter 3.

70. EPP to EWPH, February 7, 1801, Box 5 folder 3, PPHFP.

71. EPP (Litchfield) to CP, April 24, 1802, Box 5 folder 13, PPHFP. For the intriguing suggestion that Charles Phelps himself may have had some sort of relationship with a servant, see Elizabeth Pendergast Carlisle, *Earthbound and Heavenbent: Elizabeth Porter Phelps and Life at Forty Acres (1747–1817)* (New York: Scribner, 2004), 150–53.

72. EPP to EWPH, March 13, 1802, Box 5 folder 4, PPHFP.

73. EPP to Sarah Parsons Phelps, March 17, 1802, Box 5 folder 15, PPHFP.

74. EPP to Sarah Parsons Phelps, March 17, 1802, Box 5 folder 15, PPHFP.

75. EWPH to EPP, March 15, 1802, Box 13 folder 6, PPHFP.

76. EWPH to EPP, January 6, 1804, Box 5 folder 8, PPHFP.

77. EWPH to EPP, January 6, 1804, Box 5 folder 8, PPHFP. On his arrival, see EPP memorandum book, April 3, 1791, *NEHGR*.

78. Persis Morse (or Marsh, as she is also called) arrived October 12, 1803. See EPP memorandum book, December 6, 1812, Box 7 folder 4, PPFHP.

79. EPP memorandum book, April 3, 1791, *NEHGR*. She appears to have remarried; on October 16, 1796, Phelps records having "met Rubens mother & husband Mr Winchester and child."

80. EPP to EWPH, February 4, 1805, Box 5 folder 7, PPHFP.

81. EPP to EWPH, March 4, 1805, Box 5 folder 7, PPHFP.

82. EPP to EWPH, March 27, 1805, Box 5 folder 7, PPHFP.

83. EPP to EWPH, July 6, 1805, Box 5 folder 7, PPHFP.

84. EPP to EWPH, July 6, 1805, Box 5 folder 7, PPHFP.

85. For recent scholarship, see, e.g., Carole Shammas, "Child Labor and Schooling in Late Eighteenth-Century New England: One Boy's Account," *WMQ* 70, no. 3 (July 2013): 539–58; and Barry Levy, *Town Born: The Political Economy of New England from Its Founding to the Revolution* (Philadelphia: University of Pennsylvania Press, 2009).

86. EPP to EWPH, July 6, 1805, Box 5 folder 7, PPHFP.

87. EPP to EWPH, August 28, 1805, Box 5 folder 7, PPHFP.

88. EPP to EWPH, August 28, 1805, Box 5 folder 7, PPHFP.

89. EPP to EWPH, November 19, 1806, Box 5 folder 8, PPHFP.

90. EPP to EWPH, April 4, 1807, Box 5 folder 9, PPHFP.

91. EPP to EWPH, April 4, 1807, Box 5 folder 9, PPHFP.

92. EPP to Sarah Parsons Phelps, November 4, 1807, Box 5 folder 15, PPHFP.

93. EPP memorandum book, December 6, 1807, Box 7 folder 3, PPHFP.

94. EPP memorandum book, March 6, 1808, Box 7 folder 3, PPHFP.

95. EPP to EWPH, June 26, 1808, Box 5 folder 9, PPHFP.

96. EPP memorandum book, July 16, 1809, Box 7 folder 3, PPHFP.

97. EPP to EWPH, November 28, 1809, Box 5 folder 9, PPHFP.

98. EPP memorandum book, July 16, 1809, Box 7 folder 3, PPHFP.

99. Mary Turner indenture, Box 171 (oversize), folder 13, PPHFP.

100. Records of the Overseers of the Poor, May 21, 1768, BPL; see n. 24 above.

101. Pelham Vital Records. I am grateful to local historian Robert Lord Keyes for locating this and other critical information concerning Pelham's Polly Randall.

102. Massachusetts, Town and Vital Records, 1620–1988, Ancestry.com.

103. Pelham Town Meetings, 1784–1815, minutes, 313, June 5, 1809.

104. Pelham Town Meetings, 1784–1815, minutes, 312, April 3, 1809.

105. Massachusetts Vital Records, 1600s–1800s (Broderbund, 2000). For more on this extended family, see Rachel Hope Cleves, *Charity and Sylvia: A Same-Sex Marriage in Early America* (New York: Oxford University Press, 2014).

106. EPP memorandum book, July 29, 1810, Box 7 folder 3, PPHFP. Charity's daughter Huldah moved with her mother to Pelham. In 1800 she was the head of her own household, which included a boy under ten (possibly Silas), a girl between ten and sixteen, two women between sixteen and twenty-six (possibly Huldah and Polly), and two females between twenty-six and forty-five (one of whom may have been her mother, Charity Burr). On occasion, she rode down to the valley town to visit Polly in her workplace. Several of her aunt's children had settled in the area, so she had cousins to look to for aid and companionship. See, e.g., EPP memorandum book, August 12, 1810, Box 7 folder 3, PPHFP.

107. EPP memorandum book, July 1, 1810, and August 12, 1810, Box 7 folder 3, PPHFP.

108. EPP memorandum book, December 3, 10, 17, and 31, 1809, March 3, 10, 11, and 25, 1809, Box 7 folder 3, PPHFP.

109. EPP to EWPH, March 28, 1810, Box 5 folder 15, PPHFP.

110. EPP to EWPH, March 28, 1810, Box 5 folder 15, PPHFP.

111. EPP to EWPH, December 19, 1810, Box 5 folder 10, PPHFP.

112. Several books explore the advent of palm leaf to rural New England and its consequences for young working women, including Thomas Dublin, *Transforming Women's Work: New England Lives in the Industrial Revolution* (Ithaca, NY: Cornell University Press, 1994), and Christopher Clark, *The Roots of Rural Capitalism: Western Massachusetts, 1780–1860* (Ithaca, NY: Cornell University Press, 1990). C. O. Parmenter's *History of Pelham* (Amherst, MA: Carpenter and Morehouse, 1898)—while revealing late nineteenth-century inclinations to reframe this labor as leisure—explains:

> Early in this century the braiding or plaiting of split straw braid was taken up by the women. About the middle of June a rye field was selected where the growth was thick and vigorous, which was usually on new land from which the wood had been cut the year previous, and the green rank growth of rye was cut and tied in small bundles. These bundles were placed in hot water for a short time and then spread upon the ground, and in a few days was bleached nearly white. This straw was cut into lengths at the joints, submitted to the fumes of burning brimstone, and the white supple straw was split in narrow splints and the women plaited them into braids of various kinds which was gathered by dealers and sold for making ladies bonnets, it being paid for by the yard. Many women occupied their spare time from domestic duties in plaiting this domestic braid. (452–53)

113. Caroline Sloat, "'A Great Help to Many Families': Straw Braiding in Massachusetts before 1825," in Benes and Benes, *House and Home*, 89–100.

114. Jason Mixter day books, Mixter-Knight Collection, Baker Library, Harvard Business School, cited in Sloat, "'A Great Help to Many Families,'" 91.

115. EPP memorandum book, July 17, 1796, *NEHGR*.

116. Store order, August 13, 1810, William Porter Papers, Box C, OSV.

117. CP account book, 1805–1815, preserved among the papers of his son Charles Porter Phelps (vol. 1 of 5), Phelps Family Account Books, 1805–1858, Baker Library, Harvard Business School.

118. Pelham Town Meetings, 1784–1815, minutes, 324, April 2, 1810.

119. Pelham Town Meetings, 1784–1815, minutes, 325, April 2, 1810.

120. Pelham Town Meetings, 1784–1815, minutes, 336, April 1, 1811.

121. Pelham Town Meetings, 1784–1815, minutes, 324, April 2, 1810.

122. Pelham Town Meetings, 1784–1815, minutes, 351, March 12, 1812.

123. EPP to EWPH, January 4, 1802, Box 5 folder 4, PPHFP.

124. EPP memorandum book, December 29, 1805, Box 7 folder 3, PPHFP.

125. EPP memorandum book, November 29, 1806, Box 7 folder 3, PPHFP.

126. EPP memorandum book, December 7, 1806, Box 7 folder 3, PPHFP.

127. See Karen Parsons, "We Owe Something More Than Prayers," *New England Silver and Silversmithing, 1620–1815* (Boston: Colonial Society of Massachusetts, 2001), 89–112, 96.

128. EPP memorandum book, July 31, 1808, February 5, 1809, Box 7 folder 3, PPHFP.

129. EPP memorandum book, October 29, 1809, Box 7 folder 3, PPHFP.

130. *Vital Records of Conway, Massachusetts to the Year 1850* (Boston, 1943), 25, lists the 1805 birth of Erminia and the 1807 birth of Robert Goodhu Harper.

131. EPP memorandum book, January 28, 1810, Box 7 folder 3, PPHFP.

132. EPP memorandum book, February 11, 1810, Box 7 folder 3, PPHFP.

133. For discussion of a Fall 1803 bill associated with the completion of Cooley's term of service, see Marla R. Miller, *The Needle's Eye: Women and Work in the Age of Revolution* (Amherst: University of Massachusetts Press, 2006), 122.

134. See Amber D. Moulton, *The Fight for Interracial Marriage Rights in Antebellum Massachusetts* (Cambridge: Harvard University Press, 2015); see also Emily Blanck, *Tyrannicide: Forging an American Law of Slavery in Revolutionary South Carolina and Massachusetts* (Athens: University of Georgia, 2014), 142. Louis Rouchames, "Race, Marriage and Abolition in Massachusetts," *The Journal of Negro History* 40, no. 3 (July 1955): 250–73; and Carlisle, *Earthbound and Heavenbent*, 219.

135. Sarah Parsons Phelps (Boston) to EPP, February 16, 1810, Box 11 folder 5, PPHFP. Cooley seems also to be the same man Elizabeth Porter Phelps refers to in an October 14, 1804, memorandum book entry as "Prince, a Negro who lives in a house near here" who "had a child buried" that day.

136. See Carlisle, *Earthbound and Heavenbent*, 218.

137. EPP memorandum book, February 18, 1810, Box 7 folder 3, PPHFP. The child is named in the Hadley Overseers of the Poor treasurer's ledger, 1807–1852, June 29, 1813, HHS.

138. EPP memorandum book, February 25, 1810, Box 7 folder 3, PPHFP.

139. Philena's support cost the town $39.00 that year, and another $9.22 the next. For Blodgett, see Hadley Overseers of the Poor treasurer's ledger, 1807–1852, April 15, 1811, and February 19, 1812, HHS; for Smith, see April 2, 1812. Possibly this was the John Conable who in December 1810 had been published to Hadley's Abigail Congdon. On this family, see *Edwards J. Connable and John B. Newcombe, Genealogical Memoir of the Cunnabell, Conable or Connable Family, John Cunnabell of London, England, and Boston, Massachusetts, and His Descendants, 1650–1886* (Jackson, MI: Daily Citizen Book Printing House, 1886), 54.

140. EPP memorandum book, August 25, 1816, Box 7 folder 4, PPHFP.

141. EPP memorandum book, April 13, 1817, Box 7 folder 4, PPHFP.

142. Elizabeth Carlisle, in *Earthbound and Heavenbent*, 332, n. 36, notes that Arria Huntington's 1891 book *Under a Colonial Rooftree* reports that Mitte in time made a "'respectable marriage,' had children and grandchildren and continued working for the family," though Carlisle could locate no archival evidence to confirm the assertion. Although no record of a marriage has been located, there is some hint (that is, an 1864 death record for a Submit West Wright) that she may have eventually formed a union with Paul Wright, the North Hadley son of Paul Wright and Eunice Alexander, whose struggle with alcohol is considered in chapter 6; see "Massachusetts Vital Records, 1911–1915," New England Historic Genealogical Society, Boston. I have been unable to find any further documentation of Philina Cooley.

143. "Two-in-One Book," Hampshire County House of Correction, 1784–1830, FL.

144. Thomas Dwight, Boston, February 16, 1797, to Mrs. Hannah Dwight, Springfield, Dwight-Howard papers, MHS.

145. On outwork in the clothing trades, see Miller, *Needle's Eye,* 195–99; and Clark, *Roots of Rural Capitalism*, 185–89. Kathleen M. Brown discusses the cultural work of cleanliness in *Foul Bodies: Cleanliness in Early America* (New Haven, CT: Yale University Press, 2009).

146. *HG,* November 20, 1793.

147. EWPH to EPP, June 20 and July 22, 1801, Box 13 folder 5, PPHFP.

148. EWPH to EPP, September 27, 1801, Box 13 folder 5, PPHFP. On another occasion, Betsy wrote her mother that her hired girl "went off this morning, her conduct has been very bad and she needs somebody to keep her at work so much that we could not afford to give her more than 3/6—she said she could get a dollar and is gone. Candace Mr Allen's girl will come but she must have 5/ . . ." EWPH to EPP, March 20, 1805, Box 13 folder 9, PPHFP.

Chapter 5 • Making Cloth

1. Sylvester Judd, *History of Hadley: Including the Early History of Hatfield, South Hadley, Amherst and Granby, Massachusetts* (Springfield, MA: H. R. Huntting, 1905), 359. Christopher Clark reflects on Judd's ambivalence about economic change in *The Roots of Rural Capitalism: Western Massachusetts, 1780–1860* (Ithaca, NY: Cornell University Press, 1990), 3–7; Laurel Thatcher Ulrich traces the flowering of such nostalgia in *The Age of Homespun: Objects and Stories in the Creation of an American Myth* (New York: Knopf, 2009).

2. Sylvester Judd, "Miscellaneous," vol. 10, 187 (Judd Manuscript), FL.

3. Susan M. Ouellette, "All Hands Are Enjoined to Spin: Textile Production in Seventeenth-Century Massachusetts" (PhD diss., University of Massachusetts Amherst, 1996), v.

4. Ouellette, "All Hands," 136.

5. The literature here is large; key works include Adrienne Hood, *The Weaver's Craft: Cloth, Commerce, and Industry in Early Pennsylvania* (Philadelphia: University of Pennsylvania Press, 2003); Paul E. Rivard, *A New Order of Things: How the Textile Industry Transformed New England* (Hanover, NH: University Press of New England, 2002); Gail Fowler Mohanty, *Labor and Laborers of the Loom: Mechanization and Handloom Weavers*

1780–1840 (New York: Routledge, 2006); Ouellette, "All Hands"; and Ulrich, *Age of Homespun*.

6. Rabbit Goody addressed this topic in her workshop "Truth or Myth? Finding Historic Fabrics in Quilts, 1640–1860," American Quilt Study Group Annual Seminar, Manchester, New Hampshire, October 20, 2017. My thanks to Rabbit for sharing her deep knowledge of this subject with me in that setting and others. On the concept of fibersheds as environmental, economic, and cultural systems as developed by Rebecca Burgess, see http://www.fibershed.com/about/.

7. Rivard, *New Order of Things,* 191. On spinning and cloth production in Europe in this period, see Gay L. Gullickson, *Spinners and Weavers of Auffay: Rural Industry and the Sexual Division of Labor in a French Village, 1750–1850* (Cambridge: Cambridge University Press, 1986); Elise Van Nederveen Meerkerk, "Market Wage or Discrimination? The Remuneration of Male and Female Wool Spinners in the Seventeenth-Century Dutch Republic," *The Economic History Review,* n.s., 63, no. 1 (February 2010): 165–86; Arnošt Klíma, "The Role of Rural Domestic Industry in Bohemia in the Eighteenth Century," *The Economic History Review,* n.s., 27, no. 1 (February 1974): 48–56. Especially relevant here is Deborah M. Valenze, *The First Industrial Woman* (New York: Oxford University Press, 1995); and Craig Muldrew, "'Th'ancient Distaff' and 'Whirling Spindle': Measuring the Contribution of Spinning to Household Earnings and the National Economy in England, 1550–1770," *The Economic History Review* 65, no. 2 (May 2012): 498–526. Other key scholarship on the industrialization of the textile industry includes Merritt Roe Smith and Robert Martello, "Taking Stock of the Industrial Revolution in America," in Jeff Horn, Leonard N. Rosenband, and Merritt Roe Smith, eds., *Reconceptualizing the Industrial Revolution* (Cambridge: MIT Press, 2010), 169–200.

8. Clark, *Roots of Rural Capitalism,* 60, 103.

9. See Clark, *Roots of Rural Capitalism;* Laurel Thatcher Ulrich, "Wheels, Looms, and the Gender Division of Labor in Eighteenth-Century New England," *WMQ* 55, no. 1 (January 1998): 3–38, and *Age of Homespun,* especially chapters 2, 8, and 9.

10. As Ulrich writes, "To understand fully New England's peculiar arrangement of wheels and looms, more work needs to be done on artisan weaving in the early colonial period and later, on fulling and dyeing, and on the manufacture of wheels, looms, reeds, shuttles, spools, and other equipment." Ulrich, "Wheels, Looms," 35.

11. See Florence Montgomery, *Textiles in America, 1650–1870,* reprinted with a foreword by Linda Eaton (New York: Norton, 2007).

12. On the nature of Connecticut Valley wardrobes in the eighteenth century, see Marla R. Miller, *The Needle's Eye: Women and Work in the Age of Revolution* (Amherst, University of Massachusetts Press, 2006), chapter 1.

13. John Dickinson inventory, July 1763, Box 47 no. 24, HCMRP. On the proportion of references to "homemade" articles in New England wardrobes based on a large study of probate inventories, see Miller, *Needle's Eye,* 35.

14. Samuel Marsh Inventory, August 11, 1761, Box 94 no. 14, HCMRP.

15. Ulrich tracks the scholarly "devaluing of domestic production" in "Wheels, Looms," 3–5; see also her book-length inquiry into these subjects, *Age of Homespun.* Important work by Carole Shammas on cloth consumption includes "How Self-Sufficient Was Early America?," *Journal of Interdisciplinary History* 13 (1982): 247–72; and "Anglo-American

Consumption from 1550–1800," in John Brewer and Roy Porter, eds., *Consumption and the World of Goods* (London: Routledge, 1993), 177–205.

16. See Jan de Vries, *The Industrious Revolution: Consumer Behavior and the Household Economy, 1650 to the Present* (Cambridge: Cambridge University Press, 2008); and Clark, *Roots of Rural Capitalism.*

17. See Jane C. Nylander, "Textiles, Clothing and Needlework," in Gerald W. R. Ward and William N. Hosley Jr., eds., *The Great River: Art and Society of the Connecticut Valley, 1635–1820* (Hartford, CT: Wadsworth Atheneum, 1985), 373.

18. See Ulrich, "Wheels, Looms"; and Shammas, "How Self-Sufficient Was Early America?"

19. In 1774, the percentage of Hampshire County households with linen and woolen wheels as well as a loom, sheep, and flax was 14.8; see Shammas, "How Self-Sufficient Was Early America?," table 2.

20. David Smith inventory, March 3, 1772, Box 132 no. 43, HCMRP.

21. These figures are derived from the valuations attached to 104 Hadley heads of household in Judd, *Hadley*, 423.

22. Eliakim Smith inventory, February 4, 1777, Box 134 no. 19, HCMRP; and Judd, *Hadley*, 562. Indeed, at the same time, a mere 5 percent of Worcester County families owned both linen and woolen wheels as well as a loom, sheep, and flax; while still farther east in Suffolk County (which included Boston and its environs), less than a third of households owned any spinning wheel, and just 2.1 percent owned wheels to process both linen and wool, as well as raw materials to draw from and a loom on which to weave the yarn produced. Shammas, "How Self-Sufficient Was Early America?," table 2.

23. Shammas, "How Self-Sufficient Was Early America?," 257, 254.

24. On weaving, see EPP memorandum book, April 3, 1774, October 9, 1774, April 9, 1775, October 13, 1776, April 13, 1777, May 24, 1778, and December 10, 1780, *NEHGR.*

25. EPP memorandum book, August 3, 1783, *NEHGR*; and April 9, 1769, and August 19, 1770, *NEHGR.* The hired man "Rolf" may have been one of Marcy Rolf's children. Boltwood's Hadley genealogies mention a Benjamin Raulf, whose child Azubah was born April 7, 1802; see Judd, *Hadley*, 116.

26. See, e.g., Ebenezer Pomeroy (1723–1800) account book, 1756–1797, private collection (also available on microfilm at the University of Massachusetts Amherst), 11.

27. See, e.g., Ebenezer Pomeroy account book, 1756–1797, 15, 34.

28. Ebenezer Pomeroy account book, November 1764, 55.

29. Ebenezer Pomeroy account book, November 1764, 55. The accounts for what each girl received for her setting-out are contained at the back of the volume, and are probably related to the settling of Pomeroy's account at the time of his death.

30. Useful introductions to these processes include Hood, *Weaver's Craft*, chapters 3–4; and Ulrich, *Age of Homespun*, 84–92.

31. To put that another way, 32 percent of the townspeople owned 64 percent of the sheep, while another 37 percent kept none. Nancy M. Guyton, "Domestic Production of Cloth in the Town of Hadley, 1760–1800" (unpublished seminar paper, Historic Deerfield, 1981), a study based on evidence from thirty-one probate inventories and Massachusetts tax valuation lists for 1771, 1781, and 1786.

32. Guyton, "Domestic Production," appendix B.

33. Guyton, "Domestic Production," 9.

34. Susan M. Ouellette, "Divine Providence and Collective Endeavor: Sheep Production in Early Massachusetts," *NEQ* 69, no. 3 (1996): 355–80, especially 370.

35. Ouellette, "Divine Providence," 374.

36. Asa Ellis Jr., *The Country Dyer's Assistant* (Brookfield, MA: Merriam, 1798), 117; and Ouellette, "All Hands," 109.

37. Shammas, "How Self-Sufficient Was Early America?," 254.

38. Robert J. Taylor, *Western Massachusetts in the Revolution* (Providence, RI: Brown University Press, 1954; reprint, 1967), 5.

39. On patterns of planting, growing, and preparing flax, see the entry "Flax" in William Bridgwater and Seymour Kurtz, eds., *The Columbia Encyclopedia*, 3rd ed. (New York: Columbia University Press, 1964), 728.

40. *HG*, March 14, 1787.

41. Judd, *Hadley*, 392; see also Ulrich, *Age of Homespun*, 282–85.

42. Olive Cleveland Clark, "Recollections of Olive Cleveland Clark," in Phyllis B. Deming, comp., *A History of Williamsburg in Massachusetts* (Northampton, MA: Hampshire Bookshop, 1946), 57.

43. As quoted in Clark, *Roots of Rural Capitalism*, 97.

44. EPP to SPP, March 17, 1802, Box 5 folder 15, PPHFP. The amount of yarn in a run varied; see Ulrich, *Age of Homespun*, 188–89. Josiah Howard *Temple and George Sheldon's History of Northfield, Massachusetts* (Albany, NY: J. Munsell, 1875), 161, reports that one run of yarn "consisted of twenty knots, a knot was composed of forty threads, and a thread was seventy-four inches in length, or once round the reel." See also Susan McAdoo, "Stephen Brownson's Cotton Manufactory, Farmington Connecticut," in Rabbitt Goody, ed., *Proceedings of the Textile History Forum* (Cherry Valley, NY: Textile History Forum, 2018), 73–86.

45. Mary Jo Maynes, "Gender, Labor, and Globalization in Historical Perspective: European Spinsters in the International Textile Industry, 1750–1900," *Journal of Women's History* 15, no. 4 (Winter 2004): 47–66. Maynes writes: "Protoindustrial textile production relied on the labor of women and girls of age twelve or so and upwards, but it was young unmarried women as a demographic group whose efforts were most fully concentrated upon this work" (54). See also Ouellette, "All Hands," 109.

46. EPP to EWPH, December 14, 1812, Box 5 folder 11, PPHFP. The following month, when the girls were visiting the Huntington grandparents in Connecticut, Dan wrote Elizabeth, wanting to know if they were homesick, and also "how much you have spun—how much you spin in a day, how much Bethia has spun." See Dan Huntington to Elizabeth and Bethiah Huntington, January 7, 1813, Box 15 folder 7, PPHFP.

47. Moses Porter inventory, March 8, 1756, Box 177 no. 19, HCMRP. A flax wheel (accession number W023), a clock reel (W069), and two wool wheels (W070 and W071) survive in the collections of the Porter-Phelps-Huntington Museum, though whether they are the objects listed in Moses Porter's inventory is at present unknown. Also surviving is a flax breaker (W062), a hetchel (M216), two wool combs (W016.A&B), and a wool winder (W047). My thanks to Susan Lisk for this information from the collections inventory.

48. Aaron Goodrich inventory, July 4, 1769, Box 61 no. 50, HCMRP; and Josiah Dickinson, January 27, 1774, Box 47 no. 53, HCMRP.

49. Shammas, "How Self-Sufficient Was Early America?," table 2. Shammas drew from the inventories collected in Alice Hanson Jones's landmark study, *American Colonial*

Wealth: Documents and Methods, 2nd ed. (New York: Arno Press, 1977), including all the inventories proved in the Suffolk, Essex, Plymouth, Hampshire, and Worcester County Registries of Probate in the year 1774, but that data set includes only one inventory from Hadley, of Josiah Dickinson (above).

50. Hadley inventories, 1760–1790, in "The probate records for Hampshire County, 1660–1820, in the Hampshire County Registry of Probate, Northampton, Mass" [microform] (Holyoke, MA: New England Archives Center for the Connecticut Valley Historical Museum, Springfield, MA, n.d.) vols. 9–14. I say "about half" because some do not specifically describe the wheel, though it appears from context to be a flax wheel.

51. Samuel Gaylord Jr. account book (1763–1793), Memorial Libraries, Deerfield, MA: see Coleman Cooke, February 10, 1771; Enos Nash, June 23, 1776, June 6, 1779, March 31, 1786; and Daniel Marsh, December 12, 1788. My thanks to Sharon Mehrman for this and the information below from Gaylord's accounts.

52. Gaylord Jr. account book; see Elisha Cooke, January 15, 1768; Elijah "Yommans," February 13, 1781; and Ralph Way, March 5, 1781.

53. Gaylord Jr. account book; for treadles, see Ebenezer Ellis, April 14, 1788; and Aaron Cooke, February 13, 1776.

54. The Samuel Gaylord Jr. account book indicates that Gaylord recorded having made spinning wheels only once, for Elijah "Yommans," February 13, 1781.

55. Theodore Gregson Huntington, "Sketches of Family and Life in Hadley," 63, Box 21 folder 5, PPHFP. My thanks to Susan Lisk for providing dimensions of these objects in the Porter-Phelps-Huntington Collections. For the walking estimate, I am grateful to Peggy Hart (based on information provided by Susan Conover); email to author, April 3, 2017. For more on the history of wool, see Hart's *Wool: Unraveling an American Story of Artisans and Innovation* (Atglen, PA: Schiffer, 2017).

56. Judd, "Hadley," vol. 3, 220; and Josiah H. Temple, *History of the Town of Whately, Mass.* (Boston: T. R. Marvin & Son, 1872), 71–72.

57. On Sally Maminash (1765–1853), see Judd, "Northampton with Westfield," vol. 2, 372; and also Marge Bruchac, "The True History of Sally Maminash, 'The Last Indian' in Northampton," unpublished paper, 1996; see also Bruchac, "Native Presence in Nonotuck and Northampton," in Kerry Buckley, ed., *A Place Called Paradise: Culture and Community in Northampton, Massachusetts, 1654–2004* (Amherst: Historic Northampton Museum and Education Center, in association with University of Massachusetts Press, 2004), 18–38. For more on the Maminash family, see Margaret M. Bruchac, "Historical Erasure and Cultural Recovery: Indigenous People in the Connecticut River Valley" (PhD diss., University of Massachusetts Amherst, 2007). For the abandoned wife, see Judd, "Northampton," vol. 1, 492.

58. EPP memorandum book, September 11, 1768, *NEHGR*.

59. EPP memorandum book, September 18, 1768, *NEHGR*. This story is also recounted in Ulrich, *Age of Homespun*, 203–4; and Carlisle, *Earthbound and Heavenbent*, 33–35.

60. EPP memorandum book, September 11, 18, and 25, and October 2, 1768, *NEHGR*.

61. EPP memorandum book, September 11, 1768, *NEHGR*. Laurel Ulrich also discusses the incident in *Age of Homespun*, 202.

62. EPP memorandum book, January 25 and February 22, 1767, *NEHGR*.

63. Massachusetts Supreme Judicial Court, Case Papers 15747, Massachusetts State Archive, as discussed in Ulrich, *Age of Homespun*, 202.

64. EPP to EWPH, December 6, 1805, Box 5 folder 7, PPHFP.

65. See Clark, *Roots of Rural Capitalism*, 97.

66. In the mid-Atlantic colonies, it would remain work most appropriately performed by men. See Hood, *Weaver's Craft*. On weaving in seventeenth-century Massachusetts, see Ouellette, "All Hands," 118–133; and Ulrich, "Wheels, Looms."

67. Judd, *Hadley*, 386.

68. Samuel Wright inventory, June 6, 1793, Box 165 no. 44, HCMRP.

69. Judd, *Hadley*, 387.

70. See Judd, *Hadley*, 395, 430–31.

71. By the time the Revolution erupted, Gaylord's onetime apprentice Aaron Wright "wove most of the worsted cloth, called Huckabuck, for cloaks, etc." Judd, "Northampton," vol. 1, 492. For another local ledger that documents the comparative value of woven cloth, see the account book (1763–1827) of Amherst/Hadley resident Nathaniel Dickinson, in the collections of the Jones Library, Amherst, MA.

72. Goody, "Truth or Myth?"

73. Goody, "Truth or Myth?"

74. A helpful description of eighteenth-century New England looms is found in Ulrich, *Age of Homespun*, 92–93.

75. As Ulrich has proposed, "neighborhood exchanges between skilled weavers and their neighbors were essential in a production system without apprentices." Ulrich, "Wheels, Looms," 17.

76. Ulrich, "Wheels, Looms," 10, 12. By 1773, she adds, "even the wealthy Elizabeth Porter Phelps of Hadley, Massachusetts, could write that her husband had 'brought a Girl here for a Weaver.'"

77. Ulrich, *Age of Homespun*, 103.

78. Ulrich, "Wheels, Looms," 10.

79. Guyton, "Domestic Production," 10, and appendix B. Guyton also finds overall wool production appears to have dropped 26 percent between 1771 and 1786, though the cause of this decline remains unclear. Guyton, "Domestic Production," appendix B.

80. See EPP memorandum book, November 27, 1774, April 2 and 9, 1775.

81. Frances Newton inventory, July 25, 1781, Box 105 no. 20, HCMRP. On this family's work in tailoring, see Miller, *Needle's Eye*, chapter 4.

82. EPP memorandum book, June 21, 1778, *NEHGR*. Newton's birth year is given as "about 1761" in Ermina Newton Leonard, comp., *Newton Genealogy: Genealogical, Biographical, Historical* (New Haven, CT: Tuttle, Morehouse and Taylor, 1915), 81.

83. EPP memorandum book, June 14, 1778, *NEHGR*. On overshot, see Ulrich, *Age of Homespun*, 292–93.

84. My thanks to Mary Sherman Lycan for sharing with me her research on New England weaving, as well as her own experience in the weaving of overshot; see also her paper "'What on Earth Are You Going to Do with All This Yarn?' Outwork Weavers in Eastern Connecticut, 1810–1820," in Goody, *Proceedings of the Textile History Forum, 2018*, 87–104.

85. See, e.g., EPP memorandum book, April 9, 1796, April 3 and October 9, 1774, April 9, 1775; October 1, 1776; April 13 and November 2, 1777, *NEHGR*.

86. See, e.g., EPP memorandum book, April 3 and 24, 1774, and October 9 and 30, 1774, *NEHGR*.

87. On Clark, see EPP memorandum book, November 2 and 30, 1777, NEHGR.

88. EPP memorandum book, April 24, 1774, *NEHGR*; and Edwin Wilton Carpenter and Charles Frederick Morehouse, *History of the Town of Amherst* (Amherst, MA: Press of Carpenter & Morehouse, 1896), 32–33, 46.

89. Carpenter and Morehouse, *History of the Town of Amherst*, 28, 20. Pomeroy wove for the Phelps household before her marriage to Amos Nash, which occurred between October 1775 and January 1779; see EPP memorandum book, October 1, 1775, and January 17, 1779, *NEHGR*. Given that the Phelps family welcomed weaver Peggy Clark in Fall 1777, it seems likely that Pomeroy wed before this date; see EPP memorandum book, November 2, 1777, *NEHGR*.

90. The fabric set up by Pierce appears then to have been woven by Betty Newton. On Pierce and Newton, see EPP memorandum book, June 14, 1778, *NEHGR*. In the 1780s, in a pinch Phelps turned to a neighbor, Lydia Allen Hibbard; see EPP memorandum book, August 12 and October 7, 1781, *NEHGR*.

91. EPP memorandum book, December 10, 1780, July 8 and November 11, 1781; May 5, November 3, and December 15, 1782, *NEHGR*. Diademia Ingraham has not been identified; it also may be that "Lodema" is a correction or a nickname for "Diademia," which occurs only once in Phelps's records.

92. Lucy Marshall is listed as "of Amherst" when she and Shutebsury's Nathaniel Briggs Jr. published their intent to wed on October 21, 1792; see "Marriage Intentions," Shutesbury Vital Records, 14. EPP references her marriage in her memorandum book, September 29, 1793, *NEHGR*.

93. See EPP memorandum book, April 3, 1783, July 12, 1789, and December 11, 1791, *NEHGR*.

94. EPP memorandum book, April 13, 1783, *NEHGR*.

95. EPP memorandum book, July 6 and 20, 1783, July 4, 1784, *NEHGR*.

96. EPP memorandum book, September 27, 1784, *NEHGR*.

97. EPP memorandum book, January 16, 1785, *NEHGR*.

98. EPP memorandum book, July 24, 1785, *NEHGR*.

99. See, e.g., EPP memorandum book, March 7, 1790, April 26, 1790, *NEHGR*.

100. EPP memorandum book, November 4, 1787, *NEHGR*.

101. EPP memorandum book, November 4, 1787, May 13, 1787, *NEHGR*.

102. Shammas, "How Self-Sufficient Was Early America?," 254.

103. Adrienne St. Pierre, "Seeking Clues to Early American Wool Clothing in Fulling Mill Account Books," paper presented at the conference History Next to the Skin, a joint conference of the Association for Living History, Farm and Agricultural Museums and the Connecticut Historical Society, March 2003, Hartford, CT. See also Ouellette, "All Hands," 163–67; and Eliza West, "Fulling Mills, Woolen Finishing, and Changing Systems of Cloth Production on the Brandywine, 1789–1823" in Goody, *Proceedings of the Textile History Forum*, 105–20.

104. St. Pierre, "Fulling Mill Account Books."

105. Hood, *Weaver's Craft*, 107.

106. Hood, *Weaver's Craft*, 107.

107. Hood, *Weaver's Craft*, 107–8. For a wonderful description of a dye house, dyeing processes, and the work of fullers in central Massachusetts, see Ellis, *The Country Dyer's Assistant*.

108. See Hood, *The Weaver's Craft*, 107; and St. Pierre, "Fulling Mill Account Books."

109. Hood, *The Weaver's Craft*, 108–9.

110. EPP memorandum book, August 24, 1783, *NEHGR*.

111. Barry Levy, *Town Born: The Political Economy of New England from Its Founding to the Revolution* (Philadelphia: University of Pennsylvania Press, 2009), 144–46; and St. Pierre, "Fulling Mill Account Books."

112. For more on Joseph Williams's account book, see Clark, *Roots of Rural Capitalism*, 177.

113. Judd, *Hadley*, 385–86.

114. Edmund Janes Cleveland, *Genealogy of the Cleveland and Cleaveland Families* (Hartford, CT: Case, Lockwood & Brainard, 1899), 68.

115. See Cleveland, *Genealogy*, 130; Lucius M. Boltwood, "Genealogies of Hadley Families," in Judd, *Hadley*, 33; and *Vital Records of Brimfield* (Boston: New England Historic Genealogical Society, 1931), 48.

116. Hermon Alfred Kelly, *Genealogical History of the Kelly Family* (Cleveland: Privately Printed, 1897), 55. Barry Levy discusses Faxon Dean and the Dean family in *Town Born*, 277.

117. Hampshire County Court records, Inferior Court of Common Pleas, General Sessions of the Peace, University of Massachusetts Special Collections and Archives, May 25, 1765, vol. 8 (1764–1766), 83–84.

118. Cleveland, *Genealogy*, 270; and Boltwood, "Genealogies of Hadley Families," 90. Marsh did not remain long in Hadley, moving to Northampton and then Hartford, where he died in 1688. See also the November 17, 1802, *HG*, in which a "Nucom Cleaveland"— possibly a relative—advertises the sale of a fulling mill in Worthington, Massachusetts.

119. EPP memorandum book, April 13, 1767, *NEHGR*, and Judd, *Hadley*, 386.

120. Faxon Dean to Eleazer Porter, 1769, Book 9, 464, HCRD.

121. EPP memorandum book, November 18, 1770, *NEHGR*; Judd, *Hadley*, 424. Given the absence of surviving records the extent of the Deans' operation is hard to know, but Paul Rivard's work on the fulling mill in Alna, Maine, might provide a glimpse into the weaving habits of a comparable neighborhood. In Alna, over thirty-six hundred yards of locally made cloth were finished by the mill in 1809, a total supplied by 218 different customers. The yardage supplied by any one household generally never exceeded twenty yards, and many accounts fell far short of that figure. The pieces of cloth brought in for fulling, pressing, and dyeing ranged from just two or three yards to others as large as twelve yards. Lots of three, five, and seven-to-eight yards were typical. See Rivard, *New Order of Things*, 26.

122. Hood, *Weaver's Craft*, 109.

123. Hood, *Weaver's Craft*, 109.

124. EPP memorandum book, March 31 and April 7, 1776, and November 13, 1780, *NEHGR*. The reference to otter at this early date is puzzling; though otter is a breed of sheep, it is generally associated with the 1790s and later; see C. L. Bristol, "Otter Sheep," *The American Naturalist* 42, no. 496 (April 1908): 282; Timothy Dwight, *Travels in New England and New York*, vol. 3 (New Haven, CT: Timothy Dwight, 1822), 134. Perhaps the reference here is to achieving a certain color. A few weeks later, Phelps recorded that "Diademia Ingraham" had come to weave; see EPP memorandum book, November 13, 1780, *NEHGR*.

125. This and the other details in this paragraph are drawn from Ellis, *The Country Dyer's Assistant*, e.g., 43–46, 49–53, 14–16.

126. Faxon Dean to Horace Day, November 21, 1782, Book 22, 278, HCRD; see also EPP memorandum book, December 8, 1782, *NEHGR*.

127. Hood, *Weaver's Craft*, 108.

128. EPP memorandum book, February 18, March 25, April 22, September 1, 1781, *NEHGR*. Judd also notes presence of "Joseph Field, clothier," in the Oliver Smith account book, 1780–1783, in "Hadley," vol. 3, 220; this household may be related to that of Molly Marsh Field, who appears regularly in Phelps's memorandum book (e.g., July 13, 1782) doing tailoring for members of the household.

129. EPP memorandum book, January 20, 1782, and December 8, 1782, *NEHGR*. She would later conclude (December 15, 1782) that the Day family had promise, too, being "pretty sort of folks." In 1783, Faxon bought a third share on a sawmill and a third part of a gristmill in Westfield, which he sold soon thereafter to his oldest son, Samuel; the whole family relocated to Westfield, to embark on this new enterprise (on fullers who also owned other kinds of mills, see Hood, *Weaver's Craft*, 109–10). The Deans, though, kept in touch with their Hadley friends. See EPP memorandum book, August 6, 1786, *NEHGR*: "Tues Mrs Dean and her son Orang here from Westfield—they went there to live 3 years ago last spring." In 1784, Faxon Dean bought back the land he had sold to Horace Day, but the story of the fulling mill at this point becomes difficult to track. In 1785, he sold a three-acre parcel in Hadley to Charles Phelps; see Faxon Dean to Charles Phelps, June 4, 1785, Book 24, 544, HCRD. The Deans eventually moved west to Martinsburgh, New York, where Faxon died in his mill when it was washed away in a spring flood; Hitty lived on until 1812. Carpenter and Morehouse's *History of Amherst*, 470, reports a fulling mill in Amherst by 1805. In 1811, Phelps records riding to a clothier east of Forty Acres, on the "middle way"; see EPP memorandum book, September 29, 1811, *NEHGR*. This is probably the clothier and carding works owned by Sylvester Smith et al. "situated . . . one mile east of the main street, on the great road [that is, Bay road] leading to Belchertown"; in an 1818 notice advertising the works for sale, it is described as having two carding machines, a press, and "all other apparatus and tools necessary for such an establishment." See *HG*, June 30, 1818.

130. EPP memorandum book, September 30, 1798, and October 22 and November 19, 1797, *NEHGR*.

131. See, e.g., EPP memorandum book, June 21, 1795, May 15 and July 10, 1796, October 26, 1800, May 29, 1796, *NEHGR*.

132. EPP memorandum book, March 7 and April 26, 1790, *NEHGR*.

133. See, e.g., EPP memorandum book, June 1, 1794, August 8, 1802, November 4, 1804, September 8, 1805, *NEHGR*. Also August 6, 1809, September 29, 1811, PPHFP.

134. Judd, *Hadley*, 359.

135. Rivard, *New Order of Things*, 27; and Clark, *Roots of Rural Capitalism*, 140.

136. *Massachusetts Magazine, or, Monthly Museum of Knowledge & Rational Entertainment* 3, no. 5 (May 1791), 269.

137. Ulrich, "Wheels, Looms," 22.

138. Ulrich, "Wheels, Looms," 22.

139. Clark, *Roots of Rural Capitalism*, 94, 103. Also, two cotton manufacturing establishments produced 24 percent of the total yardage of "blended and unnamed cloth and stuff." "A Series of Tables of the Several Branches of American Manufacturers . . . for the Year 1810," in Tench Coxe, *A Statement of the Arts and Manufactures of the United States of America, for the Year 1810* (Philadelphia, 1814), 4.

140. "A Series of Tables," 4.

141. See Clark, *Roots of Rural Capitalism*, 93; also 96.

142. Nylander, "Textiles, Clothing and Needlework," 372.

143. Nylander, "Textiles, Clothing and Needlework," 372, citing *HG*, September 20, 1790.

144. Nylander, "Textiles, Clothing and Needlework," 372, citing *HG*, September 20, 1790.

145. Shepherd is also sometimes spelled Shephard and Shepard. For a brief biography, see http://www.historic-northampton.org/highlights/shepherd.html; see also Katherine Shepherd Smith, "More Ancient Northampton History" (undated photocopy in the Forbes Library Special Collections subject files), which explains that Levi Shephard preferred this spelling until about 1799, when the family reverted to an older spelling, Shepherd. Christopher Clark, who discusses this operation in *Roots of Rural Capitalism,* adopts the spelling Shepard; see *Roots of Rural Capitalism,* 29.

146. *Acts and Resolves of Massachusetts, 1786–87, February 1787* (Boston: Secretary of the Commonwealth, reprinted by Wright and Potter Printing Co., 1893), 881.

147. *HG,* July 30 and August 6, 1788, and September 3, 1788.

148. *HG,* October 1, 1788.

149. *HG,* December 16, 1789. On the appearance of such buildings, see Richard Candee, "New Towns of the Early New England Textile Industry," *Perspectives in Vernacular Architecture* 1 (1982): 31–50.

150. E.g., *HG,* December 15, 1790. For his advice to and encouragement of farmers to supply his manufactory, see December 7, 1791, and October 16, 1793.

151. See James Russell Trumbull, *History of Northampton Massachusetts, from Its Settlement in 1654,* vol. 2 (Northampton, MA: [Press of Gazette Printing Co.] 1898–1902), 527.

152. *HG,* January 6, 1790.

153. *HG,* March 21, 1791.

154. See, e.g., January 18, 1791, in Levi Shepherd account book, 1783–1791, FL. The manufactory persisted until Shepherd's death in fall 1805; his sons John and Thomas took over the manufactory as well as the mercantile business. See *HG,* November 27, 1805.

155. Grace L. Rogers, *The Scholfield Wool-Carding Machines*, United States National Museum Bulletin 218 (Washington, DC: Smithsonian Institution, 1959), https://www.gutenberg.org/files/27137/27137-h/27137-h.htm).

156. See Chester M. Destler, "The Hartford Woolen Manufactory: The Story of a Failure," *Connecticut History* 14 (June 1974): 8–32; and William R. Bagnall, *The Textile Industries of the United States*, vol. 1 (Cambridge, MA: Riverside, 1893), 107. The manufactory enjoyed a certain symbolic success when George Washington, among others, made a point of wearing cloth of their manufacture as a gesture in support of American manufacturing, but the enterprise itself did not survive beyond 1794.

157. Rogers, *Scholfield Wool-Carding Machines*; and Ulrich, *Age of Homespun,* 289.

158. EPP memorandum book, May 15, 29, 30, June 21, July 10 and 17, 1795, *NEHGR*. See also the entries of November 4, 1804, noting Charles Phelps's errand to bring wool home from the Amherst carding mill, and August 6, 1809, regarding a visit to another mill in Hadley.

159. Royal Chapin Taft, *Some Notes upon the Introduction of the Woolen Manufacture into the United States* (Providence, RI, 1882), 6–7; and Bagnall, *Textile Industries of the*

United States, 204. In time, as the production of woolens proved unprofitable, the manufactory shifted to cotton; that failed as well, and operations ceased in 1800.

160. Taft, *Some Notes*, 8.

161. Sarah Smith Emery, *Reminiscences of a Nonagenarian* (Newburyport, MA: Huse, 1879), 72.

162. EPP memorandum book, July 17, 1796, *NEHGR*. Persis Leonard seems likely to have been the twenty-two-year-old daughter (b. April 2, 1772) of Shutesbury's Meschach and Patience Waterman Leonard, who had only recently migrated west from Middleborough, Massachusetts. Meschach died in 1774, so this Persis would have been fatherless, making domestic service a compelling option for Persis and her mother. EPP memorandum book, July 17, 1796, *NEHGR*.

163. EPP memorandum book, September 14, 1794 *NEHGR*.

164. EWPH to EPP, May 2 and January 6, 1804, Box 13 folder 8, PPHFP.

165. Emery, *Reminiscences*, 72.

166. Emery, *Reminiscences*, 72.

167. Emery, *Reminiscences*, 72. See also Sven Beckert, *Empire of Cotton: A Global History* (London, Penguin, 2014).

168. Rivard, *New Order of Things*, 18, and Rogers, *Scholfield Wool-Carding Machines*.

169. Pittsfield *Sun*, November 9, 1801, and September 19, 1803, and (Springfield) *Federal Spy*, June 6, 1803.

170. *HG*, June 6 and 15, 1803, and (Springfield) *Federal Spy*, June 6 and August 23, 1803.

171. Ulrich, *Age of Homespun*, 289.

172. Clark, *Roots of Rural Capitalism*, 104; Carpenter and Morehouse, *History of Amherst*, 76. See EPP memorandum book entries of November 4, 1804, *NEHGR*, and August 6, 1809, Box 7 folder 3, PPHFP. Gregory Farmer and Bonnie Parsons, "MHC Reconnaissance Survey: Hadley" (July 1982), 6, says there was a carding mill in Hadley as early as 1775, at Robert Meekins's Mill River gristmill, though I cannot find the original source for that assertion.

173. See Clark, *Roots of Rural Capitalism*, 104, citing EPP memorandum book, November 4, 1804, and August 6, 1809.

174. See CP account book, vol. 1 (1805–1815), in Phelps Family account books, 1805–1858, Harvard Business School, January 8 and October 31, 1813. This Lamson is not identified, though a Charles Lamson is present in 1820 Hadley; see US Census Bureau (1820 Federal Census), Town of Hadley.

175. Judd, *Hadley*, 372.

176. Erin Judge, "Woolen Mills in Middlefield, MA (1773–1901): The Vital Role of Rural Manufacture," unpublished typescript, 2009, 11, http://middlefieldma.net/wp-content/uploads/history/middlefield-mills.pdf.

177. EPP to EWPH, March 2 and April 1, 1801, Box 6 folder 1, PPHFP.

178. EPP to EWPH, March 31, 1812, Box 6 folder 5, PPHFP.

179. EPP to EWPH, December 14, 1812, Box 5 folder 11, PPHFP.

180. CP account books, vol. 1 (1805–1815), March 1814, Baker Library, Harvard Business School.

181. Ulrich, "Wheels, Looms," 28.

182. Cf. Ulrich on Topsham, Maine, in "Wheels, Looms," 26.

183. For Elihu Cook, see January 19, 1802, Box 37 no. 25; for Warham Smith, see January 5, 1803, Box 137 no. 57; for John Montague, see August 17, 1803, Box 99 no. 29; for Benjamin Kellogg, see August 20, 1803, Box 81 no. 20; for Zera Green, see April 27, 1813, Box 64 no. 40; for Josiah Nash, see April 9, 1814, Box 104 no. 25, HCMRP.

184. *HG,* May 15, 1793; June 4, 1794.

185. *HG,* June 6 and 27, 1810.

186. *HG,* June 20, 1810.

187. *HG,* November 17, 1813.

188. *HG,* November 8, 1809.

189. *HG,* May 26, 1813. Three years later Coolidge would be putting out blue and white yarn for weaving into bedticking; see *HG,* August 16, 1816, discussed in Clark, *Roots of Rural Capitalism,* 170 and 177. See also HAD.49 (MACRIS).

190. Agnes Hannay, "A Chronicle of Industry on the Mill River," *Smith College Studies in History* 21, nos. 1–4 (Northampton, MA: Smith College, October 1935–July 1936): 31–40.

191. Hannay, "A Chronicle of Industry on the Mill River," 38.

192. *HG,* January 26, 1814.

193. *HG,* January 21, 1818.

194. Hannay, "A Chronicle of Industry on the Mill River," 39; and Asbury Dickens and James C. Allen, comps., *American State Papers,* Finance, 5 (Washington, DC: Gales and Seaton, 1859), 815.

195. *HG,* January 7, 1818. Like other woolen factories Shepherd's firm also continued to offer custom carding until about 1812. See *HG,* June 3, 1812. On merino sheep, see Mark A. Mastromarino, "Fair-Weather Friends: Merino Sheep and the Origins of the Modern American Agricultural Fair," in Peter Benes and Jane Montague Benes, eds., *New England's Creatures, 1400–1900,* Proceedings of the 1993 Dublin Seminar for New England Folklife (Boston: Boston University, 1995), 95–108. By 1837, more than thirteen hundred Hadley merinos were producing close to four thousand pounds of wool annually (worth almost two thousand dollars); see John Prescott Bigelow, *Statistical Tables: Exhibiting the Condition and Products of Certain Branches of Industry in Massachusetts* (Boston: Dutton and Wentworth, State Printers, 1838), 78.

196. See Jonathan Prude, *The Coming of Industrial Order: Town and Factory Life in Rural Massachusetts, 1810–1860* (Cambridge: Cambridge University Press, 1983; new edition, Amherst: University of Massachusetts Press, 1999); Gail Fowler Mohanty, "Hand-loom Outwork and Outwork Weaving in Rural Rhode Island 1810–1821," *American Studies* 30, no. 2 (Fall 1989): 41–68.

197. Clark, *Roots of Rural Capitalism,* 141. The latter recollection is the source for Judd's assertion in *Hadley* that "the household manufacture of wool continued in Hadley and elsewhere many years in the present century. It ceased in many families before 1822 and continued longer in some. In general, the rising generation know not how their grandmothers made cloth." Judd, *Hadley,* 380.

198. Huntington, "Sketches of Family and Life in Hadley," 46.

199. Clark, *Roots of Rural Capitalism,* 96; and Catherine E. Kelly, "'The Consummation of Rural Prosperity and Happiness': New England Agricultural Fairs and the Construction of Class and Gender, 1810–1860," *American Quarterly* 49, no. 3 (September 1997): 574–602.

200. F. W. Powell, "Industrial Bounties and Rewards by American States," *The Quarterly Journal of Economics* 28 (1914): 193.

201. D. Huntington, *Journal of the American Silk Society & Rural Economist* 2, no. 11 (November 1840): 322–25. On silk manufacture in antebellum Massachusetts, see Ben Marsh, "The Republic's New Clothes: Making Silk in the Antebellum United States," *Agricultural History* 86, no. 4 (Fall 2012): 206–34; and Jacqueline Field, Marjorie Senechal, and Madelyn Shaw, *American Silk, 1830–1930: Entrepreneurs and Artifacts* (Lubbock: Texas Tech University Press, 2007).

202. Dan Huntington account book, July 1842, Box 16 folder 2, PPHFP.

203. The Pomeroy and Gates houses, built in 1829 and 1830, respectively, are located at 4 Lawrence Plain Road (see MACRIS, HAD.367) and 119 Bay Road (HAD.177). See also Farmer et al., "Hadley Center Historic District," Gregory Farmer, Bonnie Parsons, and Betsy Friedberg, "Hadley Center Historic District (Boundary Increase)," National Register of Historic Places Nomination (1993), Section 7, 4; and Farmer and Parsons, "MHC Reconnaissance Survey Town Report: Hadley," 9.

Chapter 6 • Hospitality Work

1. Mary Smith (Mrs. John) Barstow recorded this piece of family lore in a paper entitled "Baker's or Cook's Tavern," found in the "Historians Record of the Doings of the Old Hadley Chapter of the Daughters of the American Revolution," 1908, HHS. The spelling of Cook varies in period sources, but for consistency herein, these pages prefer "Cook"; for genealogies of the "Cook, or Cooke" family, see Lucius M. Boltwood, "Genealogies of Hadley Families," in Sylvester Judd, *History of Hadley: Including the Early History of Hatfield, South Hadley, Amherst and Granby, Massachusetts* (Springfield, MA: H. R. Huntting, 1905), 23–29.

2. Newton's name is styled here as "Elizabeth," though she often signed her name "Elisabeth," and both spellings appear in period sources.

3. Hampshire County Court records, Inferior Court of Common Pleas, General Sessions of the Peace, University of Massachusetts Special Collections and Archives, vols. 14–25. Licenses were typically dispensed annually at the August meeting of the Court of General Sessions of the Peace. Sylvester Judd extracts Hadley licenses from these volumes in Judd, "Hadley," vol. 3, 86, 92–93, 174.

4. Epaphras Hoyt diary, July 17, 1790, PVMA.

5. Book-length studies that consider women as New England tavernkeepers include David W. Conroy, *In Public Houses: Drink & the Revolution of Authority in Colonial Massachusetts* (Chapel Hill: University of North Carolina Press, 1995); and Marcia Schmidt Blaine, "Ordinary Women: Government and Custom in the Lives of New Hampshire Women, 1690–1770" (PhD diss., University of New Hampshire, 1999). See also Sarah Hand Meacham, *Every Home a Distillery: Alcohol, Gender and Technology in the Colonial Chesapeake* (Baltimore: Johns Hopkins University Press, 2009).

6. My deep thanks to Margo Shea for suggesting this line of thinking here.

7. In fact, a key date in Judd's research is September 27, 1848, when he "put up" at the tavern run by Lucius and Permelia Westood Crane on the Hadley Common, to talk Hadley history with a range of individuals gathered there. See Judd, "Hadley," vol. 3, FL.

8. Sarah Hand Meacham, *Every Home a Distillery*. On women and tavernkeeping in the urban context of Boston, see Conroy, *In Public Houses*, and Jacqueline Barbara Carr, *After the Siege: A Social History of Boston, 1775–1800* (Boston: Northeastern University Press, 2005), 174; on Philadelphia, see Peter Thompson, *Rum Punch & Revolution: Taverngoing &*

Public Life in Eighteenth-Century Philadelphia (Philadelphia: University of Pennsylvania Press, 1999), 40–45.

9. Anne Digan Lanning, "Women Tavern Keepers in the Connecticut River Valley, 1750–1810," in Peter Benes and Jane Montague Benes, eds., *New England Celebrates: Spectacle, Commemoration, and Festivity,* Proceedings of the 2000 Dublin Seminar for New England Folklife (Boston: Boston University, 2002), 202–14, as well as interpretation of the Barnard Tavern and other sites at Historic Deerfield, Massachusetts, where Lanning is senior vice president. See also Amelia F. Miller and A. R. Riggs, eds., *Romance, Remedies, and Revolution: The Journal of Dr. Elihu Ashley of Deerfield, Massachusetts, 1773–1775* (Amherst: University of Massachusetts Press, 2007), 71, 146, 149; Judd, "Hadley," vol. 3, 93.

10. Thomas Paul Smith, "Farmer's Daughter, Innkeeper's Daughter, Minister's Daughter: Young Women of the Early Republic" (MA thesis, University of Massachusetts Amherst, 1976), 64.

11. EPP to EWPH, July 6, 1805, Box 5 folder 7, PPFHP.

12. For Phillis, see EPP memorandum book, May 7, 1775, *NEHGR*; on Prince, see Gretchen H. Gerzinga, *Mr. and Mrs. Prince: How an Extraordinary Eighteenth-Century Family Moved Out of Slavery and Into Legend* (New York: Amistad, 2008). Catherine Adams and Elizabeth H. Pleck discuss other enslaved women who labored in taverns in *Love of Freedom: Black Women in Colonial and Revolutionary New England* (New York: Oxford University Press, 2010), 6, 35.

13. On the Newton family's work in clothing production and maintenance, see Marla R. Miller, *The Needle's Eye: Women and Work in the Age of Revolution* (Amherst, University of Massachusetts Press, 2006), especially chapter 4.

14. Ebenezer and Mindwell Pomeroy account book, 1756–1797, private collection (also available on microfilm at the University of Massachusetts Amherst), 15, 85, 91, 135.

15. See Meacham, "Keeping the Trade."

16. Dean Albertson, "Puritan Liquor in the Planting of New England," *NEQ* 23 (1950), 483.

17. *Acts and Laws of the Commonwealth of Massachusetts* (Boston: Adams & Nourse, Printers to the Honorable General Court, 1786, reprinted by Wright & Potter, 1893), 206–16.

18. See Kelly Alisa Ryan, *Regulating Passion: Sexuality and Patriarchal Rule in Massachusetts, 1700–1830* (New York: Oxford University Press, 2014), 76.

19. Hampshire County Court records, Inferior Court of Common Pleas, General Sessions of the Peace, University of Massachusetts Special Collections and Archives, April 14, 1782, vol. 14 (1776–1790), 80.

20. EPP memorandum book, March 15, 1807, Box 7 folder 3, PPHFP.

21. Conroy, *In Public Houses*, especially 118–19, 125; Lanning, "Women Tavern Keepers," 205–8.

22. Judd, Hadley, 288–89, and "Hadley," vol. 3, 86. On the Lyman family, see Lyman Coleman, *Genealogy of the Lyman Family in Great Britain and America* (Albany, NY: J. Munsell, 1872).

23. Amelia F. Miller and A. F. Riggs, eds., *Romance, Remedies and Revolution: The Journal of Dr. Elihu Ashley of Deerfield, Massachusetts, 1773–1775* (Amherst: University of Massachusetts Press in association with the Pocumtuck Valley Memorial Association [Deerfield], 2007), 369–70.

24. Hampshire County Court records, Inferior Court of Common Pleas, General Sessions of the Peace, May 17, 1768, vol. 10 (1766–1771), 80.

25. The discussion of Lucy Hubbard herein draws on Lanning, "Women Tavern Keepers."

26. Lanning, "Women Tavern Keepers," 208.

27. See, e.g., J. Ritchie Garrison, *Two Carpenters: Architecture and Building in Early New England, 1799–1859* (Knoxville: University of Tennessee Press, 2006); Edward Strong Cooke Jr., "Rural Artisanal Culture: The Preindustrial Joiners of Newtown and Woodbury, Connecticut, 1760–1820" (PhD diss., Boston University, 1984), and *Making Furniture in Preindustrial America: The Social Economy of Newtown and Woodbury, Connecticut* (Baltimore: Johns Hopkins University Press, 1996).

28. Susan McGowan and Amelia F. Miller, *Families and Landscape: Deerfield Homelots from 1671* (Deerfield, MA: PVMA, 1996), 67–68. The below draws on Marla R. Miller, "Old Tavern Farm" (Greenfield, MA), National Register of Historic Places Nomination, 2005.

29. The below is drawn from Hampshire County Court records, Inferior Court of Common Pleas, General Sessions of the Peace, vols. 14–25, as well as Judd, "Hadley," vol. 3, 86, 92–93, 174.

30. See Judd, "Hadley," vol. 3, 86; Mary Smith (Mrs. John) Barstow, "The White Tavern," 1908, HHS; and the entry for June 2, 1775, in Miller and Riggs, eds., *Romance, Remedies and Revolution,* 216.

31. Judd, "Hadley," vol. 3, 174, and HAD.25 (MACRIS).

32. Judd, "Hadley," vol. 3, 92, and HAD.56 (MACRIS). The house appears to have been built by Lemuel's father, Jonathan Warner. There is considerable genealogical confusion about which Dorothy Phelps wed Lemuel Warner and joined him in the work of running a tavern, but it appears that this woman was the sister of Charles Phelps, and so the sister-in-law of Elizabeth Porter Phelps; Dorothy Phelps's July 1772 wedding to Lemuel Warner appears in EPP's memorandum book, though some sources describe the Dorothy Phelps who married Lemuel Warner as hailing from Connecticut. See also Judd, "Hadley," 241.

33. Judd, "Hadley," vol. 3, 77, 174, 179. See also Edwin Wilton Carpenter and Charles Frederick Morehouse, *History of the Town of Amherst* (Amherst, MA: Press of Carpenter & Morehouse, 1896), 385, which places this enterprise in North Amherst.

34. Judd, "Hadley," vol. 3, 77, 174, 179. Hadley residents today best remember the "Ben Smith" tavern, sited at the northeast corner of Middle Street and Bay Road, in part because this very large building survives. MACRIS form HAD.167 suggests that the original structure was "built as a public house by Major John Smith," and dates as early as 1774. Members of the Smith family were receiving tavern licenses as early as the 1730s and continued into the nineteenth century; see Judd, "Hadley," vol. 3, 86. According to HAD.167, a "ballroom with arched ceilings and spring dance floor, with two rooms below, was added c. 1840."

35. Stockbridge also ran a linseed oil mill in North Amherst for a dozen or so years; see Judd, *Hadley,* 385. The 1742 "Clark Inn and Toll House" (HAD.168) is also familiar to present-day residents, though this structure was moved from Northampton's Bridge Street to Hadley in the mid-twentieth century, during the construction of highway I-91.

36. *Massachusetts Spy*, December 5, 1782. According to Conroy, *In Public Houses*, 226, Northampton in 1770 had one public house for every 107 residents, a figure that seems roughly comparable to Hadley's as well.

37. Judd, "Miscellaneous," vol. 15, 163, and vol. 10, 107.

38. For consideration of women tavernkeepers and government accounts, see Blaine, "Ordinary Women." On taverns and court activity, see Martha J. McNamara, *From Tavern to Courthouse: Architecture & Ritual in American Law, 1658–1860* (Johns Hopkins University Press, 2004).

39. Judd, *Hadley,* 405, 422.

40. EPP memorandum book, March 16, 1784, *NEHGR,* and *HG,* January 3, 1798. Peter Benes writes about the latter in *For a Short Time Only: Itinerants and the Resurgence of Popular Culture in Early America* (Amherst: University of Massachusetts Press, 2016).

41. See Miller, *Needle's Eye,* 198.

42. Richard R. John and Thomas C. Leonard, "The Illusion of the Ordinary: John Lewis Krimmel's Village Tavern and the Democratization of Public Life in the Early Republic," *Pennsylvania History: A Journal of Mid-Atlantic Studies* 65, no. 1, Benjamin Franklin and His Enemies (Winter 1998): 87–96.

43. Judd, "Hadley," vol. 3, 77. See also Richard D. Brown, *Knowledge Is Power: The Diffusion of Information in Early America 1700–1865* (New York: Oxford University Press, 1991).

44. On clothing production and spaces of intimacy, see Miller, *Needle's Eye,* 158–59, 171.

45. Ebenezer and Mindwell Pomeroy account book, 1756–1797.

46. Ebenezer and Mindwell Pomeroy account book, 1756–1797.

47. Carpenter and Morehouse, *History of Amherst,* 36.

48. Patricia Laurice Ellsworth, "Hadley West Street Common and Great Meadow: A Cultural Landscape Study" (MA thesis, University of Massachusetts Department of Landscape Architecture and Regional Planning, 2007), 29. See also Jason M. Opal, "Enterprise and Emulation: The Moral Economy of Turnpikes in Early National New England," *Early American Studies* 8, no. 3, Special Forum: Markets and Morality: Intersections of Economy, Ethics, and Religion in Early North America (Fall 2010): 623–45.

49. On the John Lyman house, see HAD.393. A second generation flourished as Israel Lyman (the oldest son of Zadoc), Ethan Pomeroy (the son of Ebenezer), and Elijah Lyman (the son of Gideon Jr.) began raising their families there. Lastly, Stephen Coats, a native of the town of Westfield, Massachusetts, lived in a small house near the ferry, which he operated. As Judd notes, "These were all the heads of families previous to 1780." Judd, *Hadley,* 288–89.

50. Judd, "Hadley," vol. 3, 86.

51. Ebenezer and Mindwell Pomeroy account book, 1756–1797. Ebenezer Pomeroy appears among licensed innkeepers from 1758 to 1770; his son Ethan Pomeroy was licensed in 1772 and 1773 and again in 1783 to 1785.

52. Gregory Farmer, et al., "Hockanum Rural Historic District," National Register of Historic Places Nomination (November 1993), section 7, p. 4; and HAD.394 (MACRIS).

53. Farmer, et al., "Hockanum Rural Historic District," section 8, p. 4.

54. Farmer, et al., "Hockanum Rural Historic District," section 8, p. 4. This building was destroyed by fire in the 1880s; see Charles Forbes Warner, *Picturesque Hampshire* (Northampton, MA: Wade, Warner & Co., 1890), 80.

55. Diana D. Rockman and Nan A. Rothschild, "City Tavern, Country Tavern: An Analysis of Four Colonial Sites," *Historical Archaeology* 18, no. 2 (July 1984): 112–21.

56. The meaning of "victuals" is unclear; Pomeroy clearly distinguishes it, however, from the three meals of the day in his ledger. James Russell Trumbull suggests that this might be a cold plate in *History of Northampton, Massachusetts from Its Settlement in 1654* (Northampton, MA: [Press of Gazette Printing Co.], 1898–1902), 286.

57. Miller and Riggs, eds., *Romance, Remedies and Revolution*, 60.

58. Miller and Riggs, eds., *Romance, Remedies and Revolution*, 31, 63.

59. Unfortunately, there is enough discrepancy among early flip recipes to make it impossible to know just what these involved for the Pomeroys, and that information would shed light on the family's provisioning needs. Some recipes assume that flip calls for eggs or cream, to be combined with beer and spices; others suggest beer, rum, and a sweetener, like sugar or molasses.

60. Ebenezer and Mindwell Pomeroy account book, 1756–1797, e.g., July 1760, and May 1762, 3, 18.

61. Ebenezer and Mindwell Pomeroy account book, 1756–1797, May 1758, and October 1762, 31.

62. Ebenezer and Mindwell Pomeroy account book, 1756–1797, March 1758, 15.

63. Ebenezer and Mindwell Pomeroy account book, 1756–1797, e.g., July 1760, and May 1762, 3, 18.

64. Judd, "Miscellaneous," vol. 15, 163, and 420–28.

65. Judd, "Miscellaneous," vol. 10, 107.

66. Smith, "Farmer's Daughter," 67.

67. See, e.g., Jerusha Leonard diary, January 25, March 7, February 10, and April 26, 1791, PVMA.

68. Miriam Clapp Pomeroy died in 1793, and taverner Asahel Pomeroy remarried; presumably Hannah Whitney Pomeroy also played a role in the inn's operations. On the Pomeroy tavern in Northampton, see Nancy Bowker Brownell, "Hotels and Taverns," *The Northampton Book* (Northampton, MA, 1954), 365–67.

69. Judd, *Hadley*, 369.

70. *HG*, September 27, 1797.

71. *HG*, August 22, 1798.

72. *HG*, March 18, 1801; see also January 20, 1802.

73. *HG*, June 30, 1802; June 11, 1806; December 9, 1807.

74. Hugh and Elizabeth Queen account, 1760–1764, in Ebenezer and Mindwell Pomeroy account book, 1756–1797, 28.

75. Esther Alexander account, 1765–1766, in Ebenezer and Mindwell Pomeroy account book, 1756–1797, 22 and n.p.

76. See, e.g., William Brace account, in Ebenezer and Mindwell Pomeroy account book, 1756–1797, 87.

77. Ebenezer and Mindwell Pomeroy account book, 1756–1797, e.g., 21, 33, 47.

78. See the Fairfield and Ayres accounts in Ebenezer and Mindwell Pomeroy account book, 1756–1797, 30, 32.

79. Ebenezer and Mindwell Pomeroy account book, 1756–1797, e.g., 4, 15, 34.

80. Judd, *Hadley*, 428.

81. Ebenezer and Mindwell Pomeroy account book, 1756–1797, 116.

82. The classic study is Judith M. Bennett, *Ale, Beer and Brewsters in England: Women's Work in a Changing World, 1300–1600* (New York: Oxford University Press, 1996); other

relevant work includes Meacham, *Every Home a Distillery*, and James McWilliams, "Brewing Beer in Massachusetts Bay, 1640–1690," *NEQ* (1998): 543–69.

83. McWilliams, "Brewing Beer in Massachusetts Bay," 561.

84. Judd, *Hadley*, 66, 355.

85. Judd, *Hadley*, 366. He appears to be drawing here on an 1859 interview with Abigail Dickinson Newton, whose husband Francis was the son of Elizabeth Newton and brother of Tryphena Newton Cook; see "Miscellaneous," vol. 19, 211.

86. For Sophia Cook Clarke on brewing, see Judd, "Miscellaneous," vol. 19, 210–11.

87. These figures are derived from the valuations attached to 104 Hadley heads of household in Judd, *Hadley*, 423.

88. Francis Newton is recorded as having held a license in Hampshire County Court of Common Pleas, from 1778 to 1780; see Hampshire County Court records, Inferior Court of Common Pleas, General Sessions of the Peace, vol. 14 (1776–1790), 17, 32, 52.

89. Ermina Newton Leonard, comp., *Newton Genealogy: Genealogical, Biographical, Historical* (DePere, WI: Bernard Ammidown Leonard, 1915), 81–82.

90. Francis Newton inventory, July 25, 1781, Box 105 no. 20, HCMRP.

91. See, e.g., *Massachusetts Gazette* (Springfield), February 17, 1784; *HG*, October 5, 1796.

92. Francis Newton estate settlement, Box 105 no. 20, HCMRP.

93. Francis Newton estate settlement, Box 105 no. 20, HCMRP.

94. Francis Newton estate settlement, Box 105 no. 20, HCMRP.

95. Francis Newton estate settlement, Box 105 no. 20, HCMRP.

96. Josiah Pierce account book and interleaved almanac, March 1771, HHS.

97. EPP memorandum book, January 19, March 2, April 20, May 4 and 18, 1783, *NEHGR*.

98. EPP memorandum book, May 4, 1783, *NEHGR*.

99. EPP memorandum book, July 6, 1783, *NEHGR*.

100. Hampshire County Court records, Inferior Court of Common Pleas, General Sessions of the Peace, vol. 14 (1776–1790), 120.

101. See Judd, "Miscellaneous," vol. 19, 318, whose notes indicate that Alexander Smith had a long table and seat valued at twenty-one shillings four pence in 1759, "doubtless for bar-room in Amherst"; Moses Marsh had a long table with a leaf and a seat cut down by woodworker Eliakim Smith in 1759; Elisha Hubbard had a "tavern table" worth eight shillings; and Abner Smith owned a "bar-room table and form" worth sixteen shillings in 1777.

102. On Hubbard, see Lanning, "Women Tavern Keepers, 208–209." See also Judd, "Miscellaneous," vol. 11, 234; and "Hadley," vol. 3, 190.

103. James Kellogg inventory, 1759, as transcribed in Judd, "Hadley," vol. 3, 64, and again in Gregory H. Nobles and Herbert L. Zarov, comps., *Selected Papers from the Sylvester Judd Manuscript* (Northampton, MA: Forbes Library, 1976), 474–75. Other references to "long" and "tavern" tables in Hadley and surrounding towns are transcribed in Judd, "Miscellaneous," vol. 19, 318.

104. Chileab and Windsor Smith to Andrew Cooke, April 22, 1795, vol. 10, 449, HCRD.

105. HAD.1 (MACRIS); and Mary Smith (Mrs. John) Barstow, "Baker's or Cook's Tavern," 127–29. The upper-story hall, which included a long built-in bench along an interior wall, was dismantled when the space was divided into two rooms; extensive renovations made to the house in 2007 revealed the floor's original configuration. My thanks to

property owner Jordi Herold for sharing with me notes and images from the renovation process.

106. The Warner tavern (HAD.56.), built in 1790, has a center-hall plan, as does the Kellogg-Goodman tavern (HAD.25). The Pomeroy tavern on Hockanum Road (HAD.394) had, like the Newton-Cook tavern, a center-chimney plan. See MACRIS.

107. Judd, "Hadley," vol. 3, 3. This building would be succeeded by the 1840 Crain Tavern that rose around the same place on the Hadley Common, MHC.141 (MACRIS).

108. In Hadley, such partitions were hinged, and they collapsed back into walls, but other approaches were possible. In the Buckman Tavern in Lexington, Massachusetts, for instance, the partitions did not fold away but were completely removable; six panels "slid in a groove at the ceiling and were secured by bolts to each other and to the floor. As one of the sections contained a hinged door and frame . . . the Ballroom could quite easily be transformed into connecting bedrooms, each with its own fireplace." See Menders, Torrey & Spencer, Inc., "The Buckman Tavern Historic Structure Report" (Lexington Historical Society, 2013), 71, and figure 43; also useful here is Deane Rykerson and Anne A. Grady, "Munroe Tavern Historic Structure Report" (Lexington Historical Society, 2010). Both reports are available at Lexingtonhistory.org. In Clinton, Connecticut, near the mouth of the Connecticut River, builders of the 1791 Adam Stanton House installed "moveable wall panels in the two front parlor rooms. Designed so that the entire wall could be lifted up and hooked to the ceiling, these unique wall panels allowed the Stanton family to open both front rooms, creating an enormous space in which family worship services could be held." Description on the website for the Adam Stanton House, http://www.adamstantonhouse .org/house-and-store; my deep thanks to Myron Stachiw for bringing this example to my attention, and for so cheerfully fielding my query about the history of movable partitions in eighteenth-century Massachusetts.

109. Kevin M. Sweeney, "Meetinghouses, Town Houses, and Churches: Changing Perceptions of Sacred and Secular Space, 1720–1850," *Winterthur Portfolio* 28, no. 1 (Spring 1993): 68.

110. See SUN.35 (MACRIS). On tavern spaces associated with Freemasonry, see John Hamilton, *Material Culture of the American Freemasons* (Lexington, MA: Museum of Our National Heritage, 1994). On town houses, see Martha J. McNamara, "'In the Face of the Court . . .': Law, Commerce, and the Transformation of Public Space in Boston, 1650–1770," *Winterthur Portfolio* 36, no. 2/3 (Summer/Autumn 2001): 125–39; and Sweeney, "Meetinghouses, Town Houses, and Churches," 59–93. I am grateful to J. Ritchie Garrison for urging me to contemplate the implications of these spaces beyond their roles in tavern life.

111. See Benes, "A Time to Dance," in *For a Short Time Only*, chapter 13. Catherine E. Kelly discusses the significance of dancing instruction in *Republic of Taste: Art, Politics, and Everyday Life in Early America* (Philadelphia: University of Pennsylvania Press, 2016), 33–34.

112. Benes, "A Time to Dance," 240–44; and *HG*, e.g., March 12, 1794, September 20, 1797, November 25, 1801.

113. *HG*, December 7, 1796.

114. Catherine E. Kelly, *In the New England Fashion: Reshaping Women's Lives in the Nineteenth Century* (Ithaca, NY: Cornell University Press, 2002), 212, 196, and *Republic of Taste*, 31–34; Richard L. Bushman, *The Refinement of America: Persons, Houses, Cities* (New York: Knopf, 1992), 65; and Alicia M. Annas, "The Elegant Art of Movement," in Edward

Maeder, ed., *An Elegant Art: Fashion and Fantasy in the Eighteenth Century* (New York: Abrams, 1983), 35–60.

115. *HG*, March 12, 1794, and John Griffiths, *The Gentleman and Lady's Companion Containing the Newest Cotillions and Country Dances, to Which Is Added Instances of Ill Manners to Be Carefully Avoided by Youth of Both Sexes* (Norwich, CT: Samuel Trumbull for John Trumbull, 1798). C. Dallett Hemphill discusses dancing schools as vehicles for spreading ideas about manners in *Bowing to Necessities: A History of Manners in America, 1620–1860* (New York: Oxford University Press, 1999), 91–92.

116. Griffiths, *The Gentleman and Lady's Companion*, 21–23.

117. EPP memorandum book, April 6 and 13, 1794, *NEHGR*. See also Judd, "Hadley," vol. 3, 35, for the possibility that Betsy Phelps Huntington and her "sister" Thankful attended dancing lessons at their uncle Lemuel Warner's public house.

118. My deep thanks to J. Ritchie Garrison for suggesting how these various threads were "entangled" in nineteenth-century rural Massachusetts.

119. EPP memorandum book, November 22, 1795, *NEHGR*.

120. EPP to EWPH, November 1807, Box 5 folder 9, PPHFP.

121. See, e.g., EPP memorandum book, April 15, 1781, *NEHGR*.

122. Cook account book, HHS; and Box 104 no. 11, HCMRP.

123. EPP memorandum book, June 2, 1805, *NEHGR*; Leonard, comp., *Newton Genealogy*, 82.

124. *Columbian Centinel*, April 22, 1820; *Boston Daily Advertiser*, April 24, 1820; *The Repertory*, April 25, 1820; *Boston Commercial Gazette*, April 27, 1820; and *Boston Recorder*, April 19, 1820.

125. See the Ebenezer and Mindwell Pomeroy account book, July–October 1769, 127. On women as boardinghouse keepers elsewhere, see Ellen Hartigan-O'Connor, *The Ties That Buy: Women and Commerce in Revolutionary America* (Philadelphia: University of Pennsylvania Press, 2009), 40–66, 50–51; Cornelia H. Dayton and Sharon V. Salinger, *Robert Love's Warnings: Searching for Strangers in Colonial Boston* (Philadelphia: University of Pennsylvania Press, 2014); and Wendy Gamber, *The Boardinghouse in Nineteenth-Century America* (Baltimore: Johns Hopkins University Press, 2007). On the material culture of boarding in more urban settings, see Bernard L. Herman, *Town House: Architecture and Material Life in the Early American City, 1780–1830* (Chapel Hill: University of North Carolina Press, 2005); and John Styles, "Lodging at the Old Bailey: Lodgings and Their Furnishing in Eighteenth-Century London," in John Styles and Amanda Vickery, eds., *Gender, Taste and Material Culture in Britain and North America, 1700–1830* (New Haven, CT: Yale University Press, 2006), 66–80.

126. See Gamber, *The Boardinghouse in Nineteenth-Century America*.

127. EWPH to EPP, June 20, 1801, Box 13 folder 1, PPHFP; and Theodore Gregson Huntington, "Sketches of Family and Life in Hadley," 28, Box 21 folder 4, PPHFP.

128. Sarah Porter Hillhouse to children, September 26, 1819, Folder 54, Hillhouse Family Papers, Southern Historical Collection, University of North Carolina–Chapel Hill.

129. Hillhouse to children, September 26, 1819, Folder 54, Hillhouse Family Papers.

130. See EPP memorandum book, e.g., November 4 and 11, 1804; August 23, 1801; April 26, 1795; June 8, 1794; May 26, 1793, *NEHGR*. On Farrar's, see *History of Worcester County, Massachusetts*, vol. 1 (Philadelphia: J. W. Lewis & Co., 1889), 801.

131. EPP memorandum book, March 7, 1802; June 5, 1803; January 25, 1801; September 24, 1797, *NEHGR*.

132. EPP memorandum book, June 1, 1783; May 28, 1797, *NEHGR*.

133. The 1789, 1796, and 1800 Boston City Directories list a Catharine Gray who has a boardinghouse on State Street; she does not appear in 1803. In 1798, Gray is listed at 68 State Street. See also Carr, *After the Siege*, 59. Duncan Wu mentions the sisters in *William Hazlitt: The First Modern Man* (Oxford: Oxford University Press, 2008), 10.

134. Carr, *After the Siege*, 74.

135. EPP memorandum book, February 18, 1789, December 28, 1790, May 26, 1793, June 15, 1794, April 26, 1795, May 22, 1796, *NEHGR*. A "rare business card from Boston with elaborate border and crude eagle advertising Genteel Boarding & Lodging by Catharine Gray on State Street" was offered for sale in *A. B. Bookman's Weekly*, vol. 79 (1987), 183. No location for any extant card is known.

136. The couple also stopped, on another occasion, at the "Widow Taylours" in Hinsdale, New Hampshire; see EPP memorandum book, January 25 and 27, 1788, *NEHGR*.

137. *Report of the Record Commissioners of the City of Boston*, vol. 22 (Boston: Rockwell and Churchill, 1890), 295.

138. Carr, *After the Siege*, 59; (Boston) *Polar Star*, October 26, 1796; *Boston Price-Current*, January 5, 1797; (Boston) *Continental Journal*, August 28, 1783; *Massachusetts Centinel*, November 20, 1784.

139. EPP to EWPH, June 26, 1808, Box 5 folder 9, PPHFP.

140. Rebecca Dickinson diary, August 19, 1787, PVMA.

141. Rebecca Dickinson diary, June 15, 1788, PVMA.

142. On changes in any given landscape over the course of a day, see Dell Upton, *Another City: Urban Life and Urban Spaces in the New American Republic* (New Haven, CT: Yale University Press, 2008).

143. As quoted in Sharon V. Salinger, *Taverns and Drinking in Early America* (Baltimore: Johns Hopkins University Press, 2004), 234.

144. Hampshire County Court records, Inferior Court of Common Pleas, General Sessions of the Peace, August 28, 1803, vol. 25 (1800–1823), 84–85.

145. EPP to EWPH, June 26, 1808, Box 5 folder 9, PPHFP. Dorothy Phelps died in summer 1804. Warner remarried and was quickly widowed again; in April 1808 he married his third wife, Martha Allen, who appears to be the woman mentioned here. See Lucien C. Warner and Josephine Genung Nichols, comps., *The Descendants of Andrew Warner* (New Haven, CT: Tuttle, Moorehouse & Taylor Co., 1919), 230.

146. EPP memorandum book, May 7, 1775, *NEHGR*.

147. Dorothy Phelps Warner also seemed to have been of poor health and given to "roumatizm" and other ailments. See EPP memorandum book, April 24, 1774, January 31, 1773, *NEHGR*.

148. My thanks to Margo Shea for helping think through the implications of women's work vis-à-vis alcoholism and its effects on the community.

149. See Baron, *Brewed in America*, 351.

150. Judd, "Northampton with Westfield," vol. 2, 367.

151. EPP to EWPH, June 13, 1813, Box 5 folder 11, PPHFP.

152. See EPP to EWPH, September 11, 1814, Box 5 folder 11, for a long account of the death of John Morrison.

153. EPP to EWPH, December 20, 1802, Box 5 folder 4, PPHFP. One was a hired man named Elisha; the other probably refers to John Morrison or Reuban Debel.

154. EPP memorandum book, October 15, 1815, Box 7 folder 4, PPHFP. The records of the Northampton jail show Paul Wright (1790–1844) admitted on October 13, 1815, committed for assault. See the "Two-in-One Book," Hampshire County House of Correction, 1784–1830, FL.

155. EPP to EWPH, January 4, 1802, Box 5 folder 4, PPHFP.

156. EPP to EWPH, March 9, 1803, Box 5 folder 5, PPHFP.

157. EPP to EWPH, January 4, 1802, Box 5 folder 4, PPHFP.

158. EPP to EWPH, April 1, 1804, Box 5 folder 6, PPHFP. Paul and Deborah Sumner Wright's house, just north of the village at the mills, still stands; see HAD.219 (MACRIS).

159. EPP to EWPH, April 1, 1804, Box 5 folder 6, PPHFP.

160. EPP memorandum book, April 8, 1804, Box 7 folder 3, PPHFP.

161. EPP to EWPH, April 1, 1804, Box 5 folder 6, PPHFP.

162. EPP to EWPH, April 20, 1804, Box 5 folder 6, PPHFP. Paul Wright Jr. worked at least briefly in his teens for Charles and Elizabeth Phelps, his pay going directly to his mother; see Charles Phelps's account book, vol.1 (1805–1815) in Phelps Family account books, 1805–1858, Baker Library, Harvard Business School. Paul Wright Sr. died in 1808; it is possible that Paul Wright Jr. in time formed a union with, and possibly married, Submit "Mitte" West, whose experiences are considered in chapter 4.

163. Kelly A. Ryan, "'The Spirit of Contradiction': Wife Abuse in New England, 1780–1820," *Early American Studies* (Summer 2015): 599. In 1804, Charles Phelps was a member of the town select board, and a former representative to the state legislature; beginning in 1792 he also served several terms as a justice of the peace.

164. Massachusetts Temperance Society Constitution (Boston: Sewell Phelps, 1818).

165. See the MHC forms for the 1807 Thaddeus Smith tavern and the 1774 Ben Smith tavern, HAD.192 and HAD.169 respectively (MACRIS); see also *Emancipator and Free American* 6, no. 51 (April 21, 1842): 204. The Hampshire County Temperance Society boasted nearly twelve thousand members in 1834, and claimed to have reduced the number of outlets to acquire ardent spirits significantly in the "Twenty-First Annual Report of the Massachusetts Temperance Society: Presented by the Council, at the Annual Meeting in Boston, May 29, 1834" (Boston: Temperance Press, 1834).

166. Records of the Hadley Total Abstinence Temperance Society, founded 1837, can be found in the HHS. Scholarship on the history of alcoholism includes W. J. Rorabaugh, *The Alcoholic Republic: An American Tradition* (New York: Oxford University Press, 1979).

Chapter 7 • *Healing and Caregiving*

1. EPP memorandum book, December 19, 1773, *NEHGR*.

2. See, e.g., EPP memorandum book, September 24, 1769, January 17, 1779; April 27, 1782; September 27, 1784; and July 28, 1793, *NEHGR*.

3. EPP memorandum book, September 27, 1784, *NEHGR*.

4. The quotation is from Susan Hanket Brandt, "Gifted Women and Skilled Practitioners: Gender and Healing Authority in the Delaware Valley, 1740–1830" (PhD diss., Temple University, 2015), 192; see also her article "'Getting into a Little Business': Margaret Hill Morris and Women's Medical Entrepreneurship during the American Revolution," in *Early American Studies* 13, no. 4 (Fall 2015): 774–807.

5. These musings are prompted by Andrew W. Jones, "Caring Labor and Class Consciousness: The Class Dynamics of Gendered Work," *Sociological Forum* 16, no. 2 (June 2001): 281–99.

6. Nancy Folbre writes about this form of labor in *The Invisible Heart: Economics and Family Values* (New York: New Press, 2001). Massachusetts women's work in health care occupations is comparable to that of their counterparts elsewhere; see, for instance, Elizabeth C. Sanderson, *Women and Work in Eighteenth-Century Edinburgh* (New York: St. Martin's, 1996).

7. Brandt, "'Getting into a Little Business,'" 774–807, especially 778.

8. As Susan Brandt has noted, "apart from a few notable monographs, eighteenth-century American women healers' practices and the medical marketplace in which they worked remain understudied." See Brandt's "'Getting into a Little Business,'" citing major works, including Laurel Thatcher Ulrich, A *Midwife's Tale: The Life of Martha Ballard, Based on Her Diary, 1785–1812* (New York: Knopf, 1990); Rebecca J. Tannenbaum, *The Healer's Calling: Women and Medicine in Early New England* (Ithaca, NY: Cornell University Press, 2002); and Susan E. Klepp, *Revolutionary Conceptions: Women, Fertility, and Family Limitation in America, 1760–1820* (Chapel Hill: University of North Carolina Press, 2009), 776. An essay specific to the region under consideration here is Paul Berman, "Medical Practice in the Connecticut River Valley, 1650–1750," *Historical Journal of Massachusetts* 18, no. 1 (Winter 1990): 27–36.

9. On Elizabeth Allen, see her obituary: *HG*, January 15, 1800, January 23, 1855. Allen is remembered in Northampton by the local chapter of the Daughters of the American Revolution, organized in April 1896 as the "Betty Allen chapter" (see http://www.massdar.org/BettyAllenStory.html). Though no records survive to document Allen's practice, records of five births she attended appear in Elizabeth Phelps's memorandum book; see September 13, 1772 (Phelps's son Porter); August 7, 1774 (Mary Bartlett, daughter of Nicholas and Mary Bartlett); April 16, 1775 (Phillis, the daughter of enslaved woman Rose); March 21, 1779 (Elizabeth Whiting Phelps); and September 15, 1782 (a child born to one-time hired man Daniel Worthington and his wife Margaret), *NEHGR*. Laurel Thatcher Ulrich draws out the differences in the ways in which the work of physicians and that of midwives has been documented and understood in *Midwife's Tale*, 27–29. See also Emily K. Abel, *Hearts of Wisdom: American Women Caring for Kin, 1850–1940* (Cambridge: Harvard University Press, 2000). Richard Crouch's accounts survive in the Forbes Library, Northampton: see Dr. Richard Crouch ledger, Hadley, MA, 3 vols., 1730–1761; and also Sylvester Judd, "Medicines, etc. Including Dr. Crouch's Practice," n.d.

10. The 1771 Hadley tax valuation is available in Bettye Hobbs Pruitt, ed., *The Massachusetts Tax Valuations of 1771* (Boston: G. K. Hall, 1978), 394–96.

11. EPP memorandum book, January 1, 1775, February 26, 1776, March 19, 1776, April 16, 1776 (death), *NEHGR*.

12. Interestingly, a nineteenth-century history noted with a wink (though one born of respect, it seems) that "Old Rhoda could cure anyone outside of the grave, and—almost—those who had lain in it only a little while." See Marge Bruchac, "In Search of the Indian Doctress," unpublished typescript of essay published in condensed form in the *Old Sturbridge Visitor* 39, no. 1 (Spring 1999): 6–7; I am grateful to Marge for sharing her fascinating and important research with me. See also Daniel R. Mandell, *Tribe, Race, History: Native Americans in Southern New England, 1780–1880* (Baltimore: Johns Hopkins University

Press, 2008), 32–33. For discussions of native healers in the mid-Atlantic, see Brandt, "Gifted Women," chapter 2; and Patricia E. Rubertone, "Archaeologies of Native Production and Marketing in 19th-Century New England," in Craig N. Cipolla, ed., *Foreign Objects: Rethinking Indigenous Consumption in American Archaeology* (Tucson: University of Arizona Press, 2017), 204–21.

13. See Elizabeth Pendergast Carlisle, *Earthbound and Heavenbent: Elizabeth Porter Phelps and Life at Forty Acres (1747–1817)* (New York: Scribner, 2004), 19–21.

14. EPP memorandum book, June 30, 1767, *NEHGR.*

15. See William Young, comp., *Stafford Illustrated* (Young & Cady, 1895), 15–17. My thanks to Becky Kraussmann of the Stafford Historical Society for her assistance in understanding the early history of these springs.

16. See Young, comp., *Stafford Illustrated,* 15–17.

17. EPP memorandum book, August 20, 1809, Box 7 folder 3, PPHFP.

18. EPP memorandum book, September 12, 1784, *NEHGR.*

19. EPP memorandum book, November 14, 1784, *NEHGR.*

20. EPP memorandum book, August 30, 1795, *NEHGR.*

21. EPP to EWPH, January 6, 1804, Box 5 folder 8, PPHFP.

22. Cornelia Hughes Dayton, "Taking the Trade: Abortion and Gender Relations in an Eighteenth-Century New England Village," *WMQ,* 3rd ser., 48 (1991): 19–49.

23. EPP to EWPH, August 17, 1803, Box 5 folder 5, PPHFP.

24. Before Pomeroy appeared, townspeople called Northampton's Betty Allen, or Southampton's Mrs. Burt; see Sylvester Judd, "Northampton with Westfield," 373 (Judd Manuscript), FL.

25. EPP memorandum book, September 11, 1769, *NEHGR.* For deliveries by Montague, see EPP memorandum book, e.g., March 31, 1782, May 16, 1784, March 5, 1786, *NEHGR.*

26. See, e.g., EPP to EWPH, March 4, 1805, Box 6 folder 2, PPHFP.

27. Ulrich, *Midwife's Tale,* 40.

28. Lisa Forman Cody, *Birthing the Nation: Sex, Science and the Conception of Eighteenth-Century Britons* (New York: Oxford University Press, 2005), 37.

29. EPP memorandum book, December 8, 1811, Box 7 folder 3, PPHFP.

30. Hopkins to Elizabeth Phelps (at Watertown), July 6, 1775, PPHFP.

31. The book was T. Dawkes, *The Midwife Rightly Instructed* (London: J. Oswald, 1736); for discussion of these events, see George Marsden, *Jonathan Edwards: A Life* (New Haven, CT: Yale University Press, 2004), 292–95. See also Thomas H. Johnson, "Jonathan Edwards and the 'Young Folks' Bible," *NEQ* 5, no. 1 (1932): 37–54; and Ava Chamberlain, "Bad Books and Bad Boys: The Transformation of Gender in Eighteenth-Century Northampton, Massachusetts," *NEQ* 75, no. 2 (June 2002): 179–203.

32. For her 1798 will and 1800 inventory, see Box 2 no. 36, HCMRP. The 1826 will of daughter Eunice Breck makes no reference to the midwifery library; see Box 19 no. 24, HCMRP.

33. William Smellie, *Treatise on the Theory and Practice of Midwifery* (London: Printed for D. Wilson, and T. Durham, 1752) and the companion volume *Collections of Cases and Observations in Midwifery* (London: Printed for D. Wilson, and T. Durham, 1754); and Alexander Hamilton, MD, *Outlines of the Theory and Practice of Midwifery* (London:

Printed for T. Kay, 1786); Hamilton's volume was reprinted by Worcester printer Isaiah Thomas in 1794, and by Northampton's William Butler in 1797.

34. On these events, in Middletown, Connecticut, see EPP memorandum book, February 28, 1813, Box 7 folder 4, PPHFP.

35. EPP memorandum book, September 13, 1772, *NEHGR*.

36. EPP memorandum book, August 7, 1774, April 16, 1775, *NEHGR*.

37. EPP memorandum book, August 20, 1775, *NEHGR*.

38. Lydia Peters Baldwin diary, 1768–1821, Vermont Historical Society.

39. EPP memorandum book, December 4, 1808, Box 7 folder 3, PPHFP.

40. Tannenbaum, *Healer's Calling*, 37–39.

41. Dayton, "Taking the Trade," 21–22.

42. Hampshire County Court records, Inferior Court of Common Pleas, General Sessions of the Peace, University of Massachusetts Amherst Special Collections and Archives, May 15–19, 1787, vol. 14, 233.

43. Hampshire County Court records (1776–1771), May 21, 1771, vol. 10 (1776–1790), 175.

44. EWPH to EPP, June 12, 1801, Box 5 folder 6, PPHFP.

45. EPP to EWPH, July 6, 1805, Box 5 folder 7, PPHFP.

46. EPP memorandum book, July 14 and 21, 1811, Box 7 folder 3, PPHFP.

47. EPP memorandum book, July 15, 1804, Box 7 folder 3, PPHFP.

48. See Janet Golden, *A Social History of Wet Nursing in America: From Breast to Bottle* (Columbus: Ohio State University Press, 2001); Valeria Fildes, *Wet Nursing: A History from Antiquity to the Present* (Oxford: Basil Blackwell, 1988); and Doyle, *Maternal Bodies,* chapter 4, "Good Mothers and Wet Nurses: Breastfeeding and the Fracturing of Sentimental Motherhood," 115–45. On the lack of stigma, see Jonathan Judd Jr., as noted in Judd, "Miscellaneous," vol. 12, 188.

49. Golden, *A Social History of Wet Nursing*, 12–13.

50. Golden, *A Social History of Wet Nursing,* 19–20; and Doyle, *Maternal Bodies,* 128–29.

51. Paula A. Treckel, "Breastfeeding and Maternal Sexuality in Colonial America," *Journal of Interdisciplinary History* 20, no. 1 (Summer 1989): 25–51.

52. On maternal grief, see Lucia McMahon, "'So Truly Afflicting and Distressing to Me His Sorrowing Mother': Expressions of Maternal Grief in Eighteenth-Century Philadelphia," *JER* 32, no. 1 (2012): 27–60.

53. Golden, *A Social History of Wet Nursing,* 20–21. See also Doyle, *Maternal Bodies,* 134.

54. EPP memorandum book, December 29, 1776–February 2, 1777, *NEHGR*.

55. Karin Wulf, *Not All Wives: Women of Colonial Philadelphia* (Ithaca, NY: Cornell University Press, 2000), 140.

56. Doyle, *Maternal Bodies,* 130.

57. *Boston News Letter,* August 4, 1768.

58. *HG,* May 9, 1787.

59. *HG,* August 19, 1789; repeated August 26 and September 4.

60. *HG,* December 22, 1790; repeated January 4 to 26, 1791.

61. *HG,* November 27, 1793; repeated December 4, 1793, to January 1, 1794.

62. *HG,* July 4, 1810.

63. Golden, *A Social History of Wet Nursing,* 28–29.

64. *HG,* August 19, 1789.

65. See Lewis Tappan, "Reminiscences of Northampton," letter to Reverend William Allen, October 25, 1854, published in *HG,* January 23, 1855. The identity of Hodge is unknown.

66. EPP memorandum book, March 14, 1773, *NEHGR.*

67. EPP memorandum book, March 26, August 27, and December 31, 1769; May 17, 1771, *NEHGR.*

68. EPP memorandum book, July 10, 1773, August 8, 1773, *NEHGR.* The following year, the little boy was again injured when he had a "bad blow by the kick of a horse." EPP memorandum book, August 21, 1774, *NEHGR.* Which of Hadley's several "Mrs. Alixanders" this was remains unclear.

69. Mary Crouch (d. 1781), Box 41 no. 50, HCMRP.

70. Mary Crouch's nurse may have been Miriam Cook Pierce, the sixty-five-year-old wife of Hadley's longtime town clerk (Pierce had been a witness to Richard Crouch's 1761 will, so perhaps tended him as well), or her daughter-in-law, Lucy Fairfield Pierce, then in her mid-forties. Either woman could have tended to her ailing neighbor, probably, given the sum due, for a period of two to three weeks as Mary's health failed. See the Richard and Mary Crouch probate files, Box 41 nos. 52 and 50, HCMRP, respectively.

71. Wulf, *Not All Wives,* 139.

72. See Rose Lockwood, "Birth, Illness and Death in 18th-Century New England," *Journal of Social History* 12, no. 1 (Autumn 1978): 111–28, especially 119. On the work of nursing within informal, non-monetary systems of exchange, see Daniel Vickers's discussion of the diary of Martha Ballard in his important article, "Errors Expected: The Culture of Credit in Rural New England, 1750–1800," *The Economic History Review,* n.s., 63, no. 4 (November 2010): 1032–57, especially 1051–54.

73. Judd, "Miscellaneous," vol. 9, 160.

74. In that same year, Smith was paying two shillings eight pence per week for domestic service. Judd, "Hadley," vol. 3, 120, 218; see also Judd, "Miscellaneous," vol. 18, 416b.

75. List of expenses submitted by guardian Stephen Webster, February 22, 1803, Thankful Coates, Box 33 no. 56, HCMRP. By comparison, the executors of the estate of West Springfield's Elizabeth Lankton in 1804 "paid for a housekeeper 9 weeks at .75 per week." See her estate settlement, Box 86 no. 28, HCMRP.

76. Juliana Dickinson (Amherst), 1803, Box 48 no. 2, HCMRP.

77. Judd, "Miscellaneous," vol. 9, 322.

78. Jonathan Atherton (Amherst), 1781, Box 6 no. 23, HCMRP.

79. RD diary, November 15, 1787, PVMA.

80. Reuban Belden (Hatfield), 1776, Box 13 no. 15, HCMRP.

81. Mary Ann Jimenez, "Madness in Early American History: Insanity in Massachusetts from 1700 to 1830," *Journal of Social History* 20, no. 1 (Autumn 1986): 25–44.

82. EPP memorandum book October 10, 1784, *NEHGR.*

83. See EPP memorandum book February 6, 1744, January 4, 1781, October 20 and 27, 1782, November 30, 1783, January 8, 1786, June 21, 1789, and May 16, 1790, *NEHGR;* and Carlisle, *Earthbound and Heavenbent,* 99–101. This may have been a second attempt, as in 1780 Phelps recorded that "Brother Sol broke his skull with an axe"; see EPP memorandum book, November 26, 1780, *NEHGR.*

84. William Williams to Dolly Williams, January 16, 1802, Williams Family Papers, Box 7 folder 10, PVMA. For a comparable case of a later date, see Laurel Thatcher Ulrich,

"Derangement in the Family: The Story of Mary Sewell, 1824–25," in Peter Benes and Jane Montague Benes, *Medicine and Healing*, 168–84.

85. See Williams Family Papers, Box 7 folders 9–10, PVMA.

86. Jimenez, "Madness in Early American History," 27.

87. Springfield select board on Sarah Ball, December 2, 1773, Box 8 no. 19, HCMRP. On the guardianship of "distracted" people, see Jimenez, "Madness in Early American History," 28.

88. Guardianship records, Bethia Hawley and Ann Bartlett, Box 10 no 42, HCMRP.

89. EPP memorandum book, September 12, 1784, *NEHGR*.

90. EPP memorandum book, November 7, 1784, *NEHGR*.

91. EPP memorandum book, November 7, 1784, *NEHGR*.

92. EPP memorandum book, November 14 and 21, 1784, *NEHGR*. Elizabeth Carlisle also recounts these events in *Earthbound and Heavenbent*, 108. Elizabeth Porter Phelps may well have been mindful of the 1775 suicide of thirty-two-year-old Faith Trumbull Huntington, the daughter of Connecticut's Governor Jonathan Trumbull. See Ann Brandwein, "An Eighteenth-Century Depression: The Sad Conclusion of Faith Trumbull Huntington," *Connecticut History* 26 (1985): 19–32. Hadley had also experienced the suicides of two men, which Phelps recorded in her memorandum book, March 21, 1771, and April 25, 1779, *NEHGR*. See Richard Bell, *We Shall Be No More* (Cambridge: Harvard University Press, 2012); and also the discussion of "distraction" and suicide in Rose Lockwood, "Birth, Illness and Death in 18th-Century New England," *Journal of Social History* 12, no. 1 (Autumn 1978): 111–28, especially 115.

93. EPP memorandum book, September 30, 1798, *NEHGR*.

94. Receipt, March 29, 1786, Town Papers, HHS. For more on the making of grave cloths elsewhere in the Atlantic World, see Sanderson, *Women and Work in Eighteenth-Century Edinburgh*, 64–71.

95. Wulf, *Not All Wives*, 140.

96. See Georganne Rundblad, "Exhuming Women's Premarket Duties in the Care of the Dead," *Gender and Society* 9, no. 2 (April 1995): 173–92. The diary of Martha Ballard contains several references to the midwife preparing corpses for burial; see, e.g., Ulrich, *Midwife's Tale*, 37, 39, 72, 236.

97. Charles H. LeeDecker, "Preparing for an Afterlife on Earth: The Transformation of Mortuary Behavior in Nineteenth-Century North America," in Teresita Majewski and David Gaimste, eds., *International Handbook of Historical Archaeology* (New York: Springer, 2009), 142; and Mary Carolyn Beaudry, *Findings: The Material Culture of Needlework and Sewing* (New Haven, CT: Yale University Press, 206), 35, 38. See also Gary Laderman, *The Sacred Remains: American Attitudes toward Death, 1799–1883* (New Haven, CT: Yale University Press, 1996). The Connecticut Historical Society holds a shroud (1985.165.0a, b) from the second quarter of the nineteenth century; it is described in the museum's online catalog (accessible at http://emuseum.chs.org/emuseum/) as "hand-stitched, brown glazed cotton 'cambric,' with a drawstring neck and drawstring wrist openings." The garment "was hastily made; stitching is coarse and edges are left raw. The neckline, wrist openings, and hem are cut (pinked) in a zig-zag or 'Van Dyke' edge. It has a matching cap."

98. Beaudry, *Findings*, 35–38.

99. See, for example, EPP memorandum book, July 24, 1774, and August 4, 1776, *NEHGR*.

100. On Jenny Dodge, see *HG*, April 20, 1796.

101. James Wynbrandt, *The Excruciating History of Dentistry: Toothsome Tales & Oral Oddities from Babylon to Braces* (New York: St. Martin's, 1998), 214.

102. *HG*, April 20, 1796.

103. EPP memorandum book, February 10, 1811, Box 7 folder 3, PPHFP.

104. Peter Benes, "Itinerant Physicians, Healers and Surgeon-Dentists in New England and New York, 1720–1825," in Benes, ed., *Medicine and Healing,* Proceedings of the 1990 Dublin Seminar for New England Folklife (Boston: Boston University, 1992), 95–112. Some itinerant practitioners used only initials, so their gender is unclear; Dodge, however, identified herself as "Mrs Dodge" or "Jenny Dodge."

105. See Benes, "Itinerant Physicians," appendix B; for Skinner, see *HG,* November 7, 1798. From there she may have moved on to Portsmouth, NH: see the *United States Oracle,* January 10, 1801.

106. *HG,* January 6, 1808.

107. Benes, "Itinerant Physicians," 105.

108. Jonathan Judd diary, August 24, 1768, FL.

109. EPP memorandum book, January 28, 1798, *NEHGR*; and Frederick C. Warner, "List of Births Attended, 1805–1833, by Isaac G. Cutler of Amherst," *Detroit Society for Genealogical Research Magazine,* 35, no. 1 (Fall 1971), Jones Library Special Collections, Amherst, MA.

110. Carlisle, *Earthbound and Heavenbent,* 202.

111. Richard L. Bushman, *The Refinement of America: Persons, Houses, Cities* (New York: Knopf, 1992), 81.

112. Rundblad, "Exhuming Women's Premarket Duties."

113. Brandt, "Gifted Women," xx.

114. Brandt, "Gifted Women," xxi.

115. Mary Palmer Tyler, *The Maternal Physician: A Treatise on the Nurture and Management of Infants, from the Birth until Age Two Years Old* (New York: Isaac Riley, 1811); see Kathleen M. Brown, *Foul Bodies: Cleanliness in Early America* (New Haven, CT: Yale University Press, 2009), 224–30; and "The Maternal Physician: Teaching American Mothers to Put the Baby in the Bathwater," in Charles E. Rosenberg, ed., *Right Living: An Anglo-American Tradition of Self-Help Medicine and Hygiene,* published in cooperation with the Library Company of Philadelphia and the College of Physicians of Philadelphia (Baltimore: Johns Hopkins University Press, 2003), 88–111. See also Christina Gibbons, "Mary Tyler and *The Maternal Physician,*" *Journal of Regional Cultures* 3 (Fall/Winter 1983): 33–45.

116. Jacqueline S. Reinier, "Rearing the Republican Child: Attitudes and Practices in Post-Revolutionary Philadelphia," *WMQ* 39, no. 1 (1982): 150–63, 160; Marilyn S. Blackwell, "The Republican Vision of Mary Palmer Tyler," *JER* 12 no. 1 (1992): 11–35.

117. The entrepreneurial Tyler also launched a notable cloth making enterprise, discussed in Brown, "The Maternal Physician," 98, and Laurel Thatcher Ulrich, "Wheels, Looms, and the Gender Division of Labor in Eighteenth-Century New England," *WMQ* 55, no. 1 (January 1998): 30–32.

118. Brown, "The Maternal Physician," 107.

119. For these developments in the clothing trades, see Marla R. Miller, *The Needle's Eye: Women and Work in the Age of Revolution* (Amherst: University of Massachusetts Press, 2006); and "The Last Mantuamaker: Craft Tradition and Commercial Change in Boston, 1760–1845," *Early American Studies* 4, no. 2 (Fall 2006): 372–424.

120. Golden, *A Social History of Wet Nursing*, 39. On changing perceptions of motherhood in this period, see Nora Doyle, "The Highest Pleasure of which Woman's Nature Is Capable": Breast-Feeding and the Sentimental Maternal Ideal in America, 1750–1860," *The Journal of American History* 97, no. 4 (March 2011): 958–73; and her book *Maternal Bodies: Redefining Motherhood in Early America* (Chapel Hill: University of North Carolina Press, 2018).

121. My thanks to Susan Brandt for this important point, grounded in her own research on women's roles in health care and healing. On women's work and rising standards of cleanliness, see Brown, *Foul Bodies*, 215, 221; and "The Maternal Physician," 95–97. On the material culture and infrastructure of personal and household cleanliness, see Ruth Schwartz Cowan, *More Work for Mother: The Ironies of Household Technology from the Open Hearth to the Microwave* (New York: Basic Books, 1983); and Richard L. Bushman and Claudia L. Bushman, "The Early History of Cleanliness in America," *The Journal of American History* 74, no. 4 (March 1988): 1213–38.

122. Doyle, *Maternal Bodies*, 135.

123. Doyle, *Maternal Bodies*, 145.

Chapter 8 • Working Women and the Domestic Landscapes of Forty Acres

1. EPP to EWPH, April 10, 1803, Box 5 folder 5, PPHFP. "Mrs. Lord" is probably Mary Lyman Lord, the daughter of Joseph Lyman of Northampton, who married Lynd Lord Jr. of Litchfield, Connecticut. She and Elizabeth Whiting Phelps Huntington were acquaintances from the latter's residence in Litchfield while Dan Huntington was pastor there, and Lord traveled often to Northampton to visit family and friends.

2. Robert Blair St. George, "Artifacts of Regional Consciousness," in Gerald W. R. Ward and William N. Hosley, eds., *The Great River: Art & Society of the Connecticut Valley, 1635–1820* (Hartford, CT: Wadsworth Atheneum, 1985), 36. Richard Bushman has proposed a narrative in which eighteenth-century elite gentility gave way to nineteenth-century middle-class "refinement" in his influential book *The Refinement of America: Persons, Houses, Cities* (New York: Knopf, 1992).

3. Another study that explores "liberty" in the context of labor is Paul Gilje's *Liberty on the Waterfront: American Maritime Culture in the Age of Revolution* (Philadelphia: University of Pennsylvania Press, 2004).

4. On Elizabeth Phelps's liberty, see EPP to EWPH, August 6, 1802, Box 5 folder 4, PPFHP; on Peg's, see Elizabeth Porter Phelps's memorandum book, June 9, 1782, *NEHGR*.

5. Important early contributions to this literature include Bushman, *Refinement of America;* and Ronald Hoffman, Cary Carson, and Peter J. Albert, eds. *Of Consuming Interests: The Style of Life in the Eighteenth Century* (Charlottesville: University of Virginia Press, 1994).

6. Quartus Wells, 1825 Division of Estate, and (below) Nathan Catlin (1794) as quoted and paraphrased in Susan McGowan and Mimi Miller, *Family and Landscape: Deerfield Homelots from 1671* (Deerfield, MA: PVMA, 1996), 108 and 110.

7. This analysis takes a page from Robert David Sack's discussion of consumption, which "creates places that simultaneously weave together and alter forces and perspectives."

See *Place, Modernity, and the Consumer's World: A Relational Framework for Geographical Analysis* (Baltimore: Johns Hopkins University Press, 1992), 2.

8. See Adam Smith, *The Theory of Moral Sentiments* (1759) and *An Inquiry into the Nature and Causes of the Wealth of Nations* (1776), vols. 1 and 2 in the Glasgow Edition of *The Works and Correspondence of Adam Smith* (New York: Oxford University Press, 1976). My thanks to Tom Paske for showing me this physical feature.

9. Jane Whittle, in "The House as a Place of Work in Early Modern Rural England," *Home Cultures* 8, no. 2 (2011): 133–50, observes that "there was a trend to separate work from living space well before industrialization but, importantly, this trend did not apply to elements of women's work, which remained located within the house, or to laborers' houses, which have often been omitted from discussions." This distinction remains relevant in rural western Massachusetts as well, even at this later date.

10. Sister Lyman to Sylvester Judd, October 9, 1859, in Sylvester Judd, "Miscellaneous," vol. 18, 387 (Judd Manuscript), FL.

11. The following paragraphs are deeply indebted to Gregory Clancey, "Historic Structure Report," Adams and Roy Consultants, Inc., of Portsmouth, New Hampshire, 1987–1988, Box 178, PPHFP, and Tara Gleason, "The Porter Phelps Huntington Family: The Social Position and Material Wealth of an Elite Family in Eighteenth-Century Hadley, Massachusetts" (honors thesis, Amherst College, 1994).

12. Clancey, "Historic Structure Report," ix.

13. William N. Hosley, "Architecture," in Ward and Hosley, eds., *The Great River*, 73.

14. On the significance of this series of barriers, see Robert Blair St. George's introduction to Dell Upton's "White and Black Landscapes in Eighteenth-Century Virginia," in Robert Blair St. George, ed., *Material Life in America, 1600–1860* (Boston: Northeastern University Press, 1988), 357.

15. Robert Blair St. George, "Artifacts of Regional Consciousness," in Ward and Hosley, eds., *The Great River*, 33. See also Alexandra A. Chan, *Slavery in the Age of Reason: Archaeology at a New England Farm* (Knoxville: University of Tennessee Press, 2007), 104–5.

16. Kevin M. Sweeney, "Mansion People: Kinship, Class, and Architecture in Western Massachusetts in the Mid Eighteenth Century," *Winterthur Portfolio* 19 (1984): 231–56. See also Charles Bergengren, "From Lovers to Murderers: The Etiquette of Entry and the Social Implications of House Form," *Winterthur Portfolio* 29 (1994): 43–72. On the way the hall functioned, see Kevin M. Sweeney, "High Style Vernacular: Lifestyles of the Colonial Elite," in Carson, et al., *Of Consuming Interests*, 1–58, especially 19.

17. Elvira Casal, "'Rooms Concise, or Rooms Distended': Space in Jane Austen's Novels" (PhD diss., Vanderbilt University, 1993), 78.

18. EPP memorandum book, August 29, 1779; see also May 20, 1781, *NEHGR*.

19. Sylvester Judd, *History of Hadley: Including the Early History of Hatfield, South Hadley, Amherst and Granby, Massachusetts* (Springfield, MA: H. R. Huntting, 1905), 445–52.

20. EPP memorandum book, May 4, 1788, *NEHGR*.

21. EPP memorandum book, September 15, 1793, *NEHGR*, and April 19, 1815, Box 7 folder 4, PPHFP. Again, I do not mean to suggest that Elizabeth Phelps was not herself well or widely traveled; indeed, the opposite is true. But while she traveled more often than many of her Hadley neighbors, travel was not as much a part of her normal routine as it was for her husband Charles.

22. EPP memorandum book, August 3, 1794; see also October 26, 1794, and August 26, 1797, *NEHGR*.

23. Judd, *Hadley*, 383.

24. Dorothy Ashley Williams to Mrs. Dorothy Williams, June 25, 1795, Williams Family Papers, Box 7 folder 9, PVMA.

25. See Elizabeth Pendergast Carlisle, *Earthbound and Heavenbent: Elizabeth Porter Phelps and Life at Forty Acres (1747–1817)* (New York: Scribner, 2004), 11.

26. See EPP memorandum book, May 5, 1782, *NEHGR*. On intersections between modes of conveyance and quilting among women of the rural gentry, see Marla R. Miller, *The Needle's Eye: Women and Work in the Age of Revolution* (Amherst: University of Massachusetts Press, 2006), 105.

27. EPP memorandum book, October 30, 1790, *NEHGR*.

28. On the ways in which both petticoats and architecture communicated "kinship, group cohesion and cultural leadership," see Sweeney's description of architecture in "Mansion People" and my own discussion of the production of petticoats in *Needle's Eye*, chapter 2.

29. Marla R. Miller, "'. . . And Others of Our Own People': Needlework and Women of the Rural Gentry," in Lynne Bassett, ed., *What's New England about New England Quilts?* (Sturbridge, MA: Old Sturbridge Village, 1999). See also Rodris Roth's excellent study, "Tea-Drinking in Eighteenth-Century America: Its Etiquette and Equipage," United States National Museum Bulletin 225, Contributions from the Museum of History and Technology, Paper 14:61–91 (Washington DC: Smithsonian Institution, 1961), republished in St. George, ed., *Material Life in America*, 439–62; also Kevin M. Sweeney, "Furniture and the Domestic Environment in Wethersfield, Connecticut, 1639–1800," also republished in St. George, ed., *Material Life in America*, 261–90.

30. Anne Smart Martin, "Common People and the Local Store: Consumerism in the Rural Virginia Backcountry," in David Harvey and Gregory Brown, eds., *Common People and Their Material World: Free Men and Women in the Chesapeake, 1700–1830* (Richmond, VA: Dietz Press for the Colonial Williamsburg Foundation, 1995), 40.

31. In central Massachusetts' Worcester County, Michael Steinitz found that 24 percent of the dwellings enumerated in the 1798 federal direct tax were less than six hundred square feet in area, and 14 percent were less than five hundred square feet. There, one-story dwellings out-numbered two-story dwellings two to one. In parts of western Massachusetts, nearly 90 percent of the houses were one story. Unfortunately, these detailed 1798 census schedules do not survive for many Hampshire County towns, although figures for some communities, such as South Hadley, Granby, and Easthampton, suggest that in older, more prosperous, and more densely populated villages, two-story houses made up as many as half the houses. See Steinitz, "Rethinking Geographical Approaches to the Common House: The Evidence from Eighteenth-Century Massachusetts," in Thomas Carter and Bernard L. Herman, eds., *Perspectives in Vernacular Architecture*, vol. 3 (Columbia: University of Missouri Press, 1989), 24–25. Carole Shammas in her study of the 1798 direct tax notes that Massachusetts compares favorably to other states and regions in terms of the overall quality of its housing stock; see "The Housing Stock of the Early United States: Refinement Meets Migration," *WMQ* 64, no. 3 (July 2007): 549–90. The Commonwealth's proportion of buildings that fell beneath the taxable threshold was lower than that of any other state; however, the percentage of nontaxable housing stock was higher in western communities than coastal cities and towns.

32. Judd, "Hadley," vol. 3, 18; Olive Cleveland Clark, "Recollections of Olive Cleveland Clark," in Phyllis Baker Deming, comp., *History of Williamsburg in Massachusetts* (Northampton, MA: Hampshire Bookshop, 1946), 62.

33. As observed by Michael Steinitz, "The Evidence from Eighteenth-Century Massachusetts," "these variations in the landscape must have been readily observable as signs of individual affluence or poverty." John L. Brooke suggests, "that Shays' Rebellion pitted one-story regulators against two-story gentry-merchants." See Brooke, "Society, Revolution, and the Symbolic Use of the Dead: An Historical Ethnography of the Massachusetts Near Frontier, 1730–1820" (PhD diss., University of Pennsylvania, 1982), as discussed in Steinitz, "Rethinking Geographical Approaches to the Common House," *Perspectives in Vernacular Architecture*, vol. 3 (1989), 24.

34. Gleason, "The Porter Phelps Huntington Family," 106; see also EWPH to CP, September 28, 1800, Box 12 folder 13, PPHFP.

35. EPP to EWPH, September 13, 1802, Box 5 folder 4; also EPP to EWPH, March 2, 1801, Box 5 folder 3, PPHFP. Elizabeth Carlisle writes of Elizabeth Porter Phelps's particular fondness for writing and reading in *Earthbound and Heavenbent*, 14, 22.

36. Sweeney, "Furniture and the Domestic Environment in Wethersfield," 285; and Gleason, "The Porter Phelps Huntington Family," 70–71. As Barbara Clark Smith writes, "although many men and some women" in the late-eighteenth-century Connecticut Valley were literate, "few people besides merchants needed desks, commonly using tables for writing surfaces instead." See *After the Revolution: The Smithsonian History of Everyday Life in the Eighteenth Century* (New York: Pantheon, 1985), 22; and also Gloria L. Main, "An Inquiry into When and Why Women Learned to Write in Colonial New England," *Journal of Social History* 24 (1990–1991): 579–89.

37. EWPH to Charles Porter Phelps, April 23, 1798, Box 12 folder 14, PPHFP.

38. Quoted in Bushman, *Refinement of America*, 65.

39. Richard Sheridan, *The School for Scandal: A Comedy in Five Acts* (Boston: Belknap, 1792), Act II, Scene I.

40. EPP to EWPH, March 1801, Box 5 folder 3, PPHFP.

41. Several engravings in the collection of the American Antiquarian Society illustrate tailors sitting in such a manner. See, for example, the tale of "The Elephant and the Tailors" in William Cowper, *The History of John Gilpin of Cheapside* (Philadelphia: John Jacobsen, 1807). Such images can be accessed through the Catalog of Early American Engravings Project database at the American Antiquarian Society.

42. Madeleine Ginsberg, "The Tailoring and Dressmaking Trades," *Costume* 6 (1972): 64–71; and Ebenezer Cobham Brewer and Adriane Room, *Brewer's Dictionary of Phrase and Fable*, 15th ed. (New York: HarperCollins, 1995).

43. R. Campbell, *The London Tradesman* [1747] (New York: Kelley, 1969), 193.

44. Dolores Hayden, *The Power of Place: Urban Landscapes as Public History* (Cambridge: MIT Press, 1995), 48.

45. Jonathan Judd diary, 1822–1837, FL.

46. Central halls first appeared in the Connecticut Valley about 1750, some of the earliest examples being the Dr. Thomas Williams house in Deerfield, the Seth Wetmore house in Middletown, Connecticut (ca. 1750, extant), the Reverend Eliphalet Williams house in East Hartford, Connecticut (1751), and the Joseph Webb house in Wethersfield, Connecticut (1752, extant). Nonetheless, central halls remained uncommon in the Connecticut

Valley. Even in large houses, they were rarely built before the last quarter of the eighteenth century. See Clancey, "Historic Structure Report," 15; and Sweeney, "Mansion People."

47. Tara Gleason makes this observation and describes the Porter hall in "The Porter Phelps Huntington Family," 26.

48. Massachusetts Direct Tax, 1798, vol. 18, 172–82; and vol. 17, 170–78, as discussed in Sweeney, "Mansion People," 244. Older towns in the valley certainly contained a larger proportion of two-story houses, but how high a proportion is unfortunately not known.

49. The paragraphs here discussing the Phelps house and its renovations rely heavily on Clancey, "Historic Structure Report"; and Gleason, "The Porter-Phelps-Huntington Family."

50. EPP memorandum book, April 14, 1771, *NEHGR*: "Monday, our kitchen raised."

51. Some oven, though it is not clear which, was added in 1783, when EPP recorded, "Monday Mr. Abraham Billings here to make a new oven"; see her entry for December 7, 1783, *NEHGR*.

52. See, for example, EPP memorandum book, August 30, 1771, *NEHGR*: "I moved out of my room and into the keeping room."

53. Clancey, "Historic Structure Report," 47.

54. See Clancey, "Historic Structure Report," 43 and 47.

55. Alexander Ormond Boulton, "New England's Slave Quarters," *Journal of Regional Culture* 5 (1985): 6–12.

56. Upton, "White and Black Landscapes in Eighteenth-Century Virginia," 365. On servants' "transparency" in urban residential contexts, see also Barnard L. Herman, *Town House: Architecture and Material Life in the Early American City, 1780–1830* (Chapel Hill: University of North Carolina Press, 2005), 134–45, 147–149.

57. Chan, *Slavery in the Age of Reason*, 218.

58. Clancey, "Historic Structure Report," xi.

59. Here see also Gleason, "The Porter Phelps Huntington Family," 60.

60. This work was performed by Samuel Gaylord Jr., the father-in-law of gown maker Lucretia Smith Gaylord, and father of gown maker Betsy Gaylord, each of whom was employed at one time for the Phelps household. Gaylord's account book, preserved in the collection of the Pocumtuck Valley Memorial Association and housed at Memorial Libraries in Deerfield, Massachusetts, shows a number of transactions with the Phelps family, including the construction of six banister chairs, at least three of which survive and can be found in the collection of Historic Deerfield, Inc. I have benefited from Sharon Mehrman's research into Gaylord's craft practice. See Mehrman, "Samuel Gaylord Jr. (1742–1816) Rural Making in 18th-Century Hadley, Massachusetts" (Unpublished research paper, University of Massachusetts Amherst, 2017).

61. See EPP memorandum book, December 25, 1785, *NEHGR*: "Mr. Prescott and Mr. Bartlett from Northampton came this evening to paint some of our rooms"; and January 8, 1786: "Satt. the painters finished to my joy."

62. Gleason, "The Porter Phelps Huntington Family," 62–63.

63. EPP memorandum book, February 23, 1794, *NEHGR*. In 1799, Elizabeth Whiting Phelps wrote to her future sister-in-law, "[We are] in such confusion, you would not know this solitary antique habitation; the house is undergoing a complete repair—and may I not hope you will soon make it your dwelling?" EWPH to Sarah Parsons, July 12, 1799.

64. See EPP memorandum book, May 2, 1799, *NEHGR:* "The latter part of this week a great deal of business here—the new roof raised on the old house." In his memoirs Charles Porter Phelps writes: "I closed my law office and business on the 1st of April 1799 and removed to Hadley, where I was occupied till late in the autumn superintending the alterations and repairs of my fathers home to render it convenient for the accommodation of two families, as I proposed to bring my wife there in the early spring." See Box 10 folder 21, PPHFP.

65. Clancey, "Historic Structure Report," 56.

66. EPP to EWPH, August 6, 1802, Box 5 folder 4, PPHFP. Elizabeth Porter Phelps recorded in her memorandum book of October 26, 1797, "We [are] all in confusion, the hearths laying," which is likely a reference to the hearth of this south ell, since it comes about two weeks after she recorded on October 13th, "Fryday—this day our woodhouse [part of the south ell addition] raised as far as the roof. Satt. finished."

67. EPP to EWPH, February 7, 1803, Box 5 folder 5, PPHFP.

68. EPP to EWPH, August 4, 1802, Box 5 folder 4, PPHFP.

69. EPP to EWPH, March 27, 1805, Box 5 folder 7, PPHFP.

70. EPP to EWPH, December 15, 1809, PPHFP.

71. EPP memorandum book, May 17, 1795, *NEGHR.*

72. EPP to EWPH, October 13, 1797, Box 5 folder 3, PPHFP.

73. These were dismantled by James Lincoln Huntington in 1923, and the present balloon-frame replicas were later erected on their site.

74. EPP memorandum book, May 20, 1782, *NEHGR*, and June 9, 1805, Box 7 folder 3, PPHFP.

75. Thomas C. Hubka, "The New England Farmhouse Ell: Fact and Symbol of Nineteenth-Century Farm Improvement," in Camille Wells, ed., *Perspectives in Vernacular Architecture*, vol. 2 (Columbia: University of Missouri Press, 1986), 166.

76. Clancey, "Historic Structure Report," 29.

77. For instance, Richard Bushman notes the "Long Room" created by John and Abigail Adams (at about the same time, in 1800) in *Refinement of America*, 121; Henry Adams describes the room (and calls it a drawing room) in *The Adams Mansion* (Quincy, MA: Adams Memorial Society, 1935), 17–29. My thanks to Peter Benes for sharing his knowledge of Long Rooms in New England public life.

78. Clancey, "Historic Structure Report," 29; see also Gleason, "The Porter Phelps Huntington Family," 94–96.

79. EPP to CP, May 23, 1803, directs him to some "cheese cloathes" in the "press bed place in the sitting room" (Box 5 folder 13, PPHFP). She refers to this space by name again in a diary entry dated May 21, 1804, *NEHGR:* "Wednesday began to paint the floors and walls of our sitting room."

80. The relationship between servants and hallways is explored in Elizabeth O'Leary, *At Beck and Call: The Representation of Domestic Servants in Nineteenth-Century American Painting* (Washington, DC: Smithsonian Institution Press, 1996).

81. The mirror is described and illustrated in catalog entry 158 in Ward and Hosley, eds., *The Great River*, 269–70. On mirrors as markers of position and identity, see Rebecca K. Shrum, *In the Looking Glass: Mirrors and Identity in Early America* (Baltimore: Johns Hopkins University Press, 2017). On the furniture the family acquired to furnish this room, see Gleason, "The Porter Phelps Huntington Family," 97–107.

82. Bushman, *Refinement of America,* 120.

83. Even the two newest kitchens were separated by some distance, including the length of a hallway, the sitting/dining room, and another vestibule.

84. EPP to Sarah [Sally] Parsons Phelps, March 17, 1802, Box 5 folder 15, PPHFP; EPP memorandum book, March 27, 1805, August 28, 1805, April 4, 1807, April 21, 1810, May 30, 1812, April 20, 1815, Box 5 folders 7–12, PPHFP.

85. In this case, the worker was a farmhand from Pelham, and the control of access was enforced by Charles Phelps. In a letter to his wife, Charles reported that he "told him he would not have more liberty than he had and if he could not put up with such fare as he had, he was welcome to seek other quarters." The boy finished out the month and left; Charles would not yield on this point despite the fact that he was that spring "only half Mand." See CP to EPP, April 30, 1802. I am grateful to Christopher Clark for mentioning this exchange to me; he cites the incident himself in *The Roots of Rural Capitalism: Western Massachusetts, 1780–1860* (Ithaca, NY: Cornell University Press, 1990), 111. For more evidence of control of spaces, see EPP to EWPH, March 5, 1808, Box 6 folder 3, PPHFP. On the trade generated for one Hampshire County blacksmith by the need for locks and keys, see Susan Robeson McGowan, "Agreeable to His Genius: John Partidge Bull (1731–1813), Deerfield, Massachusetts" (MA thesis, Trinity College, 1988), 41.

86. On housing of enslaved people in New England, see William Pierson, *Black Yankees: The Development of an Afro-American Subculture in Eighteenth-Century New England* (Amherst: University of Massachusetts Press, 1988); and Robert K. Fitts, "The Landscapes of Northern Bondage," *Historical Archaeology* 30, no. 2 (1996): 54–73.

87. Works reviewed for this purpose include Samuel Richardson's *Pamela* (London: F. Newbery, 1769) and *Clarissa* (Dublin: Faulkner, 1748); Fanney Burney's *Evelina* (London: T. Lowndes, 1778); Hannah Webster Foster's *The Coquette; or, the History of Eliza Wharton, Founded on Fact by a Lady of Massachusetts* (Boston: Printed by Samuel Ethridge for E. Larkin, 1797); William Hill Brown's *The Power of Sympathy* (Boston: Isaiah Thomas, 1789); and the plays of Richard Sheridan. See also Caroline C. Briggs, *Reminiscences and Letters of Caroline C. Briggs* (Boston: Houghton Mifflin, 1897); Susan Lesley, *Recollections of My Mother* (Boston: George Ellis, 1889); Clark, "Recollections of Olive Cleveland Clark"; and Almedia M. Brown, *Diary of a Village Gossip* (New York: J. S. Oglevie, 1882). Also suggestive is Casal, "'Rooms Concise, or Rooms Distended.'"

88. Mary C. Beaudry, "Needlewomen of the Spencer-Pierce-Little Farm: An Archaeological Study of the Material Culture of Sewing and Needlework," paper prepared for the *Delaware Seminar in American Art, History, and Material Culture*, December 8, 1994, 18.

89. The rear stoop was also used to feed the farm's many hired hands; see EPP to EWPH, July 5, 1805, Box 6 folder 1, PPHFP.

90. EPP to EWPH, June 26, 1808, Box 5 folder 9, PPHFP.

91. EPP to EWPH, January 28, 1796, Box 5 folder 3, PPHFP.

92. EPP memorandum book, January 25, 1767, and February 22, 1767, *NEHGR.*

93. Paul Gilje offered this observation at the Society for Historians of the Early American Republic roundtable, "Reconsidering Mastery, Mobility and Community in Maritime America," July 23, 2006. See also his book *Liberty on the Waterfront.*

94. Claudia B. Kidwell, *Cutting a Fashionable Fit: Dressmakers' Drafting Systems in the United States,* Smithsonian Studies in History and Technology, no. 42 (Washington, DC:

Smithsonian Institution Press, 1979), 11; see also my own *The Needle's Eye,* particularly chapter five.

95. Patience Langdon to Sophronia Beebe, undated [ca. 1800], excerpted in Judith Knight's 1995 notes on needlework from the Beebe Family Papers, Old Sturbridge Village. My thanks to then-curator Lynne Bassett for making these available to me.

96. Margaret Miller, "Notebooks of Hatfield History," Margaret Miller Papers, Miller Family Papers, Box 1–122, PVMA.

97. Daniel White Wells and Reuban Field Wells, *A History of Hatfield, Massachusetts* (Springfield, MA: F. C. H. Gibbons, 1910), 170; and Miller, "Notebooks of Hatfield History."

98. Witold Rybczynsky, *Home: A Short History of an Idea* (New York: Viking, 1986), 15. As I have written elsewhere, in communities and economies like those of rural western Massachusetts—places where social and financial success depended on reputation—few residents had as much access to the households of the politically, socially, and culturally powerful as gownmakers; for more, see Miller, *Needle's Eye,* 159.

99. See the 1868 tell-all published by Elizabeth Keckley, the African American dressmaker to Mary Todd Lincoln, which even in its title, *Behind the Scenes,* suggests Keckley's unusual movement throughout the Lincoln White House. Elizabeth Hobbs Keckley, *Behind the Scenes: Thirty Years a Slave and Four Years in the White House* [1868] (reprint, New York: Arno Press, 1968).

100. EPP to EWPH, February 26, 1801, Box 6 folder 1, PPHFP.

101. EPP to EWPH, February 7, 1801, Box 6 folder 1, PPHFP.

102. EPP memorandum book, February 12, 1767, and EPP to EWPH, January 28, 1796, Box 5 folder 3, PPHFP.

103. Indenture of Timothy Buggy [Booge] to Charles Phelps Jr., August 15, 1774, Box 4 folder 17, PPHFP.

104. EPP to EWPH, December 20, 1802, Box 5 folder 4, PPHFP.

105. The number of women pregnant before marriage was on the rise in the early national period, a fact noticed by Phelps as well as her gown maker and neighbor Rebecca Dickinson; in 1792, Dickinson noted in the pages of her own journal the death of "a young woman who has had fore children, three by three likely young men," adding that "this Day is a Sad Day of iniquity more than half who marry are forced to joine in wedlock"; see the RD diary, August 12, 1792, PVMA. EPP herself regularly noted in her memorandum book, with some alarm, individual women who stood in the broad aisle of the church to confess to fornication; see, e.g., May 10, 1770; July 22, 1772; December 11, 1774, *NEHGR.*

106. Clarissa Foster deposition, Deerfield Town Offices, Box 7 folder 5, PVMA.

107. Sally Pitt deposition, Deerfield Town Offices, Box 7 folder 8, PVMA. Other servants had to be more resourceful; in the summer of 1805, Jemima Dodge and Elisha De-Wolf of Deerfield found some ad hoc privacy "at a Place in Deerfield Meadows called New Fort, about an hour and a half before the setting of the sun on said Day"; Deerfield Town Offices, Box 7 folder 5, PVMA.

108. Elihu Ashley diary, PVMA, as quoted in Jordi Herrold, "Personal Space and Privacy in Mid-Eighteenth Century Deerfield, Massachusetts: A Case Study" (unpublished seminar paper, Historic Deerfield, 1974), 21; and the diary of Rev. Justus Forward, January 16, 1799, in the collections of the Skinner Museum, South Hadley, MA.

109. Some employees sought even greater distance from the family than that provided by rear kitchens, or even garrets. Family tradition indicates that Phelps's gardener and

hired man John Morrison occupied the well-appointed garret over the south ell, and perhaps the attention paid to the room's finish reflected their esteem for the county's only gardener. But Phelps family correspondence suggests that he often preferred to sleep in the barn, much to Elizabeth Porter Phelps's dismay. The paneled, painted surfaces of the 1797 garret suggest an unusual attention to the comfort of the intended occupant, especially when viewed in comparison to the rough, unfinished surfaces of the 1771 garret. If the family did in fact make a special effort to provide comfortable quarters for this employee, he does not seem to have been especially attached to them, and slipped away to alternative lodgings that were, for him, more comfortable. See EPP to EWPH, April 12, 1811, Box 5 folder 10, PPHFP; see also March 15, 1807, Box 5 folder 9, PPHFP.

110. EPP to EWPH, November 12, 1807, Box 5 folder 9, PPHFP.

111. EWPH to EPP, August 20, 1787, Box 13 folder 4, PPHFP.

112. See Laura Hadley Mosely, ed., *The Diaries of Julia Cowles* (New Haven, CT: Yale University Press, 1931), 37.

113. EWPH to EPP, June 20, 1801, Box 5 folder 6, PPHFP.

114. EWPH to EPP, June 20, 1801, Box 13 folder 5, PPHFP. Apparently the Huntingtons' kitchen was to some degree separate or separable: in the spring of 1801, while planning an extended trip, Betsy Huntington wrote her mother, "We propose to send our girl and boy [their servants] to their other homes—and shut up our house, excepting the back part of it, of which we shall give the key to a faithful man that he may lodge here." EWPH to EPP, March 14, 1801, Box 5, folder 6, PPHFP. While the exact nature of the "lower kitchen" is unknown, it seems plausible that the room was at least partially below grade. J. Ritchie Garrison has observed basement kitchens in Northfield, Massachusetts, some 125 miles north of Litchfield in the Connecticut River Valley (and 36 miles north of Betsy's mother's home in Hadley); though these rooms (full kitchens "with sheathed whitewashed walls, storage rooms, and access to the dooryard, which sloped down from the street") were probably secondary kitchens, and date from a slightly later period than Huntington's, Garrison notes that their builder, Calvin Stearns, may have learned the form when working in 1806 and 1807 from Boston architect Peter Banner, with whom the Huntingtons could easily have been familiar. See J. Ritchie Garrison, *Landscape and Material Life in Franklin County, Massachusetts, 1770–1860* (University of Tennessee Press, Knoxville, 1991), 172–74.

115. EWPH to EPP, July 22, 1801, Box 5 folder 6, PPHFP.

116. EPP to EWPH, March 4, 1805, Box 5 folder 7, PPHFP.

117. EPP to EWPH, March 4, 1805, Box 5 folder 7, PPHFP.

118. Regina S. Leonard, "The Porter-Phelps-Huntington Property, 1659–1955: History of the Vernacular Landscape in Context" (thesis, University of Massachusetts Amherst, 2000).

119. Jeanne Boydston, *Home and Work: Housework, Wages, and the Ideology of Labor in the Early Republic* (New York: Oxford University Press, 1990); Nora Doyle, *Maternal Bodies: Redefining Motherhood in Early America* (Chapel Hill: University of North Carolina Press, 2018), 5.

120. Garrison, *Landscape and Material Life*, 163–64.

121. See Ronald Schulz, *The Republic of Labor: Philadelphia Artisans and the Politics of Class, 1720–1830* (New York: Oxford University Press, 1993).

122. Timothy John Cresswell, "In Place / Out of Place: Geography, Ideology and Transgression" (PhD diss., University of Wisconsin–Madison, 1992), 34.

Chapter 9 • New Labor, New Landscapes

1. EPP memorandum book, November 15, 1807, Box 7 folder 3, PPHFP.

2. Some key contributions here include Catherine E. Kelly, *In the New England Fashion: Reshaping Women's Lives in the Nineteenth Century* (Ithaca, NY: Cornell University Press, 1999); Mary Kelley, *Learning to Stand and Speak: Women, Education, and Public Life in America's Republic* (Chapel Hill: Omohundro Institute of Early American History and Culture and the University of North Carolina Press, 2012); Nora Doyle, *Maternal Bodies: Redefining Motherhood in Early America* (Chapel Hill: University of North Carolina Press, 2018); and of course Nancy Cott's pioneering *Bonds of Womanhood: 'Women's Sphere' in New England, 1780–1835,* 2nd ed. (New Haven, CT: Yale University Press, 1997).

3. Mary Babson Fuhrer, *A Crisis of Community: The Trials and Transformation of a New England Town, 1815–1848* (Chapel Hill: University of North Carolina Press, 2014), 2.

4. Fuhrer, *A Crisis of Community,* 9.

5. Key works and historiographical reviews include C. Dallett Hemphill, "Middle Class Rising in Revolutionary America: The Evidence from Manners," *Journal of Social History* 30, no. 2 (Winter 1996): 317–44; Kelly, *In the New England Fashion*; Jennifer L. Goloboy, "The Early American Middle Class," *JER* 25, no. 4 (Winter 2005): 537–45; and Simon Middleton and Billy G. Smith, *Class Matters: Early North America and the Atlantic World* (Philadelphia: University of Pennsylvania Press, 2008), 9–15, and particularly Konstantin Dierks, "Middle-Class Formation in Eighteenth-Century North America," 99–108, and Seth Rockman, *Scraping By: Wage Labor, Slavery, and Survival in Early Baltimore* (Baltimore: Johns Hopkins University Press).

6. Robert Paynter, "Epilogue: Class Analysis and Historical Archaeology," *Historical Archaeology* 33, no. 1, Confronting Class (1999): 184–95 (quotation, 191). I have benefited greatly from my colleague Bob Paynter's conversation on these and other subjects through the years.

7. Johann Nee, "Creating Social Capital," *Journal of Interdisciplinary History* 39, no. 4 (Spring 2009): 471–95; an important contribution grounded in the Connecticut River Valley is J. Ritchie Garrison, *Landscape and Material Life in Franklin County, Massachusetts, 1770–1860* (Knoxville: University of Tennessee Press, 1991).

8. Richard L. Bushman, *The Refinement of America: People, Houses, Cities* (New York: Knopf, 1992).

9. C. Dallett Hemphill, "Manners and Class in the Revolutionary Era: A Transatlantic Comparison," *WMQ,* 3rd ser., 63, no. 2 (2006): 345–72 (quotation, 355).

10. EWPH to EPP, August 20, 1787, Box 13 folder 4, PPHFP.

11. Jeanne Boydston, "The Woman Who Wasn't There: Women's Market Labor in the Transition to Capitalism," *JER* 16 (Summer 1996): 203.

12. Boydston, "The Woman Who Wasn't There," 203.

13. Stephen A Mrozowski, "Landscapes of Inequality," in R. H. McGuire and R. Paynter, eds., *The Archaeology of Inequality* (Oxford: Blackwell, 1991), 79–101.

14. See, e.g., EWPH to EPP, October 22, 1801, Box 13 folder 5, PPHFP. EPP also used the phrase to describe Lawyer Porter's distressed situation: "He is to have no mankind to help him, nor any body but the little black girl he must be his own negro." See EPP to EPWH, March 25, 1806, Box 5 folder 8, PPHFP. Employing a similar metaphor, Westborough, Massachusetts, minister Ebenezer Parkman's wife, lacking a maid, was "engag'd in

much Slavish work." See Ross Beales, "'Slavish' and Other Female Work in the Parkman Household, Westborough, Massachusetts, 1724–1782," in Peter Benes and Jane Montague Benes, eds., *House and Home,* Proceedings of the 1988 Dublin Seminar for New England Folklife (Boston: Boston University, 1990), 48–57.

15. William D. Pierson, *Black Yankees: The Development of an Afro-American Subculture in Eighteenth-Century New England* (Amherst: University of Massachusetts Press, 1988), 19; and Lorenzo Johnston Greene, *The Negro in Colonial New England, 1620–1776* (New York: Columbia University Press, 1942), 217.

16. Joanne Pope Melish, *Disowning Slavery: Gradual Emancipation and "Race" in New England, 1780–1860* (Ithaca, NY: Cornell University Press, 1998), 133–34.

17. Catherine Adams and Elizabeth H. Pleck, *Love of Freedom: Black Women in Colonial and Revolutionary New England* (New York: Oxford University Press, 2010), 116.

18. Town meeting records, April 5, 1797, and April 7, 1800, Hadley Town Records, 1659–1805, 457, 473, Hadley Town Hall. Levi Prutt died in July 1825; see "Records of the Church of Christ in Hadley, Kept by John Woodbridge, Pastor," Hadley First Congregational Church. On Levi Prutt Jr., see Hadley Overseers of the Poor treasurer's ledger, 1807–1852, HHS.

19. Town meeting records, December 14, 1795, Hadley Town Records, 1659–1805, 452. Prutt's larger story is recounted in James Avery Smith, *History of the Black Population of Amherst, Massachusetts, 1728–1870* (Boston: New England Historic Genealogical Society, 1999), 3–11.

20. See Hadley Overseers of the Poor, November 13, 1809, and January 1, 1810, HHS.

21. US Census Bureau (1800 United States Federal Census), Hadley, 479; and Hadley Overseers of the Poor ledger, 1807–1852, HHS.

22. Town papers, Box 1 folder 5, HHS; and Hadley Overseers of the Poor ledger, 1807–1852, HHS.

23. On the funeral, see EPP memorandum book, January 19, 1806; for the death of Boston, see "Records of the Church of Christ in Hadley, Kept by John Woodbridge, Pastor," HCC; and US Census Bureau (1820 United States Federal Census), Hadley, 161.

24. See the probate records of Ralph Way, particularly the distribution of real estate, November 10, 1790, Box 156 no. 2, HCMRP.

25. "Records of the Church of Christ in Hadley, Kept by John Woodbridge, Pastor," HCC; US Census Bureau (1800 United States Federal Census), Town of Hadley.

26. EPP memorandum book, October 27, 1799, *NEHGR.*

27. See Ousmane K. Power-Greene, *Against Wind and Tide: The African American Struggle against the Colonization Movement* (New York: New York University Press, 2014); see also John Wood Sweet, *Bodies Politic: Negotiating Race in the American North, 1730–1830* (Baltimore: Johns Hopkins University Press, 2003), 349–52.

28. Bruce Laurie, *Beyond Garrison: Antislavery and Social Reform* (New York: Cambridge University Press, 2005), 29; EWPH to Frederic Huntington, June 10, 1840, Box 12 folder 4, PPHFP. On Woodbridge, see *The African Repository and Colonial Journal* 18 (1842): 238; and *The African Repository and Colonial Journal* 22 (1846): 70. In 1842, the society reported gifts of five dollars from the Porter and Phelps households, and other donations totaling fourteen dollars from Hadley Center, and seven dollars from North Hadley village.

29. See EWPH to William Lloyd Garrison, January 22, 1834, Box 12 folder 20; William Pitkin Huntington to EWPH, February 11, 1839, Box 19 folder 5; and Charles Phelps Huntington's Fourth of July Address, 1830, Box 17 folder 17, PPHFP; see also Elizabeth Pendergast Carlisle, *Earthbound and Heavenbent: Elizabeth Porter Phelps and Life at Forty Acres (1747–1817)* (New York: Scribner, 2004), 289; and Laurie, *Beyond Garrison*, 29, 89–91.

30. Liberty Hall Johnson was born July 2, 1845, which helps explain the unusual name; see the grave of sixteen-month-old Johnson in Hockanum cemetery. A number of anecdotes survive in local memory that preserve moments of hostility toward reformers. One story recalls a schoolteacher who mentioned, in class, plans to colonize Liberia; when the daughter of an abolitionist family raised her hand to join the discussion, a classmate sneered "[and] thus the little abolitionist sticks out her paw." See Clifton Johnson papers, ser. 1: Writings, "The Abolitionist" (Box 1 folder 1) and "Odds" (Box 4 folder 1), Special Collections, Jones Library, Amherst, MA. For a close look at the abolition movement in other Massachusetts communities, see Fuhrer, *Crisis of Community*, 223–44, and Laurie, *Beyond Garrison*.

31. Town Meetings, 1803–1833, October 19, 1808, Hadley Town Hall.

32. Town Meetings, 1803–1833, October 19, 1808, Hadley Town Hall.

33. First Congregational Church of Hadley, Church Meeting Records, 1832–1936. My thanks to Mary Thayer for sharing notes from these records with me.

34. Asa B. Munn to George Sheldon, November 8, 1874, PVMA, as transcribed in "Seating 'Negroes' in the Old Hadley Meetinghouse," http://www.memorialhall.mass.edu.

35. Munn to Sheldon, November 8, 1874, PVMA. Judd calls these pews "conspicuous" in "Hadley," vol. 3, 32.

36. Theodore Gregson Huntington, "Sketches of Family and Life in Hadley," Box 21 folder 5, PPHFP; also discussed in Laurie, *Beyond Garrison*, 105.

37. On the Massachusetts General Colored Association's 1830 attempt to integrate the whites-only pews of Boston's Park Street Church, and attacks on racism in churches more generally, see Marc M. Arkin, "'A Convenient Seat in God's Temple': The Massachusetts General Colored Association and the Park Street Pew Controversy of 1830," *NEQ* 89, no. 1 (March 2016): 6–53; see also Karen Anne Hutchins, "In Pursuit of Full Freedom: An Archaeological and Historical Study of the Free African-American Community at Parting Ways, Massachusetts, 1779–1900" (PhD diss., Boston University, 2013); and Anthony F. Martin, "On the Landscape for a Very, Very Long Time: African American Resistance and Resilience in 19th and Early 20th-Century Massachusetts" (PhD diss., University of Massachusetts Amherst, 2016). The evidence as to when Hadley ceased segregating seating by race is unclear, but it seems likely that it was one consequence of the 1840s relocation and renovation of the meeting house.

38. Clifton Johnson, "Hockanum in the Past," ser. 1, Writings, Box 2 folder 23, Clifton Johnson Papers, Special Collections, Jones Library, Amherst, MA. Which Jackson this might be is as yet unknown, but see Smith, *History of the Black Population of Amherst*, 81–84. As historian Thomas Dublin notes, by 1860, "although blacks numbered only 1.8 percent of Boston servants, they constituted 5.5% of washerwomen in the city"; see Thomas Dublin, *Transforming Women's Work: New England Lives in the Industrial Revolution* (Ithaca, NY: Cornell University Press, 1994), 159. See also Adams and Pleck, *Love of Freedom*, 41. George Sheldon also mentions "Jenny," and other African American women

"frequently employed in the families of our citizens as a washerwoman" in his essay, "Slavery in the Connecticut Valley," *Papers and Proceedings of the Connecticut Valley Historical Society, 1876–1881* (Springfield, MA: Connecticut Valley Historical Society, 1881), 207–18.

On African American women in the clothing trades in nineteenth-century Hartford, Connecticut, see Marla R. Miller, "Mehitable Primus and Addie Brown: Women of Color and Hartford's Nineteenth-Century Dressmaking Trades," in Peter Benes and Jane Montague Benes, eds., *Dressing New England: Clothing, Fashion, and Identity*, Proceedings of the 2010 Dublin Seminar for New England Folklife (Deerfield, MA, 2014), 64–84. Kathleen M. Brown contemplates laundry as part of women's rising involvement in "body work" in *Foul Bodies: Cleanliness in Early America* (New Haven, CT: Yale University Press, 2009).

39. See James Deetz, *In Small Things Forgotten: An Archaeology of Early American Life* (New York: Anchor, 1977, revised edition, 1996); and Bridget T. Heneghan, *Whitewashing America: Material Culture and Race in the Antebellum Imagination* (Jackson: University Press of Mississippi, 2003).

40. Sylvester Judd recorded the recollection of one informant who said that, in the Hadley of the 1760s, "most of the buildings were old and dark colored, and . . . no dwelling was painted on the outside." See Sylvester Judd, *History of Hadley: Including the Early History of Hatfield, South Hadley, Amherst and Granby, Massachusetts* (Springfield, MA: H. R. Huntting, 1905), 377; and Kevin M. Sweeney, "Mansion People: Kinship, Class, and Architecture in Western Massachusetts in the Mid Eighteenth Century," *Winterthur Portfolio* 19 (1984): 243. The second meetinghouse, built in 1713, had been "colored" at least by the 1750s, but when that building was replaced in 1808, the successor was the brilliant white we today associate with the iconic New England meetinghouse. Peter Benes, *Meetinghouses of Early New England* (Amherst: University of Massachusetts Press, 2003), 193. For Charlotte Porter, see Charlotte Porter to Caroline Porter, April 29, 1813, Box 7 folder 12, Williams Family Papers, PVMA.

41. Quoted in Roger W. Moss, *Paint in America* (Washington, DC: Preservation Press, 1994), 129. See also Joseph S. Wood, *The New England Village* (Baltimore: Johns Hopkins University Press, 1997), 122.

42. Heneghan, *Whitewashing America*, xiv; see also Brown, *Foul Bodies*, 260.

43. "Town Meeting Affairs, 1834–1856," Hadley Town Hall, April 6, 1840. Margaret M. Bruchac, in "Historical Erasure and Cultural Recovery: Indigenous People in the Connecticut River Valley" (PhD diss., University of Massachusetts Amherst, 2007), 101–2, notes that this same period witnessed tensions between impulses to romanticize local native histories and to celebrate Anglo-American conquest of the area. See also Karen Halttunen, "Mountain Christenings: Landscape and Memory in Edward Hitchcock's New England," in Peter Benes, and Jane Montague Benes, eds., *New England Celebrates: Spectacle, Commemoration, and Festivity*, Proceedings of the 2000 Dublin Seminar for New England Folklife (Boston: Boston University, 2002), 166–77.

44. The following draws on Bruchac, "Historical Erasure and Cultural Recovery," 222–23.

45. *Northampton Courier*, Northampton, MA, June 6, 1838, as quoted in Bruchac, "Historical Erasure and Cultural Recovery," 222.

46. *HG*, June 6, 1838, as quoted in Bruchac, "Historical Erasure and Cultural Recovery," 222–23.

47. Elizabeth Huntington to Edward Phelps Huntington, May 20, 1838, Box 12 folder 4, PPHFP.

48. Clifton Johnson (and Sylvester Judd before him) preserved Crow's storytelling in "Witchcraft," ser. 1, "Old Town in New England," vol. 13, Box 4 folder 13, Clifton Johnson Papers, Special Collections, Jones Library, Amherst, MA; and Judd, "Hadley" (Judd Manuscript), FL. For scholarship on the active effort to advance claims that native peoples had disappeared (sometimes in the face of clear evidence to the contrary), see Jean O'Brien, *Firsting and Lasting: Writing Indians out of Existence in New England* (Minneapolis: University of Minnesota Press, 2010); and Bruchac, "Historical Erasure and Cultural Recovery."

49. See Judd, "Miscellaneous," vol. 19, 141; Boltwood's "Genealogies of Hadley Families" in Judd's *Hadley* (117) would also mention a Phinehas Sampson as well as his daughter, Eliza, born in 1800. On the tendency for local history to mourn the passing of the "last" Native American residents, see Bruchac, "The True History of Sally Maminash, 'The Last Indian' in Northampton," unpublished paper, 1996 (many thanks to Marge for sharing this work), and also her "Historical Erasure and Cultural Recovery"; also Colin G. Calloway, ed., *After King Philip's War: Presence and Persistence in Indian New England* (Hanover, NH: University Press of New England, 1997). A valuable essay in this volume is Jean O'Brien, "'Divorced' from the Land: Resistance and Survival of Indians in Eighteenth-Century New England"; see also her book, *Firsting and Lasting.*

50. See EPP to EWPH, September 15, 1814, Box 5 folder 12, PPHFP, on the burial of "Poll Sampson who has kept house for Boston a long time."

51. Levi Prutt, born about 1760, served in the American Revolution; see *Massachusetts Soldiers and Sailors*, vol. 12 (Boston: Wright and Potter Printing Co, 1896–1908), 830; his July 1825 death is recorded in "Records of the Church of Christ in Hadley, Kept by John Woodbridge, Pastor," Hadley Congregational Church. On Levi Prutt Jr., see Hadley Overseers of the Poor ledger, 1807–1852, HHS.

52. Annual Report, American Board of Commissioners for Foreign Missions, 1820 (Boston: Crocker and Brewster, 1820), appendix, 37. The Young Ladies Benevolent Society concentrated their attention on "wearing apparel for females," though where these recipients were is unclear. Barry O'Connell observes and explores the irony of these charitable impulses given local histories of Anglo/native relations in "Converting Cherokees and Disappearing New England Indians: A Mysterious Story," paper presented at "Visible Images, Invisible People: Four Centuries of Wampanoag History," Wampanoag Conference, Plimoth Plantation, 3–5, as quoted in Bruchac, "Historical Erasure and Cultural Recovery," 98.

53. Cash Book, Onondaga Missionary Society, 1819–1841, First Congregational Church, Hadley.

54. Holly Izard, "The Ward Family and Their 'Helps,': Domestic Work, Workers, and Relationships on a New England Farm, 1787–1866," *Proceedings of the American Antiquarian Society* 103 (1993): 79. See also Izard and Andrew H. Baker's article, "Farmers' Adaptations to Markets in Early Nineteenth-Century Massachusetts," in Peter Benes and Jane Montague Benes, eds., *The Farm*, Proceedings of the 1986 Dublin Seminar for New England Folklife (Boston: Boston University, 1988), 95–108.

55. EWPH to EPP, August 12, 1802, Box 13 folder 6, PPHFP.

56. EWPH to EPP, February 1, 1802, Box 13 folder 5, PPHFP.

57. EWPH to EPP, October 8, 1802, Box 13 folder 5, PPHFP.

58. See Carlisle, *Earthbound and Heavenbent*, 203, citing EWPH to EPP, September 27, 1801, Box 13 folder 1, PPHFP. Ellen Hartigan-O'Connor notes the "revolving door" of household labor in urban settings as indentured servitude gave way to shorter-term arrangements in *The Ties That Buy: Women and Commerce in Revolutionary America* (Philadelphia: University of Pennsylvania Press, 2009), 28.

59. EPP to EWPH, August 6, 1802, Box 5 folder 4, PPHFP.

60. EWPH to EPP, August 10, 1801, Box 13 folder 5, PPHFP.

61. EWPH to EPP, November 11, 1815, Box 13 folder 13, PPHFP.

62. EWPH to EPP, March 18, 1801, Box 13 folder 1, PPHFP. Catherine E. Kelly includes Huntington in a larger consideration of the shortage of domestic help in the nineteenth-century Connecticut Valley in the chapter titled "All the Work of the Family," in her book, *In the New England Fashion*, 19–63.

63. *HG,* April 19 and 26, 1809; and May 3, 1809; on the mill, see Josiah Gilbert Holland, *History of Western Massachusetts* (Springfield, MA: Bowles, 1855), 466.

64. EWPH to EPP, March 20, 1805, Box 13 folder 9, PPHFP.

65. Christopher Clark, *The Roots of Rural Capitalism: Western Massachusetts, 1780–1860* (Ithaca, NY: Cornell University Press, 1990), 146.

66. See Miller, *Needle's Eye.* Also relevant, of course, is Phelps's own aging process, as clothing acquisition slowed with age.

67. Kelly, *In the New England Fashion*, 65.

68. Karen V. Hansen, *A Very Social Time: Crafting Community in Antebellum New England* (Berkeley: University of California Press, 1994).

69. See Mary Kelley, *Learning to Stand and Speak: Women, Education, and Public Life in America's Republic* (Chapel Hill: University of North Carolina Press, 2006); Jo Ann Preston, "Domestic Ideology, School Reformers, and Female Teachers," *NEQ* 66 (December 1993): 531–51, as well as Kathryn Kish Sklar, "The Schooling of Girls and Community Values in Massachusetts Towns, 1750–1820," special issue on women's education, *History of Education Quarterly* (Spring 1994 and Fall 1994): 511–42. An excellent discussion of the lives of female teachers in the early republic is Rachel Hope Cleves, *Charity and Sylvia: A Same-Sex Marriage in Early America* (New York: Oxford University Press, 2014).

70. Joel Perlmann and Robert A. Margo, *Women's Work? American Schoolteachers, 1650–1920* (Chicago: University of Chicago Press, 2001); and E. Jennifer Monaghan, *Learning to Read and Write in Colonial America* (Amherst: University of Massachusetts Press, 2005).

71. Carlisle, *Earthbound and Heavenbent*, 22.

72. *The Constitution of the State of Massachusetts, adopted 1780* (Boston: Richardson and Lord, 1825), 35.

73. Hadley was fined "£8/6/8 of lawful silver money, to be to the use of the towns of Shutesbury and Ware in equal proportion, for and towards the support and maintenance of schools." Town coffers paid the court costs as well. Hampshire County Court records, Inferior Court of Common Pleas, General Sessions of the Peace, February 2, 1781, vol. 14 (1776–1790), 59.

74. Dickinson, August 19, 1787, PVMA. Also, in summer 1786, EPP mentioned a school mistress named Betty Reynolds, who may be related; see EPP memorandum book, June 25, 1786, *NEHGR*.

75. See EPP memorandum book, May 29, 1791, and May 27, 1792, *NEHGR*; and Jerusha Leonard, diary, 1791–1792, PVMA.

76. Jerusha Leonard diary, April 22 and May 9, 1791, PVMA.

77. Jerusha Leonard diary, May 2 and October 22, 1791, PVMA. Leonard married Captain William Ashley about 1802, and moved west to New York; Francis Bacon Trowbridge, *The Ashley Genealogy* (New Haven, CT: Tuttle, Morehouse and Taylor, printed for the author, 1896), 113.

78. Town meeting records, October 17, 1791, Hadley Town Records, 1659–1805, 433.

79. *HG,* February 8, 1804.

80. *HG,* November 5, 1806.

81. Sweeney, "Mansion People," 241–42.

82. See HAD.34 (MACRIS). Another generation, Charlotte's granddaughter and namesake Charlotte Williams Porter (1840–1930), would also establish a school here in 1866; known as "The Elms," it moved to Springfield in 1881.

83. William Williams to Dolly Williams, January 18, 1805, Box 7 folder 10, Williams Family Papers, PVMA.

84. Sellon has not yet been identified. The staff at Historic Deerfield speculates that the figure may be "Pauline Sellon (b.1782), the daughter of Dr. William Sellon (b.c.1753) who died in Amherst, Massachusetts, around 1844, or she may have been a niece or other relative of Dr. William F. Sellon (1786–1842) of Amherst who married Fanny Williams of Amherst in 1817." See the Five Colleges and Historic Deerfield Museum Consortium, HD96.002, HD, http://museums.fivecolleges.edu.

85. Carlisle, *Earthbound and Heavenbent,* 129.

86. Carlisle, *Earthbound and Heavenbent,* 129; and Judd, "Hadley," vol. 3, 34.

87. Jason M. Opal, "Exciting Emulation: Academies and the Transformation of the Rural North, 1780s–1820s," *The Journal of American History* 91, no. 2 (September 2004): 445–70; Kelley, *Learning to Stand and Speak*; and Kelly, *In the New England Fashion.*

88. Kelley, *Learning to Stand and Speak,* 25.

89. *HG,* May 3, 12, 19, and 26, 1802; March 28 and 30, April 6 and 13, 1803. See also Leon Monroe Orcut, "The Influence of the Academy in Western Massachusetts" (MS thesis, Massachusetts State College, 1934), 109–20.

90. *HG,* February 25, 1806. An excellent discussion of the needlework produced in these academies, and the instructors who guided that work, is Carol Huber, et al., *With Needle and Brush: Schoolgirl Embroidery from the Connecticut River Valley, 1740–1840* (Middletown, CT: Wesleyan University Press, 2011).

91. In Amherst, women were allowed to enroll in Amherst Academy's first decade, instructed in "summer quarters" by a preceptress; by 1815, some ninety were enrolled in summer sessions. See Edward Wilton Carpenter and Charles Frederick Morehouse, *History of the Town of Amherst, Massachusetts* (Amherst: Carpenter and Morehouse, 1896), 144–49, 273; Mary Lyon, future founder of Mount Holyoke Female Seminary (later Mount Holyoke College), would be among those early students.

92. Hopkins Academy, *History of the Hopkins Fund, Grammar School and Academy* (Amherst, MA: Amherst Record Press, 1890), 81.

93. Hopkins Academy, *History of the Hopkins Fund,* 152. For a list of prominent alumni—which includes Lucy Stone Blackwell and Eunice Bullard Beecher—see 152–55.

94. *HG,* November 19, 1819. Williston was baptized March 30, 1800. See *Massachusetts, Town and Vital Records, 1620–1988,* Ancestry.com.

95. Hopkins Academy, *History of the Hopkins Fund*, 86.

96. See John A. Andrews III, *Rebuilding the Christian Commonwealth: New England Congregationalists and Foreign Missions, 1800–1830* (Lexington: University Press of Kentucky, 1976).

97. Hopkins Academy, *History of the Hopkins Fund*, 86.

98. Catherine E. Kelly, *Republic of Taste: Art, Politics, and Everyday Live in Early America* (Philadelphia: University of Pennsylvania Press, 2016), 6.

99. *HG*, December 1, 1818, and "Catalogue of the Trustees, Instructors, and Students of Hopkins Academy, Hadley" (Greenfield, MA: Denio & Phelps, Printers [1819]).

100. Kelly, *In the New England Fashion*, 43.

101. Perlmann and Margo, *Women's Work?* 28–29.

102. See Cleves, *Charity and Sylvia*, especially 19.

103. Clark, *Roots of Rural Capitalism*, 31. See also Cott, *Bonds of Womanhood*; and Richard M. Bernhard and Maris A. Vinovski, "The Female Schoolteacher in Antebellum Massachusetts," *Journal of Social History* 10 (1977): 332–45.

104. Gregory Farmer and Bonnie Parsons, "MHC Reconnaissance Survey: Hadley" (Massachusetts Historical Commission, 1982), 9.

105. Gregory Farmer, Bonnie Parsons, and Betsy Friedberg, "Hadley Center Historic District (Boundary Increase)," National Register of Historic Places Nomination (1993), Section 8, 3–4.

106. Gloria L. Main, "Inequality in Early America: The Evidence from Probate Records of Massachusetts and Maryland," *The Journal of Interdisciplinary History* 7, no. 4 (Spring 1977): 559–81, especially 573–75.

107. This and below from Gregory H. Nobles, "Commerce and Community: A Case Study of the Rural Broommaking Business in Antebellum Massachusetts," *JER* 4, no. 3 (Autumn 1984): 287–308, especially 294.

108. Farmer et al., "Hadley Center Historic District," Section 8, 3. By 1850, forty-one Hadley broom shops employed over one hundred hands; see Nobles, "Commerce and Community," 302, n. 26. See Farmer and Parsons, "MHC Reconnaissance Survey: Hadley," and *Documents Relative to the Manufactures in the United States* (Washington, DC: Duff Green, 1833), 298. These wire firms were "probably responsible for initiating the major wire companies in Holyoke and Northampton"; see Farmer and Parsons, "MHC Reconnaissance Survey: Hadley," 9.

109. Darwin P. Kelsey in "Early New England Farm Crops: Broom Corn" (unpublished research report, OSV, 1980, http://resources.osv.org/explore_learn/document _viewer.php?Action=View&DocID=727), found that "by the late 1830's at least four known varieties were being grown in the area around Hadley."

110. Dan Huntington to Bethiah Huntington, January 3, 1823, and October 31, 1822, Box 15 folder 4, PPHFP. Broom carts from Hadley often offered the means of travel for their correspondence, as the Huntingtons asked drivers to carry letters to their children in Troy.

111. Edward Markunas, "Brooms and Broom Making in Massachusetts 1790–1840" (unpublished research report, OSV, 1980, hhttp://resources.osv.org/explore_learn /document_viewer.php?Action=View&DocID=851).

112. A small broom tool shop on Ferry Road (HAD.221) is all that remains of Dickinson's elaborate manufacturing enterprise.

113. Dan Huntington to Bethia Huntington, January 3, 1823, Box 15, folder 4, PPHFP.

114. Nobles, "Commerce and Community," 301, n. 22.

115. See Clark, *Roots of Rural Capitalism*, 181–90.

116. Clark, *Roots of Rural Capitalism*, 182–83, citing Huntington's store ledger, PPHFP. On straw braiding, see also Caroline Sloat, "'A Great Help to Many Families': Straw Braiding in Massachusetts before 1825," in Benes and Benes, *House and Home*.

117. Clark, *Roots of Rural Capitalism*, 182–83.

118. HAD.205 (MACRIS).

119. This and below from Gregory Farmer and Bonnie Parsons, "North Hadley Historic District," National Register of Historic Places Nomination (1993), who also found that the "largest producers of corn" were Thaddeus Smith (HAD.192), Charles Lamson (HAD.238), Erastus Smith (HAD.204), and Francis Smith (HAD.205). See MACRIS.

120. See MACRIS forms HAD.205, HAD.194, HAD.182, HAD.208, and HAD.231. Rental properties in town housed temporary farm help, especially later on, after broom corn became well established. Thaddeus Smith, for instance—the largest producer of brooms—built three cottages on French Street to house his laborers, managing them as rental properties. Smith's home was on River Drive (HAD.192); the rental houses were HAD. 224, HAD.225, and HAD.226. See Farmer and Parsons, "North Hadley Historic District."

121. Garrison, *Landscape and Material Life*, 83.

122. See Nobles, "Commerce and Community," 299. A later remnant of this landscape—a broom tool shop, ca. 1900—is documented in MACRIS, HAD.221.

123. HAD.227 (MACRIS).

124. HAD.190 (MACRIS), and Farmer and Parsons, "North Hadley." These authors further note that "Greek Revival houses outnumber other types in the clustered, more densely-built part of the village, particularly along River Drive."

125. See HAD.230, HAD.202 (MACRIS). See also the 1835 parsonage, HAD.207. The home of the parsonage's builder, Elam Cutter—among the earliest examples of Hadley's transition from the Federal to the Greek Revival style—also still stands; see HAD.212.

126. See HAD.202 (MACRIS).

127. Judd, *Hadley*, 370.

128. Judd, *Hadley*, 422.

129. Within five years, the "Lombardy Poplar could be found in every thriving city from Bangor, Maine to New York City"; however, within ten to fifteen years, the trees began to fail, and in Hadley as elsewhere, they were eventually cut down and replaced with buttonwood, American elm, and red maple, or sugar maple. Frank White, "Early New England Landscapes," *The Journal of The Society of Municipal Arborists* 36, no. 4 (July/August 2000); and Ellsworth, "Hadley West Street Common and Great Meadow," 35.

130. See Garrison, *Landscape and Material Life*, 115.

131. Martha J. McNamara, *From Tavern to Courthouse: Architecture and Ritual in American Law, 1658–1860* (Baltimore: Johns Hopkins University Press, 2004).

132. On Pratt and the Greek Revival style, see Richard C. Cote, "Rethinking the Early Greek Revival: The Successes and Failure of a Builder," *Old Time New England* 64, nos. 3–4 (January-June 1974): 61–76; see also Cote, "Thomas Pratt and Greek Revival Architecture in Northampton, Massachusetts: A Study of New England Architecture" (BA thesis,

Hampshire College, 1972). For reference to the Hatfield town hall and the quotation above, see Kevin M. Sweeney, "Meetinghouses, Town Houses, and Churches: Changing Perceptions of Sacred and Secular Space in Southern New England," *Winterthur Portfolio* 28, no. 1 (Spring 1993): 59.

133. See Marla R. Miller, "The 'Feud of the Streets': The 1841 Move of Hadley's 1808 Meetinghouse," in Peter Benes and Jane Montague Benes, eds., *Religious Spaces: Our Vanishing Landmarks,* Proceedings of the 2018 Dublin Seminar for New England Folklife, forthcoming.

134. David Jaffee, *A New Nation of Goods: The Material Culture of Early America* (Philadelphia: University of Pennsylvania Press, 2010).

135. Judd, "Hadley," vol. 3, 18, in Gregory Nobles and Herbert L. Zarov, *Selected Papers from the Sylvester Judd Manuscript* (Northampton, MA: Forbes Library, 1976), 237.

136. Priscilla J. Brewer, "'We Have Got a Very Good Cooking Stove': Advertising, Design, and Consumer Response to the Cookstove, 1815–1880," *Winterthur Portfolio* 25, no. 1 (Spring 1990): 35–54; and Garrison, *Landscape and Material Life,* 176.

137. Garrison, *Landscape and Material Life,* 176. On cleanliness, see Brown, *Foul Bodies.*

138. Judd, "Miscellaneous," vol. 19, 353, as transcribed in Nobles and Zarov, *Selected Papers from the Sylvester Judd Manuscript,* 238.

139. See, e.g., Ruth Schwartz Cowan, *More Work for Mother: The Ironies of Household Technology from the Open Hearth to the Microwave* (New York: Basic, 1983); Sally McMurray, *Families and Farmhouses in 19th Century America: Vernacular Design and Social Change* (New York: Oxford University Press, 1988); Garrison, *Landscape and Material Life.*

140. Nora Pat Small, "The Search for a New Rural Order: Farmhouses in Sutton, Massachusetts, 1790–1830," *WMQ,* 3rd ser., 53, no. 1, (January 1996): 83.

141. J. Ritchie Garrison, *Two Carpenters: Architecture and Building in Early New England, 1799–1859* (Knoxville: University of Tennessee Press, 2006). Elsewhere Garrison suggests that the shift antedated the advent of the Greek Revival style, that domestic spaces were reorganized to "nurture social rituals, family life and work." See *Landscape and Material Life,* 169.

142. Garrison, *Landscape and Material Life,* 116.

143. Historians who have drawn this connection between the material culture of the Gothic Revival and Protestant religiosity include Bushman, *Refinement of America*; Clifford Edward Clark Jr., *The American Family Home, 1800–1960* (Chapel Hill: University of North Carolina Press, 1986); and Kathryn Kish Sklar, *Catherine Beecher: A Study in American Domesticity* (New Haven, CT: Yale University Press, 1973). On the Connecticut Valley, see Garrison, *Landscape and Material Life,* xviii; and Deborah Rotman, *Historical Archaeology of Gendered Lives* (London: Springer, 2009), 88.

144. In addition to the Cook house (HAD.6), surviving examples include the 1840 Porter Cowles house (HAD.315); the 1856 Dwight Marsh house (HAD.87); and the 1857 home of Theodore Huntington—grandson of Elizabeth Porter Phelps (HAD.317). On 1830s fashion, see Lynne Z. Bassett, *Gothic to Goth: Romantic Era Fashion and Its Legacy* (Hartford, CT: Wadsworth Atheneum, 2016).

145. EPP memorandum book, July 17, 1796, *NEHGR*; EPP to EWPH, August 13, 1801, Box 5 folder 3, and December 19, 1810, Box 5 folder 10, PPHFP; and Clark, *Roots of Rural Capitalism,* 181–90.

Coda • Remembering Women and Work

1. MACRIS, HAD.39. On the Andrew Cooke structure, see Irene Gillette Steiner, "History of Saltbox House from Hadley, Massachusetts Built between 1692 and 1710 Moved and Restored 1952," typescript, February 14, 1992, Irene Gillette Steiner, "Papers Related to a Saltbox House, 1692–1992, Mount Holyoke College Library Archives and Special Collections.

2. Patricia Laurice Ellsworth, "Hadley West Street Common and Great Meadow: A Cultural Landscape Study" (MA thesis, University of Massachusetts Department of Landscape Architecture and Regional Planning, 2007), 47.

3. Theodore Gregson Huntington, "Sketches of Family and Life in Hadley," 23, 13, Box 21 folder 5, PPHFP.

4. Farm Lane was named by vote October 20, 1994; see "Town Roads," Town Clerk's Office, Hadley Town Hall. My deep appreciation to Janice Kangas for her work compiling this research, and many thanks to her for making it available to me.

5. See Margaret M. Bruchac, "Historical Erasure and Cultural Recovery: Indigenous People in the Connecticut River Valley" (PhD diss., University of Massachusetts Amherst, 2007), 224, 5, 41–46. Though it is rare that baskets can be matched with makers, an ash-splint storage basket survives in the collections of Deerfield's Memorial Hall Museum, which Bruchac attributes to Marie Saraphine Watson (ca. 1809–1882). See "Historical Erasure and Cultural Recovery," 231.

6. Prutt was supported by the town toward the end of his life; accounts by 1807 indicate annual expenditures. See Hadley Overseers of the Poor treasurer's ledger, 1807–1852, HHS. Like fascination with the so-called last Indian, New England towns also observed the last traces of slavery in their communities. Clifton Johnson would note that the "last negro who had been a slave" in Hadley was a man named Jake, who died in 1845, having reached more than one hundred years of age. Johnson recorded that Jake, once owned in the Porter family, "slept in a bunk in the woodshed attic." When Jake died, a later effort to mark his final resting spot failed, apparently due to local opposition. See Johnson, "Old Town Chronicles" loose writings, Clifton Johnson papers, ser. 1, Box 4 folder 9, Special Collections Jones Library, Amherst, MA. It is possible that this is Eleazer Porter's "negro man James"; Porter's will instructed his heirs "equally to make provision in the support of my negro man James during his life (if he so long continues to live with them). After he is unable to support himself and sd James is to have the use of the bed and bedding whereon he now sleeps so long as he continues with them." See Porter, 1797, Box 117 no. 11, HCMRP.

7. Bob Drinkwater posits that Prutt's stone may have been the work of Belchertown gravestone cutters Joseph Sikes and sons, and was possibly a pre-cut blank left behind by the family when they left the area, and inscribed by another hand; see his *In Memory of Susan Freedom: Searching for Gravestones of African Americans in Western Massachusetts* (Amherst, MA: Levellers Press, 2019).

8. On power, memory, archival preservation, and historical narratives, see Michel-Rolph Truillot, *Silencing the Past: Power and the Production of History* (Boston: Beacon, 1995).

9. David Danbom, *Born in the Country: A History of Rural America* (Baltimore: Johns Hopkins University Press, 1995), 65, 68; Catherine E. Kelly, *In the New England Fashion: Reshaping Women's Lives in the Nineteenth Century* (Ithaca, NY: Cornell University Press,

2002); and Richard L. Bushman, *The Refinement of America: Persons, Houses, Cities* (New York: Knopf, 1992).

10. Kelly, *In the New England Fashion*, 241.

11. Laurel Thatcher Ulrich, *The Age of Homespun: Objects and Stories in the Creation of an American Myth* (New York: Knopf, 2001), 29, 389.

12. Ulrich, *Age of Homespun*, 29, 389. See also Ruth Schwartz Cowan, *More Work for Mother: The Ironies of Household Technology from the Open Hearth to the Microwave* (New York: Basic, 1983); and Kathleen Brown, *Foul Bodies: Cleanliness in Early America* (New Haven, CT: Yale University Press, 2009).

13. Bruce Laurie, *Rebels in Paradise: Sketches of Northampton Abolitionists* (Amherst: University of Massachusetts Press, 2015), 17. See also Mary Babson Fuhrer, *A Crisis of Community: The Trials and Transformation of a New England Town, 1815–1848* (Chapel Hill: University of North Carolina Press, 2014), 46–73.

14. Laurie, *Rebels in Paradise*, 18.

15. Judd, "Miscellaneous," vol. 15, 366, 420–28 (Judd Manuscript), FL.

16. Judd, "Miscellaneous," vol. 15, 366.

17. Arria Sargent Huntington, *Under a Colonial Rooftree: Fireside Chronicles of Early New England* (Syracuse, NY: Wolcott's Bookshop, 1905). Huntington was born in Massachusetts but spent most of her life in Syracuse, New York. In addition to the areas of engagement listed here, Huntington was a cofounder of the Visiting Nurses Association and Syracuse Memorial Hospital. She was also the first woman elected to the Syracuse Board of Education, serving from 1898 to 1904.

18. Huntington, *Under a Colonial Rooftree*, 32, 57–58, 56, 57. See chapter 4, note 142.

19. Huntington, *Under a Colonial Rooftree*, 57.

20. On other female pastkeepers of this time and place, see Susan Williams, *Alice Morse Earle and the Domestic History of Early America* (Amherst: University of Massachusetts Press, 2013); Julie Des Jardins, *Women and the Historical Enterprise in America: Gender, Race, and the Politics of Memory, 1880–1945* (Chapel Hill: University of North Carolina Press, 2003); Michael C. Batinski, *Pastkeepers in a Small Place: Five Centuries in Deerfield, Massachusetts* (Amherst: University of Massachusetts Press, 2004); Ellen Fitzpatrick, *History's Memory: Writing America's Past 1880–1980* (Cambridge: Harvard University Press, 2002); and Kate Silbert, "Committed to Memory: Gender, Literary Engagement, and Commemorative Practice, 1780–1920" (PhD diss., University of Michigan, 2017).

21. James Lincoln Huntington, *Forty Acres: The Story of the Bishop Huntington House* (New York: Hastings House, 1949).

22. Daniel Horowitz, "Creation and Recreation: Dr. James Lincoln Huntington's Forty Acres: The Story of the Bishop Huntington House (1949)," typescript, Porter-Phelps-Huntington Foundation, September 20, 1992, 3.

23. James Lincoln Huntington tracked his work on the house in a journal and scrapbook filled with diary-like entries, photographs, and notes from houseguests. See "Journal and Scrapbook of the House at Forty Acres in Hadley," Box 80a and 80b, PPHFP.

24. An image of the farmyard before the barn's removal can be found in the *Springfield Republican*, December 8, 1929, 5E. In summer 1935, the mansion house (as well as the Porter Store on the Hadley Common) was documented by the Historic American Building Survey; see the PPHFP, Box 82 folder 12. The Samuel Porter house was documented in spring 1934.

25. See Marla R. Miller, "Introduction," *Cultivating a Past: Essays on the History of Hadley, Massachusetts* (Amherst: University of Massachusetts Press, 2009), 15; and Clifton Johnson, "The Tribulations of Founding a Farm Museum," *Old-Time New England* 23, no. 1 (July 1932): 3–16, quotation, 6.

26. "Farm Museum . . . Dedicated at Hadley," *Springfield Republican*, May 24, 1931.

27. "Old Hadley Farm Museum Dedicated to Commemorate Antiquities of Agriculture," *Springfield Republican*, May 28, 1931.

28. See "Museum to Be Housed in Barn," *Springfield Republican*, December 8, 1929. The antebellum changes to the Hadley town center are explored in Marla R. Miller, "The 'Feud of the Streets': The 1841 Move of Hadley's 1808 Meetinghouse," in Peter Benes and Jane Montague Benes, eds., *Religious Spaces: Our Vanishing Landmarks,* Proceedings of the 2018 Dublin Seminar for New England Folklife, forthcoming.

29. "Old Hadley Farm Museum Dedicated." In the late 1950s, the museum was gifted by the Johnsons to the Massachusetts Society for Promoting Agriculture (MSPA); Dorothy Potter, "'Old Hadley Farm Museum' Changes Hands," *HG,* November 1, 1957. Five years later, the MSPA turned the museum back to community members, in the form of the Hadley Farm Museum Association.

30. See Miller, "Introduction," *Cultivating a Past.*

31. F. C. Reynolds to Irene Gillette Steiner, February 1, 1955, Irene Gillette Steiner collection, MHC.

32. Steiner, "History of Saltbox House"; and Lillian Davey, "Like the House? Then Why Not . . . Move It!" *The Greenwich Social Review* 18, no. 5 (May 1965). Gass believed that after 1710, carded wool would have been the likelier insulation material.

33. See Miller, "Introduction," *Cultivating a Past.*

34. On the Award of Merit, see PPHFP, Box 82 folder 55.

35. See Thomas Eliot Andrews, ed., "The Diary of Elizabeth (Porter) Phelps," *New England Historical and Genealogical Register*, vols. 118–120, January 1964–October 1966; Laurel Thatcher Ulrich mentions this source in her watershed article "Of Pens and Needles: Sources in Early American Women's History," *The Journal of American History* 77, no. 1 (June 1990): 200–7. The next decade saw a flowering of research grounded in these materials, particularly among students in the Five College Consortium; see "Bibliography of Research," Porter-Phelps-Huntington Museum, https://www.pphmuseum.org/bibliography.

36. Several papers generated by a two-phase reinterpretation initiative, in 1992 and 1994, including the 1994 colloquium "Through Women's Eyes: A Colloquium Presenting New Research on Women at 'Forty Acres,' 1750–1850," are available on the foundation's website: http://www.pphmuseum.org/bibliography/. A doctoral student at the time, I was pleased to contribute to those efforts, alongside historians Christopher Clark, Daniel Horowitz, Elisabeth B. Nichols, Laurel Thatcher Ulrich, and others.

37. My dissertation, "'My Daily Bread Depends Upon My Labor': Craftswomen, Community and the Marketplace in Rural New England, 1740–1820," grounded in the papers associated with the Porter-Phelps-Huntington family, was completed at the University of North Carolina–Chapel Hill in 1997; see also my *The Needle's Eye: Women and Work in the Age of Revolution* (Amherst: University of Massachusetts Press, 2006); and Elizabeth Pendergast Carlisle, *Earthbound and Heavenbent: The Life of Elizabeth Porter Phelps and*

Life at Forty Acres (1747–1817) (New York: Scribner, 2004). Other important scholarship that draws on these papers and dates from this general historiographical moment is Christopher Clark, *The Roots of Rural Capitalism: Western Massachusetts, 1780–1860* (Ithaca, NY: Cornell University Press, 1990); Jane Nylander, *Our Own Snug Fireside* (New York: Knopf, 1993); Catherine E. Kelly, *In the New England Fashion: Reshaping Women's Lives in the Nineteenth Century* (Ithaca, NY: Cornell University Press, 1999).

Individuals who are not discussed in detail appear under their family name.